Lighten Their Darkness

From Gustave Doré and Blanchard Jerrold, *London*, London, 1872, p. 139.

LIGHTEN THEIR DARKNESS

The Evangelical
Mission to
Working-Class
London,
1828–1860

DONALD M. LEWIS

CONTRIBUTIONS TO THE STUDY OF RELIGION,
NUMBER 19

GREENWOOD PRESS

NEW YORK
WESTPORT, CONNECTICUT
LONDON

First published in USA in 1986 by Greenwood Press, Inc.,
88 Post Road West, Westport, Connecticut 06881

This edition published in 2001 by Paternoster Press

07 06 05 04 03 02 01   7 6 5 4 3 2 1

Paternoster Press is an imprint of Paternoster Publishing,
PO Box 300, Carlisle, Cumbria, CA3 0QS, UK
www.paternoster-publishing.com

British Library Cataloguing in Publication Data

A catalogue record for this book is available
from the British Library

ISBN 1-84227-074-5

Cover design by Four Nine Zero
Printed in Great Britain by
Bell & Bain Ltd., Glasgow

For my grandfather, Bob Munro, and my parents

Contents

Illustrations

Series Foreword

Students of religion and society have often investigated the function of Protestant activities in industrial England. A spectrum of viewpoints ranges from observations that religious groups actually accomplished some good for urban workers to the conviction that they simply placated them and thereby undercut serious concern for temporal justice. Did evangelical Christianity have a social conscience or was it the opium of the people? Such extremes are too broad to admit of resolution, but this study is relevant to that debate, and it sheds light on today's more sophisticated formulations of the general problem.

Beginning with the most elementary aspects of a missionary outreach program, missionaries in Victorian England utilized basic scriptural teachings and stressed the need for instruction among young people. Professor Lewis details for us both the message and methods of urban evangelical work. His study concentrates on the growth of such activities in London, but since it was the largest metropolitan area, the program there was representative of most other British cities. He shows that the alienation workers felt towards formal Christianity was not a recent phenomenon and that industrial conditions had little to do with creating that attitude. Moreover his research makes clear that urban evangelical work helped sensitize the general public to social problems and focused attention on slum conditions. Mission workers helped alleviate some of those conditions and promoted peaceful, gradual change rather than radical reform. On the strictly religious side they succeeded in proselytizing people to some degree too. But missionaries were not satisfied with the results of their efforts in either category. Judging from the size and duration of their organizations, though, it is fair to consider their collective exertions "the most influential religious crusade to affect Victorian working classes."

If part of this book focuses on large questions of religious values and general culture, another part concerns the internal developments of religious groups themselves. Its elemental finding is that a shared concern for urban evangelism helped bring the established church and dissenting bodies closer together. Anglicans and Nonconformists (primarily Congregationalists, Baptists, and Methodists) were able to establish links among themselves through dedication to a challenge too large for any single church. Professor Lewis shows that churchmen interested in urban missions bridged the gap between denominations before 1850, not afterwards as conventional wisdom has supposed. This historical revision is an important contribution of his book, as is his demonstration that Anglican Evangelicalism remained continuous and active throughout the middle third of the nineteenth century. Besides these revisions Lewis brings out new information by charting an urban world few have explored before. His description of what city mission work was and what it really did among the working poor will now have to be assimilated into overviews of Victorian religious life.

So readers have before them a wealth of detailed information, assiduously gathered to describe a poorly understood phase of religious activity in Britain. We now have a thoroughgoing depiction of how interdenominational societies such as the London City Mission aided the growth of evangelical fraternity. This plank in the ecumenical platform is crucial to subsequent interchurch cooperation, and Lewis clarifies its nature and strength. He alludes to possible reasons for increased membership among evangelical churches and for expansion of Evangelical convictions among Anglicans. These aspects are important at home and have implications for understanding events abroad too, especially those related to American revivalism and foreign missions around the globe. But the central focus is cooperative work in English cities, and a convincing thesis found in these pages is that "the catholicity of the lay and clerical supporters of the London City Mission represents an aspect of Victorian evangelicalism that is often ignored by historians and demonstrates a liberality of spirit rare to that age."

—Henry W. Bowden

Acknowledgments

First, I wish to express thanks to Dr. P. B. Hinchliff of Balliol College, Oxford, for his insights and direction, which were of great assistance. Other historians to whom I owe a debt of gratitude for their criticism, encouragement, and advice include: Ian S. Rennie, John Walsh, Brian Heeney, and John Wolffe. Several anonymous reviewers of the work whose observations and comments have helped in broadening the scope of the book should also be thanked, although I am afraid that they may not feel that their suggestions were properly heeded.

In addition, the librarians of the Bodleian Library in Oxford, the British Museum in London, and the Cambridge University Library should be thanked for their assistance in the task of research. Richard Budgen of the Bodleian Library deserves special thanks for his delivery of countless volumes to my desk in the typing room of that library. Gratitude also should be expressed to the Reverend G. C. Taylor, rector of the Church of St. Giles-in-the-Fields in London, for permission to use the Oppenheimer papers.

My thanks are also due to the British Library, the Bodleian Library, the University of British Columbia Library, and the Vancouver Public Library for permission to duplicate the illustrations used in the book. In this regard I should also express my appreciation to the Audio-Visual Department of the University of British Columbia and to Dal Schindell of Regent College for their assistance in the preparation of the illustrations.

This book has been published with the help of a grant from the Canadian Federation for the Humanities using funds provided by the Social Sciences and Humanities Research Council of Canada. I would like to thank the Canadian Federation for the Humanities for its subvention of this work and also those at Greenwood Press who have been so helpful in the preparation of this work for publication.

Abbreviations

BFBS	British and Foreign Bible Society
CIS	Christian Instruction Society
CMS	Church Missionary Society
CP-AS	Church Pastoral-Aid Society
DVS	District Visiting Society
GSPDV	General Society for the Promotion of District Visiting
LCM	London City Mission
LDOS	Lord's Day Observance Society
LMS	London Missionary Society
RBM	Ranyard Bible Mission
RTS	Religious Tract Society
SRA	Scripture Readers' Association
WMEU	Working Men's Educational Union
YMCA	Young Men's Christian Association
YMSAM	Young Men's Society for Aiding Missions

Lighten Their
Darkness

Introduction

Many historians have emphasized the impact that popular evangelicalism had on the British working classes in the late eighteenth and early nineteenth centuries. Twentieth-century evangelicals like Drs. J. Edwin Orr and John W. Bready have made grand claims for evangelical strength and influence.[1] Others, however, have often taken their cue from J. L. and Barbara Hammond, whose *Town Labourer* did much to popularize the view that "evangelicals had chloroformed the people" against revolution, thus rendering the working classes compliant and placid in the face of oppression.[2] Elie Halévy's seminal work *Methodism in 1815*, published in 1905, laid the groundwork for such twentieth-century views. Discussion of Halévy's views has tended to dominate the debate over religion and the British working classes. Even in the 1980s, Halévy's thesis still prompts discussion, as is to be expected of an appealing, yet unprovable hypothesis.[3]

Recent scholarship has attempted to account for the rapid growth of both Methodism and the New Dissent (the Congregationalists, the Particular Baptists, and the New Connexion General Baptists) in the period after 1790. Alan Gilbert has demonstrated that "these bodies were linked in a single, if multiform, social and religious phenomenon" and that they all followed a similar pattern of growth from the 1790s until the end of the 1830s; during this time their membership expanded much more rapidly than the total adult population.[4] In 1964 Professor Hobsbawm attempted to explain this growth in his work, *Labouring Men*. In his view, popular evangelicalism and popular radicalism grew up at the same time and in the same places, both representing different responses to rapid social change. Both were, in a sense, sides of the same coin—one the political and the other the religious.[5] E. P. Thompson offered a much less sympathetic interpretation of popular evangelicalism in his book, *The Making of the English*

Working Class in which he viewed it as an essentially counterrevolutionary force which was embraced by elements of the working class as they despaired of temporal political solutions to their problems. Methodism's heavenly vision effectively obscured the perception of temporal injustices and thereby undercut revolutionary fervor.

Professor W. R. Ward has advanced quite a different explanation by focusing on the significance of the French Revolution for both the political and religious establishments in England. The challenge to the established church in England came from the rise of evangelical voluntarism whose appeal undermined the Church of England's exclusive claims. For Ward, the New Dissent was a religious expression of radicalism, not of conservatism. While the radical leaders viewed Methodism as a conservative force, the Anglican establishment often feared it as a radical, if not a downright dangerous movement because it was tainted with French Jacobinism. Alan Gilbert in his book *Religion and Society in Industrial England: Church, Chapel and Social Change 1740–1914* argues in a way similar to Ward. He maintains that the emergence of religious pluralism in a period of rapid social change created a situation of conflict between the Church of England and popular evangelicalism. He sees the emergence of this conflict and its gradual resolution as a key aspect of English social change in the period.[6] Significantly, he contradicts Thompson's view that Methodism appealed to the despair of the working classes and maintains the opposite—that evangelical Nonconformity's attractiveness was due to its appeal to the aspirations of those workers who were breaking free of the traditional social system; it legitimated their desire for "improvement" while its social structure relieved the anomie experienced by many in early industrial England.[7]

This work deals with an important aspect of the conflict between evangelical Nonconformity and the Church of England, which Gilbert identifies. It begins with the divided state of Evangelicals in the 1820s and seeks to demonstrate how the chasm that existed between Anglican and Nonconformist evangelicals was bridged between 1828 and 1860. Its focus is thus upon an aspect of the gradual resolution of the long-standing enmity between the establishment and Dissent. While indebted to the helpful analysis of Professor Ward, it differs from him in emphasis. His stress in analyzing the 1830s and 1840s was upon the divisions among (and within) denominations during those decades. This work seeks to demonstrate that although interdenominational tensions were real, too much has been made of their significance. There were important theological, polemical (anti-Catholic and anti-Tractarian), and practical factors which mitigated the impact of such divisions. The key factor—the hinge upon which such early cooperation turned—was a shared concern for urban evangelism. Therefore, the work argues for a significant broadening of links between evangelicals inside and outside of the Church of England prior to 1850, in spite of increased social tensions. (Professor Ward indicates that such links were only forged after that date, "when the steam went out of English social tension after 1850.")[8] Thus the book contends that the beginning of the resolution of the great conflict between

Church and Dissent began earlier than most historians acknowledge and high-lights different reasons from those traditionally argued.

Recent scholarship has tended to pay attention to evangelical Nonconformity and has had little to say about evangelicalism within the Church of England, especially during the second third of the nineteenth century. For the most part, the observation made in 1962 by Dr. Kitson Clark still holds true:

The Evangelical Movement [within the Church of England] is studied until the death of Wilberforce in 1833 or possibly that of Simeon in 1836, after that no one knows what happened to the Evangelicals or much cares....

. . . But after 1836 the social and political distinction of the Evangelicals seems to fade with Lord Shaftesbury as a notable exception. They became people on the periphery working in the dim streets of provincial towns, while for many people their ideas remained, what they had always been, intellectually beyond the pale.[9]

This work attempts to remedy this imbalance. In examining the cooperative effort made by Victorian evangelicals to sow their seed on the barren soil of the working classes, this study must of necessity pay special attention to the Anglican Evangelicals as they were the least inclined toward interdenominational coop-eration, having (it was felt) the most to lose. (It should be noted at the outset that throughout the book the words "evangelical" and "evangelicalism" are capitalized when referring exclusively to Anglicans and Anglicanism.)

Few historians have explored the underworld of Victorian evangelicalism, and even of those who have, very few have ventured into the uncharted territory of its urban mission. This neglect has resulted in a rather distorted view of what was actually happening. Geoffrey Best has commented that High Church An-glican historians often have written up Ritualists "as the only Christians who evangelized the slums" in nineteenth-century England.[10] The view is so wide-spread that it has been repeated by historians like A. D. Gilbert who has written that it was "the Ritualist clergy of the late Victorian era whose efforts contributed most to the modest achievements of the Church in the urban working-class parishes."[11] The resulting impression is unfair to several generations of evan-gelicals, ignores the significant efforts of Roman Catholic missions, and fails to acknowledge the efforts of Broad Churchmen.[12]

The particular neglect of the period from 1830 to 1850 is related to the fact that leading works dealing with organized evangelistic efforts in the Victorian era have concentrated on the period after 1850. K. S. Inglis's *Churches and the Working Class in Victorian England* is essentially a study of the late nineteenth century; his first chapter opens with the words "Between 1850 and 1900,"[13] and the book is based on his doctoral thesis, which concentrated on the two closing decades of the century.[14] It is rather surprising that such a significant and helpful work should have only three passing references to the London City Mission and be oblivious to the existence of the Anglican Scripture Readers' Associations. Such organizations were key to the Anglican approach to the poor from the 1840s and employed numerous lay agents well before the emergence of the Church Army in the 1880s. Another reason for such omissions (aside from his concentration on the latter part of the century) has been pointed out by John Kent; Inglis is much more concerned with the churches' indirect attempt to conciliate the workers "through various social expressions" of Christianity than with the direct attempt to convert.[15] Two important recent works also concentrate on the latter part of the century: Hugh McLeod's *Class and Religion in the Late Victorian City* (1974) and Jeffrey Cox's *The English Churches in a Secular Society: Lambeth, 1870–1930* (1982).

This work thus seeks to examine a much less researched period in Victorian religious history. Its major theme is the changing lines of division and cooperation between evangelicals within the Anglican church and Nonconformity during the period from 1828 to 1860. Yet there are several minor themes: the content of the message and the strategies employed by the evangelicals in their efforts to spread Protestant observance among the urban poor and the response of the poor to the same. These themes—while intrinsically interesting—are minor, not major, concerns. The sociocultural foundations of Anglican Evangelicalism have yet to be studied in depth, and this work does not pretend to have laid them bare.

A significant limitation of the study is that it concentrates on the formative years of the enormous evangelical efforts to evangelize London. For several reasons, however, the work is of broader significance than it might initially appear. The pan-evangelical character of the London experience is representative of what happened in city missions throughout England. David Nasmith, the founder of the London City Mission, organized similar interdenominational societies in other cities throughout Great Britain and even overseas. In Liverpool he reorganized an existing society into the Liverpool Town Mission.[16] In Manchester, he founded another interdenominational society, while at a national level he established the pan-evangelical City and Town Missionary Society in 1837. By 1862 this society had 155 agents at work in cities and towns throughout England.[17] For other reasons as well the London experience can be regarded as representative. London was seen throughout Britain as a unique mission field which required a coordinated national effort, and only a united evangelical front was seen as equal to the task. Furthermore, the means used to convert the working-class Londoner set the pattern for the smaller interdenominational ventures throughout England and the English-speaking world.

While London had been a center for Evangelical Anglican activities in the days of the Clapham Sect and the headquarters of the leading evangelical societies were in the capital, it was not until the 1830s that Anglican Evangelical clergy really began to make their presence felt in the city. Indeed, probably the most important factor that has led historians to relegate Anglican Evangelicals to the "dim streets of provincial towns" is that during the period of the ascendancy of the Clapham Sect there were only a handful of Evangelical incumbents in London. At the turn of the century it was normal (out of necessity rather than choice) for the few Evangelical clergy in the diocese to hold appointments in proprietary chapels or in lectureships. W. E. Gladstone was to recall in 1878 that "not a single London parish, west of Temple Bar, was in the hands of the Evangelical party" during the first third of the century.[18] Nationally the story was quite different. The proportion of Evangelical clergy overall in England grew steadily from about one-twentieth of the total in 1800 to at least one-quarter (and perhaps one-third) by mid-century. Only after 1835, however, did Evangelical clergy become a significant force in London.

The very rapid growth of Evangelical strength in early Victorian London is most clearly seen in a secret report prepared for the editor of the *Times* in 1844. As he was anxious to have at hand a thumbnail sketch of the positions of the leading London clergy vis-à-vis the Tractarian issue, his reporters were instructed to analyze the eighty-nine leading clergy, the majority of whom were Evangelicals.[19] Over two-thirds of the Evangelicals had been presented to their livings after 1835, and of those appointed before that year a significant number were incumbents of proprietary chapels. These facts serve to underline a change in attitude in favor of Evangelicals by those exercising ecclesiastical patronage in London during the period under study.

The year 1828 is a convenient date for the commencement of this study. Although originally chosen because of the founding in that year of the first Evangelical society specifically concerned with promoting lay evangelism, a number of other events conveniently coincide with the date: Bishop Blomfield's translation to London; the establishment of the *Record* newspaper; and the inauguration of the annual Islington clerical conference by Daniel Wilson, Sr. These meetings quickly became an important focal point for many Evangelical clergy and were the closest Evangelical approximation to a national party conference. Charles Sumner's move a year earlier from the Bishopric of Llandaff to Winchester was also to have important consequences for Evangelicals in the neighboring Diocese of London. And, of course, another event of 1828 was to have an even more profound effect on Anglican–Dissenting relations: the repeal of the Test and Corporation Acts.

The choice of 1860 as a cut-off date for this study has allowed the author to deal with the impact of the 1859–1860 Irish Revival on interdenominational relations. In addition it was only by 1860 that it became clear that a pan-evangelical approach to evangelism had won the day; strictly Anglican societies had already peaked in terms of receipts and the number of agents supported, while interdenominational agencies were recording impressive gains. But before one can appreciate the significance of this change, one needs an introduction to English evangelicalism in the 1820s.

Part One

The Evangelicals

1

The Divided Evangelicals

The Evangelical Awakening had a profound impact upon the English-speaking Protestant world in the eighteenth century. Beginning with the preaching of George Whitefield in England and Jonathan Edwards in the Massachusetts colony, the movement was to reinvigorate much of the Protestant church and created a missionary thrust which in large measure was responsible for the worldwide expansion of Protestant Christianity in the nineteenth century. "Throughout the mid-Victorian age," Owen Chadwick has acknowledged, "the evangelical movement was the strongest religious force in British life."[1] Few would dispute Chadwick's assertion. However, while much has been written about the overseas missionary enterprise that the English evangelicals undertook, the evangelical movement has yet to be examined in the way that Chadwick has probed the mind of the Oxford Movement.[2] The sociocultural foundations of Evangelicalism within the Church of England also need to be studied in depth.[3] Their efforts in home missions have also largely been neglected; the significance of these home missions for Victorian evangelicalism is the theme of this book.

In approaching the question of interdenominational relations, historians stress the political and social differences between Anglicanism and Nonconformity and emphasize the growing rivalry between the two in the late 1820s and early 1830s. In 1828 Nonconformists achieved the repeal of the Test and Corporation Acts, the long-standing restrictions upon the political rights of English Nonconformity. Roman Catholic emancipation in 1829 brought similar relief to Catholics. Both measures symbolized the failure of the old monopoly that the Church of England had once enjoyed and set the stage for demands for full religious equality. The established church was in desperate need of reform and hence was a favorite target of radicals. Vast differences existed in the incomes of the bishops, several receiving princely payments while some incumbents lived in poverty. The parochial system had undergone little change in five centuries, and high rates of pluralism and absenteeism were ammunition for the radicals. In 1827 less than half of the benefices were reported to have resident clergymen, a statistic which "afforded a formidable stick to the critics."[4]

In 1831, the very popular Reform Bill was defeated in the House of Lords, and it was quickly pointed out that if the twenty-one Anglican bishops who had voted against the measure had supported it, the bill would have passed. In Regent's Park, the chairman of a meeting was handed a placard that read: "Englishmen—remember it was the bishops, and the bishops only, whose vote decided the fate of the Reform Bill." Popular speakers denounced the bench of bishops, "compared their wealth and state with apostolic simplicity, demanded that they be excluded from the House of Lords, asserted that they had no right to interfere in politics, but ought to be about their pastoral duties."[5] This agitation occurred at a time of general social unease, economic recession, and agrarian strife (due to several poor harvests). People could be forgiven for feeling that the nation was on the verge of revolution and that the unreformed Church was about to be disestablished.[6]

All these factors did serve to heat up Anglican–Dissenting relations during the 1830s, but one needs to appreciate that prior to 1828 there had been little common ground between evangelicals within the Church of England and those outside of it. Victorian evangelicalism was a complex phenomenon, and crucial differences existed among evangelicals. From the mid-eighteenth century on there was a small but growing group of Evangelicals within the establishment. From the late 1780s to the 1820s effective leadership was given to this party by the "Clapham Sect," a group of socially concerned Evangelical laymen (along with a few clergy) under the leadership of William Wilberforce (1759–1833). This was the group which fought long and hard for the outlawing of the British slave trade (achieved in 1807) and the abolition of the institution of slavery itself within the British colonies in 1833. The leading Evangelical periodical of the early nineteenth century was the *Christian Observer*, which had been established by the Clapham Sect.

In 1828, well before the troubled times of the early 1830s, an American minister visiting London was surprised to observe that most of the *Christian Observer*'s supporters, "while they are men of distinguished worth, and of truly evangelical views, have but little religious sympathy with any, who do not happen to be within the pale of the Establishment."[7] Yet, in the course of the next third of the century, this situation had greatly changed. By 1860 a number of the leading Evangelical Anglican clergy were advocating and supporting close co-operation with Nonconformists, not only cooperation in pursuit of common moral–political goals, but also in evangelism. This is of special significance, as evangelism is a field in which interdenominational cooperation is notoriously difficult because of doctrinal and denominational differences. In order to understand the roots of the problem, one needs to appreciate the situation in which Anglican Evangelicals found themselves during the 1820s.

ANGLICAN EVANGELICALS: THE CLAPHAM HERITAGE

One of the most significant effects the French Revolution had on the Church of England was to induce its Evangelical clergy to withdraw "from close association with Dissent," so that they might clearly dissociate themselves from Nonconformists who had voiced pro-Jacobin sentiments.[8] Fears that French revolutionary fervor would grip the growing Methodist movement led the British government to consider measures to restrict itinerant preachers in 1800.[9] This suspicion as to the political loyalty of the Methodists was part of the legacy of the Puritan Revolution; religious "enthusiasm" had once succeeded in overthrowing the British Crown, and it was feared that it might do so again if unchecked. Anglican Evangelicals were suspect because of their association in the public mind with the Methodists; thus Evangelicals were increasingly anxious to distance themselves from Nonconformists, a point that the same American visitor noted in 1828:

The Evangelical party . . . are more rigid in their peculiar notions of church government, and more disposed to talk of Episcopalians as *the* Church, than are those who are most lax in their views of Gospel truth. The solution which I have heard of it is, that the Evangelical party are apprehensive that they shall not be suspected, on account of their rigid adherence to the Gospel, of verging towards Puritanism; and in order to keep down such a suspicion, they manifest their attachment to the Church by an increased degree of zeal for her particular forms of government.[10]

The anxiety created by the French Revolution brought this political concern into sharp focus once again and led Evangelicals to express "a greater respect for the church as an institution."[11] From the 1790s on, however, this trend toward a stricter churchmanship was encouraged by the Evangelicals' growing hopes of capturing the established Church from within, thereby rendering it useful in the cause of Gospel religion. Church order had to be closely observed, and most Evangelical clergy were careful to limit their ministries to their own parishes rather than intrude Wesley-like into areas where they would upset incumbents who disliked their Evangelicalism and would oppose their ministrations. As this concern intensified between the 1790s and the 1820s, the Evangelical clergy were transformed from "being a scattered and powerless minority to becoming the most highly organized, power-conscious party within the Church of England."[12] Fraternizing with Dissenters or ignoring constituted church order lent credence to the often-repeated charge that the Evangelicals were merely "Church Methodists," undeserving of the Anglican name. Expediency in ecclesiastical politics demanded that Evangelicals keep their distance from Nonconformists.

Theological considerations also influenced this trend. The two leading groups in the eighteenth-century Church of England were the High Churchmen (who were strongly Erastian in politics and orthodox in theology—often called the

"High and Dry" party) and the Latitudinarians or Low Churchmen (who were anti-Erastian and whose theology had been strongly affected by Enlightenment thinking—sometimes spoken of by detractors as the "Low and Slow"). Both groups had long suspected that the distinctive Evangelical emphasis on justification by grace through faith was a dangerous doctrine. Many were convinced that in the end it would lead to an undervaluing of good works, there being little incentive to Evangelicals to do such as they relied upon faith alone for their salvation. Also, it was thought that such teaching focused too much upon the individual. In so doing, it encouraged a hyperindividualism, thereby producing a loosening of personal restraints and the disparaging of ecclesiastical traditions. It might even lead to the defiance of the civil law as each man did what was right in his own eyes. In order to counteract the effects of this hostility, the Clapham Sect sought to buy up church presentations (the right to appoint the minister to a specific church). In this way they could secure an ongoing succession of Evangelical clergy in particular parishes. Charles Simeon, the leading Evangelical cleric of the period, was especially effective in raising funds for the trust which still bears his name.[13] (See Illustration 1).

Thus the attitude of the *Christian Observer* and of many of the Evangelical clergy toward Dissent had long been one of antipathy, a point that needs to be underlined in view of contrary assertions by other historians. Charles Simeon held such a view. He described Dissent as "an evil," although he had acknowledged that he could not blame a man for turning to it "where the Gospel truth is not declared in the Church pulpit."[14] Not only did numerous Evangelical clergy strive to keep their distance from Dissent, but some also continually emphasized the superiority of the Church over Dissent. This hostility toward Dissent was undoubtedly further fueled during the 1830s by evangelical secessions from the established Church.[15]

In fact, the avowed aim of the *Christian Observer* had not been cooperation with, but the reincorporation of Dissenters. As late as 1841 the *Observer* was defending itself against the charge that this self-distancing from Dissent was for it a novelty, a reaction to Tractarian influence. Not so, maintained the periodical, which claimed that the policy was in the distinguished tradition of Lord Teignmouth, who in 1799 had determined never to frequent a place of worship that did not belong to the establishment for fear of influencing his servants, as he did not want them to "follow preachers in whom that essential quality was lacking."[16] This persistent opposition to Nonconformity thus had its roots in the heritage bequeathed to Anglican Evangelicalism by the Clapham Sect.[17]

Nevertheless, the concern of the Clapham Sect Evangelicals for the spread of foreign missions and for the distribution of religious literature and Bibles had served for a time to effect a loose form of pan-evangelicalism. Between 1795 and 1808, four religious societies were established on a broad evangelical basis; within a few years two of the four (the London Missionary Society and the London Society for Promoting Christianity amongst the Jews) fell under denominational control. The remaining two societies continued to thrive despite the

PARTICULARS

AND

CONDITIONS OF SALE,

Of a very Valuable

CHURCH PREFERMENT,

COMPRISING

THE NEXT PRESENTATION

TO THE

RECTORY OF RADWINTER, IN THE COUNTY OF ESSEX,

WITH MODERN-BUILT RECTORY HOUSE,

EXCELLENT OFFICES, GARDEN, & PADDOCK,

CONVENIENT FARM YARD, AND BUILDINGS,

WITH SIXTY-FIVE ACRES OF GLEBE LAND,

LAND-TAX REDEEMED, AND

THE GREAT & SMALL TITHES OF THE PARISH

CONTAINING 2300 ACRES & UPWARDS,

EXCLUSIVE OF 400 ACRES WHICH ARE SUBJECT TO MODUSES IN KIND,

AND OTHER LANDS THAT ARE TITHE FREE,

THE WHOLE AT A MODERATE CALCULATION IS WORTH

700 GUINEAS PER ANNUM,

Which will be Sold by Auction,

BY MR. CHEFFINS

AT THE

AUCTION MART, LONDON,

On *TUESDAY,* the 7th of *JUNE,* 1825, at One o'Clock,

IN ONE LOT,

Unless previously disposed of by private Contract of which due notice will be given.

Radwinter is situated 44 miles from London, 19 from Cambridge, and 3 from Saffron Walden; in a pleasant and healthy part of the County of Essex, with good Roads.

Particulars may be had at the Eagle Inn, Cambridge; Saracen's Head, Chelmsford and Dunmow; Sun, Walden; White Hart, Bocking; Crown, Hockerill; of Messrs. Toplis and Son, 22, St. Paul's Church Yard; at the Auction Mart, London; and of the Auctioneer, Bishops Stortford, Herts.

MULLINGER, PRINTER, BISHOPS STORTFORD, HERTS.

Illustration 1

Securing an Evangelical Succession

Well into the 1800s Evangelical clergy were excluded from the more important and lucrative church appointments. In order to secure a place for their party within the Church of England, special trusts were created to buy up church "preferments." These "preferments" entitled the owner to appoint the minister to a particular church whenever the position became vacant. From the John Johnson Collection, Religion, Box 2. Used with the permission of the Bodleian Library, Oxford.

forces ranged against them, but by the 1820s no new ventures of this kind were feasible. The weakness of pan-evangelicalism at this time is clearly seen in the societies which did not succumb to sectarian forces: the Religious Tract Society (RTS) and the British and Foreign Bible Society (BFBS).

Only by co-operating in enterprises that avoided denominational issues—like the distribution of tracts and Bibles—could all the denominations successfully co-operate with each other. But even then, the Tract and Bible Societies functioned under the continual fear that their simple alliance might break up over issues of polity and church government.[18]

By the mid–1820s some Dissenters viewed these societies as the "Trojan horses of the establishment."[19] The Wesleyan Methodists, the largest Nonconformist denomination, were an important exception to this trend. From the early 1790s to the late 1820s, Wesleyanism had become increasingly conservative and at the same time more vocal in its support for the established church.[20] Anglicans were soon to learn, however, that the Wesleyans did not represent the wider evangelical community. The age of Nonconformist docility had passed.

CHALLENGING THE CLAPHAM HERITAGE

While some Dissenters questioned the wisdom of their stance vis-à-vis the Church of England, many Evangelicals were having doubts about their own course of action within the establishment. During the 1820s a power struggle began to develop within Anglican Evangelicalism, between those desiring a "moderate and cultured" Evangelicalism, which would accommodate itself to the surrounding culture, and those who considered such "accommodation" to be unacceptable compromise. The issue centered on the use of "means," or what might today be termed "technique." Some expressed concern that there was not only "an over-dependence on human means" within the fold, but also "a supineness, a love of ease, growing complacency and a lack of self denial."[21]

Rumblings of discontent among Evangelicals can be traced as far back as 1816.[22] By the early 1820s serious expressions of ideological doubt were being voiced. In 1821 James Haldane Stewart, one of London's most respected clergymen, questioned the usefulness and effectiveness of the Evangelical machinery in the conversion of souls and threw doubt on the widely accepted Evangelical belief in "gradually and soberly conducted progress towards world conversion."[23] He also called into question Evangelicalism's optimistic postmillennial eschatology, which had argued for the eventual universal triumph of Christianity, a view that in the eighteenth century had accorded so well with the prevailing liberal idea of progress.[24] Anglican Evangelicals had come to accept the need for aggressive missionary efforts to hasten the spread of the millennial light of the Gospel in lands where it had never been seen, but no such urgency was thought to be necessary at home because of the comprehensive nature of the parochial system.

The most vocal and colorful spokesman for those dissatisfied with the status quo was Edward Irving, the immensely popular Church of Scotland minister in London. It was he who "challenged the complete Anglican Evangelical framework, its love of order, moderation, piety and prudence."[25] Irving spared no pains in denouncing as expediency the accommodating policy of the older generation, convinced as he was that the Clapham Sect was compromising its Protestant principles for political ends. Furthermore, Edward Irving's scorn of the postmillennialist's optimism was unbounded.[26] While reaction to Irving among most Evangelicals was predictably hostile, his questioning had nevertheless served to cause confusion and to raise doubts about the basis of Evangelical missions and evangelism. These tensions within Evangelicalism led to a collision between the two groups in the mid–1820s. The first open defeat of the old guard, headed by Charles Simeon, came in the Apocrypha controversy of 1825–1826 over the issue of the Bible Society's policy of circulating the Apocrypha bound with the Canon in order to conciliate Catholic sensibilities on the Continent. The anti-Apocrypha lobby under the leadership of the fiery Scottish evangelist Robert Haldane won the day. "No longer was Simeon's Evangelical *via media* beyond dispute."[27]

The strains within Evangelicalism, however, were to be even more evident in 1829 over the issue of Catholic emancipation. In Parliament, the Claphamites and the Whig Evangelicals for the most part favored Catholic emancipation, as did the Evangelical Bishops (Ryder and the Sumner brothers) in the House of Lords. The Tory Evangelicals, along with the majority of Evangelical clergy and at least a large minority of laymen, were opposed.[28] David Hempton has noted that the division for and against emancipation was not a straightforward split along party lines, but rather was based on opposing views of its impact on Ireland:

Optimistic evangelicals voted for emancipation on grounds of imperial and missionary expediency, whereas pessimistic evangelicals, who were usually those with the closest Irish connections, believed that emancipation would ruin Protestantism in Ireland. The former were neither pro-Catholic nor advocates of religious pluralism; they simply believed that Ireland could not be made Protestant by discriminatory legislation.[29]

Evangelical support for emancipation was due in large measure to hopes that it would be the panacea for the situation in Ireland. By 1830, however, these hopes had been dashed. "Catholic emancipation," Professor Machin has observed, "had not quietened the Irish but groomed them for further conflict."[30] Some of the Evangelicals who had been pro-emancipation soon began to regret the 1829 decision.

The Evangelical leaders who had rejected the accommodating policy of the Clapham Sect were also those who were strongly opposed to Catholic emancipation. By 1830 they had found their rallying point in the *Record* newspaper. During the debate leading up to emancipation, the paper had declined to take a

specific stand on the issue although its anti-Catholic credentials were impecca-
ble.[31] Concerned to discuss political activity only insofar as it affected specifically
religious issues, the *Record*'s early management avoided taking a position because many Evangelicals believed that it was purely a political matter. By 1830,
however, the *Record*'s tone had changed. In July of that year it published an
address that underlined the Protestant nature of the British constitution and
accused the Evangelicals in Parliament of wholesale capitulation. As a remedy,
it urged the election of more staunchly Protestant members.[32]

The change that came over the *Record* also reflected the increasing influence
of Alexander Haldane, a cantankerous Scottish lawyer who had settled in London
in the early 1820s. Although he disclaimed the title of "editor" of the *Record*,
for half a century he was so in all but name and as such "might well be considered
the most important single influence on the Evangelical party in the Victorian
age."[33] Writing in 1853, Haldane summarized the estimate many of the younger
generation of Evangelicals in the 1820s had of their elders:

We have no hesitation in avowing the belief, that when the *Record* commenced its labours,
a wide-spread spirit of worldly wisdom and sinful compromise had come over a considerable portion of the Evangelical party in the Church. There is no doubt that the great
anti-slavery struggle had induced an amalgamation between its leaders and Socinians
[Unitarians], Romanists, and worldly men. We have heard of a distinguished Prelate,
who was arguing with Mr. WILBERFORCE, Mr. MACAULAY, and others, on the danger of
the combination, who thus concluded his prophetic warning, "It may not injure you, but
what will be the influence on your sons?" Thirty years before, Evangelicalism had been
persecuted and evil spoken of; but it had now become comparatively fashionable. It was
no longer a mere stigma of reproach, as it had been to ROMAINE, and VENN, and NEWTON,
and CECIL, and even to CHARLES SIMEON in his earlier years, when the pure light of his
noble profession burned so brightly in the sepulchral darkness of Cambridge.[34]

Haldane's domination of the *Record* seems to have come about a step at a
time; in fact he had not been involved in its original foundation. The establishment
of the newspaper was due to a coterie of Evangelicals, many of whom had
Scottish connections.[35] With the backing of three wealthy laymen, the newspaper
had published its first edition on January 1, 1828; within six months the publication was faltering and about to fold. One of the owners then introduced two
new figures to his partners: the above-mentioned Alexander Haldane (who was
also a nephew of Robert Haldane, the central figure in the Apocrypha Controversy), and the Reverend Henry Blunt,[36] the rector of Chelsea.[37] Another person
who appears to have been a leading figure behind the *Record* was another Scot,
Captain James E. Gordon, who became the leading figure in nineteenth-century
No Popery. (Gordon, when returned in 1831 as the M.P.—Member of Parliament—for the Earl of Roden's pocket borough of Dundalk, led the hard-line
Evangelicals in their opposition to the continuation of the annual grant to the
Roman Catholic college at Maynooth.[38]) The youthfulness of many of the Re-
cordites as well as their Scottish roots set them apart from the older generation

of Evangelical leaders.[39] Undoubtedly this common background also did much to intensify their anti-Catholicism. Never having been accepted by the English Evangelical establishment, these Scots, like their fellow countrymen Robert Haldane and Edward Irving, were disposed to criticize freely aspects of the English Evangelical establishment.

By the mid–1830s "it had become clear that the older tradition of the Clapham Sect—*Christian Observer*, an optimistic, accommodating evangelicalism, could no longer command general Evangelical consent."[40] Instead it was the *Record*, opposing any concession to liberalism, which "represented the political stance of most Evangelical Anglicans."[41] The leadership that the newspaper exercised led a large segment of Evangelicalism in the direction of conservatism in politics and moderate Calvinism in theology but "also bequeathed to the Evangelicals a reputation for violent and intemperate utterance."[42] Indeed, many of its own constituency were from time to time upset by the paper's tendency to overstate its case and its use of offensive language. Even so, the *Record* was very popular as is evidenced by the fact that by 1838 it had "the largest circulation by far of the religious prints."[43]

Any observer of Evangelicalism in 1828 who was hoping for a change in its attitude toward Nonconformity might have hoped that the *Record*'s repudiation of Evangelical accommodation and compromise would lead them to cooperate more closely with Nonconformity. The Recordites, however, were very dedicated to the establishment of the Church of England and were soon to emerge as its most vocal champions. If the "old-guard" Evangelicals were unwilling to countenance Dissent, the Recordites seemed even less likely to do so because the Nonconformists were beginning to attack their cherished establishment.

EVANGELICALS AND THE DEFENSE OF THE CHURCH ESTABLISHMENT

While the unwillingness of Anglican Evangelicals to associate with Nonconformists had its roots in the heritage bequeathed to it by the Clapham Sect, it was soon to be reinforced by the strife of what became known as the Voluntary Controversy. The Controversy was about whether churches should be supported "voluntarily" by their members or receive state support (as the Church of England did through church rates and grants for church extension). The Voluntaries, as they were known, insisted that the state churches in the British Isles should be disestablished and receive no further government monies. A related issue, of course, was the confessional nature of the British constitution; disestablishment was feared by many as another step (following Catholic emancipation) toward a secular, nonconfessional state.

The 1820s had been both a crucial and an awkward time for those who cherished the Protestant Constitution. In the face of a liberal press, Whig politicans and the political situation in Ireland, it was becoming ever more difficult for those who believed in a Protestant confessional state to advocate their views, without appearing to be religious bigots.[44] As David Hempton has observed:

With the basis of politics being widened and with the growth of a liberal intelligentsia outside aristocratic patronage, it became increasingly difficult for English and Anglo-Irish landowners, Church of England supporters and evangelical anti-Catholics to defend the Protestant Constitution in style.[45]

Following the repeal of the Test and Corporation Acts, most Evangelicals were genuinely surprised by the hostility expressed by some Dissenters toward the establishment, although those who attacked the establishment in the late 1820s and in the 1830s represented only a small minority within Protestant Nonconformity. (At that time the great bulk of the Dissenters were content with petitions for relief on lesser matters, the overt demand for disestablishment being viewed "by some as an obstruction to the settlement of tangible grievances."[46]) Most Evangelicals had assumed in 1828 that Nonconformity was "politically innocuous,"[47] and Sir Robert Inglis, a leading Tory Evangelical M.P., had gone unheeded when he warned Parliament that the disabilities should be continued "just in case the Dissenters should launch any future attack against the Church of England."[48] Once the measure had passed and the dissenting attacks began, many Anglicans overreacted and quickly became convinced that Inglis's warnings had been vindicated. In July of 1828 the *Record* made it clear that it would never have supported repeal "if we believed that it added any real power to the Dissenters to the disadvantage of the Church; still less, if we thought . . . that it was tantamount to a casting off of the allegiance which this kingdom professed to Christ and his religion."[49] By 1829 the paper was appealing for peace in what it perceived to be an escalating war of words between evangelicals, but without effect.[50] Few things infuriated Evangelicals more than to see devout Nonconformist brethren join political radicals and "Socialists" in their struggle against the Church establishment. In October of 1830 the *Record* warned:

There is no doubt the attack upon the establishment will be made, and *that* under various pretexts, and with great force and impetuosity. With the great mass of the invaders, the overthrow of the Establishment is only a present step to an ulterior object, *viz.*, the overthrow of Christianity altogether. They will gladly take the assistance of the orthodox Dissenters as far as they will go, in destroying those with whom, on all that is vital and essential, they agree,—and then turn upon, and rend them. Paganism has persecuted; Popery has persecuted. Can Infidelity not persecute?[51]

Even with the passage of the Reform Bill of 1832, the strength of evangelical Dissenters in Parliament was negligible. The new House of Commons in 1833 saw only two evangelical Nonconformists on its benches, but this did little to quiet Anglican fears.[52]

Appeals such as the one by the *Record* fell on deaf ears, and the controversy heated up in the early 1830s. Bishop Blomfield remarked in his 1834 *Charge* that at the time of his last address to his clergy in 1830, he had not perceived "amongst the dissenters, any symptoms of increased hostility towards the established church," but that in view of recent events, he could only conclude that "the spirit of bitterness . . . waited only for an opportunity to break forth."[53] In the same charge, however, Blomfield did much to aggravate the situation by recommending a work to his clergy that contained a savage attack on Dissent.[54] The *Record* regarded publication of *The Case of the Dissenters* in 1833, an anonymous work by a Nonconformist minister, as a serious escalation of the controversy over disestablishment, and the newspaper attacked it repeatedly— even years after its publication.[55] The *Evangelical Magazine*, the respected spokesman of moderate evangelical Dissent, hailed the book as "mild, dignified, charitable and firm" and estimated that "In the present age, no wiser defence of the Dissenters has made its appearance."[56]

The Reverend Hugh McNeile, the fiery Irish Evangelical who was to dominate the religious life of Liverpool for decades, made his national reputation as a leading anti-Catholic orator. He was no friend of Dissent either and in 1834 exacerbated denominational tensions by a series of lectures in defense of church establishments. In them he alleged that much of Nonconformity's growth was due to sheep stealing from Anglican congregations.[57] Perhaps such losses would not have been so galling if Evangelicals had had a high estimation of Dissenting spirituality. McNeile's second charge was typical of the attitudes of many Evangelical clergy toward the effects of Voluntaryism's "free trade" in religion:

To obtain a voluntary support the man must dilute his teaching to meet the prejudices of fallen man; he must only assail the natural character as far as conscience will bear it, setting forth, what they know already, that they are indeed what they ought not to be, so as to do it gently, so as not to alarm and disturb too much; and thus measuring his statements of doctrine, so that he may not bring forward what may make them recoil from him; seeking to be palatable, instead of seeking to be true; he must consider the prejudices of his people in preparing his discourses, instead of considering the contents of the word of God.[58]

This low view of Dissenting ministrations had been bolstered by the enumeration of the many weaknesses and failings of Dissent by one of its chief spokesmen, J. Angell James.[59]

Hugh McNeile was far from alone among Evangelicals in his disparaging of Nonconformity. Even Thomas Chalmers, the leading Church of Scotland evangelical, in an 1833 sermon on church establishments which he preached in London, indulged in what the *Evangelical Magazine* considered "very bigoted representations of the state and character of Dissent."[60] The temptation to make personal attacks on those who seemed to threaten the establishment remained powerful throughout the decade. In 1839 a Nonconformist minister, anxious for reconciliation among evangelicals, wrote to the *Evangelical Magazine* and outlined the significance of this barrier to closer pan-evangelical cooperation:

Another obstacle arises from the serious provocation which dissenters have lately suffered. Not only have bitter taunts and degrading representations been employed against them; not only have the lamented expressions of a few individuals been reiterated, month after month, from one end of the country to the other, and charged upon the general body; but they have been cruelly represented as willing to sacrifice the interests of vital Christianity to the extension and secular aggrandizement of their own party. In truth, the more liberal and pious members of the establishment would feel an honest indignation, could they be fully acquainted with the unjust reproaches and the supercilious contempt which many holy and devoted nonconformist ministers, even of the most quiet and peaceful spirit, have now to endure from bigoted or worldly-minded Churchmen. Such treatment, although it cannot justify retaliation, may naturally induce a reluctance to any measure which might, however mistakenly, be regarded as somewhat apologetical.[61]

Personal invective was not limited to Anglicans, however. In responding to McNeile's "stupid and vulgar attacks upon dissent" in his 1834 lectures, the normally placid *Evangelical Magazine* wondered whether his "almost insane deviation from truth" was not perhaps due to McNeile's flirtation with Irvingism, a Pentecostalist sect that had grown up around the figure of Edward Irving, for McNeile had briefly embraced the movement: "Perhaps the Rev. Gentleman takes his view of dissent from a certain *gifted school*, which he first supported and then denounced."[62]

It was the strife engendered by the Voluntary Controversy that led Evangelicals to reexamine their support for church establishments. The doubts being raised about the same within the Anglican communion caused them little worry. In 1830, some three years before John Keble's assize sermon at Oxford (which many have mistakenly regarded as the beginning of the Oxford Movement) the *Record* commented:

> The proposition that all alliance between Church and State is unscriptural and prejudicial, is received by many, in the present day, as demonstrated.
>
> . . . we believe, some learned Churchmen of Oxford, more distinguished for their logic or poetry, than for their theology or orthodoxy, have signified their adherence to it. This new light, however, whether it be pure or false, has penetrated the Establishment to so trifling an extent, that we may be excused from combating the opinion as embraced by Churchmen, and consider it only as held by our non-conforming brethren.[63]

In December 1833 the *Record* launched an onslaught on the doctrines of the early Tracts emanating from Oxford, but it was not until 1841 that the *Record* considered the disestablishment views of the Oxford Movement worthy of a refutation.[64]

The basis for the shift in Evangelical attitudes toward the establishment was laid in the late 1820s, and in this regard it is interesting that the *Evangelical Magazine* linked Hugh McNeile with Edward Irving, as it was Irving who laid the foundation for the change of the 1830s. Under pressure from hostile Dissenters, Anglican Evangelicals turned to the sort of views that Irving had advanced in the late 1820s. Before Irving's emergence on the London scene Evangelicals had generally followed the *Christian Observer*'s leadership when defending the establishment. The *Observer* had long advanced the very pragmatic defense of the establishment principle developed by William Warburton and Archdeacon Paley in the eighteenth century.[65] They had "abandoned appeals to doctrinal truth as the basis for establishments and had appealed to utility to justify the direction of ecclesiastical polity."[66] In 1824 the *Christian Guardian*, another Evangelical periodical, had stressed that the Old Testament union of church and state was a divinely given pattern, God's highest design for his people.[67] This emphasis, however, had little appeal for the *Christian Observer*, which was "never impressed by Old Testament precedent in the matter."[68]

In 1828 Edward Irving published a book entitled *The Last Days* in which he attempted to revive the Puritan concept of a "covenant people" "bound to Christ, and recognizing his headship in all things."[69] A minister of the Scottish establishment, Irving became particularly hostile toward Nonconformists whom he argued were aiding and abetting liberalism. He insisted "that rulers must be prepared to enter into covenant relation with God, or else face national judgment. And since Nonconformists placed themselves outside the National Church—the Church of the covenant—they should be debarred from Parliament."[70] Irving's views, however, were so extreme and couched in such extravagant language that they were bound to be dismissed by Evangelicals. The *Christian Guardian* presented its readers with an extract from *The Last Days* that dealt with Dissent and suggested that the passage "combining at once some truth with no small share of extravagance may perhaps amuse our readers, and leave them in good humour with Mr. I."[71] But many were not amused. The shock of Roman Catholic legislators in a Protestant parliament and emancipation's failure to ameliorate the Irish situation soon pushed many Evangelicals into a reactionary position and inclined many to some form of Irving's covenant nation theory. As Ian Rennie has commented, "there can be no doubt that the Catholic emancipation crisis made the Evangelicals the most self-conscious and determined upholders of national Christianity. At the very time when the ancient Christian ideal of the confessional state was running into its stiffest opposition, the Evangelicals were emerging as its champions."[72]

The persistent attacks by Dissenters on the older, more pragmatic apologetic maintained by the *Christian Observer* and by its most eloquent spokesman, Thomas Chalmers, also served to induce Evangelicals to consider these new arguments in favor of the establishment principle. In 1833 the *Evangelical Magazine* dismissed a sermon that the Scottish divine had preached in London on the question: "Most of the Doctor's arguments were based in mere human expediency; while the appeal to the word of God was so scanty as scarcely to be perceptible in the entire composition."[73] Anglican Evangelicals had justified their participation in the British and Foreign Bible Society with the maxim "The Bible and the Bible only is the religion of the Protestant" and effectively used the slogan in their anti–Roman Catholic polemics. Dissenters thus challenged

Anglicans to justify church establishments on the same basis—that of Scripture. As Irving's arguments were rooted in Old Testament precedent, they were especially suited to meet this criterion.

THE NEW CALVINIST APOLOGY FOR CHURCH ESTABLISHMENTS

The shift in Evangelical arguments occurred in the 1830s and was effected not by Irving directly, but by three Anglicans who had been closely associated with him in the 1820s: Hugh McNeile, Robert Benton Seeley, a leading Evangelical publisher, and Alexander Haldane of the *Record*.[74] The Calvinistic stance of all three inclined them to embrace an understanding of establishments which drew heavily from the Old Testament, as Calvinism had traditionally stressed the unity and continuity of the whole canon of Scripture.

Seeley's views were first published in a series of articles in the *Christian Guardian* in 1833 and then in book form the following year.[75] At the root of his view was an organic understanding of the state resting upon the Old Testament concept of a nation having a corporate responsibility to God. A Christian king, like any Christian father with family responsibilities, had a duty before God to provide spiritual guidance and instruction to those for whom he was responsible. Seeley argued that if the king (and Parliament) fulfilled this duty, God's blessing would be poured out on the nation:

England, when her Protestant church was formed, held, perhaps, about the tenth place among the nations; but England is now far above the mightiest of the empires . . . she owes it to that special favour and protection of God, which is never withheld from any nation which publicly honours him; and who, as he gave her a pure and scriptural church at first; gave he also wealth, and power, and prosperity, as a closely-connected consequence.[76]

To deny or neglect this duty would invite God's wrath; hence, even the mild and saintly Edward Bickersteth could write to a friend and tremble at the consequences of disestablishment: "The rejection of God's true Church by the Nation would be a national crime to be visited by awful national judgments."[77] Seeley was careful to distinguish between the government's obligation to support the national church and any attempt by the rulers to interfere with its functioning.[78] In his view, the doctrinal purity of the Church was safeguarded by the Thirty-Nine Articles, which constituted "a formidable bulwark against the encroachments of error and corruption."[79] Practical arguments were also advanced by Seeley. The Evangelical conviction about the inadequacy of Dissent either to evangelize Britain or to stand against infidelity was central to this line of defence. The comprehensive nature of the parochial system was intended to assure that all areas were supplied with spiritual oversight, a task for which he felt Dissent was numerically, financially, and spiritually inadequate.[80]

The *Record* especially emphasized points that endeared Evangelicals to the hearts of the Protestant constitutionalists. In its view, the basis of the constitution was the state's public acknowledgment of God in its support of the established churches. This was clearly represented in the sovereign, who as head of state and head of the Church of England, categorically repudiated Romanism:

> Does anyone doubt these facts? Let him read the Coronation Service, and he will see from what hand our monarchs acknowledge they receive their crown. Let him read the oath they take on their accession, and he will mark their repudiation, with a solemn oath, of the idolatry of the Papal apostasy.[81]

In so arguing, the newspaper was playing the last card in the hands of the Protestant constitutionalists, what Wellington in 1826 had called their "last entrenchment."[82] In keeping with the views of the Protestant Tories, the *Record* maintained that British prosperity and worldwide expansion were evidence of the Almighty's blessing upon a nation that had remained faithful to its Protestant calling:

> It was given of God to its founders to perceive the only rock on which a nation's prosperity can be securely and permanently built, according to the revelation he had vouchsafed of his Divine will. That foundation these master builders laid, and of the same materials raised they the superstructure. And what nation has been so blest, so prosperous, so happy as this? It is nowhere to be found.[83]

Paranoia that Rome would capitalize on the vacuum created by disestablishment was especially fanned by the *Record*, with great effect. Geoffrey Best correctly acknowledges that there was an influential body of Evangelicals in 1829 who believed "that old Rome's days were numbered"[84] and hence had not gone along with the Protestant constitutionalists on Catholic emancipation. Daniel Wilson, Sr., who had been so optimistic in 1829 about the decline of Rome,[85] had reversed his view by 1845.[86] In the same year yet another Evangelical bishop was repenting of earlier mistakes concerning Romanism. C. R. Sumner, who had jeopardized his friendship with the king in 1829 by voting for Catholic emancipation, acknowledged in his 1845 *Charge* that he had been wrong to have so voted.[87]

Anglican Evangelicals thus trembled for their church and for their nation when they contemplated the possibility of disestablishment, and it is important to note that many of them did so for theological reasons. Dr. Machin has suggested that the Tractarians were the first to "make the question of Church defense subordinate to theological conviction,"[88] but the Evangelicals developed their own theological defense of the church well before the emergence of the Oxford Movement. In so doing, however, they were forced into a politically unpopular and reactionary position and developed a defensive mentality that came to characterize much of Anglican Evangelicalism during the rest of the nineteenth century. They

were convinced that God would judge the nation if it spurned its spiritual responsibilities; it would justly forfeit God's blessings. Only the Evangelical revival
within the Church of England could hope to reverse this trend, as the *Record*
so strongly argued:

THE ACTS OF NATIONS are ever and anon referred to in the word of God. By these they
are justified or condemned. And as among individuals, so among nations, the acts of
primary importance and which determine the character of all the rest, are those which
immediately refer to the acknowledgment and worship of the one living and true God.
Let these be wanting, and the rest is refuse. They may exist, and be hollow and false,
and in this case (as in individuals so in nations) the tendency is to corruption and apostasy.
Our profession *has been* most hollow. We are now trembling on the next step of apostasy.
And it remains to be seen, whether the revival of Evangelical truth among us during the
last and present generations, will save us from the perpetuation of this crowning national
sin.[89]

In response to this perceived threat, the Evangelicals formed several organizations designed to defend the establishment—both from the threat of disestablishment and from the challenge of Romanism. The debate over the establishment
question took two forms: that of series of public lectures, upon conclusion of
which they were usually published; and that of a more direct pamphlet warfare.[90]
The most prominent of these organizations was the Christian Influence Society,
which was formed in 1832 and dominated by Alexander Gordon, a Recordite
commercial man. It was this society which sponsored Chalmers' well-known
lectures on church establishments given in London in 1838.[91] These in turn
induced the Protestant Dissenting deputies to invite Dr. Ralph Wardlaw, another
Scottish divine, to answer his arguments.[92] The Christian Influence Society in
response requested Hugh McNeile to reply to Wardlaw in another series the
following year, hoping to place the defense of the establishment on a more
biblical basis.[93] These lectures solicited yet another response from the Nonconformist evangelicals.[94]

Alexander Gordon was instrumental in setting up another organization similar
to the Christian Influence Society called the "Established Church Society" and
dominated by laymen who were later involved in the establishment of the Church
Pastoral-Aid Society (CP-AS).[95] A similar society but with a broader basis of
support was the Lay Union in defense of the established church. Although only
about one-third of the members of this committee are easily identified as Evangelicals, the fact that its most important officers were Lord Ashley and Sir Walter
Farquhar is indicative of its being dominated by Evangelicals.[96]

The ultra-Protestant Evangelicals, in forging an alliance with Protestant constitutionalists in defense of the establishment did just what they decried the
extreme Dissenters for doing in their attacks on the establishment. Both worked
in close cooperation with groupings in British political life with whom they were
at theological variance. Some of the evangelical Dissenters were willing to work
with Radicals (who were liberal Anglicans or "free thinkers") and with Roman

Catholic Irish Repealers because of their common interest in undermining the establishment.[97] The relation of the Dissenters to the Whigs was more complex, for "the Whigs desired, as they constantly stated, to keep Dissenting support without deserting the Establishment."[98] On the other side of the issue, Anglican Evangelicals allied with the "Protestant Constitutionalists, who numbered in their ranks the ultra-Tories and most of the Orthodox clergy."[99] The latter alliance, initiated in 1829 over the issue of Catholic emancipation, continued throughout the 1830s and 1840s. The Evangelical Protestant Association even took to reprinting anti–Roman Catholic speeches delivered in the House of Lords by Bishop Phillpotts of Exeter, a bishop well known for his antipathy to Evangelicals.[100] Dr. Ian Rennie has commented on their ties with the other elements of this pro-establishment and anti–Roman Catholic alliance: "By attaching themselves to the No Popery movement the Evangelicals aligned themselves not only with the most reactionary but perhaps also the most truly irreligious section of English public life."[101]

DISSENTING LOGIC: ESTABLISHMENTS IMPEDE EVANGELISM

Dissenters for their part justified their unholy alliance on the same basis as did Anglican Evangelicals: their piety, and especially their concern for evangelism, demanded it. J. A. James, the well-known Congregationalist minister, insisted, "Establishments necessarily annihilate the distinction between the church and the world, and render good men less useful than they would have been in other circumstances."[102] Greatly sharpening his concern for disestablishment was his linking it with progress in evangelism. In 1828 he wrote the following to a friend:

I must say, that I feel so deeply interested in the subject of revivals, that I am anxious to have every objection to them removed. The existence of our National Establishment is, in this country, a great impediment in the way of such a state of things here. I am quite convinced that, had not the Church of England been set up again at the Restoration, religion would have been in a far better state in the British empire than it is now. There was piety enough in the land at that time, had it been left to its own unrestricted energy and influence, to have filled the country by this time.[103]

In 1831 James demonstrated how seriously he misread Anglican feelings when he privately expressed his view that "by and by many of the evangelical clergy will come out and select a voluntary, unendowed Episcopal Church."[104] Assuming that Dissenting pressure for disestablishment would bring Evangelicals around to their position, orthodox Dissenters like James joined in the attacks on the establishment to the great detriment of pan-evangelical unity.

To Anglican Evangelicals the growth of their own party within the established Church was a sign of God's vindication of the establishment, whose parochial system was best suited to the evangelization of the nation. Thus the *Record*'s editor maintained:

A revival of true religion of the most striking character has taken place within her during the last thirty years. It is the work of the Spirit of God; and the most striking, in some respects, since the period of the Reformation. Does not God thus mark her for his own? If this is to go too far, Does it not prove her a true Church? Was a false Church ever thus revived?—If so, let us fear to inlist ourselves against her, "lest haply we be found even to fight against God."[105]

Dissenters like James, however, came to different conclusions:

One of the most extraordinary circumstances connected with the Church of England is, the vast increase of evangelical clergymen, in connexion with a system so manifestly and notoriously corrupt as is the Church of England. I cannot interpret this circumstance; a vast nucleus of piety has been forming in the midst of surrounding evils of an enormous character. The mischief of the present state of things is, that all hopes of a revival of religion are at present checked. . . . I am inclined, upon the whole, to regard the present situation of things as the commencement of a great conflict against organised systems of ecclesiastical corruption.[106]

Thus while Anglicans reasoned that state support of the establishment was a divinely appointed responsibility incumbent upon the government of a Christian nation, radical Dissenters argued that the state had no right to favor one religious group among Christians. In their view, state support of the Church was inevitably counterproductive because it identified the sacred with the secular. Anglican Evangelicals hoped that they would eventually leaven the whole church and so render the establishment effective in the cause of "Gospel religion." Nonconformists, on the other hand, were perplexed that so corrupt an institution could harbor a large and growing number of Evangelicals, and were convinced that disestablishment would benefit the evangelical cause.

Both sides were agreed on one thing: the Church of England was being profoundly affected by Evangelicalism. The movement was reinvigorating the establishment in a remarkable way, after almost a century of steady decline. A. D. Gilbert has commented, "The period 1740–1830 was an era of disaster, for whereas the Church of England had controlled something approaching a monopoly of English religious practice only ninety years earlier, in 1830 it was on the point of becoming a minority religious establishment."[107] In the view of most evangelicals, both inside and outside the Church, the resurgence of Evangelicalism was strengthening and reviving the Church and thus making it more competitive with evangelical Nonconformity. In the past the Methodists and New Dissent had grown best in areas "where the Church was either too weak or too negligent to defend its traditional monopoly of English religious practice."[108] By the 1830s, however, evangelical Nonconformity was coming to the end of its period of rapid expansion and was showing signs of being more concerned with protecting its territory than with enlarging its borders. It was felt that a Church of England reinvigorated by Evangelicals posed a serious threat to Dissenting gains. That Anglican Evangelicals were reasserting the monopolistic claims of the Church was seen as adding insult to injury.

Thus, during the 1830s, Anglican–Dissenting relations would appear to have reached their nadir, with apparently little prospect for any improvement in the situation. The Evangelicals who had long distanced themselves from Dissent were becoming more and more disaffected by the increasing attacks of Voluntaries upon the church establishment and personal invective on both sides of the divide was deepening and broadening the rift. The younger generation of Evangelicals represented by the *Record* seemed so intent on defending the establishment against Voluntary attacks that to contemporary observers it seemed that there was little hope for a cessation of hostilities among evangelicals.

2

Evangelicalism in Flux: Changes in the Evangelical Theology and Strategy of Evangelism

Both Anglican and Nonconformist evangelicals argued that their particular stance on the question of church establishments would best promote evangelism. In the long run the issue of urban evangelism was the most important factor in leading Anglican Evangelicals to question their unwillingness to work with Dissent at a local level. The thaw in the cold war between evangelicals came slowly. In order to appreciate why the evangelicals made the immense effort to evangelize the urban poor when they did, one must understand the changes occurring in the evangelical theology and strategy of evangelism during the 1820s and 1830s.

EVANGELICAL THEOLOGY OF CONVERSION

Since the beginning of the evangelical revival in the eighteenth century, there had been great differences of opinion over the important question of Christian assurance. How could one be assured that he was a Christian? How could one be sure that one had "faith"? The questions, of course, were not new and had been a central concern of seventeenth-century Puritanism. Three different answers had been developed by the eighteenth-century evangelicals. The Wesleyan Methodists had stressed personal religious experiences as the basis on which one could be assured. Most Anglican Evangelicals, however, were wary of the Wesleyan approach. They argued that a Christian might have faith and yet at the same time be plagued with doubts and fears; he was thus not to evaluate his condition by the state of his erratic emotions or give undue attention to any single religious experience. The real proof of faith was not to be found in anything so ephemeral, but rather in the gradual change which occurred in the life and character of a true believer. "Experience," not "experiences" was the key.[1] Anglican Evangelicals, like their Puritan forebears, found that this approach also had its problems in that it tended to encourage introspection. Individuals were to evaluate regularly their own spiritual condition, searching for evidence which would confirm to them the validity of their faith. The clearest statement of this Evangelical view can be found in Thomas Scott's *Treatise on Growth in Grace* first published in 1795, a work that was cited time and again in Evangelical writings.[2]

The third approach was developed by a small group of hyper-Calvinists. Their own experience of conversion often brought with it an intense conviction that God in his "Sovereign Grace" had elected them to salvation and that this choice had nothing to do with their own efforts or merit. To the more robust among them there was no problem with assurance. What was worrisome to the moderate Evangelicals, however, was the tendency of some of these hyper-Calvinists to take the logic of their views in a rather odd direction. Some of them became Antinomians—that is, they denied that as members of the elect they had any responsibility to obey the moral law. Indeed, as some of them reasoned, might not the breaking of the moral law demonstrate Christian freedom? God, having elected them with no regard to their works, was determined to redeem them with no regard to their deeds.

The mainstream Anglican Evangelicals reacted in horror to such views. Dr. Robert Hawker, vicar of Plymouth, angered Charles Simeon with his refusal to preach the need of holiness of life; he informed Simeon that the only reason the Apostles had bothered to preach it at all was because of the infant state of the church. William Wilberforce was equally appalled. Whenever Hawker was the visiting preacher at the Locke Chapel in London, Wilberforce avoided the services, anxious as he was to shield his children from Hawker's "poison." It was not a coincidence that most of the secessions of Evangelical clergy from the Church of England in the first half of the nineteenth century were led by men influenced by Hawker.[3] Concerned that Antinomian conduct would jeopardize their attempt to establish themselves as a leading party within the Church, fully deserving of its blessings and high ecclesiastical appointments, the Claphamite Evangelicals had strongly emphasized the need for caution and self-doubt in these matters.[4]

By the 1830s the Recordites had concluded that the view developed by the Evangelical mainstream had overemphasized the subjective side of faith in its reaction to the Wesleyans and the hyper-Calvinists. As befitting the mind of a lawyer like Alexander Haldane, the *Record* defined conversion in terms of an objective, legal, covenantal relationship that could be entered into and could be clearly recognized. The Calvinist Recordites rejected religious subjectivity and introspection as eminently unsound. The caution about religious certitude that had led the Clapham Sect to emphasize the importance of self-doubt and self-questioning was thus dismissed by the Recordites.[5] The importance of this shift was brought out in the *Record*'s replies to attacks made upon Evangelical preaching in the *Edinburgh Review* in 1837. It acknowledged that assurance could be gained from self-examination; a true Christian should be able to observe progress in his moral life. A more solid basis, however, was found in resting upon the promises of the covenant which he had embraced. Conversion was viewed in covenantal terms and assurance involved acknowledging the covenant and confessing its promises. Salvation was thus seen in an objective, contractual manner; it could be offered by an evangelist, and then both accepted and acknowledged by the convert.[6] This straightforward approach to assurance made evangelism a clear-cut matter of offering a contract and expecting a positive or negative response and was undoubtedly an impetus to evangelism.

It would be wrong, however, to suggest that the new emphasis led to a focusing upon a "conversion experience," something that had long been foreign to the Anglican brand of evangelicalism. Such a charge was made by the *Edinburgh Review* and refuted by the *Record*, which allowed for a variety of experiences: an imperceptible growth into faith during childhood; a gradual dawning upon the realization of an adult over the period of several years; and for "a large class whose conversion has been far more rapid, and is to be traced to some particular event."[7] The *Record*'s concern with these distinctions as to how the Holy Spirit brought people to conversion was closely related to Evangelical concern with the lapse of seventeenth-century Puritanism into Deism and Unitarianism during the eighteenth century. Having led the forces against Unitarianism in the Bible Society in the early 1830s and then for a time having supported the establishment of the rival Trinitarian Bible Society, the *Record* was especially concerned with anything which could be interpreted as denigrating the Person and place of the Holy Spirit.[8]

Clearly the Recordite approach to evangelism reflected its moderate Calvinist theology which sought to exalt the divine role in election and calling and to emphasize personal commitment and growth. This brand of Calvinism did not lead to paralysis, but rather to aggressive evangelistic efforts. The leading influence in this matter was exercised by Thomas Chalmers, the outstanding figure in the Scottish establishment. Steeped in a Calvinist distrust of human nature, Chalmers argued against the traditional Evangelical expectation that people would be drawn to the Gospel by the agency of the established church:

Nature does not go forth in search of Christianity; but Christianity goes forth to knock at the door of nature and, if possible, awaken her out of her sluggishness.... And seeing, that the disinclination of the human heart to entertain the overtures of the gospel, forms a mightier obstacle to its reception among men, than all the oceans and continents which missionaries have to traverse, there ought to be a series of aggressive measures in behalf of Christianity, carried on from one age to another, in every clime and country of Christendom.[9]

Thus the attempt by the Clapham Sect to strike a balance between Wesleyan subjectivity and the extremes of Antinomianism was rejected by the Calvinists associated with the *Record*. Furthermore, some Recordites were becoming concerned that there be a more aggressive response to the problems posed by urban evangelism. These theological considerations helped to induce some to challenge the traditional Simeonite acceptance of the limitations of the parochial system. Such an abandonment of church order would, in the long run, bring these Evangelicals much closer to cooperating with Nonconformists.

In the last few decades, historians have come to recognize the great influence that different understandings of biblical prophecy had on the development of popular culture in the late eighteenth and nineteenth centuries. E. P. Thompson has described the appearance of millenarian concerns among the lower classes in the 1790s and early 1800s, and argued that prophetic fantasies compensated for revolutionary fervor once the latter was frustrated.[10] J. F. C. Harrison has demonstrated in his work on popular millenarianism that the expectation of Christ's second coming provided many ordinary people with a belief system that gave meaning to the bewildering changes they experienced in industrializing Britain.[11] Fascination with biblical prophecy was not limited to a lunatic fringe nor was it merely a concern of the poor. R. A. Soloway has pointed out that such interpretations were more common than Thompson realized. Even in the 1790s, they "were prevalent among the higher orders as well, where they often became confused with revelations about age-old super-secret societies dedicated to the destruction of the monarchy and religion."[12] The French Revolution was undoubtedly a major factor in the rise of such speculation at this time. High Churchmen like the aged Bishop Samuel Horsley and his protégé, William Van Mildert (bishop of Llandaff from 1819–1826 and of Durham from 1826–1836), both preached and published on millenarian topics.[13]

By the 1820s, millenarianism was a preponderant concern of many Anglican Evangelicals. Edward Bickersteth, who was perhaps the best known Evangelical clergyman in England after Simeon, decided to write a book on the subject in the 1830s because people were so preoccupied with the question. His work was designed "to quiet the minds of those Christians, who were in danger, of forsaking plain and immediate duties for the path of thorny and doubtful speculation."[14] Before finishing the work, however, Bickersteth himself had abandoned the traditional Evangelical expectation concerning the future of Christianity. Rather than the gradual improvement of human history and the expansion of Christianity to the point where its triumph would be manifest to all, Bickersteth concluded that the current age would end cataclysmically with the literal, personal return of Christ to earth to establish his kingdom. The thousand-year reign of Christ spoken of in Scripture would not well up from below to engulf human history; rather it would descend from above and consummate it. Christ would not return after a period of peace and tranquility (the *post*millennial view); rather his return would precede and inaugurate the millennium (hence the *pre*millennial view).[15] From his new understanding, however, "he found new motives for diligence in the shortness of time, and the prospect of a speedy recompense from the Lord in the day of His appearing."[16]

Attacking the widely held postmillennial view in a letter to a friend, he wrote; "by a spiritual millenium yet to come, the Church cannot now be expecting his coming—but is brought to the false position 'My Lord delayeth his coming' & loses all the peculiar graces connected with that joyful hope.''[17] In another letter he drew out the implications for evangelism:

Look at his gracious promises; he means to gather a people out of the Gentiles . . . before he returns. . . . My mind is clear, a blessed harvest is to be gathered in before the Lord comes in the last tribulation near at hand. Rev. 7.14.

When we see these things we see the proper foundation for mis' [missionary] labours. Not to bring in the Millenium, the Lord will do that at his coming, but to gather a rich harvest of souls before he come, by spreading far & wide his glorious Gospel & preparing men for the great day of tribulation.[18]

This growing sense of urgency to the task of evangelism and the dissatisfaction with the established Anglican means partly explains the willingness of men like Bickersteth to consider new methods and efforts in evangelism. Bickersteth's change of views both signified and hastened the breakup of the consensus within Anglican Evangelicalism over a host of issues. Given his stature within the Evangelical community and the conviction with which he promulgated his views, Bickersteth was probably the single person most responsible for popularizing premillennialism in Britain during the 1830s and 1840s. In so doing he was able to make respectable views that had been brought into disrepute by the fact that they had been advocated by the Irvingites and the Plymouth Brethren.

Another issue disturbing evangelicalism at this time was the issue of revivalism. W. R. Ward has criticized R. A. Soloway's work *Prelates and People* for assuming that Evangelical clergy in this period were revivalistically inclined.[19] Yet, it is true that the progress of the religious revivalism in the United States in the late 1820s was affecting Evangelical attitudes toward evangelism. Even the staid *Christian Observer* was moved to comment, ''The well-judging portion of our American brethren seem justly jealous of what are called the 'revivals' which have lately taken place in the various parts of the Union.''[20] Cautious of such movements, the magazine recommended to the consideration of the Americans Jonathan Edwards's *On the Religious Affections*. The same journal also published a letter from Lyman Beecher, the Boston Congregationalist preacher who was a key figure in the revivals, a letter in which Beecher outlined a number of his own reservations.[21] The *Christian Observer*'s final verdict was that the American revival was to be regarded as a blend of good and evil in which it could not but ''rejoice with trembling.''[22] An American minister visiting England in 1828 reported, ''The subject of American revivals has often been introduced into the circles in which I have fallen, and always in a manner indicating a deep and serious interest.''[23] The *Record* was also curious about the American phenomena and on its publication of what it considered ''well authenticated'' reports, its editor praised them as being ''solid and highly important.''[24]

Individual Anglican leaders were also impressed. Daniel Wilson, Sr., citing ''the authentic reports of our American brethren,''[25] concluded in 1829 that ''the revivals of religion are actually commencing."[26] In a letter to William Sprague, the American author of *Lectures on the Revivals of Religion*, Edward Bickersteth confessed his deep interest in the subject and acknowledged of the work that "It has tended also to weaken if not remove many doubts and suspicions which I freely confess were in my mind concerning revivals."[27] The British religious press had reported that one of the chief means used in promoting the American revival was house-to-house visitation,[28] and Bickersteth was particularly impressed with this aspect of the American movement.[29]

The fact that Bickersteth promised William Sprague that he would promote consideration of his book among Anglican clergy was perhaps in part responsible for the agenda of the Islington Clerical Conference in January 1834.[30] The topic for discussion was "What may be regarded as the marks of a general revival of religion & what [are] the best means of promoting it."[31] While Baptist Noel lectured the conference at length on the nature and means of revivals, and Henry Blunt, the leading clergyman behind the *Record*[32] "spoke with much favour of the means adopted in America in reference to revivals,"[33] others doubted their effectiveness. John Hill, vice principal of St. Edmund Hall, Oxford, noted in his diary that Charles Bridges[34] "made a just remark on the deficiency of the American preacher in statement of Gospel truth."[35] Although, as Professor Ward suggests, Evangelicals were generally cautious about revivalism, it is clear that it was leading some to consider new means and methods of evangelism.

CHANGING STRATEGIES

While theological factors such as American revivalism, shifting views of biblical prophecy, and changing attitudes toward the basis of Christian assurance were all having their effect on Evangelical attitudes in the 1820s and 1830s, other more practical considerations were having an impact upon Evangelical strategy toward urban evangelism. The first significant challenge to Evangelicals to reexamine their traditional approach to the evangelization of the working classes came in 1815 with the publication of Richard Yates's *The Church in Danger*. Marshalling an impressive battery of statistics, he demonstrated the need for more churches and concentrated especially on the deficiency in London.[36]

Both the Parliamentary grant of £1 million and the establishment of the Church Building Commission in 1818 were partial answers to the problem outlined by Yates, but they were not the panaceas that many anticipated. While some churchmen may have tended to have become rather complacent as a result of the 1818 grant, supplemented as it was by another £500,000 in 1824, this was not the case with the Evangelical clergy.[37] In fact, they were the leaders when it came to parochial organization, initiating a multiplicity of parochial schemes from blanket societies to cottage lectures, from annual pastoral letters to parishioners to the use of lay agency.[38] As R. A. Soloway has demonstrated, parochial innovation and reform were major Evangelical concerns.[39]

While many did try to adapt and innovate within the traditional parochial framework in order to deal with the problems of the new urban growth, others were prepared to experiment with new methods. As early as 1822 a rather short-lived attempt was made to found a "city mission" in London,[40] and two years later two different groups of evangelicals endeavored to succeed where others had failed.[41] Of these only one demonstrated any ability to survive. The Metropolitan City Mission was formed in August 1824 and was a small, weak, and primitive attempt to evangelize the poorest of the poor.[42] An interdenominational mission, it used unpaid lay workers to visit in rotation a handful of preaching stations (usually rented rooms) that the society occupied. Meetings were held once or twice on weekdays in addition to Sundays, with agents preaching and praying. Later the workers tended to make their homes in rented accommodation in a specific area, either in rooms or in a house, and would then use them as rallying points and refuges.

The society continued many of its activities on a small but growing scale into the 1830s: opening Sunday schools, rescuing prostitutes, leading meetings in prisons and hospitals, distributing tracts. The work was never large. In 1835 it had only thirteen "stations" and twenty voluntary workers.[43] A major problem for the Metropolitan City Mission was the lack of attention it received from the evangelical press. An 1832 advertisement in the *Record* acknowledged that it was but a "small and almost unknown society."[44] In spite of its size, this mission was significant for several reasons: its interdenominational character, its lay control, and its use of lay agency. Its board was dominated by Anglican laymen, but others active in it included a handful of Anglican and Dissenting ministers. The willingness of these Anglican laymen to work with Dissenters, to disregard parochial boundaries, and to encourage lay agency in this manner all set them apart from other Anglicans.

Traditionally, Anglican Evangelicals had regarded evangelism as something that was to take place within the parochial system, rather than considering the alternative of forming specialized societies through which to proselytize. The leading influence on Evangelical views on the strategy of evangelism in this period was Thomas Chalmers. His book *Christian and Civic Economy* outlined the principles he had put into practice in his Glasgow parish in the late 1810s.[45] Possibly working from a German model, Chalmers adapted the large city to the rural parish by subdividing his own charge into twenty-five sections and appointing an elder in each area, both to oversee spiritual affairs and to handle social welfare.[46] Chalmers hoped that this principle of "locality" would strengthen the establishment by making it more efficient. Not to concentrate one's efforts in a specifically defined geographical area was in his view greatly detrimental to the success of many relief and instruction societies. While the bulk of the Scottish professor's writings were to become the basis of subsequent Evangelical pastoral manuals and were to be very influential abroad, London Evangelicals were relatively slow to adopt his evangelistic model.[47]

The first English organization to follow Chalmers's example appears to have been an Anglican district visiting society established at Brighton in the early

1820s.[48] Interest in the method was first aroused in London in 1826 when a committee was formed to promote the evangelization of the Irish poor in the parish of St. Giles. Using a paid lay agent and voluntary unpaid lay visitors, the whole area was brought under systematic visitation along the lines of Chalmers's model. By 1828, however, the costs had proved prohibitive. The committee published a book outlining the religious and physical conditions, stating that in its view "a more appalling or melancholy statement has seldom issued from the press of a civilized country."[49] Supporting the appeal, the *Record* noted that the committee had aroused the concern of a number of individuals who were establishing a "Central Metropolitan Visiting Society" whose design would be to publicize and relieve "the moral and physical evils" of the London poor.[50]

Two months later the establishment of the District Visiting Society (DVS) was announced.[51] In effect it was the result of the union of the St. Giles Committee with two other recently formed district visiting societies. The new committee appears to have been composed of wealthy young professionals, one-third of whom had served or were yet to serve as M.P.s. Several had a special interest in Evangelical missions to Ireland, and a few had close connections with the *Record*, although the views expressed in that paper did not always dominate in the committee.[52] Similarities between the new committee and the fledgling Metropolitan City Mission did exist. The youth and lay character of the committee, its advocacy of lay agency, and the presence of three leading Evangelical laymen on the boards of both organizations were all significant points of continuity. An important difference between the two was the DVS's hope of mobilizing large numbers of laymen in a systematic approach to urban evangelism. Chalmers's plan was to be the blueprint.

The use of laymen for other forms of domestic visitation was not new to the evangelicals; in fact they had used voluntary visiting for other purposes for a number of years. As early as 1777, London had known such organizations for charitable ends. John Gardner, a Methodist, had established the Benevolent, or Strangers' Friend Society, in London in 1785, and this society had set the pattern adopted by other similar organizations.[53] In both the Bible Society and the Religious Tract Society, as well as in the campaign against the slave trade, the Evangelicals developed techniques that allowed them to canvass from house to house for whatever purpose.[54] The use of laymen in a form of systematic and aggressive evangelism, however, represented a change from the traditional Evangelical Anglican approach. While eighteenth-century Evangelical clergy were generally diligent in the care and visitation of their flocks, they had hesitated to use laymen for the task of pastoral visiting.

Henry Budd was one of the first to break with the generally accepted practice. In 1810 he had explained to one of his laymen, the yet-to-be-ordained Edward Bickersteth, that, "In such a place as London it is quite impossible for the ministers to visit all their poor."[55] He thus justified his use of laymen to visit and relieve "the aged and the sick with families."[56] By the 1820s Budd's solution to the problems faced by overworked urban incumbents was being recommended by other leading clergy. In his introduction to an 1829 edition of Baxter's *Reformed Pastor*, Daniel Wilson, Sr., admitted that the Evangelical clergy were failing in the area of personal pastoral oversight. They were able to devote time to preaching, to ecclesiastical duties and they paid the occasional visit to the sick; "but what," Wilson asked, "have we done in personal care and direction, in affectionate catechetical conferences, in going from house to house, in visiting every family and individual in our districts?"[57] Given the exigencies of the urban setting, he felt that the clergy had to turn to lay agency: "Others must be set to work, and a machinery be erected, of which he [the clergyman] takes only the general guidance."[58] The willingness of Anglicans to make use of lay agency in this new, systematic form of evangelism was important for the subsequent development of pan-evangelicalism. Also significant was the fact that the DVS, which directed the agents, was itself under lay control. Only with the acceptance of these evangelistic methods and their promotion by Anglican laymen would Anglicans come to cooperate with Nonconformists in prosecuting the mission to the working class.

In turning to district visiting, Anglican Evangelicals testified to their disillusionment with the adequacy of the Church of England on several accounts: its resources were insufficient to provide adequate accommodation for the poor; its clergy unable to give effective pastoral oversight; its parochial system unequal to the task of being comprehensive; and its established Evangelical organizations inadequate to meet the challenge of the new urbanization. The situation in the 1820s and 1830s seemed to be deteriorating and the working classes' ignorance of, and apathy toward religion was an oft-repeated lament in DVS meetings and advertisements: "many individuals, and even whole families being found who seem scarcely aware of the existence of a Supreme Being, or their accountability as rational beings."[59] Their infrequent church attendance was more evidence of the same.

District visiting was advanced as a means of remedying this disturbing situation. By the employment of a citywide strategy which involved the formation of local district societies throughout London and with a carefully laid out procedure for visitors, it was hoped that the volunteers would be able to establish long-term relationships with those assigned to their oversight. The central committee would provide paid agents to survey the proposed district or parish, and these surveyors would gather information about the poor in the area: their names, occupations, size of family, and other data. Using this study, the district would then be subdivided, allowing a maximum of thirty families per section. Registers and journals were available for the visitors at the expense of the central committee, and detailed monthly reports were to be submitted to the local committees.

The district visitors were required to keep very detailed records of those under their care. If such records could be located, they would be of great interest to social historians, as the visitors were to determine and record numerous factors, including size of the family, ages of the children, schooling, literacy, ownership of a Bible and other religious books, frequency and place of attendance at public

worship, occupation, means of relief received, period of residence in accommodation, amount of rent paid, and how Sunday or leisure hours were spent!
These records were to assist the directors of the society in providing continuity
to its efforts. It would appear that the agents were diligent enough in their task
to enable close bonds to be formed. The detailed statistics that have survived
from 1831 to 1832 show that on average each volunteer had seventeen families
under his care and that he paid eighteen visits yearly to each family, or about
one visit every three weeks.[60] The religious tracts were central to the means, as
they were to be lent to the poor and regularly exchanged at each visit. In 1830
the DVS changed its name to the General Society for Promoting District Visiting
(GSPDV) in order to distinguish itself from the numerous local societies. Although primarily concerned with the establishment of such societies in London,
its impact was felt throughout Britain through the publicity it received in the
Record. The annual meetings of the society frequently mention the extension of
district visiting to various provincial cities and towns.

ANGLICAN DISTRICT VISITING SOCIETIES

In some respects the establishment of the DVS can be seen as a setback for
pan-evangelicalism, for from its inception the object of the society was clear: it
was to be an Evangelical Anglican organization, similar in form and mission to
the London Christian Instruction Society (CIS), an interdenominational mission
established by Dissenters in 1825 to evangelize the London poor. Membership
of the DVS's Central Committee was restricted to members of the established
church. Initially Dissenters were welcome to assist in the formation of district
committees; indeed they were "cordially invited" to lend their assistance.[61] The
gulf between the two societies was evident in 1829, however, when the DVS
declined to cooperate with the Dissenting society on the matter of Sabbath
observance, even though some DVS committee members had close connections
with the CIS.[62] With the increasing bitterness of the debate over Voluntarism,
the desire to cooperate with Dissenters seems to have disappeared altogether and
was replaced with an emphasis upon the importance of the society in drawing
the poor to the ministrations of the established Church.[63] By 1834 the revised
aims of the society included attracting the poor to the Church of England,[64] and
the following year the organization was advanced as evidence against the Dissenters' charge of inefficiency.[65]

Significantly the directors of the society were unwilling to budge on the
question of church order. While hoping for clerical support, the committee
cautioned in 1829 that "where it cannot be obtained, they will feel themselves
at full liberty to open communications with other individuals desirous of establishing Local Committees in connection with the Society."[66] Pressure from
Evangelical clergy was forthcoming, and it was argued that respect for parochial
boundaries be shown so that the society not lose "the cordial sanction and
approbation of the highest ecclesiastical authorities."[67] Thoroughly unrepentant,

the society incorporated the following statement in its "Plan of Operation": "It is . . . to be distinctly understood, that even should the sanction of the Clergyman be withheld, a Society may *still be formed where circumstances render it expedient.*"[68] By 1832 a quarter of the local associations were under the control of committees operating without clerical patronage. This disregard for church order clearly made the GSPDV unacceptable to the bishop of London, and while he came to accept the agency of district visiting, Bishop Blomfield made it clear that such activities had to be carried out "in subordination to the clergy."[69]

The fact that these Evangelical laymen were determined to ignore parochial barriers reflects in part the influence of the theological considerations discussed above. It also underlines a point which can hardly be overemphasized: the strong anticlericalism of many of the Evangelical laymen, especially those associated with the *Record*. The Recordites were as one in their rejection of the accommodating policy of the Clapham Sect; they risked nothing by ignoring ecclesiastical decorum. The important influence Scottish Presbyterianism had in the Recordite circle—with its strong emphasis on lay leadership—undoubtedly had a significant impact. Ian Rennie has commented, "Although Evangelicalism had always attracted laymen . . . there was always enough anticlericalism among Evangelical laymen to make them suspicious of any suggestion of clerical pretension whatsoever."[70]

The determination by the Evangelical laymen in control of the District Visiting Society to ignore parochial boundaries and to steer a course independent of the Evangelical clergy in order to evangelize reflected in part this strong anticlericalism. It is noteworthy that until the mid–1830s the only societies in which Anglican Evangelicals could prosecute the urban mission (the Christian Instruction Society, the General Society for Promoting District Visiting, and the Metropolitan City Mission) were all controlled by laymen, all committed to disregarding parochial boundaries, and all used lay agency. In spite of its irregularity, the DVS did receive the support of the Evangelical bishops. J. B. Sumner, who in his 1829 *Charge* had urged his clergy to establish such parochial societies for the purposes of evangelism and relief, gave his backing 1831.[71] The following year he was joined by Dudley Ryder, bishop of Lichfield and Coventry, both in advocating district visiting and in countenancing the GSPDV.[72]

PROBLEMS OF DISTRICT VISITING

Even with this episcopal support the central society struggled simply to survive during the 1830s. Plagued by a continual lack of finances, due in part to structural problems, the society was chronically in debt to its treasurer. Another obstacle to the success of the organization was its lack of clerical support, in part because of the scarcity of Evangelical incumbents in London during the early 1830s. Although the number of local associations was rapidly expanding, it was widely felt that the recruitment of visitors was the greatest problem that faced the society. In 1832 the *Christian Observer* expressed the view that

the main fault is with the laity, especially persons of local weight and influence, who
are not sufficiently zealous in coming forward to assist their ministers in this interesting
duty. In some district societies, the visitors are chiefly very young persons, and persons
in the less influential departments of society; many of whom spend almost the whole of
the little leisure they can command, at great personal sacrifice, in works of Christian
mercy, while the great majority of their richer neighbours, including many strenuous
"professors of religion," and men and women who have ample time, and few pressing
occupations, stand aloof.[73]

The squalor and misery of the slums combined with the social opprobrium
connected with such religious activity undoubtedly served to deter many. While
still a layman, Edward Bickersteth was discouraged by his parents from visiting
the "sick poor." They feared that familiarity with other visitors of lower rank
might cause him to "forget his position in society."[74] Opposition to such evangelism in the religious press did not help. A hostile *British Critic* delighted in
caricaturing district visitors and in an article portrayed one poor woman who
was plagued by a host of warring Anglican and Nonconformist evangelicals.[75]

The majority of visitors were women, and the focus of district visiting came
to be on the conversion of their working-class sisters: "Go on, Ladies, visit the
houses of the poor, and when you administer comfort and consolation to the
wife who, perhaps, is neglected for the alehouse dramshop, teach, oh! teach her
those ways by which she may bring her husband back."[76] The treasurer of the
society eventually acknowledged that there was "a disinclination on the part of
men to engage in this work" and thus urged them to support the society financially
instead. F. K. Prochaska has pointed out that in terms of charitable visitation

one of the secrets to successful visiting was a knowledge of domestic management;
everyone agreed that female volunteers moved more easily amongst wives and mothers
and were more sympathetic to their problems; and some argued that they were also more
likely to uncover female dissimulation. Moreover, the use of women as visitors was in
accord with society's deeply ingrained beliefs about the family. The protection of the
family was the cornerstone of nineteenth-century social policy; within the family the role
of wife and mother was thought crucial.[77]

The same historian has written an insightful study of the sort of women who
undertook this sort of volunteer work.[78]

In spite of the problems with finance, recruitment, and clerical support, the
number of district visitors and local visiting associations increased steadily during
the early 1830s. It was estimated that there were 300,000 families in London in
1830.[79] By 1833 the GSPDV had 10,455 families under regular visitation through
the agency of 573 visitors, in association with twenty-two local societies. In the
same year the Nonconformist CIS reported that it had 1,300 workers in the
metropolis, sixty-three associations and 32,452 families under systematic visitation; Dissenting efforts continued to grow throughout the decade.[80] The impact
of these figures was not to be lost on the Anglican laymen concerned with

evangelism. If in London, where Dissenters were relatively weak, they could still muster enough visitors to cover three times the number of families visited by Anglican volunteers, then urban evangelism was inevitably going to be directed by Nonconformists who might be hostile to the establishment.

During the 1830s Anglican Evangelicals were becoming increasingly dissatisfied with the effectiveness of district visiting as an evangelistic tool, but much of this dissatisfaction stemmed from factors unrelated to the problems of organization, finance, and recruitment. From its very inception the society had attempted to combine evangelism with the distribution of relief, something that Thomas Chalmers strongly opposed. Previously Evangelical benevolence had expressed itself through numerous but often uncoordinated societies, some organized on a city or national basis; others were associated with the local parish machinery. Opposition to the use of district visitors as dispensers of relief was offered by the *Record*. The paper, while it enthusiastically supported the evangelistic aim of the society, strongly opposed its distributing charity, arguing that such aid should be given privately and not through such a public organization. The *Record* feared that such a publicly acknowledged aim would encourage "dissimulation and hypocrisy" among the poor and would weaken the spiritual aims of the society.[81]

The society responded that the disruption caused by urbanization rendered anachronistic the form of paternalism advocated by the *Record* and pleaded that the anonymity of the poor and the magnitude of the destitution effectively dulled the sympathies of the higher classes. In order to convince the doubtful that the poor could not manage without the aid the district visitors gave them, descriptions of utter destitution were paraded by the society in their advertisements. One local association reported that they often had "the satisfaction of preventing absolute death by starving."[82]

In order to counter criticism that it was merely fostering duplicity and indolence among the poor, the role of the visitors in discerning fraud came to be stressed and offered as evidence that people could safely channel money through the GSPDV. Thus the visitors, whose primary role was to have been evangelism, became the "moral and spiritual police" of the poor, reassuring the wealthy that the fruits of their benevolent paternalism were not being squandered.[83] Such a concern may seem harsh and mean-spirited to modern readers accustomed to the welfare state, but as one historian has pointed out:

We must remember something which those who worked for nineteenth-century charities never forgot: there was not enough money to go around, and that those in need were often so desperate that funds must not be wasted on fraudulent cases. When it was common for from 5 to 10 per cent of those admitted to a visiting society's books to die soon after, imposters took on a sinister importance.[84]

To meet the charge that charitable relief was fostering a dependence on the society, the visitors' promoting of self-help came to be stressed. This emphasis was wholly lacking in the original statement of the DVS's aims.[85] Yet another concern that served to divert attention from the original evangelistic emphasis was the apology advanced on behalf of the society as a valuable agent of social control. While the society attempted to promote itself in terms of its social utility, it also strove to prevent its lapsing into a welfare service. It emphasized that its leading object was "to improve the religious and the moral state . . . of the poor,"[86] and when one of its local societies forsook evangelism, the Central Committee declared that it "ceased to exist, for they could not consider a Benevolent Society, into which it had lapsed, however intrinsically valuable, as in any material degree supplying the place of a really efficient and well conducted District Visiting Society."[87]

By 1835 the apology advanced by the advocates of district visiting had significantly changed. Some of the changes represented accommodations by the GSPDV to its Evangelical constituency, but the total effect of these was to shift the original focus from evangelism to other concerns. The visitors had become the "moral and spiritual police" of the poor, ferreting out the undeserving and the unscrupulous; instructors in self-improvement, collecting pennies from the poor for a variety of schemes; promoters of the establishment principle among the "lower orders"; and in the view of some they were emissaries of the higher classes who were to render the working classes dutifully obedient and compliant.[88] These factors, combined with the problems of recruitment, organization, and finance, all contributed to Evangelical disillusionment with voluntary district visiting as a means of evangelism. While the strategy had been particularly effective in areas of London like Islington, where a strong Evangelical incumbent ruled, its overall impact on the metropolis was a disappointment to Evangelicals, as Hugh Hill, the secretary of the GSPDV acknowledged in 1835.[89]

In spite of the decline and the eventual demise of the GSPDV in the late 1830s and its reorganization as the Metropolitan Visiting and Relief Association in 1843, district visiting was itself to continue as an important part of nineteenth-century parish life.[90] The method was adopted by clergy of all shades of churchmanship as well as by Dissent and was used in support of a host of philanthropic activities as well as evangelism. By 1850 virtually every parish church in London had a visiting society attached to it; only thirty-six churches were without one by then, and most of these were located in wealthy areas of the city.[91] Promoted as a means of bridging class barriers, the societies normally consisted of middle-class ladies, who, by the end of the century handled much of "the regular distribution of money, food, and clothing" that the churches had to dispense.[92] By 1914, however, most of the societies had disappeared because of the transformation of attitudes toward the relationship between the churches and society which occurred in the 1890s and 1900s.[93]

THE IMPACT OF DISTRICT VISITING ON EVANGELICAL STRATEGY

As Evangelicals came to doubt the effectiveness of voluntary district visiting in the early 1830s, they considered the possibility of using a paid lay agency instead. As early as 1832 the committee of the GSPDV had considered whether to recommend the employment of full-time paid lay agents to its local societies. A motion to that effect failed, not because of opposition to the principle, but because the committee members doubted that competent Anglican laymen could be found for the work.[94] Unable to match the Nonconformists in voluntary efforts, Evangelicals did not expect to fare much better with their own paid lay agency. It was becoming more and more clear that the Evangelicals could not alone effect the evangelization they so earnestly desired.

Thus in a number of ways these early efforts were to shape future Evangelical strategy in regard to urban evangelism. They had spotlighted concern on domestic missions at a time when the foreign mission scene was attracting the overwhelming amount of money, personnel, and attention. The efforts had enlisted the cooperation and talent of key clergy and laymen who were to mold Evangelical opinion over the next few decades. They had popularized Chalmers's systematic, aggressive approach to evangelism and had promoted the widespread use of laymen in parochial activities that had long been regarded by many Evangelicals as the preserve of the clergy.

Especially significant for the development of pan-evangelicalism was the experience gained from district visiting. It had helped to uncover the serious dimensions of spiritual destitution while proving itself inadequate to alleviate the situation. By the early 1830s a number of prominent Anglican laymen had concluded that a paid lay agency was imperative for the proper, systematic evangelization of the metropolis. At the same time they doubted that Anglicans had the manpower resources to accomplish the task. These men had demonstrated that while they were prepared to take the steps they deemed necessary to defend the establishment, they were also willing to ignore ecclesiastical order, and if necessary, to take action independent of and unpopular with the Evangelical clergy. The interdenominational Metropolitan City Mission, which had been organized in the 1820s, had not been able to attract a broad following; the District Visiting Society had proved itself inadequate to the task at hand. By the mid–1830s the Recordites had come to the conclusion that measures to employ full-time lay agents were needed.

While many laymen stopped short of cooperating with Dissent, some did not; they had concluded that such Evangelical unwillingness sacrificed souls to the idol of ecclesiastical expediency. Evidence of the radicalizing of Recordite laymen on this score can be seen in the calls made for the establishment of an Anglican home mission society in the early 1830s.[95] Some correspondents with the *Record* made it clear that they were willing to work with Dissent and hoped that such an organization would ignore parochial boundaries.[96] Others, like Frederick Sandoz, who emerged as the chief organizer of the Church Pastoral-Aid Society (CP-AS), wanted an ostensibly Anglican society, but one that would employ laymen who would officiate at services held in buildings owned by the society. If necessary, he suggested, the buildings could be registered as Dissenting chapels![97]

While Anglicans discussed the possibility of establishing a Church home mission, others were busy organizing the London City Mission (LCM), which sought to appeal to a broad cross section of evangelicalism. In fact its founders were counting on the financial support of Anglican laymen willing to dispense with church order.[98] The founding and early development of the LCM will be discussed in detail in the next chapter, but its establishment cannot be ignored in the formation of what became the Church Pastoral-Aid Society.

The *Record*, which initially endorsed the interdenominational London City Mission, also approved of Sandoz's plan for a distinctly Anglican home mission. Indeed, it argued that the formation of the City Mission would "facilitate and quicken" the establishment of a society "now so long delayed," by provoking Anglicans to jealousy.[99] For conservative Evangelicals this was the case; their disapproval of the LCM was "among the causes of the origination of the Pastoral-Aid Society itself."[100] For the radicals, however, even Sandoz's plan was not adequate,[101] their objection being that "it does not prominently propose interfering with parishes where there are unfaithful pastors, and therefore . . . [it is] too restricted compared with the magnitude of the evil."[102] In his efforts to organize the Church Pastoral-Aid Society, Frederick Sandoz used the threats of the radicals to put pressure on the bishop of London to patronize the new society. He wrote to Bishop Blomfield cautioning him that the more extreme among the laymen were prepared to form an independent evangelistic society should the CP-AS fail.[103] Such threats reportedly led the bishops to fear that irresponsible laymen "were beginning to train up an army of unordained and unsubjected lay-agents" over whom the bishops would have no control.[104]

There were in effect two issues at stake: lay agency, and Evangelical party control of the new organization. The bishops succeeded in forcing the CP-AS to back down on the issue of its directly employing lay workers; it agreed that such workers would be employed only by the clergy.[105] When a proposal to exclude lay workers altogether was made in 1837, the *Record* vehemently objected to such a fundamental change.[106] The newspaper felt that lay agency was not only necessary, but would insure Evangelical domination of the society. Concession on this issue would swamp the society with High Churchmen who would "insist that the erroneous doctrines contained in so many of the tracts of the Christian Knowledge Society, shall be circulated through the country."[107] Although the proposed change was defeated and the organization progressed and flourished, its constitution was a far cry from what Sandoz originally proposed. Great pressure had been put on the lay organizers to conform to church discipline and order. (Even a few leading Evangelicals had urged the new society to concede the issue of lay agency, notably Christopher Benson, William Carus of Cambridge, and Edward Bickersteth.)[108] If, as the *Record* seemed to suggest, there were some laymen who had withheld support from the LCM because of their hopes of a somewhat irregular Anglican home mission, then they were sure to be disappointed with the final outcome of the CP-AS.[109]

The consensus among Anglican Evangelicals had begun to break up in the 1820s, and the debates over the establishment of the CP-AS demonstrate the lack of agreement among Anglican Evangelicals on the crucial issue of evangelism. Evangelicals were not even in full agreement on the propriety of using a paid lay agency. And those who supported its use were split into three camps: those who insisted it be done through a church society that respected parochial divisions, those who desired an unauthorized Anglican society that would ignore such limitations, and those (mostly laymen) who were willing to cooperate with Dissenters in order to see the task carried out.

Anglican Evangelicalism was thus in great ferment in the mid–1830s, especially over the question of evangelism. Many factors were working to arouse Evangelical interest in missions to the working classes, but at the same time there was great uncertainty as to what was the proper course for them to follow. Their interest in urban evangelism had grown at the same time that they organized to defend the establishment. As such evangelism had been promoted as an important means of strengthening the establishment, of demonstrating its efficiency, and of countering the advances of Dissent, one might have expected little progress for pan-evangelical cooperation. Yet there remained a group of Anglican laymen who were willing to cooperate with Dissent in evangelism, provided that they could be assured that it would not endanger the establishment. Initially only the *Record* was willing to approve such a radical approach.

Part Two

The Urban Mission

3

New Approaches to Urban Evangelism

The founding of what was to become the largest and possibly the most enduring interdenominational mission in Britain, the London City Mission, resulted from the efforts of an eccentric Scotsman, David Nasmith.[1] Arriving in London in March 1835, Nasmith visited Bishop Blomfield to inform him of his intention to establish an interdenominational mission similar to the ones he had pioneered in Glasgow, Dublin, and New York City.[2] His arrival in London coincided with the publishing of an important pamphlet by Baptist Noel, a leading Evangelical clergyman in the metropolis. Noel's work, *The State of the Metropolis Considered*, was to evangelicals of the early Victorian period what Richard Yates's *The Church in Danger* had been to the initiators of the first phase of the Church Building Commission. It received prominent attention in the *Record*, which reprinted long excerpts from its pages.[3]

Central to Noel's argument was the conviction that aggressive means must be employed to reach the poor:

It is vain to expect, that, by a proper and primary impulse, originating with themselves, those aliens from Christianity will go forth on the inquiry after it. The messengers of Christianity must go forth upon them. Many must "go to and fro" among the streets and lanes, and those deep intricacies which teem with human life to an extent far beyond the eye or the imagination of the unobservant passenger, if we are to look for the increase, either of a spiritual taste or of Scripture knowledge, among the families.[4]

The isolation of social classes one from another in London was a complaint often heard in the religious press. The *Christian Observer* decried the fact that the "great and prevailing evil amongst the members of the Established Church in the metropolis is that gulf and *hiatus* between the higher and lower classes of society, which nearly precludes all communications, whether social, civil, or religious, between them. . . . the poorer classes live and die quite in a world by themselves."[5]

Noel sought to use statistics on available church accommodation to demonstrate the extent of the spiritual destitution of the metropolis. He maintained that despite the efforts at church building there were over half a million Londoners "living without a public acknowledgment of God, and in contempt of all the means of grace."[6] Appalled by the conditions of the working classes, Noel particularly attacked Sabbath breaking, spirit drinking, the growth of mendicancy, gambling, prostitution, robbery, and prisons, which in his view were providing 12,000 children with "training for theft and vice."[7] His solutions may have been "wildly impractical," but they do illustrate the seriousness with which Evangelicals regarded the situation.[8] Noel proposed increasing the number of Sunday services while shortening their length, the subdivision of large urban parishes, the building of proprietary chapels, episcopal approval for services in unlicensed rooms, greater use of the laity, and open-air preaching. In fact a number of his proposals were later adopted by Anglican clerics. Although Noel's pamphlet was addressed to Bishop Blomfield, it came as a clarion call to Evangelicals, who like its author were anxious that the Church of England should not "die of dignity."[9] His statistics were repeatedly cited in sermons, articles, and lectures. The pamphlet also aroused the attention of Nonconformist evangelicals and did much to facilitate Nasmith's establishment of the LCM.[10]

Nasmith was doggedly determined that the mission he wanted to organize be interdenominational in character despite the numerous warnings he received about the impracticality of the scheme. He corresponded with Baptist Noel, who told him that the clergy would not act without the consent of the bishop and the laymen would not move without the support of the clergy. Interdenominational rivalry meant that one had to choose between Nonconformity and the Establishment.[11] One factor that did augur well for the formation of the new society was Nasmith's experience in organizing other such missions. While Anglicans discussed the spiritual destitution of the masses and pleaded with the ecclesiastical hierarchy to take special action, Nasmith proceeded with organizing the LCM. Within a month of its inception the new society had agreed to appoint its first agent, who was to work under the supervision of an Anglican clergyman.[12]

Nasmith gave top priority to seeking the support of leading Anglican laymen and succeeded in inducing one of the best known Evangelicals of the day, Thomas Fowell Buxton, to act as treasurer. In the first six months of the LCM's existence, however, the donations to the society were very limited and were largely confined to Buxton's wealthy family and relatives. Buxton himself was hardly a typical Anglican. While he had been baptized at the insistence of his father, he was more indebted to his Quaker mother for his religious upbringing than to Anglicanism.[13] Until his marriage (to a Quaker) he often attended Friends' meetings in the home of his sister-in-law, the well-known prison reformer, Elizabeth Fry.[14]

Besides this Nonconformist influence on him, Buxton was unusual in that he was unrepresentative of what had become the political mainstream of Anglican Evangelicals. A life-long Whig, he was typical of the second generation of the Clapham Sect, which Clyde Ervine has demonstrated was moving in a Whig/ Liberal direction at a time when Evangelicalism was heading in the opposite direction.[15] Central to the Whig philosophy was the "attainment of perfect civil and religious liberty" and they "could never see why members of a Protestant establishment should shun Protestant Dissenters."[16] Bishop Bathurst, an earlier Whig appointee, had maintained an openness to all Christians, including Roman Catholics, demonstrating a breadth of tolerance uncommon for clerics of his day.[17] To be sure, the common Whig view of Christianity fell far short of the Evangelical view. Geoffrey Best has described Whig Christianity as "largely a blend of the classical precepts of morality and the moral sense of the Scottish philosophers, improved by Christ's special injunctions to toleration and forbearance, and substituting for the dreamy ambition of establishing Christ's kingdom on earth, the nearer but no less desirable object of the Reign of Liberty."[18] Individual Evangelicals, while unhappy with such a theology, did embrace Whig politics in the same way that many of their Dissenting brethren had and objected no more than moral Dissenters to "the political leadership of immoral Whigs."[19]

This Whig broadmindedness is important, for it is unlikely that Nasmith's dream of a pan-evangelical mission would have been realized without it. Key to the success of the struggling organization was Nasmith's enlisting of another well-known Evangelical Whig—Baptist Noel. The son of a prominent Evangelical Whig M.P., Noel had himself been urged to enter politics rather than the Church.[20] His family connections gave him influence with Whig aristocrats and M.P.s.[21] His devotion to the Whig cause, however, was not simply out of family loyalty. In 1836 he toured Ireland for the Melbourne government and published a work in 1841 that attacked the Corn Laws.[22]

It is evident that he was instrumental in persuading leading Evangelical Whigs to lend their public support to the LCM at a time when many Evangelicals were putting the greatest possible distance between themselves and Dissent.[23] In 1840 the LCM Magazine acknowledged that without his support and advocacy during the first seven months of its existence, the LCM's "success and operations . . . [were] very limited," and credited his efforts with being crucial to its becoming "known to the religious world, and widely supported."[24] With Noel's backing and influence the LCM's funds increased dramatically. Receipts in the first six months of its operation—before Noel joined the LCM—were £176; in the following six months, they were £2,539.[25]

The significance of the "Whig factor" can be further seen in the fact that the first Anglican bishop to support an interdenominational city mission was Edward Stanley, the Whig bishop of Norwich, appointed by Melbourne in 1837.[26] Stanley, while by no means an Evangelical, was averse to High Church and Tractarian views[27] and was remarkably active in the Church Missionary Society (CMS) and the CP-AS in the 1840s.[28] He freely cooperated with Nonconformists in his diocese[29] and was the first bishop to show an interest in "Ragged Schools."[30]

His embracing of Nonconformist denominations seems to have been an extension of his liberalism generally and was not impelled by the necessity to cooperate for evangelistic purposes.

THE LCM'S RECEPTION BY ANGLICANS

Initially only a handful of London clergy were willing to risk their bishop's wrath and cooperate with the LCM. Bishop Blomfield's displeasure with the mission was first expressed in December 1835, when he instructed one clergyman to withdraw his name from the published list of superintendents while saying nothing to other clergy who were advertised as being connected with the society.[31] The reception given the LCM by the leading Evangelical publications is indicative of the extent of the division within Evangelicalism on the issue of such cooperation. The *Record* was the first to notice the new society's existence, but even then only did so six months after its founding—despite the fact that the mission had been advertising on its front page.[32] The delay in the *Record*'s declaration of support was not due to ignorance of the LCM's existence but to uncertainty, as its editor explained, "as it has only been after much consideration, so it has not been without difficulty that we have reached the conclusion that it is our duty to recommend it to the countenance and support of our readers."[33] This division of opinion among the paper's owners underlines the uncertainty among Evangelicals. It is difficult to assess what Alexander Haldane's view was at this time, although as both the son and nephew of prominent Scottish congregationalist evangelists, he might be expected to support the LCM. Certainly the *Record* was unlikely to have lent its support in the face of determined opposition from Haldane.

Three leading figures behind the *Record* were clearly in favor of the policy adopted. These included two of the three original proprietors of the newspaper. Andrew Hamilton, the person responsible for introducing both Alexander Haldane and the Reverend Henry Blunt to the *Record* in 1828,[34] was one of the original owners and one of the chief writers for the journal. He was also one of three friends of David Nasmith who agreed to join him in founding the LCM in 1835 and undoubtedly strongly urged its promotion in the *Record*.[35] It is likely that Hamilton and Nasmith had come to know one another in their native Scotland. A second figure prominently associated with the paper was J. S. Reynolds, another of the original owners.[36] Reynolds, like Hamilton, was among the first supporters of the LCM.[37] It is significant that Reynolds was also a founding member of the District Visiting Society, and it was he who had proposed its employment of paid lay agents in 1832.[38] The third person associated with the *Record* was one of the chief spokesmen in defense of the establishment. Alexander Gordon,[39] the organizer of both the Christian Influence Society and the Established Church Society, was involved with the LCM almost from its inception.[40] Opposition to the scheme in Recordite circles was likely to have been offered by the Reverend Henry Blunt, who remained aloof from the LCM till his death in 1843. Blunt's unwillingness to cooperate in such evangelistic efforts with Dissenters was common to the majority of the Evangelical clergy in the 1830s and 1840s. While few London clergy were willing to countenance such cooperation with Nonconformity, a number of Recordite laymen were. Much of this openness to Dissenters was probably due to the strong influence on the Recordites of non-Anglican, reformed theology from Scotland and the Continent.[41]

Thus the *Record* declared that while it was aware of "the dangers of infringing on Church discipline and order," it yet considered that "the gigantic good" of evangelizing the poor outweighed the disadvantages and it expected that the effect of the scheme would be to "fill the churches, not to empty them." The other alternative, that of leaving the control of the LCM in the hands of the Dissenters would have, "to an incomparably greater degree," strengthened Dissent and weakened the Church.[42] Still, the greatest problem in such cooperation was the voluntary issue, but the *Record* was willing to accommodate.[43]

In part this new willingness was due to an increasing sense of frustration of Evangelicals within the establishment, especially with restrictions hampering them from building and endowing their own chapels to evangelize the destitute. The Evangelicals had lost a major battle in regard to such restrictions in 1818. During the Parliamentary debates on the legislation to establish the Church Building Commission, Sir William Scott had successfully moved an amendment that deleted clauses that would have permitted subscribers to erect a church with the bishop's permission and to exercise the patronage themselves. This was a severe setback for Evangelical laymen who were anxious to endow churches, as they wanted the assurance that these churches would have an Evangelical succession. Such obstacles, argued the *Record*, only facilitated the growth of Dissent and prevented the Church from being strengthened by conscientious Churchmen:

How deplorable, how foolish, how wicked a system is this. Let it be continued, and this new Society may assuredly injure the Church. And what is more galling and mournful to her attached members, it ought to do it. Let the Church be injured rather than men's souls be lost.[44]

While able to rejoice at the founding of the LCM and convinced that it would result in "great good," the *Christian Guardian* was somewhat more cautious than the *Record*. Although able to support such interdenominational organizations as the Bible Society, it stopped short of offering the same to the LCM, doubting the validity of such a society.[45] Instead the journal proposed that Anglican clergy set up their own city mission which would simply ignore parochial boundaries! Reflecting the same sense of frustration which the *Record* had expressed, the *Christian Guardian* declared, "We are aware that some difficulties and impediments of a legal nature exist . . . but it is really time that this POPISH SYSTEM should be exploded."[46]

Steadfast opposition to the LCM was expressed in the *Christian Observer*, the organ of conservative, mainstream Evangelicalism. The editor decried the scheme as "neither desirable nor feasible,"[47] while one contributor reasoned that it "invades the principle of our Establishment, spoils it of its due agency, and by a fallacious liberalism levels constituted order with dissent. Hence confusion and disorganization under the semblance of piety, charity and usefulness."[48] By violating the parochial plan of the Church of England, the LCM was felt to be destroying the prominence of the Church and was also weakening its ability to evangelize by directing Anglican resources away from their proper channel. Cooperation with Dissenters might be justified for narrow, limited activities such as those of the British and Foreign Bible Society and the Religious Tract Society but not for such wide-ranging purposes as proposed by the LCM. Fears were also expressed in the *Observer* that the city missionaries would form their own churches or that the Mission might "generate a lawless schism, without the master-mind and the commanding influence of a Wesley either to shape or controul [sic] it." Furthermore, reflecting fears of the blurring of doctrinal distinctions, the writer objected that "There are no articles, no test; and the word 'Evangelical' contains no spiritual virtue to ensure the orthodoxy, the piety, or the prudence, either of the managers or the agents."[49] It was this sort of criticism that the LCM Committee tried to counter in its management of the mission. The LCM could not deny the charge that it violated the parochial plan of the Church of England. Indeed, this was the very basis of much of its appeal to Anglican Evangelicals. The LCM was eager to demonstrate that it alone was adequate to address the task at hand, and that in doing so, it would not be to the detriment of the Church.

A fourth periodical that wielded considerable influence among Evangelicals was the *Christian Lady's Magazine* edited by Charlotte Elizabeth, who was undoubtedly one of the most influential popular religious writers of the nineteenth century. Nasmith wisely and successfully elicited her backing for the LCM.[50] Charlotte Elizabeth's promise to promote the society in the pages of her monthly magazine gave the infant organization valuable national attention among the evangelical women, who provided the grass-roots support for the innumerable evangelical societies.[51] Although Charlotte Elizabeth was strongly attached to the Church of England and its establishment principle, her spiritual pilgrimage had been greatly affected by the ministry of Dr. Caesar Malan,[52] a Genevan Protestant minister who had close connections with Alexander Haldane, the leading figure behind the *Record* newspaper.[53] It is paradoxical that much of the early Anglican support for the LCM came from the two political extremes within Evangelicalism: Whigs like B. W. Noel and T. F. Buxton, and the ultra-Protestants associated with the *Record* and the *Christian Lady's Magazine*. Charlotte Elizabeth had no qualms about using her journal both to promote pan-evangelical cooperation in the LCM and to attack the views of Evangelical Whigs who promoted political liberalism.[54]

DEFENDING THE LONDON CITY MISSION

The LCM was very aware of its dependence on Anglicans for financial support and therefore directed its appeal for funds to those laymen who shared the *Record*'s frustration with ecclesiastical hindrances to evangelism and especially tried to attract those who might have been disaffected with the CP-AS. Baptist Noel was particularly adroit in pointing out its lack of influence in London, citing publicly the anti-Evangelical stance of many incumbents as the key factor in its failure.[55] Noel noted that in the first year of its operations only one of the fifty-eight clergymen the CP-AS recruited was assigned to London, and only five of the thirteen laymen.[56] He repeated the comparison at successive meetings of the LCM, and in 1838 when the CP-AS appointments in London had declined to five curates and three laymen, he pointed out that none of these were even being used in the populous parishes.[57]

With the failure of the CP-AS to meet many Anglican hopes for the evangelization of London, the LCM supporters pressed their case, arguing that no properly organized church society would be able to be comprehensive.[58] LCM backers reasoned that the combination of Anglican money with the use of a largely Dissenting lay agency was the only possible way to meet the evangelization need. Noel had "no hope" that the CP-AS could find a sufficient number of Anglicans equal to the task when the Church Missionary Society (CMS) was obliged to employ foreign workers to fill missionary vacancies.[59] The Reverend John Garwood, the Anglican secretary of the mission, took the position that Dissent was simply inadequate to the task: "nor can they who do not belong to the Church of England on their part, in their present position, do the work, a very large amount of *wealth*, if not of influence, being requisite."[60]

Other considerations favored the LCM's scheme of employing lay agency: the cost and their ability to identify with the working classes. With the difficulty experienced in obtaining funds for church building it was not practical to consider providing London with clergymen at £300 a year, an amount that was enough to support five LCM agents.[61] Even if it were possible to provide more clergymen, some agreed with Thomas Chalmers that laymen were better evangelists in some situations. Garwood put the case as follows:

If we cannot support an educated ministry in a class of life raised above the greater part of the people we must send men . . . whose rank in life will enable them to support themselves on less, and who, it is found, can sometimes, from the very circumstances of their situation and previous habits, better understand the difficulties and dangers of a life devoted to the visiting of the depraved poor in low districts, and more easily comprehend the cases of those with whom they come in contact.[62]

Although the view was not widely popular with Anglicans in the 1830s, by the mid–1840s it had gained much ground. Even Bishop Blomfield was moving toward the view that laymen might be more effective in winning the poor back to the Church than the clergy had been. In an 1845 letter to another bishop he acknowledged that in the poorer sections of London "a great part of the population is of such a description as to be inaccessible, for some time to come, to the Clergy, unless they are brought within the scope of their ministrations by the efforts of others, less removed from them in respect of worldly conditions, & manners."[63]

The City Mission, eager to use any apology on its own behalf, even promoted itself as a means by which American-style revivals could be encouraged. The *London City Mission Magazine* recommended the society on this basis, drawing attention to the testimony of a visiting American minister in 1836:

Since his arrival in this country he had been asked what he conceived to be necessary in the economy of the British Churches to promote revivals of religion. He believed that the formation of Societies such as the present would bring the truths of the Gospel to square with the consciences and feelings of a large mass of the population.[64]

Such a recommendation may have sat well with the society's Dissenting supporters but was hardly likely to be welcomed by most Anglican Evangelicals.

While these and other arguments were to be advanced in favor of Anglican support for the LCM, the need for a complete reorganization of the society was proposed as a way of securing their participation. A crisis in 1837 provided the opportunity for Anglicans to reshape the society, if not in their own image, then at least into one that was more acceptable to them. Many of Nasmith's previous attempts to found city missions had failed because of his independent attitude and his unwillingness to cooperate with local churches.[65] The LCM committee had proved to have a mind of its own and on several occasions had voted down the founder's proposals.[66] Early in 1837 his involvement in establishing other religious societies in London became a contentious issue in the committee, but Nasmith adamantly refused to relinquish these activities in favor of the LCM. The withdrawal of the leading Nonconformist minister did not move Nasmith, nor did the resignation of the two Anglican clerical examiners of the agents; however, Baptist Noel's letter of resignation did.[67] His chief complaint was that scarcely any Anglicans were employed as agents and that the society was likely to become a Dissenting institution.[68] In order to prevent a complete debacle, Nasmith withdrew.[69]

In the twenty-two months that Nasmith was secretary of the LCM much had been accomplished. A systematic plan to deal with the spiritual destitution had been proposed, money raised, fifty-six agents employed, and the *LCM Magazine* published.[70] Key to its growth and expansion during the period was Nasmith's ability to enlist the support of influential Anglicans like T. F. Buxton, Charlotte Elizabeth, and Baptist Noel. Noel's backing was crucial, as Nasmith's biographer was to acknowledge in dedicating the work to him: "you did more than any man of your class—more, indeed, than all of them united,—to assist Mr. Nasmith in founding and establishing the London City Mission."[71]

The LCM had only managed to prosper because of Anglican backing; Nasmith was forced to resign because of Anglican pressure. The LCM was only to be rescued from collapse by Anglican financing and organizational expertise, and the price for all of this was to be effective Anglican control of the society. The reorganization of the LCM was effected along the lines of the BFBS and was calculated to attract the support of Anglican Evangelicals by reassuring them that it would not be used as a tool against the Church in the Voluntary Controversy. The new committee was comprised of an equal number of Churchmen and Nonconformists, a change that Nasmith had long resisted.[72] Following a period of active solicitation of Anglican clergymen to act as clerical examiners, the LCM published the first public notice of the reorganization.

The revamping of the society also needs to be seen in the context of the continuing debate among Anglican Evangelicals over the efficiency of the CP-AS and the need for a more flexible use of paid lay agency. As early as 1828 contributors to the *Record* had been urging the formation of a society to employ lay agents on the model of the "Scripture Readers' Society for Ireland," which had been established in 1822.[73] While similar appeals were made throughout the 1830s, most of the support for such an agency seems to have dissipated for a time with the formation of the CP-AS.[74] That society's adherence to ecclesiastical order, however, made it unacceptable to the more radical Evangelical laymen.

A call for the formation of yet another Anglican society was made by a correspondent to the *Record* in April 1837 at the very time of the LCM's reorganization.[75] The directors of the LCM wrote to the newspaper to contradict the suggestion made by the author of the appeal to the effect that the LCM was controlled by Dissenters.[76] In publishing the committee's letter, however, the *Record*, while high in its praise of the LCM's work, announced its change of attitude toward the Mission. Only the establishment of a strictly Anglican society would remove the "Great and *unnecessary* difficulties" that were experienced in such joint ventures. It offered the view that "right feelings would, in the long run, be advanced instead of injured, by missionary work being prosecuted in the metropolis, as in other parts of the world, on this distinct footing."[77] The reorganization had highlighted the LCM's problems and apparently swung the *Record*'s management to the Reverend Henry Blunt's position of refusing to cooperate with it. Blunt's hand may have been strengthened by the disaffection of Andrew Hamilton with the LCM, following the forced resignation of his friend, David Nasmith.

In the interim there was no alternative to the LCM. The strength of opposition within the Anglican Church to lay agency had been demonstrated in the battle over the CP-AS, and despite the *Record*'s approval the suggestion of a new Anglican society had failed to elicit a response from other readers.[78] Even the proposer of the new society was willing to countenance supporting the LCM to evangelize London:

Members of the Church of England are limited to one of two courses—either to join the "City Mission" already established, and inviting their cooperation, or else to form a new and exclusively Church Society. Most unhesitatingly do I, for one, maintain . . . that love for the souls of men and desire for the extension of the kingdom of the Redeemer, ought to lead us to join that Society, and to labour in every manner for its advancement, *sooner than that we should do nothing.*[79]

Anglican hesitation was partly due to the fact that many were convinced that the LCM would eventually fall victim to the denominational forces which had robbed the London Missionary Society of its pan-evangelical design, and Anglicans were for the most part unwilling to work in such an apparently fragile alliance:

It is a *fact*, that Churchmen in general do not think themselves at liberty to join the "City Mission." It has now been established for two years, and how very few of the clergy, or even of the laity, has it numbered among its members or its agents: perhaps I am not wrong in attributing it mainly to the steadfastness and devoted zeal of one beloved and honoured brother, that even these few have been found in its ranks.[80]

The simple fact was that the CP-AS was too restricted in its constitution to cope effectively with the situation, leaving the LCM as the only organization for Anglicans concerned with the systematic evangelization of the metropolis to support. With its new constitution it could plead neutrality in the Voluntary Controversy and it could argue that it served to lessen the contentiousness and competitiveness that would have resulted from strictly denominational missions. Furthermore, most Evangelicals realized that no episcopally sanctioned church society could ever operate in parishes where incumbents opposed its activities. Only a "neutral" evangelical society could meet the need. With Anglicans effectively in control of the LCM, what better assurance could one have that the society would not be used against the church establishment and would still effectively penetrate otherwise neglected areas? The longer the proposed Anglican society using lay agency was delayed, the more time the LCM had to establish itself as a pan-evangelical society with an established pattern of Anglican support. Anglican opponents of lay agency thus in effect drove Evangelicals to support a more radical solution and helped to create a pan-evangelical approach to urban evangelism in London.

It would be naive to assume that doctrinal matters alone constituted the divide between Anglican and Nonconformist evangelicals. The social distance between those within and without the establishment was deep and marked, even between evangelicals. The *Record*, the paper most willing to countenance Dissent, could at the same time grind the faces of the Dissenters in the dirt:

We have always made a marked distinction between the pious Dissenter, who objects to the Church of England on conscientious grounds, but who would allow the majority of his countrymen to retain their conscientious opinions with as much freedom as he is allowed to retain his, and the political Dissenter, who is ready to connect himself with those who would destroy all that is sacred and valuable in the institutions of his country, provided he could succeed in overthrowing an Establishment of which the purposes it serves he has not the capacity to comprehend, and the superiority of whose members in rank, in learning, in all that gives moral influence in society, is a perpetual eye-sore to his pride, and an object of cupidity to his avarice and selfish passions.[81]

Undoubtedly these social distinctions did much to affect Anglican willingness to cooperate with Nonconformity. Elizabeth Jay has suggested that the social gulf widened throughout the nineteenth century[82] and demonstrates that even novelists who were theological neophytes were "perfectly capable of distinguishing between Evangelicals and Dissent in social terms."[83] If Jay's assessment is correct, then interdenominational cooperation flew in the face of social trends. However, two factors need to be considered. First, one needs to realize that such hostility was "most intense among literary people."[84] "Popular hostility," maintains Jeffrey Cox, "does not appear to have been very intense except among the immediate targets of puritanicalism, such as pub-owners, and a kind of amused contempt or a light dismissal was more common than outright bitterness."[85] Second, of all the nineteenth-century Anglican Evangelicals, it would seem that the Clapham Sect were among those most aware of social distinctions and eager to esteem highly "those who count" in society; hence, they were the least eager to associate with Dissenters. They were "in Ford K. Brown's phrase, 'firm believers in the sacredness of rank, position, office, and property and profoundly respecters of persons.' "[86]

If these barriers—doctrinal, political and social—were to be surmounted by the LCM, then definitive action was required by the society. The annual reports of the LCM in this period took care to stress the harmony and unanimity prevailing within the LCM: "Within your Committee room, though some events have occasioned discussion and much prayerful anxiety, there has been no dissension, no strife, and no party feeling. The storm was without—not within."[87] In order to preserve this unanimity and to minimize the conflicts between Church and Dissent within the society, the committee was quick to dismiss agents who violated the neutrality of the Mission.[88] In doing so it demonstrated its willingness to enforce discipline, allaying Anglican fears that the missionaries would be agents of "a lawless schism."[89]

Aside from pouring oil on the troubled seas of denominational rivalry, the LCM needed new positive initiatives to demonstrate its unique features and the practical benefits flowing from such an interdenominational mission. Aware that a parallel Anglican mission had been proposed, but had yet to be established, the LCM sought to launch programs that would attract the backing of a broad cross section of evangelicalism. These ventures would serve not only to meet special needs, but would also establish the LCM as the accepted canopy under which pan-evangelical activities in the metropolis would function, and in each case the unwillingness and/or inability of a strictly Church society to perform the same task was to be made crystal clear.

WOOING THE EVANGELICAL COMMUNITY: THE FIASCO OF THE SCRIPTURE CAMPAIGN

The first major initiative launched by the LCM committee was a Scripture distribution project, which aimed to supply the destitute poor of London with copies of the New Testament. Hoping that such a laudable project would elicit broad evangelical support, the LCM applied to the BFBS for assistance. The response from the Bible Society was most encouraging, as it offered to prepare a cheap edition of the New Testament and Psalter, the cost to be borne by its local associations. This venture involved the organization of evangelicals on a grand scale. The whole metropolis was divided into 433 districts,[90] and 121,080 houses were canvassed by volunteers from local Bible societies (32 districts), the Wesleyan Tract Society (2 districts), the Christian Instruction Society (104 districts), City Missionaries (191 districts), and by private individuals (104 districts).[91] About one-third of the families visited (35,393) were without any form of the Scriptures and were willing to accept the offer of a New Testament. Illiteracy was not seen as a problem, as the canvassers reported that in almost every family there was someone who could read. The chief reason for the lack of the Scriptures was said to be ignorance, with one distributor reporting, "Several persons inquired what I meant by a Bible or a Testament, not even understanding the meaning of the term; others said, they had had one left last week, but on producing it, it was a tract published by the Religious Tract Society."[92] The offer was declined by most infidels and Jews, but some of the strongest resistance to the project apparently came from Roman Catholics who viewed the offer with suspicion.[93] One city missionary reported:

On the New Testament being presented to one woman, who is a Roman Catholic, she sternly refused to have it, saying, that she would rather be drawn to pieces by horses than she would have it and deny her religion. She said, that if she received it she must make confession of it to the priest, and she was sure that he would not grant her absolution for such a sin. Two other women were also present, and they all appeared highly offended with me for bringing them a book which was intended to draw them from the religion in which they had been baptized and also to deny the blessed Virgin Mary, which they never would do for any body.[94]

Such accounts undoubtedly were emphasized to promote the mission's effectiveness in reaching Roman Catholics, but the accounts of the responses given are not unusual, especially in light of papal pronouncements that forbade the reading of the Scriptures by the Catholic laity in the nineteenth century.

While the scheme may have been popular with many evangelical laymen, it soon involved the City Mission in a quagmire of ecclesiastical politics. In recruiting people both to survey the houses of the poor and to distribute the Scriptures, the mission had issued separate circulars to Anglican and Nonconformist ministers requesting their assistance.[95] The solicitation of Anglican clergy to aid the interdenominational mission led the LCM into direct clashes with Bishop Blomfield and the *Record*. Blomfield was particularly upset with the Reverend John Garwood, who had signed the circular to the Anglican clergy in his role as secretary to the LCM. Garwood was informed by his superior that he was not to join with Dissenting ministers in prayer meetings for the mission, nor was he to sign circulars addressed to London clergy by the mission; furthermore, the Bishop forbade the preaching of any sermon in an Anglican church in support of the LCM and opposed any of the London clergy preaching on the mission's behalf.[96]

When a deputation from the LCM sought to dissuade Blomfield, they were informed that "he disapproved of lay agency altogether, on which ground he objected to the Church Pastoral-Aid Society; but he had a stronger objection to the London City Mission because of the Union of Churchmen with Dissenters."[97] The Bishop promised that while he would not actively oppose the work of the LCM, he would "offer it . . . a passive opposition."[98] Much to Blomfield's chagrin, both the secular and the religious press publicized reports of the disagreement.[99] The Bishop's instructions to his clergy were sufficiently strong to lead Garwood and another London clergyman, the Reverend R. E. Hankinson, to resign from the LCM;[100] they were also sufficiently vague for Blomfield to deny having ever specifically ordered such withdrawals.[101] Garwood therefore rejoined the LCM in his former capacity but was again reprimanded by his bishop, who attempted again to clarify what he was prohibiting him from doing.[102]

The reaction of the *Record* was both more distressing and damaging than anything Blomfield said or did. As a means of wooing Anglican cooperation with the LCM the Scripture distribution project was turning into a fiasco. At the time of the LCM's reorganization the newspaper had suggested that it would be better for Anglicans to support a strictly denominational society to do a similar work. While it lamented the further fracturing of evangelical unity, the *Record* at that time had squarely placed the blame for the disunity on the Nonconformists involved in the disestablishment campaign:

Now we see them united even with Papists, speaking and spouting together with O'Connell on the same platform, for the accomplishment of this wretched end. Their doctrine may be sound, but their course is perverse. And if we concealed or passed over the matter, under the plea of promoting love and unity, we should be partakers in their sin.[103]

The dispute between Blomfield and the LCM had alienated the *Record* from the mission. Such interdenominational cooperation was no longer simply ill advised; the paper now argued that the LCM in itself constituted a threat to the establishment. Noting that the whole question "has undergone a very radical change within these few years" since the beginning of the mission in 1835, it reasoned that while the Nonconformists associated with the LCM were not involved in direct attacks on the establishment, they had not actively opposed the same. It went on to allege that the city missionaries were in effect undermining the establishment "in another and quieter way." As the meetings held by the LCM for the poor did not accord "with the *formula* of the Church," they inevitably favored Dissent. In deference to Blomfield's stated opposition, incumbents were urged to give "careful consideration" to his orders, "with a view to compliance with them, if they conscientiously can."[104]

The responsibility for responding to such charges was assigned to Baptist Noel, whose argument was largely a pragmatic one: the LCM had investigated the destitution of the Scriptures in London and relieved the need; the LCM was successful in reaching the poor, much more successful than any other society; the proposal to build more churches was laudable, though expensive, but Noel asked "how would they do the work of this Institution? It might provide for the respectable part, who would be attracted to the house of prayer, but it would do next to nothing for the less respectable." On the issue of the bishop's refusal to countenance the LCM, Noel appealed to each believer individually to judge the case:

When a man attained his maturity of understanding, he must weigh argument and not authorities. If authority were to take the place of argument, they might have been debarred the privilege of aiding the Bible and Church Missionary Societies. They had been told not to read the *Record* because it was a Presbyterian, pestilential journal—more mischievous than all the other journals, and, if he yielded to authority, he must no longer be a subscriber to it, as he had the pleasure of being.[105]

In the succeeding few months Noel and the *Record* kept up their exchanges on the case, with the latter insisting that the LCM had been worked "to the prejudice of the Church and the advantage of Dissent," and it alleged that the LCM was "in effect a Dissenting Society."[106]

The crucial question for the *Record* was whether such cooperation was necessary for evangelism. Foreign missions operated effectively on denominational lines, so too could home missions. If such was the case, then "why," the newspaper asked, "amidst at least equal inconvenience, in circumstances injurious to the Church, offensive to our Christian brethren, and in opposition to the highest ecclesiastical authority, are we to insist on departing from a generally established rule?"[107] A precondition for the *Record* considering further cooperation with Dissent was then laid down: "till a public protest is offered against them [the "Political Dissenters"] by such of their body as oppose them (if such there be), they must all be concluded as participating in those principles and in those aspirations."[108]

Noel defended the LCM against the charge that it had become a Dissenting institution, noting that the new constitution assured members of the established church that this could never be the case. If the *Record* considered it wrong for Anglicans to cooperate with Dissenters in the LCM, why, asked Noel, did it not adopt a similar view regarding cooperation in other societies like the Tract and the Bible Societies? His central appeal was again to the LCM's proven effectiveness:

You cannot point out any means by which the poor may be visited except this. I know of many souls saved through this instrumentality. . . . I know that the poor of London are famishing by thousands for the lack of knowledge. The District Visiting Society cannot visit them because you cannot get district visitors in those parishes in which the clergymen do not favour their efforts. The Pastoral-Aid Society cannot, because the rule forced upon them by circumstances has been, that they will *send no agents except where invited by the clergyman.* So that they are shut out from all the most populous parishes of London. . . . Nor can you even *sketch, much less form,* a Church Society which could send either lay-agents or curates to *these perishing creatures,* in these and similar parishes.[109]

The *Record*'s insistence that Dissenters had to make amends before consideration could be given to the issue of cooperation apparently led to the publication later in the same year of a "Remonstrance by certain Evangelical independent ministers in London and Neighbourhood." This document decried the bitterness and acrimony among evangelicals and pleaded for reconciliation which would remove the stumbling block of disunity presented to the world. The ministers made the sort of statement that the *Record* wanted: "*We have no desire to interfere in the regulation or adjustment of the internal affairs of other ecclesiastical communities—least of all, have we any wish to participate in their property and possessions.* We are simply concerned for our liberty, and the true prosperity of the Church of Christ."[110] While the *Record* appreciated the Remonstrance, it gave no indication that it regarded it as sufficient to establish the truce that it professed to desire.[111]

The wisdom of the LCM's selection of a Scripture distribution project as an evangelical common cause can hardly be questioned, in view of the success of the British and Foreign Bible Society. In the highly charged atmosphere of the disestablishment debate, however, Blomfield's opposition to the city mission produced an acrimonious public quarrel, which undoubtedly stiffened the resolve of many clergy and laymen to keep their distance from an organization involved in a public dispute with their bishop.

THE SECOND INITIATIVE: SUPPRESSING VICE

In selecting their next project designed to promote evangelical unity, the mission demonstrated that it was aware of the great responsibility that evangelicals felt toward suppressing blatant manifestations of public vice, even at the price of making themselves opprobrious to their contemporaries. It is important to understand that many evangelicals held the view that Christians have a responsibility to rebuke boldly those who sin boldly. In the Middle Ages wandering "preachers of repentance" had often taken this role upon themselves, and this concern reemerged in the Evangelical revival of the eighteenth century as a central theme in the preaching of both John Wesley and George Whitefield. The early Methodists often saw themselves in the role of modern-day John the Baptists who were to "bear testimony against sin" and declare "the whole counsel of God" to their hearers. By this they meant that Christians had a peculiar responsibility to identify and denounce both social and personal sins regardless of the consequences; if one failed in this duty, one was in effect condoning and thus participating in the sin. Put simply, the options were condemnation or commendation. Much of the anti-Methodist rioting of the 1730s and 1740s was related to such rebukes.[112]

The denominational bureaucracies that emerged within Nonconformity in the late eighteenth and the early nineteenth centuries were designed to meet peculiar ecclesiastical tasks and not to fill a political role as guardians of the nation's morals. Before the repeal of the Test and Corporation Acts in 1828, this role was fulfilled by Anglican Evangelicals. Upon his conversion in 1785, William Wilberforce felt the call of the Almighty to bring about "the reformation of manners" (morals) of the British nation. Thus he wrangled a declaration from the king against vice, and in 1787 established "The Society for Giving Effect to His Majesty's Proclamation Against Vice." The Proclamation Society was clearly intended to rebuke the sins of the age, and it was later augmented by the Society for the Suppression of Vice. Both of these strictly Anglican societies had relatively short lives: the former was in decline by the early 1800s and then merged with the latter.[113] The "Vice Society" itself was in serious trouble by the early 1840s, limited as it was by its constitution to prosecuting cases that involved clear violations of the law,[114] and restricted by a lack of funds.[115] By the early 1830s, the district visiting societies had been promoted as the agency that could provide Anglicans with the most effective "moral and spiritual police" of the poor, and the district visitors had been instructed to rebuke "open vice."[116] With the faltering of the District Visiting Society in the late 1830s, the lack of a large and effective evangelical organization to suppress public vice was being felt by Anglican Evangelicals, particularly in London.

The LCM advanced itself as the agency to fill this vacuum in moral leadership. Its first target was one at which English preachers had taken aim for centuries: the immensely popular public fairs held in the vicinity of the capital. As these fairs were exempt from normal licensing restrictions until 1874, liquor flowed freely at them. In 1638 one preacher told his congregation: "Go but to the town's end where a fair is kept, and there they lie, as if some field had been fought; here lies one man, there another."[117] Wilberforce's "Vice Society" had attempted to deal with such fairs and in 1803 had argued that as their original commercial purposes had long since been forgotten, they could all be suppressed "without being productive of the smallest inconvenience to the public."[118] Such a hope was fostered by many nineteenth century preachers. But while they denounced the fairs and their vices and may have prevented some among their flocks from straying toward the fairs, they had singularly failed to suppress the fairs themselves.[119]

The popularity of these amusements among the poor can be seen in the fact that the Fairlop Fair, which extended over four days, managed to attract over 70,000 people on a Sunday.[120] (See Illustration 2). In memorializing Lord John Russell, the LCM Committee noted that this fair was legally restricted to a Friday, but that:

now, the fair is continued beyond the Friday till the Monday following; and booths of all descriptions, even the most disreputable, are kept open during the Sunday. One hundred and seven drinking-booths, seventy-two gambling-tables, and about twelve brothels, were counted on the last occasion; Sunday, July 7, 1839.[121]

Two different tacks were adopted in dealing with the fairs. The first was the standard, direct evangelistic approach. Ten missionaries were assigned to distribute tracts at the Fairlop Fair on Friday and Saturday, but the LCM, "knowing that the chief day of concourse and wickedness was the Sabbath," doubled its contingent on that day. Graphic details of the fair recorded by the city missionaries provide interesting descriptions of early Victorian popular amusements; they also illustrate the agents' none-too-subtle evangelistic techniques. The evangelicals were perhaps most outraged at the prostitution associated with the fairs, and the *LCM Magazine* was remarkably candid in the attention it gave to this aspect of the fair:

BROTHELS.—Temporary places were erected in the wood for the filthiest crimes. One missionary states, "I saw about a dozen places of seclusion formed around different trees, about six feet or more in height. The sides were sheets, and the tops of some of them were covered with blankets." Another missionary saw seven young females all dressed in white under a tree a short distance from one of these temporary brothels. He gave tracts to all of them, and shortly after he saw two young men follow one of the young girls into the place, and they were all admitted by an old woman lifting up a stick fastened to the ground. One of these females passing the missionary in the afternoon in the fair, seized his hand and looking him in the face said, "Are you ready to die?" The words being the title of the tract he had given her in the morning.[122]

The following account by a city missionary gives one an appreciation of the sort of theological beliefs the evangelicals were trying to spread:

In the afternoon I saw a young Gipsy kneeling down washing her clothes, her husband and relations sitting by. I offered her a handbill. "I cannot read it, Sir; I wish I could. Will you be so kind as to read it to us?" "Yes, I will." I did so: when they put several questions to me, evidently very desirous of knowing the meaning.

I said, "if it were not for trespassing on your time, I would just sit down with you and show unto you from the Bible the way of salvation." "O, Sir," she said, "I am not too busy for that. We should like to hear you; come, Molly," addressing her sister, "bring something for the gentleman to sit down upon." However, I preferred the green

Illustration 2
The Fairs

This 1843 sketch of Fairlop Fair in Epping Forest gives the impression of a respectable middle-class event, a view which many Victorians would not have endorsed. *Illustrated London News* 3 (July 15, 1843):44.

grass to a dirty piece of carpet, which Molly had provided, and proceeded to show them their sinful state by nature, from Psalm li.; their need of regeneration, justification, and sanctification, before they could be happy here, or have any well-grounded hope of happiness hereafter. The woman said, "Sometimes the children upset me and I can't help swearing at them. I know it is wrong; but will not God forgive me?" The man said, "I have the rheumatism so bad at times that I swear at God for sending it, and sometimes I pray to him to remove it." I showed him the sin and folly of swearing, and then praying; and read to them Matthew v.32–37, "Swear not at all,"&c.

Others who were approached were not as welcoming, as another agent reported:

I arrived on friday, just at the time when one of the ships drawn by six grey horses was going to open the fair. As they were stopping I gave the postilions tracts, also each of the gentlemen in the ship, one of whom commenced reading the handbill "Why should I not be saved" aloud. Heard him say, "I am a sinner," and the ship moved on amid a concourse of people nearly as infatuated as the Eastern worshippers before an idol's cart! Afterwards saw a number of young men together, much like pickpockets, in deep consultation; gave each of them a handbill. One said, sneeringly, "I cannot read, perhaps you will read it for me." "O yes," I replied, it was "Scripture admonitions." I then read aloud, "The wages of sin is death." "Whoremongers and adulterers God will judge." "The wicked shall be turned into hell," &c., &c., asking them after every passage, "Do you understand this?" They quickly dispersed, unaccustomed, I suppose to such appeals.[123]

The London City Mission was not prepared to limit its activities to evangelism and mounted a direct attack on the continuation of the fairs, aware that outrage at their proceedings was not limited to evangelicals or to churchmen; even the secular press was upset with the proceedings at the fairs and the annoyance that they caused to people in the vicinity.[124] A great boost to such efforts came from the new police legislation enacted in 1839.[125] Armed with this new weapon, the LCM succeeded in having the Fairlop Fair restricted to one day in 1840[126] and routinely reported the diligence with which the police enforced the legislation.[127]

In petitioning London's City Council for the discontinuance of the large, popular Bartholomew Fair, the committee of the LCM knew that it could count on the support of the mayor and an alderman, both of whom had presided at public meetings for the mission.[128] Approval was also forthcoming from the Council's Market Committee, and from the city solicitor, who concurred with the Market Committee "in the confident belief that not many years will elapse ere the Corporation may omit to proclaim the fair, and thus suppress it altogether, without exciting any of those feelings of discontent and disapprobation with which its compulsory abolition would probably now be attended."[129] The vigilance needed to maintain pressure on the Council was provided by the LCM which kept its constituency informed about the state of the fairs.[130] In 1842 the London City Council followed through with its stated intention and limited the Bartholomew Fair to its original commercial purposes.[131] Important for the reputation of the mission was the fact that LCM attacks on local fairs effectively galvanized religious and political opinion in a parish under the standard raised by the society.[132]

With the effective suppression of these fairs, the LCM took on another activity popular with the poor—the horse races—which evangelicals declared were merely excuses for gambling, prostitution, and drunkenness. Francis Close, the noted "Evangelical Pope of Cheltenham,"[133] had launched a successful attack on the races in his county in the late 1820s, arguing that Christian avoidance of the races was not adequate and "that it is the duty of every virtuous citizen, and every pious Christian, not only to absent himself from this scene of vanity, but to endeavour, as far as in him lies, to stem the torrent of iniquity."[134] Close's view excited considerable response, both in the local press and in an ensuing pamphlet warfare.[135] (See Illustration 3).

In 1838 the LCM drew up a petition to oppose the erection of a hippodrome in the vicinity of London,[136] which Bishop Blomfield presented on the mission's behalf in the House of Lords.[137] "It is not the mere fact of racing horses," explained the *LCM Magazine*, "comparatively few care about that part of the matter, except as they are pledged for gambling speculations."[138] The very activities that the mission had sought to curb through the suppression of the fairs were emerging at horse races such as the one begun at Romford in 1839. The LCM complained that

it is, in fact, the establishment of a new fair in connexion with horse-racing, and should be immediately suppressed by the Commissioners of the Police summoning the proprietor of the ground before the magistrates. We have the particulars of scenes of drunkenness, of public indecency, and of whoredom, which we cannot publish, but which call for the immediate interference of the magistracy, and of every respectable inhabitant of Romford.

In support of this, the following City Missionary's report was cited:

Three principal vices on the ground were gambling, drunkenness, and whoredom, all of which were carried on to a great extent, but on account of the brilliancy of the moon the last was greatly curbed. About eleven o'clock on the second night a disturbance was created in—booth, by a band of ruffians, headed by two Romford men. The object of these men was to raise a fight, in order that they might rob and plunder. . . . During the whole of this dangerous and excited period, policemen were called for, but in vain. Seventeen men, with an inspector, had been on the ground, to keep it clear for the races during the day, but the races over, the force was entirely withdrawn, and the ground left unprotected amid the most violent and dangerous scenes. . . . We succeeded in delivering about 3,800 tracts, which, upon the whole, were received well, with the exception of a sincere desire to "duck me in the horse pond," some curses, a half-brick thrown at my head, which had not commission to hit me, and a close interrogation by a leading man of the town, who intends to examine into the nature of my commission for visiting them. My conviction is, that the establishment of these races, now only three years old, will tend greatly to demoralize the town of Romford, as well as the adjacent villages, and will no doubt increase crime.[139]

THE

Spiritual Quixote,

GEOFFRY WILDGOOSE,

IN

CHELTENHAM:

OR, A

DIS-COURSE

ON A

Race-Course.

" His occupation's new—
" The Gospel fires his soul;
" Hell-flames roar out like thunder,
" Which make the old wives wonder;
" Hard-words, grimace, and noise,
" Now scare the girls and boys;
" His rage without control."—

Rev. W. Hett

THIRD EDITION.

Cheltenham:

PRINTED FOR G. A. WILLIAMS;

SOLD BY WASHBOURN, AND HOUGH, GLOUCESTER; KNIBB AND LANGBRIDGE, WORCESTER; BENNETT, TEWKESBURY; MEYLER, AND COLLINS, BATH; STRONG, BRISTOL; SLATTER, OXFORD; LONGMAN AND CO. AND G. B. WHITTAKER, LONDON AND ALL RESPECTABLE BOOKSELLERS.

Price Sixpence.

Illustration 3
The Race Course

An example of the works published in the pamphlet warfare over the horse races. Bodley pamphlets 1419 f. 2094 (3) T.P. Used with the permission of the Bodleian Library, Oxford.

Clerical opposition to the races continued throughout the century, with suppression being advocated as the only solution. One author wrote in 1858 that the races were "so helplessly rotten that you might as well talk of reforming a cancer."[140]

Other objects of the LCM's ire included "penny theatres" which had long been decried in the Evangelical press. In 1829 the *Record* had expressed the view that "The minor theatres we consider as incomparably more pernicious than the great ones. The exhibitions in the former have seldom, if ever, one solitary redeeming quality."[141] In 1833 the same journal labeled the theaters "those pest-houses of vice" and defended Blomfield's questioning of their usefulness, noting that "the scenes of indecency exhibited rise occasionally even beyond the endurance of such a censor of morals as the *Times* journal."[142]

Such complaints had failed to have an impact upon the theaters. In 1839, however, the LCM privately lobbied Middlesex magistrates with the result that only four of thirty-three applications for licences of so-called "music halls" were granted. The mission argued that the "music halls" were being used illegally by their owners as "penny theaters."[143] The society was quite prepared to oppose such permits annually and marshaled its agents to gather information and to testify in court. One magistrate gave vent to his frustration with such evangelical activities when the LCM agents appeared to oppose licences to allow music and dancing in Sunday taverns:

This Society, however good its intentions may be, is calculated to interfere with the entertainments and amusements of the people; and it appears to me that they are a set of spies and informers. Are we to read all the reviews that are published by the saints in the county?[144]

The LCM took this complaint as a compliment and rejoiced that the remark was dismissed by the other magistrates who heeded most of the mission's recommendations in refusing licences; much of the credit was due to the leadership of two evangelical magistrates.

The complaint about the attitude of "the saints" toward amusements was largely justified. David Hempton has observed that "in both the eighteenth and nineteenth centuries, Methodist opposition to all manner of entertainments, both for the rich and poor, was probably its biggest millstone in the passionate quest for new members."[145] Even a clergyman decried this fact:

There are many really pious people who . . . do not believe in recreations. They utterly ignore them; they say that man's only recreation should be in the worship of God, in the study of His word, in the holy exercises of prayer and praise. They seem to assume that prayer and recreation are two things, the antipodes of each other—that all amusements have a savour of sin in them—that if all mankind were perfectly religious and thoroughly devoted to God, there would be no amusements of any kind; men would not need them.[146]

The LCM protested that it did not subscribe to such a narrow view, and that it did not want to interfere with the proper amusements of the poor, but its activities to suppress popular amusements struck a chord with its evangelical constituency and served the aim not only of "preventing iniquity" but also of promoting the society itself. While courting unpopularity with the poor, these actions served to establish the LCM as the primary agency of moral leadership among evangelicals in London.

While the "saints" may have felt an obligation to safeguard public morality, these conflicts over recreation strongly influenced popular attitudes to religion and, as Brian Harrison has suggested, they probably accelerated secularization.[147] In Victorian Britain there were three reforming movements that were predominantly evangelical in origin and aim, which sought to interfere with popular recreations: the temperance movement, sabbatarianism (which found expression in the Lord's Day Observance Society, founded in 1831), and the campaign against animal cruelty, which produced the Royal Society for the Prevention of Cruelty to Animals (RSPCA).

These moral crusades and the efforts of the London City Mission are interesting in light of discussion of the censorious aspect of the Nonconformist conscience of the late nineteenth century.[148] They serve as a link in a long chain: the emphasis upon personal rebuking in Wesleyan and Whitefieldite Methodism; the institutionalizing of these functions by Wilberforce in the Proclamation and Vice Societies; the reconstituting of similar concerns in organizations like the City Mission, the Lord's Day Observance Society, and the RSPCA in the 1820s and 1830s; and the full-blown development of this moral-watchdog approach by Nonconformists in the late nineteenth century in league with Gladstonian Liberalism. It would seem that only after the repeal of the Test and Corporation Acts in 1828 were Nonconformists willing to appeal to the magistrates—those who had persecuted them in the past—for assistance in dealing with their moral (or immoral) enemies. As the century progressed, however, and the memory of their more serious disabilities faded, the tendency for such appeals increased; the Sabbatarian cause and the prohibitionist phase of the Temperance Movement giving them plenty of scope.

THE THIRD CRUSADE: "INFIDEL SOCIALISM"

Alarm over the prospects of social disintegration in England was strong in the first two decades of the nineteenth century but diminished somewhat during the relatively stable and optimistic 1820s. The economic and social developments of 1830–1831, which produced widespread disturbances, renewed such concerns. In urban areas the problem seemed most acute because it was here that the old alliance of gentry and clergy had disappeared, and the clergyman as social ameliorator made little sense. The economic depression of the late 1830s was accompanied by a seeming explosion of radical lower-class organization and agitation.[149] The shock waves of this explosion seemed to threaten that the base of the social pyramid would crumble. Thus, in 1839 the LCM turned its attention to this ominous foe. Its annual meeting was warned:

Never before did men calmly and openly unite together, organize institutions, frame laws, and employ missionaries to overturn the constitution of society, destroy the social relations, abolish marriage, and blot out from the mind the belief and love of the one living and true God. All that was bad in the atheistic doctrines of the French Revolution is embodied in socialism, with the addition of the fixed purpose of the socialists to propagate their errors by tracts, public discussions, and missionary operations, not only through the length and breadth of Britain, but of the whole world.[150]

In these solemn tones the LCM announced the object of its third crusade: evangelical warriors were to do battle with the "threatening scourge" of Owenite socialism.

Political radicalism in Britain drew much of its leadership from the elite of the working class. Following in the traditions of Thomas Paine's (1737–1809) humanistic deism, the "radicals" embraced a form of environmental determinism and opposed orthodox Christianity. They were particularly scandalized by the evangelical doctrine of the Atonement upon which they lavished contempt.[151] Anglican Evangelicals had long been in the forefront of efforts to silence the radicals. In 1797 the "Proclamation Society"[152] had instituted the original prosecution of Tom Paine's *The Age of Reason*, and twenty years later the Evangelical "Vice Society" did the radical cause a great favor by prosecuting Richard Carlisle (1790–1843) for reprinting the same work. While the action led to Carlisle's fining and imprisonment, it also promoted the circulation of a book, which had been selling poorly, and hardened the radicals' determination to publish other illegal works.[153] Such prosecutions of sinners had earned the evangelicals a great deal of working-class bitterness and hostility. One of Carlisle's associates, an ex-Methodist lay preacher, offered the following as a reason for his renouncing Christianity:

Because, though Atheists, Deists, and Skeptics are all willing to be convinced by fair argument and reason—the supporters of the Christian system not being able to do it, resort to the unconvincing arguments of fine, imprisonment and brute violence.[154]

The high priest of this rival "socialist" faith was Robert Owen (1771–1858), who qualified both as an "infidel" and a "socialist." The word "infidel" was generally used at the time as a term of abuse "to signify anyone who rejected orthodox Christianity and who combined with such a rejection a low social position or an appeal to those in such a position."[155] Owen's "socialism" combined "infidel" beliefs with a paternalistic doctrine that advocated alternative cooperative communities shaped (in Owen's own words) by the guidance of "those who have influence in the affairs of men."[156] Two of the tenets of Owen's system which were especially obnoxious to his opponents were his belief in human moral nonresponsibility and his views on divorce, which he advocated "on the grounds that individuals, having no free will, could not continue loving their partners if circumstances changed during the course of their marriage."[157] Many equated "Owenism" with immorality. (Samuel Wilberforce referred to

Owen as the "chief apostle [of] . . . a debasing sensual atheism."[158]) In attacking Owenism, then, the evangelicals were not simply taking on a political movement. In fact, after 1834 Owenite "organizations became religious bodies, and his followers drew in on themselves to preserve their purity from the world. They acquired buildings and their lecturers took out licenses to preach."[159]

Evangelicals were not alone in their fear of the workings of these radicals. During the 1840s the episcopal bench was acutely aware of the threat posed by the socialists and by the Chartists and "felt that they were in a desperate race against the forces of anti-civilization and class warfare."[160] Samuel Wilberforce argued that the two movements "were essentially secularized forms of Methodist dissent" and saw in them the Church's great failure to provide for the spiritual needs of those who had turned to such secular creeds.[161] The most vocal bishop was Henry Phillpotts, who repeatedly attacked the "socialists" in the House of Lords in 1840.[162] (See Illustration 4).

If the LCM committee had hoped that by raising the spectre of a host of infidels overturning society they could thereby enlist evangelicals in a campaign against socialism, they had rightly judged at least a part of their constituency. Early in 1839 an evangelical, T. H. Hudson, had published what appears to be the first of many such works countering Owenism.[163] Edward Bickersteth warned the LCM's annual meeting that year that evangelicals must "Realise the active energetic working of Socialism at this moment."[164] Another minister spoke in a similar vein:

Never was there a time when it will take a greater exertion, and well have they used the word "grapple", for they have something to contend with when there seems to be an associated body of seven or eight thousand people, bound together by the ties of Satan, to endeavour to uproot, if they could, but they cannot, the cause of God and our Saviour Jesus Christ.[165]

To some extent this fear of popular political agitation among evangelicals was strengthened by the growing acceptance that millenarian views were receiving, especially by Anglicans who were shaken by the constitutional revolution of 1828–1832. Many were convinced that the world situation was rapidly deteriorating and that the final judgment was imminent. Edward Bickersteth, who had emerged in the 1830s as a leading writer on biblical prophecy, used his premillennial views in explaining the "mushroom growth" of Socialism. His brand of premillennialism was given to date setting, both of the return of Christ and of specific events leading up to it. Socialism thus was a manifestation of the "Spirit of Infidelity" to be discerned by the prophetically aware.[166] Bickersteth was further able to pinpoint Socialism as the working of "the unclean spirit from the mouth of the dragon"[167] of Revelation, Chapter 12, while Chartism and the Anti-Corn Law League were identified with "the unclean spirit out of the mouth of the beast."[168] Even for evangelicals who rejected millenarianism, the forces contending for popular self-government were often regarded as dia-

Illustration 4
Protestantism versus Socialism

Religious opponents of Robert Owen's brand of ''Socialism'' were attacked in the popular press as intolerant bigots. Here Bishops Phillpotts of Exeter and Blomfield of London are vilified for their anti-Owenite speeches in the House of Lords. *The Penny Satirist*, March 7, 1840, p. 1. By Permission of the British Library.

metrically anti-Christian, and it was not unknown for Evangelical incumbents to preach sermons against Chartism.[169] In 1840 even the staid *Christian Observer* trembled for God's hierarchically structured society:

Rank, birth, station, princes, nobles, priests, honorary distinctions, and established institutions, are all under the disintegrating process; and not one movement, upon a large scale and permanent, has occurred for many years, to raise privilege and restrain popular power . . . democracy in the end rights itself through the medium of usurpation and tyranny; and the nation which could not appreciate true liberty, passes on to despotism by its abuse.[170]

The LCM's campaign overlapped with an anti-Socialist lecture series sponsored by the Christian Instruction Society in London and also came at a time when numerous Dissenting ministers in the provinces were taking their stand against these "missionaries of atheism."[171] The LCM adopted the same format as the Christian Instruction Society, and ten public lectures were delivered in January and February 1840. They attracted considerable public attention with Robert Owen personally attending one of them[172] and were subsequently published to achieve a wider circulation.[173] The *Christian Observer* concurred with this sort of evangelical activism: "We are constantly witnessing new efforts of vice and infidelity;—Socialism is the climax and what can put them down but the faithful preaching and strenuous inculcation of evangelical truth, we say emphatically 'evangelical', meaning specifically what is couched in that emphatic word."[174]

In its mission to defend both orthodox Christian beliefs and the social order, the LCM hoped to gain the support of evangelicals who had previously stood aloof from the society. In so doing, however, the LCM was straining the limits of its comprehensive design. Professor Machin has observed that "it is difficult to establish a direct link between evangelicalism as such and political conservatism" as "Congregationalists, Baptists and seceding Methodists, who were inspired by evangelicalism, did not share the conservatism of the leading Wesleyans"[175] or of most Anglican Evangelicals. Baptist Noel, undoubtedly reflecting his optimistic Whig political views, made it clear to the London City Mission's annual meeting in 1839 that he discounted the danger facing society discerned by some evangelicals:

Here are times, when so many principles . . . are combined—I do not say, to destroy this empire, for still I believe it is sound at heart, our commerce well based, a sound and wholesome education gaining ground . . . there are various breakwaters to this deluge of evil . . . but if these misguided persons cannot destroy society, . . . still there is an association of evil strong enough to make us fear for them, if it does not make us fear for society.[176]

Noel's concern was that the poor should not be alienated by actions that they might perceive as politically self-seeking. This could be avoided by the pan-evangelical approach of the LCM, which comprehended different political views and various social and denominational groupings. Working-class support for the radicals, Noel argued, had "its roots in the poverty and want of employment of many of the labouring classes":

Now such being the case, if the Church of England alone were to organize a set of measures to endeavour to overcome this Socialism, it might be ascribed to our own party feelings and our political leanings; if it were done by any body of Christians alone, it might be supposed that there was something of sectarian zeal, combating their own sectarian zeal. But when Christians of all denominations are combined, and men of all political creeds united, when it cannot be said that we are prompted either by sect or politics, or anything but a wish to disabuse them from errors we believe to be mischievous or fatal, and to save their souls, we have at once access to their hearts and consciences.[177]

While Noel's plea pointed the LCM back to its original evangelistic calling, the fact that many perceived the operations of the LCM agents as counterrevolutionary and as a stabilizing, pacifying influence on the poor, undoubtedly did much to commend the work of the LCM to its many conservative, middle-class supporters.

The LCM's initiatives in Scripture distribution, the suppression of various forms of amusement, and the campaign against socialism were supplemented by yet another venture: an attack on the growing problem of metropolitan intemperance. Reflecting contemporary evangelical unease over teetotalism, the LCM committee was unwilling to endorse the practice of taking the pledge of total abstinence.[178] The campaign strategy which was adopted to combat excessive use of alcohol was borrowed from the earlier efforts: the missionaries distributed tracts to the same constituency that had been the object of its 1838 Scripture distribution project, and the LCM began to play watchdog of taverns as well as of theaters in its self-appointed role as guardian of London's morals.[179] It did not hesitate to appeal to the justices of the peace when it judged that a tavern had broken the terms of its licence.[180]

The establishment and survival of the LCM was undoubtedly the most important development for pan-evangelicalism in the 1830s. The support of Evangelical Whigs had been crucial to the LCM during its early years and was particularly important following the *Record*'s withdrawal of its backing for the venture. The various campaigns mounted by the LCM in the late 1830s and the early 1840s were specifically calculated to woo Evangelical Anglican support. These capitalized on the fact that Evangelical societies which had previously provided such moral leadership were in decline and lacked the organization and manpower to wield and direct evangelical energies. Thus even by the late 1830s the London City Mission was beginning to be a significant factor in the evangelical world. For the first time in over three decades (since the formation of the British and Foreign Bible Society in 1804) the evangelicals had successfully created an interdenominational society which would be able to endure and thrive.

The society's influence was to extend far beyond London itself, as it was eventually to develop a national constituency and to be the model for countless similar societies throughout the English-speaking world.

The Church of England and evangelical Nonconformity were affected in different ways by the pan-evangelical approach. While many Anglicans were aware of the manifest failings of the parochial system, they had not despaired of it and viewed the LCM with hostility. Yet, as early as the 1830s others had given up on it. Some Anglican Evangelicals were abandoning their allegiance to the parochial system by creating a pan-evangelical alternative to it. This new system included parishes that would accept city missionaries, but would establish its hegemony in Anglican parishes that were hostile to evangelicals, or where the provision was simply inadequate.

Pan-evangelicalism had a different appeal to evangelical Nonconformity. The fact that use of a paid lay agency came into its own in the 1830s needs to be seen in light of the changes occurring within evangelical Dissent at the time, and particularly within Wesleyan Methodism. In the earlier period evangelical Nonconformity had been largely concerned with growth and expansion, and called upon those in the wider society to join the new movement. Signs of a change were evident in the 1820s when the Wesleyans tried to take over many nondenominational Sunday schools in their attempt to consolidate their denominational position, a clear indication of the shift from recruitment of new members to the retention of existing ones. By the mid–1800s organizational changes had occurred that reflected the different complexion of the movement; consolidation rather than expansion was becoming the key concern and accommodations with the wider society were being sought.

W. R. Ward has demonstrated that the role and status of Wesleyan ministers had changed dramatically between Wesley's death in 1791 and the 1820s. "It was now too," he writes, "that the preachers laid claim to the full dignity of the Pastoral Office which Wesley and some of his immediate successors had been so anxious to deny them, and the emphasis was subtly transferred from feeding and guiding to the teaching and ruling" of the flock.[181] Evangelistic work, which had previously been carried out largely by itinerant lay evangelists, was no longer expected of the Wesleyan ministers whose administrative duties were increasing and whose rising salaries reflected their increased social status. New responsibilities were robbing the ministers of time that they would have previously given to evangelism. House-to-house visitation was coming to be seen as somewhat below their calling in life. This professionalization of the ministry was characterized by the increasing institutionalization of Methodism and New Dissent, and by this greater "role differentiation between minister and laymen."[182] In sociological terms the professionalization is an aspect of its slow shift "from a *sect* type religious culture of the early industrial age towards a new and patently *denominational* orientation to the wider society."[183]

The employment of lay agents by interdenominational societies served this process well. While the employment of lay agents was ostensibly out of a desire to recruit new members, the fact that such lay agents could not aspire to full ministerial roles within evangelical Nonconformity underscored the role differentiation between the professional clergy and the laymen. Lay workers could be given the tasks that were now seen to be below the dignity and station of the clergy; such workers could perform the evangelistic role which the Nonconformists still acknowledged as important, but which they no longer expected their ministers to be doing themselves. Furthermore, because the lay agents were under the control of an interdenominational organization, and were ordered not to exercise "ministerial" functions, they would pose no threat to Nonconformist clergy. A few decades previously, such laymen would have been the ministerial recruiting ground for Wesleyanism and New Dissent, but now "The colleges were training, and the local churches were calling to the ministry, men whose aspirations and talents fitted them less for personal work and popular evangelism than for the maintenance of standards of preaching and worship acceptable to discriminating, theologically informed congregations."[184]

The changes demonstrated the extent to which evangelical Nonconformity was losing touch with its working-class heritage. The very sort of people whom Wesley had used to build his movement were no longer welcome in leadership roles. The employment of such a form of lay agency was itself an indication that the steam was going out of evangelical Nonconformity, even in the early 1830s, something that soon became evident in the declining growth rates experienced by the movement from the early 1840s on until World War I.[185] Recruitment was still regarded as important, and evangelical leaders became increasingly aware of a fact about which twentieth-century historians are agreed: that Wesleyanism and the New Dissent were having "little impact on the unskilled masses."[186] The period from 1790 to 1830, which witnessed the conservatizing of Wesleyanism, had also seen "the end of Wesleyan Methodism as a force in working-class culture and politics."[187]

The LCM's plan to use lay agents was thus meeting the needs of the changing world of evangelical Nonconformity as well as those of many Anglican Evangelicals. In terms of the early impact of the mission through its various campaigns of the late 1830s (conversions aside), the society was making the working classes aware of aspects of evangelical morality: its strong Sabbatarianism, its concern for temperance (if not in its teetotal and prohibitionist refinements), its views on what constituted proper recreations (or more correctly, improper recreations), and its strong polemic against Owenite socialism. Yet the mission also had an impact among the increasingly affluent middle classes where evangelicalism was at its strongest: it was providing them with a means of supporting evangelistic efforts in the poorest areas of London, even as they prepared to retreat to the suburbs.

4

The Influence of Issues of Church and State on Pan-evangelicalism during Peel's Second Administration

The various factors that served to heat up Anglican–Dissenting relations during the 1830s have been discussed in chapter 1. The author's contention is that other forces were at work to induce Anglican Evangelicals to cooperate with evangelical Nonconformity. Both W. R. Ward and A. D. Gilbert have emphasized the rivalry between the Establishment and Dissent during the 1830s and 1840s. This chapter will argue that rivalry among parties within the Church of England, which prior to 1828 had served to prevent interdenominational cooperation, eventually became an important factor in promoting evangelical unity. Rivalry within the Establishment led many Evangelicals to play down their differences with Dissent.

As has been seen, the establishment of the London City Mission in the 1830s clearly went against the strongly sectarian trend of that decade. At the very time that denominationalism appeared to be at its strongest, a small group of evangelicals had launched an interdenominational society that few expected to survive. The political events of the early 1840s had a decisive impact upon the future of such an ecumenical approach. The changes that occurred during this period enabled evangelicals to build upon the foundation already laid. We now turn to consider the political factors that facilitated such changes.

When Sir Robert Peel became prime minister in 1841, he had support from all shades of Anglican churchmanship. His Whig predecessors were in large measure responsible for this. From 1835 to 1841 the Whigs had affirmed their devotion to the Establishment while effecting moderate internal reforms. They had also tried to conciliate their Dissenting supporters by reasonable concessions to their grievances. The policy had not been very successful and its numerous failures were conspicuous. The Irish Church Bill of 1835 was abandoned because the House of Lords was adamant against any appropriation of Church of Ireland revenues. Church rates survived the attempt made in 1837 to abolish them and were to remain a point of contention between Anglicans and Nonconformists until their final abolition in 1868. In 1839 the Whigs' educational proposals had angered many supporters as well as opponents, with the Anglicans winning significant concessions.[1]

Anglicans had been alarmed by the Whig measures and were suspicious of their intentions toward the Church; hence, they looked to the Tory leader as the defender of "the Church as by law established." Both the essence and the genius of Peel's policy toward the Church had been that he sought not merely to reconcile it to reform but to make it "the instrument of its own regeneration."[2] It was largely due to him that the Ecclesiastical Commission had been established in 1835 and the process of church reform put on a footing acceptable to Anglicans. "The actual legislation by which the delayed reformation of the Church of England was partially effected was passed by his Whig successors in office between 1836 and 1840, but the initiative had been that of Peel."[3] Not only had Peel staunchly defended "the Church's inalienable right to its property"[4] throughout the 1830s, but he also in conjunction with Bishop Blomfield had "enabled the defence of the Establishment to be undertaken jointly by both State and Church."[5]

Evangelical enthusiasm for church reform had declined sharply during the 1830s. Few of them had approved the proposals advanced by Peel's Evangelical brother-in-law, Lord Henley, in his influential *Plan for Church Reform* published in 1832.[6] Their caution increased during the decade as they came to fear that Voluntaryism would use reform as a tool to destroy the establishment or that Tractarians would employ it for their own ends.[7] Although some of Peel's Anglican support was out of gratitude for the services he had rendered to the Church, much of it was also related to the fact that the Whigs were the only alternative. Not all could forgive Peel his liberal Tamworth Manifesto or forget his assistance given to "the greater apostasy of 1829."[8] While Evangelicals and Tractarians tended to support Peel politically, neither group approved of his religious views or expected to benefit in terms of preferment from a Conservative government.[9] Evangelicals did, however, expect better church measures from Peel, particularly as regards church extension.

EVANGELICAL SUPPORT FOR PEEL AND THE CAMPAIGN FOR CHURCH EXTENSION

During the late 1830s many Anglicans assumed that the administrative reform of the Church, coupled with significant voluntary efforts toward church building, would dispose Parliament to look favorably on a grant for church extension. If a Whig-dominated House refused, then certainly a Parliament in which Conservatives were in the ascendancy would agree. The need for church extension had been demonstrated in the 1836 report of the Ecclesiastical Commission, which had announced that 279 new churches were required to supply the metropolis's need adequately. When Bishop Blomfield issued his proposal to create the Metropolis Churches Fund in 1836, Evangelicals came forward to back the effort with significant contributions and personal involvement.[10] At a time when few Evangelicals were willing to cooperate with Dissent in the evangelization of the working classes, their concern was being expressed through parochial efforts, the exertions of the CP-AS, and voluntary church building.

Evangelicals were not content with these means, and they led the campaign for a government grant. The Whig government's opposition to such a proposal reinforced the Evangelicals' tendency to see their interests as bound up in the Tory cause. In 1837 Charlotte Elizabeth had expressed the typical view in her *Christian Lady's Magazine*: "We earnestly hope that as Christian and Conservative principles gain ground, and Conservative strength waxes, we shall find our parliament aroused to the duty and privilege of voting large grants for the increase of churches, and of provision for their ministers."[11] Two years later Baptist Noel put the Evangelical case for a church extension grant in a published letter to Lord Melbourne, stressing as Yates had done earlier the particular lack in London.[12] The appeal focused Evangelical concern on the issue,[13] and an 1839 public meeting, called to put pressure on the government, was organized and directed by leading Evangelical figures, both lay and clerical.[14]

The campaign for a church extension grant set the stage for another head-on clash between Anglican and Nonconformist evangelicals. In the same edition of the *Record* in which its editor was rejoicing over the Remonstrance signed by Nonconformist ministers, it also reported the formation of the Evangelical Voluntary Church Association, a society headed by Sir Culling Eardley Smith and dedicated to coordinating evangelical support for disestablishment.[15] The *Record* made no attempt to hide its fury with evangelicals such as Eardley Smith, who on the one hand could be a significant contributor to the LCM, but who, because of his antiestablishment stance, could also oppose government aid to church extension:

Yet these men, some of them professing to be the true and devoted servants of the Most High, unblushingly present themselves to obstruct the impartation to their fellow countrymen of "God's unspeakable gift," and to exert every nerve to seal up their souls in present darkness, the sure presage of that darkness which is eternal! O, who can adequately describe the scandal, the danger, the shame of such a course![16]

The campaign for the grant culminated in a parliamentary motion in June 1840 by Sir Robert Inglis, the Evangelical M.P. for Oxford University. Inglis, a well-known Ultra-Tory, petitioned that a significant but unspecified amount of public funds be made available for the Church. In a lengthy speech Inglis employed many familiar arguments: he warned Parliament of its national responsibility; he commended the social benefits accruing from the Church's influence on the community; he even appealed to the "lowest view" that "religion is the cheapest and most effective police."[17] Inglis especially praised effective Evangelical incumbents (notably his "excellent friend," John Venn,[18] and his two other "friends," Bishop Wilson of Calcutta and Daniel Wilson, Jr.). Significantly Inglis also argued against the Voluntary system from the viewpoint that was central to Evangelical thinking regarding evangelism:

All legislation ought, I think to be based on the principle that we have no natural inclination for religion or for instruction. There is no natural hunger or thirst for the bread and water of life. Mankind are under no influence by nature to go to Church: and, therefore, the doctrine of the demand regulating the supply, however true in respect to the wants of the external man, is utterly unapplicable to his spiritual necessities. Reason and experience confirm the truth, that our need is greatest where our sense of it is the least; and therefore, according to the memorable sentiment of Chalmers, we must not wait till men go to the Church or to the school; the Church and the school must go to them.[19]

Although the overwhelming majority of M.P.s were nominal members of the Church of England, Inglis tried to nurture the view that those who opposed his motion were strongly opposed to the church. His opponents were "The Papist and the Dissenter, in unholy alliance with the Infidel and the Socialist; the Papist, who, to this day, tolerates no other worship than his own in some of the chief states of the Continent, and the Dissenter, whose war-cry is religious liberty."[20] The division saw Sir Robert Peel and other leading Conservatives vote for the motion, while the Whigs were largely against; in fact three leading Evangelical Whigs (Sir George Grey, Lord Robert Grosvenor, and Viscount Morpeth) even voted against Inglis's proposal.[21]

The defeat of the church extension motion served to exacerbate Evangelical–Dissenting relations. The *Record* noted the decisive effect of the twenty Roman Catholic votes, but the alliance of Nonconformists with Chartists and "Socialists" elicited the following denunciation: "Such associates might teach these Political Dissenters the character of their work, if their eyes were not fast closed by the scales of prejudice, and their hearts deluded by the lust for personal aggrandizement."[22] The *Christian Observer* and the *Christian Guardian* both echoed the thunder claps of the *Record*. The former, in an uncharacteristic outburst declared: "The voluntary principle, important as it is, both as auxiliary to legislative provision and in regard to each Christian's private responsibility, is, nationally speaking, infidel and practically ineffective."[23] The latter journal moaned that with various reforms recently effected "it can scarcely now be said, as heretofore, that the State must wait till the church has first done her duty in the matter."[24] At the same time, however, the *Christian Guardian* took consolation in the closeness of the vote (168 to 149), especially in view of the Whig government's opposition to the motion, and it called for renewed pressure to force the Commons to act. The identifying of Evangelical interests with the Tory cause frustrated Whig Evangelicals. This can be seen in a letter of Walter Shirley to a friend, written in 1841: "The worst of it is, that the said evangelical body do not know who are their best friends, and fraternize with the Tories, who have ever been their most determined opponents and persecutors, instead of the Whigs, from whom we have had admirable church measures, and the best church appointments."[25]

While the Evangelicals were putting more and more trust in the Tory party, they were also drawing farther away from Dissenters who favored disestablishment and therefore opposed a church extension grant. Conservative Evangelicals who looked to the *Record* for spiritual and political leadership were encouraged to wait out the storm created by their opponents, in the belief that it would eventually dissipate. Buoyed up by such a hope, Inglis urged the London clergy to petition parliament in 1841.[26] The earnest of this hope seemed to the *Record* to be the election of the Peel government in July 1841. The *Record*'s editorial was rapturous:

The Whigs found they could not maintain themselves in place without yielding to the pressure of democracy, Dissent, and Popery; in other words, without endangering our glorious Constitution in Church and State—that palladium of the civil and religious liberties of the world—that honoured fabric which, in the mercy and through the blessing of God, has raised this nation to the highest pinnacle of power, riches, and honour. And when the nation's eyes, though late, were at last fairly opened to this enormous danger which threatened them, down have gone Whigs, Radicals, Dissenters, and Papists together! . . . No, the *nation*, the PEOPLE of *Great Britain and Ireland*, have now declared in favour of the British Constitution in Church and State, in opposition to the democracy of America, the latitudinarianism of Dissent, the degrading superstition of Popery, and the demoralizing nonentities of scepticism and Infidelity.[27]

Central to this Evangelical alliance with the Tory party was the assumption that the Conservatives would be generous in their assistance to the establishment. The *Churchman's Monthly Review* expressed the common Evangelical view in 1841 when it attacked those who embraced "modern liberalism": "that lowest of all exhibitions of human degradation." The journal was convinced that at the very minimum Peel would follow through with his commitment of 1841: "We have already said that one particular matter—Church Extension—has been so far advanced so as merely to wait for a vote of the House of Commons; which, constituted as that assembly now is, cannot, surely, be long withheld."[28] This it regarded as only "an important and excellent beginning" to measures favorable to the Church of England. Both the *Record* and the *Christian Observer* identified themselves closely with the Tory party, and once Peel was in office, it was not unknown for leading Evangelicals to use their influence among the brethren on behalf of the Tory government. An instance of this can be seen in the lobbying of Recordite publisher Robert Benton Seeley. Seeley was an important figure in Tory party circles in London and served party interests by seeking to influence Evangelicals like Lord Ashley on issues that might have jeopardized the standing of Peel's government.[29] He was particularly concerned in 1841 that Ashley's pursuit of his Factory Bill might be injurious to Peel's administration.[30] Conversely, Seeley also sought to use influence in government circles to benefit Evangelical interests.[31]

From Peel's perspective as prime minister in 1841, a church extension grant was not high on his list of priorities. The depressed state of trade, stagnating industrial manufacture, and severe distress in the textile districts occupied his attention, and these troubles were further aggravated by bad harvests.[32] The Whigs had bequeathed him a budget deficit, which led him to reimpose an income tax in the hopes of balancing the budget; furthermore, the surplus that the new tax would produce could be used to introduce tariff reform and a new Corn Law.[33] Social unrest, fanned by propaganda of the Anti-Corn Law League and the activities of the Chartists, broke into violent protest in the summer of 1842.[34] To Peel, the financial constraints on his ministry and the unpopularity of any church extension measure (especially at a time when some of the manufacturing poor were on the brink of starvation) ruled out such a measure. (See Illustration 5.) He wrote to Sir James Graham in December 1842 expressing his view on church extension:

It is very well for clergymen, and for Sir Robert Inglis, to argue that it is the duty of the State to provide religious edifices wherever they are wanted, and that Dissenters are bound to build and repair and endow their own churches and those of the Establishment also, and this by new Taxation wherever requisite. But you and I know that the Church and religion would suffer, and peace and charity would be sacrificed, were we in practice to push these arguments to their logical conclusions.[35]

Peel's arguments, however, were substantially those advanced by H. G. Ward, M.P., against Inglis's motion in 1840.[36] If plans for facilitating Anglican self-help were all that Peel could offer, his support for Inglis's motion in 1840 had certainly led many Anglicans to expect more.

The events of the first few months of 1843 served to confirm the wisdom of Peel's course. In Ireland Daniel O'Connell began to arouse the Roman Catholic population with his campaign to repeal the Union with Britain, thus making a church extension grant an inviting target for the repealers' propaganda.[37] In England, Dissent was provoked by the introduction of Sir James Graham's Factory Education Act. The measure was in part aimed "at reducing the labour of children in cotton, woolen, flax and silk factories to 6 1/2 hours per day" by requiring the children (eight years old and up) to spend three hours a day in schools, which would be supported by the rates and inspected by government officials. Rioting in the depressed industrial areas in 1842 made the issue one of pressing concern.[38] Graham's measure received strong support from Evangelicals like Lord Ashley[39] and sought to conciliate Dissenters by excusing their children from religious instruction classes and by providing for the possibility of a limited number of Nonconformist school trustees.[40] The concessions required of both sides proved to be too much for either. Although the measure was pro-Anglican, many champions of Church-controlled education opposed any form of publicly supported interdenominational education.

Illustration 5
The Church Extension Grant

Proposals for a church extension grant served to increase antiestablishment and anticlerical sentiments in the early 1840s. *The Penny Satirist*, March 13, 1840. By Permission of the British Library.

Nonconformists were fierce in their opposition to the measure. London Nonconformity was especially aroused, with Dr. Andrew Reed, a leading Congregationalist minister, heading the opposition. In the provinces, Edward Baines the younger, the evangelical Congregationalist editor of the *Leeds Mercury* played a prominent role. More significant in the long run, however, was the impact of Graham's measure upon the Wesleyan Toryism of Jabez Bunting and *The Watchman*, a weekly newspaper begun in 1835. Between 1836 and 1843 the Wesleyans had been involved in a heated theological controversy with the Oxford Tractarians, which had seriously damaged Wesleyan–Anglican relations. The nastiness of the High Church polemic which declaimed the Methodist "heresy" elicited cries of protest; in 1841 Bunting warned the Wesleyan Conference that "unless the Church of England will protest against Puseyism in some intelligible form, it will be the duty of the Methodists to protest against the Church of England."[41] Graham's measure provided the opportunity for such a protest, for the measure was popularly seen as being Tractarian-inspired. Yet the Wesleyans would not have backed the proposals even if Tractarianism had not been a factor for they "supported the Church of England not for what it might achieve if properly endowed, but for its key role in the maintenance of England's Protestant Constitution."[42] Liberal Wesleyans who felt that in practice the "no politics" rule had come to mean "no Liberal-Whig politics" could take heart from the difficulties the bill presented the Wesleyan leadership.[43] John Prest comments, "The new image that Peel had laboured since 1834 to give the Tory party vanished almost overnight."[44]

In the midst of the storm over the Factory Education Act, Peel introduced his long-awaited church extension proposal, a moment that the *Christian Observer* noted was hardly auspicious.[45] Even before the agitation over the unsuccessful education bill, the prime minister had been aware of the political alliance which would be formed to oppose such a measure. He wrote to Henry Hobhouse outlining his feelings:

Sir Robert Inglis thinks the whole difficulty would be readily solved by the proposal of a large parlimentary grant, two or three millions.

I totally differ from him. Such a grant simply proposed would meet with powerful and persevering opposition from large classes of the House of Commons; from the representatives of Ireland; in the present state of the Scotch Church, from the representatives of Scotland; from all the representatives of Dissent in its various forms; from combinations for party purposes; from, in short, all the elements of which a powerful opposition could be formed.[46]

Peel's measure reflected his unease. It was so feeble that Sir Robert Inglis, who had recently presented a petition from Oxford University on the issue,[47] told Parliament that he could not support it.[48] The *Christian Observer* also expressed disappointment that the bill did not go far enough: "it only enables the Church to borrow from itself, and to make the best use of its resources: it adds nothing to its revenues; which, however managed, are quite inadequate to the spiritual wants of the people."[49] Peel had succeeded in not arousing another storm; the measure passed without even a division in the House. The impact of the bill upon London was minimal.[50]

The disillusionment of Evangelicals with the Tory government is evident in the *Record*'s confession several months after the bill's passage: "There are many who profess not to be able to discover any material distinction between the principles of a Conservative and a Whig-Radical Government, so as to give occasion to any considerable preference to the one above the other."[51] The paper, however, dissented from this view and maintained that the Conservatives had sought to defend the church–state connection, which the Whigs had attempted to loosen. Acknowledging defeat on the church extension issue, Evangelicals were urged to channel their energies in other directions, particularly toward voluntary church-building efforts.[52] This was facilitated by Peel's Church Endowment Bill of 1843, which did much to reverse the defeat the Evangelicals had suffered in 1818 when Sir William Scott had thwarted a measure to allow greater lay influence in church building.[53] The new measure encouraged them to build churches by placing the right of presentation in the hands of the boards of trustees rather than in the hands of the bishops as was the case with the Incorporated Church Building Society. Almost immediately the Evangelicals established their own Church Extension Fund.

Until 1843 the Evangelicals had had great expectations of government assistance in the pursuit of their mission to the working classes; many had persuaded themselves that a Tory government would assist with a generous church extension grant. Only once that had failed did the long-standing alternative of establishing an Anglican society similar to the aggressive London City Mission become a serious possibility. It was no coincidence that the discussions which resulted in the formation of such a society (which will be discussed in the next chapter) began only a few months after the defeat of the church extension bill.

ENGLISH EVANGELICALS AND THE SCOTTISH "DISRUPTION"

Tory Evangelicals were disappointed with Peel and angry with Nonconformist support for disestablishment. The dispute that had been raging in the Church of Scotland since the mid–1830s caused them further concern. In 1834 the General Assembly of the Scottish Establishment had passed the Veto Act, which permitted a congregation to reject without stated cause any minister appointed by a lay patron. Supporters of the measure were known as "Non-Intrusionists" because they objected to the intrusion of unwanted ministers into parishes. The Non-Intrusionists drew their strength from the evangelical party in the Kirk, which by 1834 dominated the General Assembly. The act was despised by the "Moderates," who were strongly Erastian and the inheritors of eighteenth-century latitudinarian theology.

The Scottish Kirk was a very different sort of establishment from the one familiar to Peel and his fellow English politicians. It had a tradition of much greater independence from the state, with the northern establishment never having recognized royal supremacy.[54] Its doctrines and liturgy were also dissimilar, as was its administrative structure. Unfortunately for the Non-Intrusionists, these differences were not appreciated and the pronouncements of the General Assembly and its challenges to decisions made in civil courts struck the English politicians as odd and unreasonable. The Non-Intrusionists had little political clout in the British Parliament, and as the conflict over the Veto Act made its way through the courts to the House of Lords, successive governments, both Whig and Tory, hesitated to intervene. Furthermore, John Hope, a leading Scottish advocate and Moderate sympathizer, had the ear of Lord Aberdeen and, through him, of Peel.[55] Hope nursed the view that a secession was unlikely over the issue; in one letter to Aberdeen he insisted that "there are not six or ten who would secede."[56] Erastian predilections and dislike of a democratic veto were thus reinforced by such assurances from north of the Tweed.

Anglican Evangelicals feared that such intransigence on the part of Peel would lead to disaster; many expected a large number of the evangelical ministers to secede from the Scottish establishment if the spiritual independence of the Scottish Church was not guaranteed. As early as 1840 the *Record* had been echoing the demand that the contentious Veto Act be repealed.[57] By 1842 it cautioned that "matters are assuming that shape which may lead that Church to enter with grave and determined hostility against our own."[58] Evangelicals were particularly concerned that a schism would greatly strengthen antiestablishment forces. Right up to the time of the Disruption of 1843 the *Record* maintained its unrealistic expectation that the Tory government would intervene to prevent the division,[59] and when it occurred, the *Record* condemned the government for having "greatly failed in their duty."[60]

The secession was much more serious than the Peel administration had expected. Over a third of the clergy (451 of 1,203 ministers) left the Establishment, among them many of the Kirk's leading figures, and within a decade the number of attendants at the Free Church almost equaled those at the Established Church.[61] Even the English Evangelicals were surprised by the strength and wealth of the secession.[62] Although the *Record* praised the official stance adopted by the Free Church of Scotland in favor of the establishment principle,[63] both the *Record* and the *Christian Observer* worried that the influence of the aging Chalmers would not suffice to keep Free Churchmen from eventually joining in attacks on the English establishment.[64] Recordite concern for harmonious relations with Dissent was enhanced by the secession, as the newpaper's editor made clear early in 1844.[65] Now acutely aware of the shrinking base for the establishment as they had known it, some Anglican Evangelicals were realizing how isolated they were politically. They needed to foster a broadly based coalition of evangelicals if they were to succeed in the battles which loomed ahead. In 1844, however, Evangelicals could see no basis for such a pan-evangelical alliance.

THE SHIFT IN FAVOR OF PAN-EVANGELICALISM

At the same time, the Tory party's lack of commitment to Protestant ideals and Peel's apparent anxiety to conciliate Dissent at the expense of the Church were leading to the estrangement of the ultra-Protestant Recordites from the Tory cause. Until 1844 this disaffection had centered on issues on which Anglican Evangelicals were at odds with Dissent: the Factory Education Act, Tory unwillingness to intervene to prevent the Scottish Disruption, and the government's refusal to provide significant support for church extension. By February 1844 the *Record* had made a major about-face and was lamenting the fact that "Renewed union among Protestants is, we believe, in many cases at the present moment quite impossible."[66]

The *Record*'s new concern with evangelical unity may well have been related to the removal of the Reverend Henry Blunt from the Recordite inner circle; however, it is also clear that Tractarianism was leading the Recordites to seek better relations with Nonconformity.[67] By the mid–1840s, more Evangelicals were abandoning their self-distancing from Dissent. Much of this was due to a change in the nature of the interparty rivalry within the Church. By now many Evangelicals had concluded that they were not going to succeed in "evangelicalizing" the whole church and that ideologically they should be stressing their mutual ground with evangelical Nonconformity. By embracing Dissent one would clearly be repudiating the Tractarians who discounted nonepiscopal ministry. On the other side of the ecclesiastical divide, the continued willingness of many Nonconformists to forge links with Anglican Evangelicals was related to the change that had taken place within Nonconformity. The increasing professionalization of the Nonconformist ministry had made many more anxious for the sort of legitimization of their roles that association with Anglicans would offer.

The *Record* was especially worried by Wesleyan Methodist disaffection with the Church of England as manifested in their opposition to the Factory Education Act[68] and was now anxious to defend Dissenters against the charges of schism made against them by the Tractarians.[69] While appealing for recognition of the validity of Dissenting ministrations, the *Record* pleaded for evangelical unity against Roman encroachments and praised the Wesleyan Methodists for not joining in the disestablishment campaign. It hoped that evangelical Nonconformity would "see that the times are too critical to exhaust their strength on secondary grounds of division while the very foundations are threatened with destruction; and that all faithful men will labour, each in his own sphere, not for sectarian objects, but for the great truths of God."[70] For the Tory Evangelicals in particular, the threats to their "very foundations" seemed to be multiplying.

The political winds were shifting, and Anglican and Nonconformist evangelicals were soon to find unity in opposition to Tory policies that they felt threatened their common faith. The first major cause in which evangelicals could unite to fight a Tory proposal was provided by the Dissenters' Chapels Bill which allowed

Unitarians who had once been Presbyterians to retain their properties and endowment funds.[71] Theological considerations aside, the Wesleyan leadership was particularly alarmed by the precedent that the measure might set in allowing secessionist groups to make claims against the parent body; Bunting succeeded in securing a technical change in the bill, but more damage to Wesleyan Toryism had been done.[72] To evangelicals who still took seriously the religious office of the state it was an instance of an allegedly Protestant Parliament professing agnosticism while promoting heresy. The *Record* made an appeal for unity in order to "resist and expose this unjust, this iniquitous, this barefaced attempt to disseminate and protect the awful heresy which denies the Godhead of our blessed Saviour."[73] Exeter Hall, the standard Evangelical meeting place, hosted a large meeting of evangelicals opposed to the measure, an exercise that brought together numerous Anglican and Dissenting ministers. (See Illustration 6.)

Behind the scenes Recordites urged the government to change its course. James E. Gordon, who nine years earlier had written to Peel to express his regrets at not being able to support him in his former role as M.P.,[74] now adopted a very different tone in addressing the Tory leader:

You are acting in complete ignorance of the moral guilt of the transaction to which you have too hastily lent the sanction of your name and authority, and in still greater ignorance of the feeling of the Christian and moral wrath of this great country. In the view of that body I can honestly assure you, that the action is not only Unchristian in its essence, but Antichristian in its tendency; and the equivocal approbation of a handful of Socinian Infidels will be found a sorry compensation for the fortified confidence, and alienated feeling of all that is holy and righteous in the land. I exerted myself and my principles for my party untill [*sic*] I became incapable of further effort, and that exertion, humble as it was, has no inconsiderable relation to the increase of that noble majority which it is your pride and your privilege to wield in the House of Commons; but if that party should become the instrument of saddling the country with the guilt and with the consequences of what is proposed by the Dissenters Chapels Bill, I, and tens of thousands besides, will feel that our confidence has been grossly betrayed as our principles have been misrepresented.[75]

The unwillingness of Peel to back down on this measure was a serious blow to Recordite support for his government. The *Record* made clear its disaffection; it felt well warned of the Conservative party:

The recent proceedings in Parliament have done much to dissipate an illusion which was becoming very prevalent. The party struggles of the last ten years have had so many matters connected with the external framework of the Church mingled up with them; the Liberals have been so often placed in collision with the religious establishments of these islands; and the Conservatives have so constantly been found among the defenders of those establishments, that Christians were in danger of forgetting the greater and more permanent distinction between the Church and the world, and of almost imagining a Conservative Association to be a kind of religious Society.

The effect, however, of this piece of unjust legislation, will be, as we remarked at

Illustration 6
Exeter Hall

To Victorian Britain, Exeter Hall was synonymous with evangelicalism. Located in the Strand, it was designed as a national evangelical meeting place and housed the headquarters of a number of benevolent and evangelistic societies. Built in the early 1830s, the "Hall" was owned by a group of wealthy evangelical laymen and functioned as the evangelical "nerve center" until its demolition in the 1880s. Its "Great Hall," pictured above, could accommodate 4,000, while another room directly beneath could simultaneously host a smaller gathering. As evangelical societies held their annual meetings in London between mid-April and the end of May, their supporters in the provinces would flock to the city for extended vacations in order to attend; hence they became known as the "May Meetings." By the mid–1850s, railway companies laid on special trains to accommodate travelers from northern cities. *Illustrated London News* 4 (May 18, 1844):317.

first, to clear away one mistake,—that what is called Conservatism is *intrinsically* connected with the defence and maintenance of true religion. It may be so, it has latterly
been so, *incidentally*. But whenever the question is stripped of extrinsic circumstances,
and reduced to a simple choice between *the truth*, and any falsehood which may come
into collision with it, we are almost certain to find a combination of all parties not really
knowing and loving the Gospel to suppress and keep it down.[76]

The moderate *Christian Observer* shared the *Record*'s disapproval of the bill[77]
but maintained its steadfast support of Peel's government, fearing far worse
treatment from Peel's foes.[78] The *Record* disagreed with such an analysis and
argued that no government had been so dangerous: "we are harassed with more
alarms on the score of rash and dangerous legislation, under our present *Conservative* Government than we suffered even from their professedly reforming
predecessors."[79]

Early in 1845 a bill was introduced into the House of Lords designed to remove
certain minor disabilities from Jews. Evangelicals were again alarmed that the
de-Christianization of the nation was being carried a step further, and both the
Christian Observer and the *Record* objected. The *Record* spoke of "our national
sin, in departing from the *national* profession of Christianity"; and feared for
the time when Britain would "have to endure the punishment."[80] The *Christian
Observer* pondered as to how Jews could "duly and of good will administer the
laws of a Christian nation?"[81]

THE GREAT UNIFIER: THE MAYNOOTH GRANT

The Tory measure that did the most to unite evangelicals in a common cause
was the Peel government's decision to increase the annual grant to the necessitous
Roman Catholic college at Maynooth in Ireland from £8,000 to £25,000 and to
make the grant a permanent feature not subject to annual revision. Seven years
earlier, Sir Robert Peel had noted that the English had conspicuously failed to
establish a working relationship with the Roman Catholic church in Ireland.[82]
The need for such an understanding was brought home to the Conservative
government in 1843; the Irish repeal movement had come to life with such force
that the British government found it necessary to move against its leader O'Connell and brought him and other leading repealers to trial. By following up this
"firmness by conciliation" Peel hoped to defuse the Catholic-nationalist movement in Ireland. The grant to Maynooth was part of his broader strategy "tac-
tically to isolate O'Connell and the repeal movement by driving a wedge between
them and the Catholic hierarchy."[83] Peel fully expected that the measure would
trigger a strong outburst of popular anti-Catholicism. It did more than that: it
"occasioned a split in the Conservative party which compelled Peel to rely on
Liberal support to carry his bill, thus producing a situation which was repeated
in the Corn Law crisis of the following year."[84]

Quite understandably, Evangelical Anglicans were at the forefront of the opposition. In 1831 the Recordite M.P.s, led by Captain Gordon and in alliance with Irish Orangemen and a handful of Ultra-Tories, had tried unsuccessfully to put an end to the annual grant to Maynooth.[85] The Irish Church Temporalities Bill of 1833, which the Whig government had intended as a measure of much-needed reform, had increased fears among the Recordites that the Whigs were determined to weaken the Protestant establishment in Ireland and to strengthen the Church of Rome. The confidence that the defenders of Protestant ascendency in Ireland had placed in Peel as an antidote to Whig compromise with Anti-Christ had been betrayed. The *Christian Observer* denounced the grant as ''impolitic'' and ''anti-scriptural,'' while the *Record* took special aim at the government which sponsored it: ''the Conservative party, as now working . . . are accomplishing, not by preserving, but by departing from, the principles of our Christian and Protestant Constitution, an amount of evil incomparably greater than the Whigs could accomplish.''[86] Peel was seen by many as an opportunist; at worst, as a traitor to the conservative principles he had espoused.

The measure was, as Edward Norman has pointed out, a significant milestone along the road from a confessional state to the modern liberal state, and it was opposed as such by both Tory Evangelicals and by Jabez Bunting, the Wesleyan leader.[87] The Recordites had dismissed the eighteenth-century arguments on behalf of the establishment based on utility and had erected a defense which appealed to the Establishment's basis in truth. They now beheld with horror a professedly Protestant government willing to endow what it confessed to be error. The writing had been on the wall since the passage of the Dissenters' Chapels Bill in 1843, but few had expected such a measure from Peel.

The *Eclectic Review* opposed the Maynooth grant on the basis of its opposition to all state support for religion; it appreciated the difficulty of the situation for the Protestants who opposed Maynooth on different grounds:

The pretence of maintaining the Irish establishment because it teaches the *truth*, is now virtually abandoned; for the legislature is called upon to provide means that the effect of that truth may be contradicted—that priests may be multiplied and educated, and sent forth, to teach what our public formularies had designated ''damnable heresies.''[88]

The view of the ultra-Protestant Recordites was that the Conservative party had become leavened with the yeast of liberalism and Tractarianism and could not be relied upon as a bulwark against the encroachments of Rome. Hugh McNeile, the dominant figure in Evangelicalism in Liverpool, had a national reputation as an anti-Catholic agitator. It was he who now argued that ''it was time to throw off the name of 'Conservative', which originally wanted a more definite meaning, and which was now becoming disgusting, and to assume the plain, distinct, and intelligible title of 'PROTESTANTS.' ''[89] (See Illustration 7.)

On both sides of the evangelical divide decisions had to be made as to whether Maynooth should be opposed singly or together. The *Record* was willing to countenance such cooperation and urged Evangelicals to support the Anti-

POOR OLD BULL BETWEEN TWO WOLVES.

BULL.—Oh, mercy on me! what will become of me, poor, old, feeble wretch that I am? I've slipped down, and two ferocious wolves are fighting over me for my vitals! The Exeter Hall brute hunts me from pillar to post, and wants the whole of my carcass to himself, and won't let the other hungry beast have even a bite. Oh, Lord! I shall be devoured alive between these two wolves!

Illustration 7
"Exeter Hall" and Maynooth

These two "wolves" seriously disrupted English political life in 1845. The one labelled "Exeter Hall" represented a coalition of evangelicals and Protestant Constitutionalists who were infuriated by Peel's proposals. The "Maynooth" wolf stood for the counterclaims of the Irish Catholics. *The Penny Satirist*, May 10, 1845. By Permission of the British Library.

Maynooth Committee, which had been established to coordinate the battle. Although the *Record* had supported joint opposition to the Dissenters' Chapels Bill, it recognized that the anti-Maynooth campaign would involve a deeper commitment and a real change vis-à-vis Dissent:

We have recently been disposed to think that public and outward fraternity with them [Dissenters] was for the present inexpedient: that we might all work harmoniously for the same great ends without taking part in the same meeting, or constituting one Association for one great object. But when Popery within the Church is giving its hand to Popery without it, when the great masses of Churchmen, who neither call themselves Papists nor Tractarians, appear to sympathize and side with the Popery rather than with the Protestantism of Europe, we think it is time for true Protestants publicly to show that they are animated with a very different—with a directly opposite spirit.[90]

In this conclusion, however, the *Record* stood alone. In the year that the Oxford Movement seemed its most ominous, cooperation with Dissent was seen by many moderate Evangelicals as unwise. Lord Mounteagle correctly gauged the opinion of the Evangelicals in a parliamentary speech in which he argued that they were "alarmed by the doctrines not of Maynooth, but of Oxford."[91] The *Christian Observer* agreed with the *Record*'s analysis that "it is the anti-Protestant spirit of Tractarianism which has endowed Maynooth." At the same time, however, it was convinced that the embrace of Dissent in opposing Rome would further the supposed Romanizing tendencies of the Tractarians, because it would alienate moderate Churchmen from the Evangelical party. Moreover, the *Observer* reasoned that Sir Robert Peel, by conceding to the pro-Maynooth agitation, had infinitely strengthened Voluntaryism. It thus feared that the British government would soon decide to pay the increased Maynooth grant out of Church of Ireland revenues instead of from taxes, further subverting the Church of England of its strength.[92]

The anti-Maynooth agitation induced a small but significant number of London clergy to join Dissenters in a common cause who had not previously been willing to work openly with Nonconformists. Most notable among these were Daniel Wilson, Jr., the influential vicar of Islington, and Henry Venn, the secretary of the CMS.[93] The Central Anti-Maynooth Committee, headed by the former disestablishment agitator, Sir Culling Eardley Smith, organized large public meetings such as the conference convened in London on April 30, 1845, which attracted numerous clergymen and ministers. Nonconformists like Eardley Smith also faced a crisis of conscience. If he opposed Maynooth on the ground of his opposition to all establishments, he forfeited the possibility of working with Anglicans; they would only cooperate with him on the basis of anti-Catholicism. Eardley Smith had just returned from a tour of Italy and was sufficiently horrified by his firsthand observation of Catholicism there that he was willing to compromise.[94]

Divisions within the ranks of Voluntaryism vis-à-vis Catholicism had become evident as early as 1839. The moderate Voluntaries had been led by Eardley Smith who played a prominent role in the evangelical Voluntary Church Association whose aim had been to seek "the peaceful conversion of the established clergy to the Voluntary principle."[95] The moderates were disturbed by the methods of the militant Voluntaries who founded the Religious Freedom Society in 1838 and established their own periodical, *The Nonconformist*, in 1841, under the editorship of Edward Miall. Support for militant Voluntaryism also came from the *Patriot* newspaper and the *Eclectic Review* under Dr. Thomas Price.[96] Many of the moderates had been upset by the willingness of the militants to cooperate closely with Roman Catholics in opposing the Anglican establishment,[97] as many moderate Nonconformist evangelicals in the late 1830s did share the concern of Anglican Evangelicals about the growing strength of Roman Catholicism and Tractarianism. Apart from the Wesleyan Methodists, however, few Nonconformists seem to have shared the Evangelicals' intense concern about Irish Catholicism.[98] In 1839 the *Congregational Magazine* remarked that it considered Charlotte Elizabeth, the editor of the intensely anti-Catholic *Christian Lady's Magazine*, "a very good Christian, but a very sorry politician"[99] and dissociated itself from her estimate of "orange christianity," the character and quality of which it considered to be major barriers to evangelism in Ireland.[100]

During the late 1830s and early 1840s the moderates hesitated to join Roman Catholics in pulling down the Anglican establishment, but also refused even to consider opposing Catholicism in alliance with Anglican Evangelicals. In an 1839 review of a work published by the Reformation Society, the *Congregational Magazine* made it clear that Nonconformists put much of the blame for the growing strength of Roman Catholicism and for the emergence of Tractarianism upon the partial reformation of the Church of England in the sixteenth century. Speaking specifically of the perceived Catholic resurgence:

We hold the Church of England responsible for it. She has not given to the people, only partially, that gospel which was given to her, when the reformers put the Bible into her hands; she has taught Popery by her constitution, sacraments, rites, and divinity; she has kept the mass of the nation under her influence, so ignorant of spiritual religion, and so familiar with high notions of church authority and priestly power, that Rome has little else to do to make converts, when external circumstances are favourable.... The principles of Anglicanism, left to flow freely and unfettered, inevitably shape their course towards the gulf of the papacy; and ... our Episcopalian friends must not be surprised, if a stream of their adherents should part company with them, and pass into the communion of Rome.[101]

This stance had led John Blackburn, the editor of the *Congregational Magazine*, to urge Dissenters to unite to oppose both Rome and the Anglican establishment in the early 1840s.[102] But Blackburn, like Eardley Smith, reversed his position in 1845 so alarmed was he at the added strength that Rome would have by its effective establishment in Ireland. He urged support for the activities of the Central Anti-Maynooth Committee and pleaded, "if we sincerely desire to defeat this measure, which we can only hope to do by the union of all Protestant denominations, surely for the sake of their powerful aid, and for the pleasure of fraternal union, we may forbear, for a season, to avow extreme opinions."[103]

Unity was extremely important for the agitators. The Central Anti-Maynooth Committee, eager for a great display of Protestant unity, decided to convene a national conference in London on April 30. Once it was convened, however, a rift occurred, which came "at the most unfortunate moment for the whole agitation."[104] The extreme Voluntaries (the Independents, Methodist secessionists, and Miall's Congregationalist followers) withdrew to oppose Maynooth on an antiestablishment footing. Professor Machin has observed, "The schism in the anti-Maynooth assembly was the more effective because the conference had been meant to display the unity of the cause."[105]

The breakdown of the united front was a great encouragement to the supporters of the measure. As expected, the government tried to play down the significance of Anglican opposition, thereby fostering the impression that it was the work of disgruntled Voluntaries. Sir Robert Peel privately nurtured this view among the press. He wrote to John Wilson Croker of the *Quarterly Review*: "The opposition to the Maynooth Bill is mainly the opposition of Dissent, in England; partly fanatical, partly religious, mainly unwillingness to sanction the germ of a second Establishment, and to strengthen and confirm that of the Protestant Church."[106] Such assertions were hotly denied by the *Record* which insisted that "A continual, but very disingenuous effort has been made, in some of the journals, to represent the opposition to the Maynooth Bill as 'a Dissenting movement.' "[107] To prove its point, the paper pointed to an anti-Maynooth petition circulated among the clergy in the Diocese of London, which had been signed by 350 clergymen.[108] Anglican opposition can also be gauged by the fact that only six of the twenty-three bishops who voted in the House of Lords were in favor of the measure.[109]

Yet another of Peel's measures angered Tory Evangelicals. His Academical Institutions Bill introduced in May 1845, was designed to allow the formation of unsectarian university colleges in Ireland. It was denounced by Sir Robert Inglis as involving "a gigantic scheme of Godless education."[110] Peel was resigned to another outcry and wrote to an associate to acknowledge that he expected to be assailed by "the reproach and clamour" of Protestants like Inglis, but expressed his confidence that "We shall carry our measure in spite of Exeter Hall."[111] Once the Maynooth grant had become law, pan-evangelical unity based on opposition to the measure began to disintegrate because of Dissenting disillusionment.[112] Needful of continued Dissenting support the *Record* urged them to continue to fight Roman encroachments.[113] The paper, however, was aware that a more broadly based alliance was needed, and it threw its influence behind efforts to create a new organization.

THE ESTABLISHMENT OF AN EVANGELICAL ALLIANCE

In July 1845 the *Record* began to promote pan-evangelical unity in earnest with its publication of a series of letters "On Christian Union" written by Edward

Bickersteth. Playing down doctrinal and political distinctives,[114] Bickersteth
stressed the evangelical doctrine of an invisible church composed of "those who
truly believe in Jesus and love the brethren."[115] In October of the same year a
pan-evangelical conference was convened in Liverpool to lay the foundations of
an anti-Tractarian, anti–Roman Catholic grouping known as the Evangelical
Alliance. Although only twenty of the 250 ministers attending were Church of
England clergy, the *Record* hailed the organization as "the only apparent hope
of repelling the advances of Popery."[116] A large number of Anglican Evangelical
laymen and clergy were opposed to such cooperation with Dissent. Some clergy
were undoubtedly hampered from acting freely on this issue because of their
dependence on their bishops or on Tractarian clergy, but many of the Evangelical
clergy opposed the alliance because they were genuinely eager to demonstrate
their adherence to "Church principles."[117]

The *Christian Observer* put its case against the Evangelical Alliance in very
strong terms. It noted that the proposed alliance had grown out of the activities
of the Central Anti-Maynooth Committee and that even that body had experienced
great difficulties within its own ranks.[118] Furthermore, some of the leading
Dissenters who had withdrawn from the committee's activities in order to oppose
Maynooth on a strictly antiestablishment basis were now prominent in the efforts
of the Evangelical Alliance.[119] With three of the leading Dissenting journals in
the hands of men active in the Anti-State Church Association, a diminution of
Dissenting hostility was not to be expected.[120] Given that Dissenters conscientiously held such different views, the *Christian Observer* felt that there was no
room for cooperation:

We have no quarrel with Mr. Binney, for wishing to subvert institutions which he believes
destroy more souls than they save; or with Dr. Cox, for opposing the baptism of the
children of believers, which he considers to be an awful delusion; or with Presbyterians
and Congregationalists, for desiring to free Christ's Church from what they consider the
ungodly bane of Episcopacy; only such being their views, and ours being very different,
we cannot work cordially together in religious institutions; and it is more for union that
each should pursue his own path, than that there should be a fusion of heterogeneous
materials in which there can be no real amalgamation.[121]

The *Christian Observer* had little sympathy with the suggestion that, by joining
the Evangelical Alliance, Evangelicals would lessen the hostility of Dissenters.
Dissenting hostility might now be aggravated by Tractarianism, but it had preceded the rise of Tractarianism; furthermore the *Observer* maintained that "it
was the conduct of the political Dissenters that gave birth to the Tractarian
'conspiracy.' "[122]

The opposition of some of the members of the Free Church of Scotland to
the English establishment caused great concern to Evangelicals, and the *Christian
Observer* expressed fear that Free Churchmen were attempting to use the Alliance
as a new "Solemn League and Covenant" of Cromwellian days, which would

uproot English episcopacy.[123] So deep did its feelings run on the issue that the magazine warned of the danger of schism:

The wary Scottish sectaries have thrown a fresh bone of contention among us; and will rejoice if, by the agency of a few members and ministers of the Church of England, they can foment an intestine strife in our camp. Strife there will be; for our bishops, and the great body of our clergy, will not, and cannot, subscribe to this new anti-Church League and Covenant; . . . Mr. Bickersteth would not willingly generate a schism among us; but do it he will by persisting in this project. We have spoken to many brethren upon the subject; and this has been their unanimous voice.[124]

The fear that the Evangelical Alliance was "only a trap to draw them over to Dissent" was common among Evangelicals and was in part related to the emergence of a small Evangelical secessionist group in 1844.[125] The Free Church of England established a church in Exeter following the secession of an Evangelical incumbent harassed by Bishop Phillpotts.[126] Even the *Record* had mooted the possibility of secession, arguing that while it might at some point be justified, that point had not arrived and cautioning that "we are sure that for men of Evangelical principles at present to leave her, on account of some personal difficulty . . . is a grievous error. . . . "[127] Suspicions that the leading advocate of cooperation with Dissent, Baptist W. Noel, was about to secede in 1844 reflected similar fears; Noel denied the allegation in the strongest possible terms.[128]

Contributing to this theory of a Dissenting conspiracy was the fact that the original suggestion of such an organization as the Evangelical Alliance had been made by J. A. James at a meeting of the Congregational Union in 1842, and the whole movement had been strongly dominated by Dissenters.[129] Furthermore, the founding conference had been organized by Free Church of Scotland ministers, and this only served to increase Evangelical suspicions.[130]

For some Evangelicals, however, interdenominational cooperation was a question of degree, and it is important to appreciate that opposition to the loosely defined Evangelical Alliance did not necessarily imply opposition to other forms of pan-evangelicalism. For instance, the Reverend Peter Hall, minister of Long Acre Episcopal Chapel in London, was well known for his interdenominational activities,[131] but he published a pamphlet attacking the Evangelical Alliance.[132] Despite such anomalies, it is clear that the formation of the Alliance, given the support of the *Record*, did much to promote the concept of pan-evangelicalism among Evangelicals and provided a framework in which such cooperation could take place.

At a national level, then, Evangelicals were being divided on the issue of pan-evangelicalism by the pressure of political events. Many of the ultra-Protestant Recordites who had drawn back from cooperating with Dissent at the height of the Voluntary Controversy were now willing to reestablish working relationships with Dissent in order to counter Roman Catholicism. It would seem, however, that the majority of the Evangelical clergy sided with the *Christian Observer* and were eager to distance themselves from charges of "low churchmanship."

The *Record* was clearly disappointed with the feeble support that the Evangelical Alliance received from Anglicans and was particularly annoyed that several of the leading ultra-Protestants stood aloof. Hugh Stowell of Manchester published a declaration signed by numerous Mancunian clergy which deplored the alliance as "an Association which appears to regard all the unhappy separations from our Church as comparatively unimportant" and viewed it as subversive of the establishment principle.[133]

Hugh McNeile of Liverpool had long opposed cooperation with Dissent[134] and saw fit to preach and publish a sermon against the fledgling organization.[135] The *Record* was convinced that it could discern another theological concern motivating McNeile: his premillennial "futurist" eschatology provided him with no incentive to strive for Christian unity as the object could only be obtained by the personal return of Christ.[136] The Reverend Joshua W. Brooks, a leading Anglican writer and publisher of books on prophecy, wrote to the *Record* to support its analysis:

> Though essentially agreeing with Mr. M'Neile of Liverpool, in the views entertained by him on the Redeemer's advent, I nevertheless consider your allusion to some of the consequences of those views, in reply to one of the objections of Mr. M'Neile to the Evangelical Alliance, perfectly just and to the point. I have myself witnessed precisely the same effect follow, in some instances, from propounding Millenarian doctrine.[137]

As discussed above, in the 1820s and 1830s premillennialism had been challenging the long-accepted, optimistic postmillennial views held by most evangelicals.[138] Edward Bickersteth had played an important role in popularizing the imminent return of Christ. By the 1840s premillennialists were divided into two major camps of "historicists" (also called "presentists") and "futurists." Both were agreed on a number of points: the view that acceptance of the authority of Scripture necessitated acceptance of a literal rather than a spiritual fulfilment of prophecies; that the world would not, as the postmillennialists expected, be saved by the Gospel, but that it would become more and more corrupt and that it was in fact rushing to imminent judgment; that Christ's return was literal and personal; that the Jews would be restored to Palestine before the onset of the millennium; and that the panorama of human history was explicitly foretold and knowable.[139]

The "historicist" school argued that "in chapters 6 to 18 of Revelation, we have a symbolic representation of the history of the church and the nations and rulers associated with it."[140] They worked from a "Day-Year Theory," to compute the date and expected fall of the Papacy and interpreted contemporary European history in light of its prophetic timetable. This school of interpretation dominated the first generation of the millenarian revival until the mid–1840s when it began to lose its almost undisputed position. The "futurists" were so called because they insisted that the events of the Book of Revelation would take place at a future date, during the Tribulation, rather than viewing them as the past history of the church. They also rejected the historicists' "Day-Year Theory" and insisted on interpreting the prophetic "days" of the books of Daniel and Revelation literally. "Futurism, the competing eschatology of Irish millenarianism [as represented in Hugh McNeile] and the Plymouth Brethren, gradually became prominent during the 1840s and eventually commanded the adherence of a great part of the British . . . millenarians."[141]

The diffusion of millenarian views had received little help from the leading Evangelical periodicals. The *Record* tried to ignore the topic and only rarely expressed its own view. It held to a more optimistic, Reformed, postmillennial position.[142] The *Christian Observer* had demonstrated some interest in the late 1820s[143] and in 1843 once again took notice of the apocalyptic fervor with several articles on the subject.[144] Its concern, however, did not indicate a conversion from its postmillennial position.

Millenarianism had developed its own means of securing a hearing: prophetic journals, prophetic conferences, prophecy investigation societies. Premillennialism mushroomed so quickly that by the mid–1850s contemporary analysts claimed that "this view is now entertained by a majority of the Evangelical [Anglican] clergy of England and Ireland, and a large number of the laymen who are most prominent in works of Christian benevolence, and certainly by a large majority of recent writers on the prospects of the Church and the world."[145] It is important to appreciate that the adoption of a specific interpretation of prophecy could greatly influence an Evangelical's views both on such large issues as Roman Catholicism, evangelistic activities, and pan-evangelical cooperation and affect his everyday decisions.

The propagation of premillennial views among Evangelicals appears to have been greatly aided by the establishment in 1842 of the Prophecy Investigation Society, which sponsored an annual series of Lenten lectures in London delivered by Church of England ministers.[146] This series, which began in 1843, continued throughout the 1840s and 1850s, attracting considerable public attention.[147] The publication of the lectures did much to spread the millennial light into corners hitherto unilluminated.[148] The *Christian Observer* reported that the members of the society (which included some Anglican laymen) were somewhat inappropriately known as the "Albury School" of prophetic interpretation, a name derived from the conferences of 1828–1829 held at Albury Park in Surrey, which were foundational to millennial thinking.[149]

The Prophecy Investigation Society was dominated by leading historicist writers, including Edward Bickersteth, Thomas R. Birks, James Haldane Stewart, and Hugh Montague Villiers, although the society managed to encompass "futurists" as well.[150] Some historicists at the Albury Park conferences had spoken "confidently about the second advent happening in 1843 or 1847, but whether they set dates or not, all the participants expected Christ's return within a few

years.''[151] What was significant for the emergence of the Evangelical Alliance
in the mid–1840s was the fact that some historicists attached special importance
to these years:

Interest in the years 1843–1847 was aroused by another prophecy, the vision of the
desolation of the sanctuary for "two thousand and three hundred days" in Daniel 8.
Encouraged by the fulfillment of the 1,260 days in Daniel 7 [by their figuring this was
fulfilled in the French Revolution], prophetic scholars became convinced that the next
great event would be the fulfillment of the 2,300 days, which they dated to 1843–1847.[152]

Such conjectures and date setting bothered many Evangelicals,[153] and the *Christian Observer* made it clear that, although it respected the piety of the clergy
involved in such projections, it cautioned its readers that "we cannot see our
way to many of their conclusions; such as the personal pre-millennial advent of
Christ, and the general literal interpretation of prophecy."[154]

An example of "historicist" enthusiasm for the Evangelical Alliance can be
seen in James Hatley Frere, a leading historicist interpreter who was active in
the formation of the alliance. In 1846 he published his view that the alliance
was to be identified with the "harvest of the earth" of Revelation, Chapter 14.[155]
In 1848 Frere claimed that the alliance, although in its infancy, was preparatory
to "the union of the followers of Christ of all the various denominations of the
Church into one body, and their separation from the rest of the world, that they
may be delivered from the final judgment of the vintage of wrath, or the great
day of the wrath of Christ, about to be inflicted on his enemies."[156] Opposing
this apocalyptic speculation was the Reverend Edward Hoare, who had a different
brand of eschatology. In his work entitled *The Time of the End*, published in
1846, Hoare argued against the same Evangelical Alliance. Adopting a "futurist"
position, like Hugh McNeile's, Hoare deprecated the optimists who expected
"infallibility in the visible church"[157] and opposed the alliance as "a human
scheme for the incorporation of God's elect."[158]

It was therefore no coincidence that a number of the leading Anglican figures
in the founding of the alliance were also prominent "historicist" premillennialists: Edward Bickersteth, Thomas R. Birks, J. H. Frere, William Marsh, and
R. W. Dibdin. Their eschatological understanding was undoubtedly a major
factor in inducing them to strive for pan-evangelical unity at a time when their
prophetic timetables indicated that it was especially urgent and auspicious. Nor
was it coincidental that leading "futurist" premillennialists, Hugh McNeile and
Edward Hoare, published works attacking the alliance. To them any such efforts
were presumptuous human schemes to effect that which God alone could achieve
by ushering in the eschaton.

These eschatological understandings also strongly influenced and shaped evangelical anti-Catholicism, which as has already been demonstrated was an important unifying force among evangelicals. E. R. Sandeen has commented on
the connection between anti-Catholicism and millenarianism:

Although fear of Catholicism and alarm over Catholic emancipation can scarcely be used to explain the rise of millenarianism, it is significant to note that this pairing of anti-Catholicism and millenarianism was more than casual. Millenarians without exception were stoutly anti-Catholic and viewed every agitation by English and Irish Catholics as confirmation of the increasing corruption of the world and thus of the increasing likelihood of the second advent.[159]

The extent to which millenarianism shaped anti-Catholicism and vice versa, is difficult to assess.[160] It is clear, however, that the new millenarian views propounded by the Evangelicals did much to shape and sharpen anti-Catholic polemic and to exacerbate Evangelical paranoia about Rome. This in turn strengthened the position of those who argued that evangelical unity was necessary in order to counter Catholicism.

THE REPEAL OF THE CORN LAWS: ANOTHER BARRIER REMOVED

For many Dissenters the great political question of Peel's administration, the repeal of the Corn Laws, symbolized the social and political divide between Anglicans and Nonconformists. Kitson Clark has commented, "It is necessary to read contemporary literature to realize the full violence of the Dissenting attacks on the Church of England at this time. It is more than theological; it is pregnant with the festering bitterness of one class at another whom they believe to be insolently privileged at their expense."[161] The Anti-Corn Law League, formed in 1838, had under the influence of the Quaker activist, Richard Cobden, framed its attack on the Corn Laws in moral and religious terms[162] thereby echoing the strains of the great moral and religious crusade of the evangelicals against slavery.[163] The famous Anti-Corn Law meeting in Manchester in 1841 attracted several hundred Dissenting ministers; however, the Wesleyan Methodists held to their founder's "No Politics" rule, fearing that such discussion would only tear the denomination apart. Many other Dissenters followed the Wesleyan example and stayed away from the gathering, arguing that the Corn Law question was not a religious issue.[164] Dissenters strongly attacked laws that they felt were designed "to protect the unjust advantages of the insolent nobility, of the fat Church of England bishops and rectors and of the booby squires."[165] From the Evangelical side the *Record* favored Peel's position in 1842,[166] while the *Christian Observer* hesitated at the reduction of the tariff on imported corn, feeling that while the landed interest might lose some, that the Anglican clergy would lose most: "The clergy will suffer most, for their tithes being commuted for the price of so many bushels of corn, a fall in prices will reduce their incomes."[167]

The depth of feeling on the issue can be gauged by the decibels of the Tory outcry and Whig applause which greeted Baptist W. Noel's publication of *A Plea for the Poor* in 1841. In arguing for a reduction of the duty, Noel cited his own experience in visiting the London poor and the testimonies of city missionaries in Liverpool and Manchester in order to plead the wretchedness of the poverty and to deprecate the efficacy of charitable relief:

What is to be done for them? Soup kitchens, tickets for coals and potatoes, mendicity societies, night asylums, and charity balls, or charity sermons, will not fatten their lean visages, nor furnish their empty dwellings, nor make them bless God for plenty. And yet God has provided plenty for them all. . . . Only allow them the opportunity of laboring for the food with which Europe can supply them; only fix and reduce the duty on foreign corn, and they will be fed.[168]

No less than five counterblasts were launched in Noel's direction in an ensuing pamphlet warfare.[169] The work earned him hard words from the *Record*[170] while the *Christian Observer* disagreed with Noel's regarding the issue as at heart a religious one.[171] A Quaker visitor to his chapel in 1842 was surprised to find it "far from full" and attributed the decline in attendance to the fact that "His recent pamphlet on the Corn Laws and his well known liberality towards Dissenters have stamped him in the eyes of all Tory Churchmen as a dangerous man."[172] On the other hand, the publication won Noel a chaplaincy to the queen from the outgoing Whig administration,[173] and it was alleged that Lord John Russell used the pamphlet very effectively in the ensuing election campaign.[174]

While Peel's own attitudes toward the Corn Laws changed significantly during the course of his administration,[175] it was the spectre of the Irish potato famine and his view "that repeal would remove a sense of social injustice" that finally led him to change his public position in 1846.[176] The effect of the decision on interdenominational relations can be seen in the following appeal to Voluntaries made by a writer in the Evangelical *Churchman's Monthly Review*: "Surely it is abundantly evident that all the old questions are at an end,—the old names and phrases worn out. You have obtained 'Reform' and 'Free Trade.' There is no contest on any of these points. Church matters are now coming into first place."[177] Peel's actions had removed this contentious issue from the arena of conflict; long an impediment to evangelical unity, it would no longer so vex Anglican–Dissenting relations.

The removal of some of the thorny issues affecting interdenominational relations helped some evangelicals to draw closer to each other between 1841 and 1846. Peel's reversal on the Corn Laws reduced frictions. Both the Scottish Disruption and the alienation of the Wesleyan Methodists from the Church of England worked to isolate Evangelicals at a time when the political party which most of them looked to for leadership was proposing measures which greatly angered them. The *Record* was for the moment concerned to forge a new evangelical alliance for political and religious (anti-Catholic and anti-Tractarian) purposes; it had been confirmed in this by the Maynooth Grant, which had touched a raw nerve in evangelicalism. Millenarian concerns also reinforced the anti-Catholic sentiment, which played such an important role in fostering pan-evangelical unity.

Perhaps the most important factor in this period had been the Tory government's unwillingness to countenance a significant grant to church extension. This had a double-edged effect: in some ways it contributed to the reduction of interdenominational tensions; it also led Evangelicals unwilling to work with Dissent to consider prosecuting the task of urban evangelism through a distinctly Anglican society. Evangelical Anglicans could no longer maintain their ostrich-like stance of expecting the government to support a monopolistic establishment; they had to come to grips with the fact that Anglicanism was now, in effect, one denomination among many. As a denomination, it could either compete or cooperate, but it could no longer delude itself with the hope that it could command government help. Nor could the Evangelicals realistically hope to achieve the capture of the Church from within; the old Claphamite distancing of Evangelicalism from evangelical Nonconformity no longer made sense to many as a means of interparty rivalry. Instead, many felt that interparty rivalry demanded an emphasis upon their common ground with Dissent. We now turn to a study of those who clung to the old ways: those who decided to compete by establishing a new society under the control of the Evangelical party within the Church.

5

The Scripture Readers' Association: A Denominational Challenge to Pan-evangelical Evangelism

In the late 1830s and early 1840s, ecumenically minded evangelicals were trying to recruit Anglican support for the interdenominational approach of the London City Mission. At the very same time, however, denominational rivalry was being exacerbated by the proposals for a church extension grant, for which Anglican Evangelicals were pressing in Parliament. Some conservative Evangelicals throughout this period were determined to establish an Anglican society that would rival the London City Mission. The circumstances surrounding the formation of this society, as well as its final structure and scope, were greatly influenced by the difficulties in the relationship between Bishop Blomfield and his numerous Evangelical clergy. As this organization came to set the pattern for a multitude of similar diocesan societies throughout England in the nineteenth century, we turn to study the origins of the Anglican society that challenged the pan-evangelical approach.

BISHOP BLOMFIELD AND HIS EVANGELICAL CLERGY

Many London Evangelicals harbored suspicions of their bishop's intentions and thought that he was at heart a secret Tractarian. In fact the diocesan was an old-school Protestant High Churchman who shared the erastianism of the Evangelicals, though they criticized other aspects of his theology.[1] Bishop Blomfield was eager to establish conformity to the rubric as he understood it. In 1842 he issued a charge instructing the clergy to wear surplices (white preaching gowns) while in the pulpit and made a minor change in the order of services in which there was no communion.[2]

To many, these changes from accepted practice portended Tractarian design. The publication of Tract XC by John Henry Newman in 1841 had made the

Oxford Movement very unpopular. Given these fears, the reaction to Blomfield's actions among clergy and laity, both Evangelical and non-Evangelical, was largely negative.[3] Many clerics simply refused to comply. Sir Robert Peel hesitated to promote clergy who had obeyed Blomfield's charge, so fearful was he of abetting Tractarianism.[4] Edward Bickersteth wrote to Blomfield to explain the ferocity of Evangelical opposition to the charge:

Our congregations generally had become thoroughly alarmed by the progress of Tractarianism & the organs of the new movement had more & more manifested their papal tendencies. Hence anything of external change created suspicion and anxiety.[5]

When clergy from the Evangelical stronghold of Islington met privately with Blomfield and urged on him the claim that enforcement of his charge would force many of the "reclaimed Dissenters" in their congregations to leave the Church of England, the bishop granted special concessions.[6] Despite the accommodation, deep distrust of the diocesan remained; the original instructions had served to deepen Evangelical fears of Tractarianism.

In the early 1840s Evangelicals were having increasing doubts about the effectiveness of the church building efforts that Blomfield had championed. K. S. Inglis, in his work on this period, has acknowledged that Evangelicals were prominent in evangelistic efforts to reach the working classes in the first half of the nineteenth century.[7] He has suggested, however, that during this period most evangelistic activity "rested on an assumption that millions of people were absent from worship simply because churches had become inaccessible to them, and that they would become willing worshippers as soon as the facilities for doing so were brought within their reach."[8] Although this view may have been held by Blomfield and other advocates of church extension during the 1830s, it was not representative of Evangelical attitudes as is demonstrated in their concern to establish evangelistic district visiting societies to seek out the poor and thereby to draw them to the ministrations of the Church. Both the CP-AS and the LCM had been founded with the intention of strengthening the arm of the church in this attempt to win back the estranged laboring classes. As noted above, in 1839 Baptist Noel had publicly attacked the assumptions underlying church extension.[9]

In their support for church extension, Evangelicals had few illusions that churches by their mere presence would induce working-class attendance. The Bethnal Green experiment was a case in point. This destitute, overly populated parish had been selected by Blomfield in 1839 as an area in which the effectiveness of church building could be demonstrated. The parish was subdivided into twelve districts, and each district was to be provided with a church building.[10]

In 1844 Baptist Noel wrote to Blomfield to complain that several of the Bethnal Green churches were almost empty. The bishop privately disputed the attendance figures with Noel, but his letter shows that even the diocesan had discarded his earlier view that the churches only had to await the patronage of the poor:

It is not true that several of the new churches are almost empty . . . The churches are well attended in the Evening; and if they were not, I should not be surprised. Poor ignorant people who have been neglected for so many years passed [sic] cannot all at one [sic] be brought to Christ: but the congregations are steadily improving, and the schools will, we hope, raise up a generation of worshippers.[11]

Blomfield's persistent optimism about the fate of the churches and his confidence about the effectiveness of the schools was not shared by Evangelical incumbents. A year later Bishop Daniel Wilson recorded in his diary:

The kind Mr. Stone of Christ Church, Spitalfields said that Bethnall [sic] Green Churches had been badly filled and were a failure—he lamented the state of the Shoreditch Church— he pitied the Bp of London who was sorrowed at heart, but perplexed more than anyone c[d] [could] conceive.[12]

The reasons for the failure of these churches are complex and numerous, but:

At the root of the problem was the increasing residential segregation of classes. The ideal parish contained both rich and poor, all worshipping in the parish church and the rich supporting the parochial charities and institutions. Few of the new urban parishes matched the ideal.[13]

An important factor contributing to the residential segregation of the classes was the flight of the wealthy from the overcrowded districts, something facilitated in the 1840s by the construction of railway lines, which allowed for easy, cheap access to the suburbs.

Pew rents undoubtedly did much to offend the poor and to keep them from attending church if they were so inclined. While "the middle and upper classes on the whole found the pew rent system to their liking, and considered it a perfectly normal arrangement,"[14] many Evangelicals protested against its abuses.[15] The editor of the *Record* complained:

The higher and middle classes . . . have constructed places in which two-fifths of the community take to their own use four-fifths of the accommodation, and leave the remaining one-fifth for those who are the largest class of all. And not only so, but they allot to themselves all the most desirable seats, and condemn the poor to the dark and cold corners of the church, where all comfort is lacking.[16]

Furthermore, the system's inequities were entrenched in laws that incumbents were powerless to alter, as one complained to the *Record*:

Under the old and existing law, it is known that sittings in the church are to be allocated to the parishioners, *in order of their amount of contribution to the church-rate*. It is thus essentially a law by which the poor are sacrificed deliberately to the rich, and by which, in consequence (in the defect of church accommodation which has come to characterize our larger towns,) the poor are practically excluded from many of our churches altogether.[17]

Further complicating the situation was the fact that the new churches that Peel's church-building measures encouraged were not included under the old laws, and it was claimed that they therefore drew the poor away from the old parish churches with their provision of ample free sittings and also provided stiff competition for pew rentals.[18]

While these factors were acknowledged by Evangelicals to have hindered the success of new churches and of the progress of parish churches, they were convinced that the overriding reason for the failure of the Bethnal Green churches was their alleged Tractarian charater. It is clear that the rise of Tractarian influence did much to damage support for these new churches. In 1839 the *Christian Guardian* had advised its readers to address communications regarding the Bethnal Green Church Building Fund to the Reverend Bryan King, who soon emerged as a leading Tractarian and who was a continual trouble to Blomfield.[19] The bishop had made an effort "to exclude Tractarians from his new churches in particular, but some incumbents developed ritualistic tendencies only after appointment."[20]

Evangelicals made no attempt to hide their displeasure with Blomfield or with his appointees. In the 1843 debate on church extension in Parliament, J. P. Plumptre put the common Evangelical explanation quite bluntly: the London churches were empty because of

the character of the preaching employed before them. He remembered a saying of Rowland Hill, that the place where a cannon-ball might be fired with the least risk in London on a Sunday, would be along the aisle of a church in which the Gospel was not preached.[21]

This explanation brought cries of "Hear, hear" from sympathetic M.P.s. The *Record* put the blame squarely on Blomfield's shoulders for the appointments he had made in Bethnal Green,[22] and cited examples of Evangelicals drawing large crowds of the poor in temporary licensed buildings while the other churches in similar circumstances were "nearly deserted."[23]

Blomfield had long resisted the use of lay agency, but in 1843 he was presented with a choice that forced him to rethink his position. On September 11, 1843, the LCM Committee considered a proposal that it should especially direct its efforts to the Bethnal Green district, the same area where the Anglicans had concentrated their energies in church building. The committee agreed to the proposal and appointed twenty missionaries to the district.[24] Robert Hanbury,[25] a wealthy Anglican brewer, philanthropist, and former LCM committee member, was distressed by the poor attendance at the Bethnal Green churches and was especially upset by the appearance of ritualism there.[26] He was willing to back the LCM plan with significant financing.[27] Hearing of Hanbury's action, Bishop Blomfield sent him a letter of rebuke for supporting an interdenominational society.[28] In response, Hanbury offered to back the employment of Anglican lay agents if Blomfield would consent to patronize a new Anglican society. The bishop was also informed, however, that some Anglican laymen intended to establish such an avowedly Anglican society with or without his sanction.[29] Given the dashing of their hopes earlier in 1843 for significant government aid for church extension, those Evangelicals who had long been unwilling to co-operate with Dissent in urban evangelism were now prepared to act on their own. In this regard, it is noteworthy that Sir Robert Inglis, the M.P. from Oxford who had led the Evangelical campaign for a church extension grant, was a member of the new committee.

Hard pressed by the difficulties encountered in church extension, exasperated by Tractarian incumbents, and disappointed by the poor performance of the Bethnal Green churches in particular, Blomfield relented. In 1844 he joined with Bishop Sumner (an Evangelical) of the adjacent diocese of Winchester to patronize the Scripture Readers' Association (SRA), which in 1849 became known as the Church of England Scripture Readers' Association. The committee of the SRA was composed of prominent Evangelical laymen, thus guaranteeing the doctrinal stance of the laymen employed. The regulations of the society were similar to those of the Church Pastoral-Aid Society: laymen were to be appointed only at the request of the local clergy, and the workers were to be placed under their direction. Despite opposition to this form of lay activity from the expected quarters[30] and the Evangelical stamp of the new Scripture Readers, nine of the Bethnal Green clergy requested such assistance, including two clergymen noted for their Tractarian leanings.[31] The society was not universally welcomed, and letters attacking it appeared in *The Times*.[32]

The bishop's cooperation, however, came at a price. At his insistence careful restrictions were placed on the activities of the agents.[33] They were forbidden to preach; they were simply to read portions of Scripture from door to door; they were not allowed to distribute literature or to hold local meetings in their districts. The SRA was similar in design to and may have actually been modeled on the Irish Scripture Readers' Association, which had been active in Ireland since the 1820s.[34] The Irish society had been designed to minister to a largely illiterate peasantry, and the restriction of the SRA agents to the reading of Scripture and the prohibition on their distribution of literature limited the workers of the new society to a form of evangelism not wholly appropriate to urban realities. The agents were not able to adapt their methods to reach the increasingly literate working classes, a constituency that the LCM knew well and which it attempted to adapt its literature to suit.[35] Thus both the structure and scope of the Anglican society were limited by episcopal pressure, depriving the organization of the flexibility enjoyed by the LCM.

To some extent the emergence of the new Anglican organization in the mid–1840s reflects the stiff resistance that there was within Evangelicalism to pan-evangelical cooperation at the time. Most of those who favored such cooperation did so only when they were assured of one basic condition: effective Anglican control of the pan-evangelical society. In part, this Evangelical response can be understood as Anglican defensiveness under the strain of attacks from Dissenters and their unwillingness to work with any organization which could be used as an instrument in the battle with the establishment.

PAN-EVANGELICALISM

On the other hand, it is evident that by the mid–1840s some Anglicans were eager to demonstrate the depth of their Protestant feeling and their revulsion toward Tractarian teaching, especially in its discountenance of Dissent. This view was put clearly by the Reverend Dr. Mayo, the Anglican cleric who pioneered the interdenominational Home and Colonial School Society. In an 1845 sermon he told fellow Anglicans that in some localities their Church was being gradually converted "from a living portrait of its great and glorious head into something like an 'image of the beast.' " If the laboring classes of the next generation were not to be handed over to "Romanism—modified or unmodified, open or concealed," then Anglican Evangelicals had to support pan-evangelical societies. Surely, he reasoned, "we must look to Societies exclusively evangelical to fight the great battle of the Lord in this our day, and to meet the peculiar exigencies of these times."[36]

Dr. Mayo's views represented only one end of the Anglican spectrum. It is important to recognize that the establishment of the SRA to some extent reflected a reaction against just this sort of pan-evangelicalism. At the same time its formation also demonstrated a growing Evangelical concern to encourage lay support of and involvement in evangelism. This concern had been seen in the 1842 formation of the City of London Young Men's Society for Aiding Missions at Home and Abroad. This organization was established by a number of Evangelical clergy and was designed to provide a forum for young men connected with their Sunday schools. It was also designed to interest and involve them in evangelistic activities at home and abroad. By this means the Evangelical clergy hoped to remedy the poor recruitment record of Anglican laymen both as Scripture Readers and as foreign missionaries. The subscription revenue of the new organization was to be divided equally between three (later four) Evangelical missionary societies.[37]

It would appear that a great stimulus to the growing interest in urban evangelism in the early 1840s was the national debate over the "Condition of England Question." The debate intensified when the combination of Chartism, Anti-Corn Law League propaganda, widespread unemployment, and short-time working erupted into violence during the summer of 1842. In 1844 the Young Men's Society made it clear how the importance of domestic evangelism had been brought home by contemporary events:

The Parliamentary reports on the physical, moral and religious state of the manufacturing and mining populations, and the details respecting the agricultural classes in the "Perils of the Nation," and other works, show a fearful—an overwhelming necessity for efforts to spread at home, not ministers and churches merely, but that Gospel which alone can elevate the minds, and thus alone alleviate the moral miseries of our countrymen. Home Missions, then, should hold the first place in the attentions of a Society established for general missionary purposes.[38]

The concern for the welfare of the working classes that this agitation generated undoubtedly had an influence on the formation of both the SRA and the Young Men's Society for Aiding Missions (YMSAM) and affected the LCM as well. In 1839–1840, the LCM's income had actually declined, but from 1840 on there was a strong, steady increase in its receipts, a trend that continued throughout the decade. When the LCM's income is combined with that of the SRA's, one observes a very dramatic rise in the level of evangelical support for urban evangelism between 1842 and 1850.[39]

The new Anglican "Young Men's" society soon became national in scope and therefore dropped the words "City of London" from its title. During the 1850s the society changed its name once again, becoming the Church of England Young Men's Society and altered its regulations to stress the evangelization of young men through the society by "direct missionary efforts," which included Bible classes, devotional meetings, libraries, and lectures. The emphasis upon the importance of missionary activity abroad remained.[40] Once again, however, Evangelicals were at a disadvantage because they were following the lead taken by their Dissenting brethren. The first major initiatives in foreign missions (the London Missionary Society, 1795), domestic missions (the Christian Instruction Society, 1827), and city missions (the LCM, 1835) had all been taken by Nonconformists. The Church Missionary Society (1799), the Church Pastoral-Aid Society (1836), and the Scripture Readers' Association (1844) all followed Dissenting precedents. Even in the young men's societies, the pattern was set by a Nonconformist, in fact, the same Nonconformist who had pioneered the London City Mission. In 1844, one writer traced the first such society to David Nasmith's activities in the mid–1820s when he formed one out of his Glasgow Sunday school class, an idea which rapidly spread to other Scottish cities.[41]

Nonconformists had therefore long outdone Evangelicals in organizing laymen for religious, specifically evangelistic, activites. By the 1840s attempts by Anglicans to duplicate in Church societies what had originally been a Nonconformist design were suffering from stiff competition from pan-evangelical societies. In the case of young men's societies, the challenge to the strictly Anglican society did not come from the unsuccessful efforts of David Nasmith in that regard, but from the activities of a fellow Congregationalist, George Williams.[42] The Young Men's Christian Association (YMCA), which Williams was largely responsible for organizing in 1844, grew out of an informal gathering of apprentices to a draper, George Hitchcock. Key factors in the formal organization of the group were the evangelical conversion which Hitchcock experienced in 1843 and his invitation to John Branch, a former city missionary (by then the superintendent of the city missionaries), to lead Hitchcock's employees in "Family Prayer."[43] Williams managed to attract the participation of Anglican laymen—even of some who were involved in the Anglican Young Men's Society.[44] Clyde Binfield has noted that there is only circumstantial evidence for a link between Williams and Nasmith, the City Mission's founder, but Binfield thinks that it is highly likely that there was some contact between the two.[45] The YMCA initially directed its appeal toward young men in the drapery trade, who in social terms were upwardly mobile. Like Williams himself, they endured frightful working conditions in the hopes that they might one day have a shop of their own.[46] After 1851, when the YMCA really began to grow, it failed to broaden its appeal and did not move toward a working-class clientele.[47]

With the failure of attempts to secure a sizable church extension grant and the growing disillusionment with the effectiveness of church building itself, Evangelicals who were concerned that there be a distinctly Anglican response to the need for the evangelization of the working classes put their hopes in the SRA. The 1840s was thus a crucial time for pan-evangelicalism. If the SRA could win the solid support of Anglican Evangelicals, it could hope to repeat the success of the Church Missionary Society, which at the turn of the century had managed to outdo its pan-evangelical rival, the London Missionary Society, in soliciting Anglican backing. For the SRA to succeed in this, however, would involve winning back Anglicans already involved in the LCM; at the very least Evangelicals who shared this concern had to prevent further seepage of Anglican support to the pan-evangelical society.

Concern to counter the growing acceptance that the LCM was receiving among Evangelicals led the *Christian Observer* in 1843 to publish an article "On Co-operation Among Christians of Different Denominations." It assailed Baptist Noel for his participation in the LCM and the Reverend Thomas Mortimer, another well-known Evangelical clergyman in London, for his speech at the anniversary meeting of the Wesleyan Missionary Society.[48] The *Christian Observer* argued against cooperation with Dissenters on the bases of "consistency and example," "honest views of scriptural truth," and "due church discipline." Concern was expressed that such activities were an overreaction to Tractarianism that would "in the end cause confusion instead of scriptural order."[49] The *Record* similarly chided Mortimer for his action, fearing that some would be

shocked by levities, or grieved by questionable sallies of low-churchmanship. . . . The waverers, and the only half-informed, at the present instant, form a very numerous class. And anything like a rash and startling assertion of Low Church principles, or rather of half-hidden, half-avowed dislike to divers things in the Church, will at once drive all these into the hands of the Tractarians.[50]

A. D. Gilbert has suggested that during the 1830s and 1840s, the Church of England was, in sociological terms, shifting from a "church type" to a "de facto denominational" status. The former he defines as a type of religious organization "claiming the allegiance of the whole society, thoroughly integrated with the mainstream culture and social structure, and monopolistic in its attitude towards religious rivals."[51] The denominational type, unlike the "sect," does not involve a rejection of society, but is oriented to a particular constituency within society and regards itself "not as the one true church, but as one of a plurality of legitimate institutional alternatives."[52] The resulting situation was thus one in which active competition was to be expected and increased rivalry the norm: "rivalry was itself evidence of a closing rather than a widening of the functional differentiation between the two phenomena within the society. The history of Victorian religion took the form it did, in other words, partly because the Church of England, in the second quarter of the nineteenth century, had moved significantly toward a typically denominational solution to its intolerable situation as an ex-monopolistic institution in a pluralistic society."[53]

Rivalry and competition with Dissent did characterize the attitude of some Anglicans (including some Anglican Evangelicals) in the 1840s. Cooperation with Dissent was, however, also on the rise as can be seen in the *Christian Observer*'s concern with Noel's involvement with the LCM. Its polemic is itself evidence of the changing attitude of an increasing number of Anglican clergy who were jettisoning the Simeonite self-distancing from Dissent and demonstrates the success that the LCM was having in winning their allegiance. Thus the *Christian Observer*'s assault on pan-evangelicalism demonstrates both the wisdom and the weakness of Gilbert's analysis.

The *Record* was also reassessing its attitude to pan-evangelicalism at this time. Relations between the LCM and the newspaper had been cool in the early 1840s with the paper declining to give it the prominence it once had. In 1842 the *Record* had launched another salvo in the society's direction, protesting against its operations in Clapham, where it felt that the society was interfering in an Evangelical stronghold, operating beyond its proper boundaries and advancing the cause of Dissent in the area.[54] The LCM responded that neither of its agents in the locale—one a Churchman, the other a Dissenter—had violated the mission's neutrality and that any such activity would result in immediate dismissal.[55]

This dispute caused the *Record* to review its position regarding the mission. It noted:

while the Political Dissenters continued to make attacks so atrocious on the Church, and their brethren in the *City Mission* said not a word in opposition to them, it was contrary to duty, and just Christian feeling, to remain associated with them even in such a work.

The paper acknowledged, however, that there was now a new situation:

During the spread of Puseyism which has since occurred in the Church . . . we have been disposed to let this Society, with whatever evils associated, pursue its course in peace; . . .

Our advice to the London City Mission, if they will condescend to attend to it, is very simple. To devote themselves to making known the Gospel to the most destitute places in London, which was the object of the institution of the Society. . . . To eschew such fields of labour as Islington and Clapham, where possibly they may do as much harm as good, and where, at all events, there is no such need for their labour as exists elsewhere, and where it cannot be prosecuted without exciting suspicion as to the purity of their motives, and the integrity of their appeal for public support with a view to relieve the *extremity of London destitution.*[56]

The further mellowing of the *Record*'s attitude toward the Mission can be seen again in 1843 when it applauded its efforts in Bethnal Green: "Bethnal-green [sic] is a legitimate sphere for this Society, and not Islington or Clapham; and while we may object to it in the latter localities, we may see the necessity of its operation in the former."[57]

THE SCRIPTURE READERS' SOCIETY VERSUS THE LONDON CITY MISSION

The advent of the SRA seems in fact to have had little impact upon the progress of the pan-evangelical LCM. The Anglican society continued to expand its activities through to 1850 with its funds increasing from £3,488 in 1844–1845 to £6,063 in 1849–1850, a rise of 77 percent. During the same period, however, the LCM's receipts climbed from £9,571 to £20,320, a 112 percent increase. The steady growth of the LCM's financial support from 1840 onward seems to indicate that there was no significant shift of funds by the LCM's Evangelical constituency to the SRA. It would appear that much of the SRA's funding came from Evangelicals who were unwilling in the 1840s to support a pan-evangelical society.

A few instances of Anglican clergy switching their support from the LCM to the SRA probably occurred, but the overall picture of the 1840s shows that the seepage of Anglican support to the pan-evangelical society was accelerated rather than reversed with the formation of the SRA.[58] A careful study of Evangelical clergy in London reveals a marked rise in support for the LCM between 1844 and 1850, with about one-seventh of them supporting the mission in 1844 and about one-third aligned with it in 1850.[59] The significant increase in support for the LCM was in part due to the political considerations and the prophetic considerations (both discussed in chapter 4). Other factors were affecting London Evangelicals: the person of their bishop and the increasing attractiveness of the LCM's demonstrated effectiveness and practicality. Leading Evangelical capitalists like Robert Hanbury still continued to support the LCM financially.[60] In some cases this was undoubtedly due to the LCM's having well-established works in areas of London for which they felt a special concern, as with Hanbury, who was interested in Spitalfields as well as Bethnal Green.[61] Some undoubtedly backed the LCM because it could work freely in non-Evangelical parishes; others preferred the LCM because they disliked the restrictions placed on SRA workers.[62] In addition, however, it is evident from the numerous denunciations of Tractarianism by Evangelical clergy at LCM meetings in the early 1840s that they, like the *Record*, were anxious to dissociate themselves from the "detestable pestilence'' of ''Puseyism'' by identifying with Dissenters whom the Tractarians discountenanced.[63]

The LCM was not inclined to relax its efforts to expand its Anglican constituency with the establishment of the SRA. Its further growth was facilitated by the resignation of one of its clerical secretaries in 1844; this allowed the mission to revamp its monthly magazine. The LCM committee was concerned that the sale of the periodical till then had been largely restricted to places outside London,.[64] The appointment of a new editor brought about a much improved journal, which produced article after article that caught the eye of the religious and secular press, especially in its concern for the destitute of London.

At the 1845 LCM annual meeting the Reverend Thomas Mortimer testified to the effectiveness of the *LCM Magazine* in changing his views of the mission and urged that the LCM send regular subscriptions to the London clergy: ''there are many hundreds among them who will have nothing to do with the City Mission, because they think—as I once was simple enough to think,—that you are a parcel of heretics; . . . the best way of getting at the clergy, I believe, is, just to send them your monthly magazine.''[65] By 1849 the *LCM Magazine* had an impressive circulation of 6,750 copies, including 1,200 that were sold through booksellers, and the publication was turning a large enough profit to provide the support of a city missionary.[66]

The importance of a magazine to the financial survival of the LCM was demonstrated in an 1846 study done by the *LCM Magazine*. It showed that although London accounted for a large portion of Britain's wealth, its giving to religious organizations was not proportionate to its ability.[67] Dissenting missionary societies (the London Missionary Society and the Wesleyan Missionary Society) fared much better in the metropolis than did the Church Missionary Society and the Society for the Propagation of the Gospel, despite the fact that the 1851 religious census found Dissenters to be relatively weak in the London area. A magazine was thus essential for an organization like the LCM if it was to build the requisite national basis for its support. By establishing local associations of the LCM in country towns and assigning them specific areas of London in which they were to support missionaries, the LCM Committee effectively linked the organization with its grass-roots supporters in the provinces.[68] The circulation of a national magazine had been greatly helped by the establishment of the penny post in 1840 and was a particular boon to an organization which was unable effectively to use sermons as a means of publicizing its work among Anglicans. This was the most common means used by the strictly Church societies, such as the CP-AS and the SRA.[69]

The LCM's rapid expansion in the 1840s had much to do with its business-like management and its mastery of advertising and fund-raising techniques. Its practical effectiveness argued strongly in favor of Anglican support for the pan-evangelical approach, while both anti-Catholic and anti-Tractarian considerations reinforced the LCM's appeal. The Scripture Readers' Association, which had tried to harness the Evangelicals' zeal on behalf of the Church, had not been able to stem the current in favor of the London City Mission.

6

From Door to Door: Men, Methods, and Response

Evangelicals were not impressed by arguments about supply and demand when it came to evangelism. They did not think that their attempts to win the working classes to Christianity would be popular; they certainly did not expect to be welcomed with open arms by the poor. The evangelicals believed that the urban poor had been lost to the faith by discrimination, by neglect, and by the secularizing forces of the city. The task of reclaiming them would not be easy; they would be won back only by persistent effort. Thus Anglican Evangelicals had insisted in the Parliamentary debates concerning a church extension grant that the demand should not determine the supply. From the Protestant Reformers, the evangelicals had learned that people by their very nature resisted the truth; in their fallen state they were disinclined to seek their own spiritual welfare. The allegiance of the poor was to be sought in spite of any opposition or lack of interest.

The central focus of this work is on the factors that affected the supply side of the mission. It is concerned with the reasons why the evangelicals united behind the mission to the poor. The demand side is also important, however, and this chapter seeks to evaluate how the poor responded to the mission and what impact it had on them. We begin with an examination of the paid lay agents themselves: their numbers, their social and religious backgrounds, and the ways in which they formed their appeals to the poor. We will then attempt to assess how the poor responded to their efforts.

It is important to appreciate the size and strength of the evangelical troops marching as to war among the poor of London. Between 1836 and 1842 the number of LCM agents fluctuated between 40 and 63.[1] But evangelical interest in the use of lay agency in London began an upward swing in 1842, with the

LCM's activity continuing to expand with slight fluctuation throughout the period to 1860 (see Appendixes A and B.)

When the SRA was formed in 1844, there were 101 LCM workers regularly visiting their assigned families.[2] Two years later the ranks of evangelical workers were swelled by 50 Anglican Scripture Readers, bringing the total to 202.[3] In 1850, 340 men were at work in the metropolis,[4] and a decade later 494 men (375 LCM workers and 119 Scripture Readers),[5] and 137 women[6] were employed in full-time evangelistic work, raising the total number of full-time workers to 631. One can appreciate the significance of these figures when one realizes that in 1851 there were only 1,274 clergymen and ministers in London (including Roman Catholic clergy).[7] Outside the scope of this study, but of importance to the national scene, was the establishment of numerous parallel organizations for provincial towns.[8] The use of lay agency by the Church Pastoral-Aid Society, which is often cited by historians, was but the tip of an iceberg in terms of evangelistic missions.[9]

THE WORKERS

The religious and social background of these workers is noteworthy. In both 1839 and 1849 two-thirds of the LCM agents were Nonconformists. With the addition of the SRA workers in 1849, the overall picture changed: 162 of the evangelical workers were Anglicans; 143 were Nonconformists. Thus while the LCM continued to employ a majority of Nonconformist workers, Anglican money insured an overall dominance of Anglican workers in the metropolis once the SRA was established. An examination of the former professions of the LCM workers in 1849 reveals that 29 of the 214 had worked with other such evangelistic organizations before working with the LCM. Interestingly, most of the agents had never lived in London before they began working with the LCM.[10]

An evaluation of the former occupations of the remaining 185 LCM workers provides a profile of their social background. Here one wants to ask whether the workers were drawn from the "aristocracy of labor" posited by Marxist historians. The background to this concept is in the disappointment that both Karl Marx and Friedrich Engels experienced when the British working class failed to adopt a revolutionary stance (particularly after 1850) and seemed to be content with developing trade unions and cooperatives. To explain this, Marxist writers have made much of the concept of a "labor aristocracy."[11] This self-satisfied elite is supposed to have exercised a remarkably conservative influence, which both suppressed and concealed the militancy of the mass of workers. Dr. E. J. Hobsbawn attempted to establish the validity of this concept in an article entitled "The Labour Aristocracy in Nineteenth Century Britain," which was first published in 1954.[12] He acknowledges the difficulty of setting criteria for membership and admits that prior to 1840 it is doubtful whether one can speak of such a grouping at all. Even if one grants the existence of such a group, others have reasoned that Marxist historians like Dr. Hobsbawn "have completely got the wrong end of the stick: militancy was much more likely to be found among the better-off than among the poorer workers."[13]

In short, any interpretation of the social background of the workers runs into great difficulties. If they were from an "aristocracy of labor," are they to be regarded as conservative in outlook or tending toward a more radical stance? The LCM's descriptions of the workers are somewhat sketchy, and without specific biographical information it is impossible to assess precisely which agents were drawn from the ranks of depressed workers or from a "labor aristocracy." Two facts are clear, however: first, about a quarter of the workers were from the lower middle class or above, and second, at least half of the agents were drawn from the mainstream of the working class.[14] (See Appendix D for a breakdown of the workers' backgrounds.) Thus the majority had known, in Hugh McLeod's words, "the stigmata of the manual worker—ingrained dirt, work-man's clothes—and the contagion of a rough working environment."[15] Manual laborers were on the bottom rung of the national social status system, clearly below the poorest clerk or shopkeeper, who might have had a similar standard of living. It was from this group that the greater portion of LCM agents would appear to have been drawn.

Their numbers and backgrounds established, we now turn to an examination of the overall strategy and the tasks of the individual lay agents. Following the plan devised by Thomas Chalmers and used in the district visiting societies, the agents were to be assigned to a particular area of London, the City Mission making the poorest areas their top priority. The LCM agents were regularly to visit the same 500 to 550 families each month and were required to spend at least thirty-six hours a week in such work; in addition they were to hold a minimum of two meetings a week for the poor in their districts. Scripture readers employed by the Scripture Readers' Association were under the direct control of the Evangelical clergy in their district, but were required by the regulations of the SRA to spend thirty-six hours per week reading the Scriptures from room to room.[16] Overlapping of the work was avoided by close cooperation between the LCM and the SRA,[17] and indeed with the Church Pastoral-Aid Society as well.[18] Unencumbered with the parochial concerns that swamped the greatly overworked clergy, these agents were undoubtedly better known by the poor than the local ministers.

Because of their acquaintance with the poor, the lay agents were invaluable both to government information gatherers and to those who made their reputations by familiarizing the Victorian public with the London slums. Before the extension of the franchise "Parliament tended to obtain its information from religious bodies, missions, prison chaplains and reforming societies," and thus the better-educated missionary was often called on as "one of the few educated observers, apart from the doctor, to enter the slum."[19] Reliance upon such sources for accounts of working-class opinion naturally tended to strengthen the hands of the evangelicals in their temperance and Sabbatarian causes; few parliamentarians had any personal knowledge of the habits and dwellings of the classes for which they legislated.

Initially this information-gathering role was requested of the mission; within a few months of its founding, the LCM committee received a plea for aid from its missionaries from a House of Lords committee on prison discipline.[20] Similar appeals continued to be received by the mission and were often related to metropolitan sanitation. It was Lord Ashley (later Lord Shaftesbury), however, who continually brought the LCM to public prominence by using its magazine's statistics in Parliament and by his repeated references to the mission's agents who familiarized him with working-class life and culture.[21] Henry Mayhew was similarly indebted. In preparing his renowned *London Labour and the London Poor*, he was guided through the metropolis's slums by city missionaries, who "pointed out to the writer what they knew to exist, but what they had not the power to describe with the same skill and power."[22] We now turn to a more detailed examination of the tasks of the lay agents.

The instructions governing how the visitation was to be carried out by the Scripture readers and the city missionaries were very similar (see Appendix E). The central focus was upon the Scriptures; the workers were to emphasize their importance as "the only infallible rule of faith and practice" (SRA), inculcating in their hearers "the duty of searching the Scriptures as a revelation from God, and as the standard by which they will be judged at the last day" (LCM). If permission was given, they were to read a portion of Scripture and explain it. Aware of the religious ignorance of the poor, this was to be done with "plain remarks" (SRA), the agents being enjoined to "see that the terms used are understood" (LCM). The Scripture portions were to be selected "that bear on the depravity of man, justification by faith alone, the necessity of a change of heart and of holiness of life." Those of the poor who lacked copies of the Scriptures were to be offered them. Church attendance was to be encouraged, the Scripture readers naturally seeking to bring the poor into the parish church with which they were associated, while the city missionaries were not to specify a particular church or chapel, leaving the choice up to the poor—that is, provided that they chose an evangelical church, one in which "the great doctrines of the Reformation are faithfully taught."

While the LCM workers were cautioned to be "humble, courteous and gentle," they were also instructed to point out to the poor "as occasion may require, their relative duties, and faithfully but prudently reprove open vice, such as swearing, intemperance, and the profanation of the Sabbath." Thus the bold rebuking of those who sinned boldly was not limited to fairgoers and race-course attenders: the city missionaries brought it down to a much more personal level. All of this was to be pursued

in a spirit of prayer, and with an earnest desire that every person you visit may be brought to a saving knowledge of the Lord Jesus Christ. Your work is awfully important; you have to deal with immortal souls, many of whom may never hear the Gospel but from you, and whose eternal condition may be determined by the reception or rejection of the message which you deliver to them.

In terms of training for these workers, there seems initially to have been no set course of instruction, although from time to time the LCM required its agents to attend lectures dealing with Christian apologetics. In 1847, however, the mission began a course of instruction "in the evidences of Christianity and the doctrines of the Gospel" for all its new recruits.[23] It was expected that anyone applying for such work had already proved their effectiveness in voluntary district visiting. The agents were hired for a probationary period during which time they were given on-the-job experience by a "training superintendent," and their ongoing work was supervised by interested evangelical clergy and laymen.[24] Each agent was responsible to keep detailed records in journals provided by the society, and these were to be examined weekly by the superintendent.

In turning to consider how these agents approached the poor and how they were received by them, the historian is limited to three types of sources: the extracts from the agents' journals published in the *London City Mission Magazine* and (after 1852) in the *Scripture Readers' Journal*; the books of two City Mission agents;[25] and the manuscript diary of one city missionary. Such sources, while abundant, are necessarily limited by the fact that the writers had their own preconceptions about the poor and at times only heard what they wanted to hear. For instance, in June of 1855, the *LCM's Annual Report* argued that the city missionaries had found the working classes appreciative of the passing of the Wilson-Patten Act of 1854, which had restricted the Sunday opening hours of pubs, and it claimed, "The general regret among the poor is that the Act of Parliament did not proceed further."[26] In fact, popular sentiment was very much against the measure, as was soon to become evident in the riots against it in Hyde Park.

Another factor that one must consider in evaluating the first two types of evidence—the published reports—is the fact that the excerpts from the journals were designed to alarm and arouse complacent middle-class evangelicals to action. They were chosen with the knowledge that the home missionary societies were competing with foreign missionary enterprises, which were able to fascinate the religious public with the exciting exploits of missionaries in far-off lands. Nonetheless, the picture that emerged has some degree of consistency and can be corroborated by other sorts of evidence.

It is important to note that the great majority of the people approached by the agents in household visitation were women, as they were far more likely to be at home during the hours of the agents' visiting. It would appear from the testimony of the agents that they often encountered opposition when first oc-cupying a new district, especially from "infidels and socialists," but that quite quickly they were accepted as a standard feature of slum life in Victorian London. The fact that they were sometimes regarded as intrusive reflects the treatment received by government officials later in the nineteenth century when they attempted to enter the slums to give effect to legislation designed to improve the conditions of the poor. In this respect, health inspectors, truant officers, and evangelical lay agents often received similar receptions.

The agents were aware that they needed to vary their approach according to the circumstances. One of the better-educated of the city missionaries recalled that when he began his work in Clerkenwell in 1846,

he spoke as in usual discourse, read a portion of a chapter, prayed, and so closed his visits, pleased in very many instances with the apparent close attention paid, the ready response to the justice of his remarks, such as, "That's true, sir." "Oh, yes, indeed." "Certainly, your reverence." "What a nice prayer." etc.[27]

The new agent soon discovered that this deference was a cloak for ignorance:

After conducting visitation thus for some time, a circumstance arose which occasioned some suspicion, and led to a system of catechising, and the result so affected the writer that he had almost decided upon relinquishing his charge. Pursuing this system of inquiry after reading a portion of a chapter of the Testament, which would be listened to with the greatest attention, I would inquire, "Do you at all know what I have been reading about?" varying the interrogatory; and I found that in the great majority of instances, that no leading idea whatever was possessed of what had been read—no leading idea even of the subject: the reply would, perhaps, be, "About God;" "About good;" "Telling you to do your duty,"—some mere guess—no real intelligent attention whatever had been paid. Some pleaded that they had "such a poor head-piece;" others that they were "no scholards." [sic] I found this to be a general result of my inquiries, and that I must pursue a widely different course. The mass of these wholly uneducated people, did not possess the mental apprehension of a second class scholar in our Ragged School.[28]

The tack adopted seems very much to have depended upon the education, social standing, and religious background of the person approached. Evangelicals were well aware that for many, church going was a symbol of middle-class respectability and might have little to do with a commitment to Christian doctrine or living. Thus when an evangelical agent encountered a church goer, nothing was assumed, as the following extract from a missionary's journal reveals:

Visited Mr. King. He was playing very sweetly on the accordian when I knocked at his door. He readily accepted my tract on ascertaining that it was not to be called for, and was about to bow me out, when anxious not to leave without imparting to him some religious instruction, I pleasantly told him to attract his attention, that his music reminded me of a passage of Scripture. This appeared somewhat to surprise him. His curiosity predominated over his desire to be rid of a religious teacher, and I obtained his permission to read the passage to him. I read Ezekiel xxxiii. 32: "Thou art unto them as a very lovely song of one that hath a pleasant voice, and can play well on an instrument: for they hear the words, but they do them not." I said, "My friend, I sincerely trust this is not your case; I hope you not only hear the words of God, but do them." Mr. K. said very politely that he was a member of the Church of England, hoping perhaps thus to divert the conversation from personal religion into a controversial channel, a common expedient with unconverted persons. I asked him mildly, how he expected his soul to be saved, a question I generally ask. He hesitated, and then said there were different opinions, and added that he always endeavoured to avoid discussion on religious subjects. He spoke also of the propriety of every one being permitted to hold his own opinion.[29]

The conversation ended with the missionary appealing to the Church of England Prayer Book and by referring the man to the section in the Thirty-Nine Articles that deals with justification by faith alone.

CHARACTERISTICS OF WORKING-CLASS ATTITUDES TO RELIGION

Several characteristics of working-class attitudes toward religion can be discerned in the reports of the early years of the LCM's operations, until the early 1850s. The first is the overwhelming degree of ignorance which many people had of the basic tenets of Christianity. The following account by a city missionary outlines the content of the evangelical appeal, but more importantly, it underlines its unfamiliarity:

Missionaries who have just entered the Mission, and who have been sent to visit with me, have repeatedly been astonished. Visiting a sick man [an illiterate chimney sweep] with one new Missionary, I requested him to read and instruct him, which he did, detailing to him our fallen condition, our need of salvation, and the redemption purchased for us, in a very correct manner, and then reading a portion of a chapter in the Gospels in proof of what he had said, he replied, "Certainly, sir;" or, "In course, sir." My companion appeared pleased with the man's attention to instruction, and I thought it time to undeceive him. "Mr.—," I said, "My friend has been taking much pains to instruct you, and now I will ask you a few questions. Do you know who Jesus Christ was?" "Well, no," said he, after a pause, "I should say that's werry hard to tell." "Do you know whether He was St. John's brother?" "No, that I don't." "Can you tell me who the Trinity are?" "No, sir." "Are you a sinner?" "Oh, certainly, sir, we are all sinners."—A pause. "Have you ever done anything wrong?" "Why no, I don't consider as ever I did." "Did you never commit sin?" "Why, no, I don't know as ever I did." "But do you think you're a sinner?" "Oh, certainly, sir, we're all sinners." "What is a sinner?" "Well, I'm *blest* if I know rightly; I never had no head-piece."[30]

Even among those who had had some contact with churches, the conception which many had of Christianity was often mingled with superstition or a vague belief that religious observances would bring "luck" to the participants. The lay agents were surprised to find some of the poor attributing almost magical powers to the sacrament of baptism, such as the woman who declared to the city missionary "that before her child was christened it was very sickly, but that through being baptized it had throve amazingly." Another mother explained that she had had her baby baptized because it was her understanding "that unless a child is christened, it cannot go to heaven."[31] Working-class persistence in maintaining sacramental rites of passage such as christening and church weddings has long interested historians. At the same time, it has often frustrated clergy who have realized that "in the popular mind the Christian sacraments were associated with 'luck' more than with anything resembling Christian devotion."[32] That the city missionary heard these views expressed by the mothers and seldom by the fathers bears out Jeffrey Cox's view that "Women were almost always responsible for a family's practice of these rites of passage, which were part of an attempt to maintain a minimum level of respectability for the family."[33] Attitudes toward religious observances such as prayer were also of interest to the lay agents, as they were very concerned to encourage families to maintain daily family prayers. Among the very poor and illiterate, R. W. Vanderkiste found that in general children in his district were taught no prayers, although a few parents ventured to say to him:

"Oh! I teach them the 'Our Father' and 'Matthew, Mark, Luke and John.' " The first prayer alluded to is of course the Lord's Prayer—the last is a Romish doggrel for saintly intercession—"Matthew, Mark, Luke, and John, Bless the bed that I lay on!"[34]

Unbeknownst to the city missionary, the latter prayer, the so-called "White Paternoster," has a long history in English folklore.[35]

Ignorance of basic Christian doctrine often went hand in hand with a second feature of working-class attitudes: the strong anticlericalism that the lay agents encountered. The thoughts of one "infidel" on the subject fairly adequately represent the views of many of his peers: this religious business was "the parson's trade, just the same as painting's ours, only there's no work attached to it, and the pay's a bloody sight better than ours is."[36] Naturally the City Mission and the Scripture Readers' Association constantly emphasized the view that their workers were the most effective agents in overcoming this pervasive sentiment. Evangelical clergymen tended to agree that lay agency was necessary to overcome working-class hostility if the poor were ever to be evangelized. One cleric testified to a House of Lords committee in 1858, which was investigating religious conditions among the poor, that lay agents were most effective in "breaking up the hard ground" and thereby prepared the way for the clergy to minister.[37]

A third noteworthy aspect of working-class religious attitudes is the strong class identification with religious indifference. Although many Victorians feared that the churches were losing their hold on the lower classes, it is doubtful that they had any such grip in the first place. Organized religion was seen by most of the poor, especially by the very poor, as the preserve of those of a different social rank. In Victorian England, church going rose with social status. Hugh McLeod has observed, "Nonconformity often represented a middle-class rejection of the politics and cultural values of the gentry, [while] working men frequently signalled their rejection of both upper class [Anglican] and middle class [Nonconformist] values by Secularism or by simple indifference."[38] That

Nonconformity had little appeal in the slums of London is borne out by the testimony of one of the witnesses before the above-mentioned House of Lords Committee, who was asked if the Dissenters had any appeal in his neighborhood:

They do among a peculiar class of people; not among the very poor, but among the mechanics, and those who may be made elders, and who consider themselves as part of the establishment of the meeting-house, for that is a great attraction.[39]

A Bethnal Green clergyman supported this view when asked a similar question, reasoning that in his neighborhood, the people were "too poor to be dissenters; they are too poor to support adequately a minister."[40]

The comments recorded by one city missionary in his summary of the arguments put to him against Christianity by infidels bear out the fact that the objections were often more of a social than a religious nature:

"Religion," it has been said to me, "is all a sham. It's all very well to go to church and chapel, and very genteel, but I'll *never* believe these people consider my soul will burn in hell for ever and ever. If they do, they must be brutes indeed. Why, if I saw a poor creature under a cart-wheel, I'd try to pull him out, but hell you say is worse still. If they believed it, we should hear more about it than we do." Then would frequently follow some such statement as this:—"I worked for (so and so) so many years, regular people, paid you your wages regular; not bad masters; well, they went to their church, (sometimes it would run to their chapels;) very strict to their religion; but I never knew them to ask a man, woman, or child in their employ, where *they* went on Sundays, or anything about it: no, no; religion's for you gentlefolks, not for us poor people; still I like your conversation."[41]

Often the response included a more pointed attack on employers, as caricatured again by the city missionary:

"Do you know the firm of (A & B, etc.) Well, you see what my business is; I have to work from six in the morning generally, to eleven at night; I am paid so much per dozen; I can make up so many dozen in that time; and so, you perceive, sir, I can hardly get bread for my family *so*. My master's a strict chapeller, and is very rich; he never says anything to us about religion; and you see what wages he pays.[42]

The inconsistency of middle-class church goers insisting on strict Sabbath observance by their own family and yet creating work for their servants was also frequently pointed out. One man approached by the city missionary about the state of his soul assured him:

I'll think it over—fact is, sir, I've been set against religion. Mr.—used to drive up to London with his family on Sunday morning to go to church; very particular to his church. Well, he'd come home, and come into the yard, and keep us men there for hours, to have the horses out to try their paces. A civil man he was, but that set me against religion.[43]

A general picture thus emerges of working-class attitudes toward religion when the evangelicals began their mission to the poor. Their views were shaped by ignorance, anticlericalism, and class resentment. The response to the evangelistic efforts was one of great variety; undoubtedly there was some hostility, although this seems to have been mitigated by the low social status of the workers themselves. As well, a great deal of indifference was apparently masked v ith deference. At the same time, there was some positive response, much of which probably did not manifest itself in church attendance. Working-class antipathy to church going was strong and marked, and it would appear that the lay agents' influence cannot be measured by this standard. Many of the poor who might attend the agent's meetings on his district would have been too embarrassed to have ever entered a church.

ASSESSING THE EVANGELICALS' IMPACT

What then can be said about the evangelical impact on the poor? Undoubtedly the mission made some contribution to the improvement of social order in the slums, especially in encouraging people to see to the education of their children. In 1849 the *Annual Report of the SRA* stated that:

Unanimous evidence is given by readers whose districts have been most notorious for open profligacy and irreligion, that vice has become less bold and obtrusive. The presence of a reader in a court where he had only made one previous round of visits, has been the signal for quiet and decorum. The open drunkenness and rioting which formerly filled the streets on the Sabbath-day has been in some degree suppressed.[44]

This view was strongly supported by the LCM which asserted that "there is no question that, from the constant visitation of a reader or a missionary, very much that is outwardly evil is prevented, even when no further and more important result follows."[45] Even the popular press acknowledged the omnipresent city missionary as a regular feature of slum life and commended the Christian concern that they evidenced. Reporting on Clerkenwell, the *Illustrated London News* noted that it

is the locality of dirt, and ignorance, and vice—the recesses whereof are known but to the disguised policeman, as he gropes his way up ricketty [sic] staircases towards the tracked housebreaker's den; or the poor, shabby genteel City Missionary, as he kneels at midnight by the foul straw of some convulsed and dying outcast.[46]

At the same time, however, their impact seems to have been much more limited than the evangelicals had hoped: the number of conversions was never great, although this was not the LCM's only measure of its progress. Each year the mission produced a summary of its accomplishments, a rather dry litany for the hearing of its annual meetings, but one which indicates some of the more specific goals of the society. The following example is taken from the 1855 Annual Report, when the Mission had 328 city missionaries:

The number of visits paid by the missionaries last year was 1,484,563, which is an increase of 45,245; the number of religious tracts distributed was 2,092,854, which is an increase of 161,149; the number of books lent was 50,458, which is an increase of 13,647; the number of readings of the Scriptures in visitation was 452,851, which is an increase of 21,205; the number of Bibles distributed was 8,155, which is an increase of 1,427; and the number of meetings held for prayer and exposition of the Scriptures was 25,318, which is an increase of 2,283.

The report then turned to statistics dealing with individuals:

The number of fallen women persuaded to enter asylums, or to return to their homes, which was in 1853, 279, in 1854 was 376, and last year the number of additional cases amounted to 411. The number of drunkards reclaimed last year were 656, or 87 more than in the previous year. 479 persons living improperly together, were persuaded to marry, or 26 more than 1854. 363 families were induced to commence family prayer, which is an increase this year of 56. The number of persons admitted to the Lord's Supper by their respective ministers, as the fruit of the missionaries' labours, was last year exactly 700, which is an increase of 24. 967 cases of decided reformation of life are also reported by the missionaries this year, or 179 more than in the year preceding. And the number of children sent to school has been 9,561, which shows an increase of 708.[47]

Such bare statistics, however, do not give one a feel for what was happening at the local and personal level. Such an appreciation can only be gained by listening to the oral testimony of those directly involved.

In some locales, the lay agents were very effective, if one is to give any credence to the clerical estimates of their effectiveness. Many Evangelical clergy viewed them as essential if they were to have any impact among the poor slumdwellers. The Reverend J. Colbourne, rector of St. Matthew's, Bethnal Green, told the House of Lords committee investigating religion among the poor that he had supervised four lay agents in his parish, two from the Scripture Readers' Association and two from the London City Mission. When asked whether they had been beneficial to his parish, he responded: ''I am certain of it; I attribute my congregation to their labours.''[48]

The case of the Reverend William Weldon Champneys, rector of Whitechapel, is a most interesting example of what could be done in a poor area of London. Champneys (1807–1875) had been educated at Brazenose College, Oxford, and following graduation became a fellow of his college, was ordained, and in 1832 became rector of St. Ebbe's parish in Oxford. While at St. Ebbe's he won his parishioners' affections by visiting and caring for those sick with cholera during the 1832 outbreak.[49] In 1837 he accepted the rectorship of St. Mary's, Whitechapel, with the cure of some 16,000 souls in the East End of London, the great majority of the workers in the area being dock laborers. He took over the parish

from a "Low and Slow" rector (that being the eighteenth-century designation
for the old school of latitudinarians), who had been accustomed to reading a
sermon to his clerk and the charity children at the sole Sunday service.[50] The
1851 Ecclesiastical Census reported 1,157 adults present at St. Mary's in the
morning service, 437 in the afternoon meetings, and 1,463 in attendance in the
evening. During each service there were sizeable groupings of Sunday scholars.
In addition, there was a school, which was used twice on Sundays for services
for another 580 school children and 149 adults.[51] Champneys claimed that a
large portion of the church attendants ("perhaps the majority" were his words)
were of "the very poor, many of them of the poorest class."[52] Nonetheless, less
than half of the sittings in his church were free; thus, a good number of his
congregation must have been sufficiently well off to afford pew rents.

In working his parish Champneys had the assistance of two curates (whom
he paid out of his own pocket); one Scripture reader (whom he also paid); another
Scripture reader paid for by a friend; two more such workers from the Scripture
Readers' Association; and two city missionaries.[53] In total he had two curates
and six lay agents. The lay workers were carefully overseen by Champneys:

My practice is to have my curates and all those Scripture readers [including the London
City Mission agents] together every week on Tuesday, and on that occasion I have
frequently given points for them on which they are to give me their answers; and I have
read the answers and commented upon them, when time has allowed, and pointed out
what was deficient in the one or correct in the other.[54]

He encouraged the lay agents to get on with house-to-house visitation and assigned the most difficult cases that they encountered to the curates or dealt with
them personally. The rector saw the lay agents' work as "having been preparatory, and in many instances breaking up the hard ground; when a person has
been in a state of anxiety, and wanting to receive further instruction, they have
passed the case on to us, the clergy, for visitation." Under questioning, Champneys explained in interesting detail the degree to which his agents had assisted
him in knowing one of London's poorest slums:

I cannot speak too strongly of the great results which have been produced: we have gained
a thorough knowledge of the state of the people, which with the staff of clergy I could
command would have been impossible; we have ascertained the needs of the schools,
and also been enabled to open school after school, until we nearly have now an adequate
supply of schools for the entire parish: that is greatly owing to the work of the lay agents.
We have been able to visit, through them, every case of ascertained sickness and infirmity,
and every house, or nearly so, has had some one to go to it who has endeavoured to
draw them from carelessness to godliness. We have been able to exercise the supervision
of our communicants, who are a very large number; so that, in fact, if one of the
communicants has acted inconsistently, that has been immediately communicated to me,
and I have had the person in the library, to speak to him seriously, and in many instances
effectually to stop what was beginning, and might have been a serious evil. Generally,

I think, the result has been to bring the clergy into close contact with the people, and enabling us both to know them and them to know us; that has given us an influence in the parish over the people generally which without them I should have conceived would have been impossible in so large a number.[55]

The size and scope of Champneys's work does not seem to have been unique. The Religious Census returns indicate that the Reverend Hugh Allen, an Irish Evangelical who took over the newly consecrated St. Jude's District Church in Whitechapel in 1848, had 1,400 adults in his congregation on a Sunday morning. In the evening, all the standing room was normally occupied, the sittings of 1,900 being exceeded by 300. Allen, like Champneys, worked closely with the LCM.[56] Two other Evangelicals who were examined by the House of Lords Committee gave evidence of a similar comprehensive working of their parishes: one was the Reverend William Cadman, rector of St. George-the-Martyr, Southwark, who had six curates and seven lay agents at work (one from the CP-AS, three from the Scripture Readers' Association, and three from the London City Mission).[57] Cadman had taken charge of the parish only four years earlier, and at that time the parish church had been accustomed to a congregation of about twenty people.[58]

JOSEPH OPPENHEIMER: AN AGENT'S VIEW

A second means of assessing the evangelicals' effectiveness is the detailed study of the work of a single agent, a task that is somewhat simplified by the fact that only one of the agents' journals seems to have survived from the nineteenth century. It belonged to Joseph A. Oppenheimer, a young Jewish convert to Christianity. His diary of his visits covers the last nine months (from September 1861 to May 1862) of his almost four-year stint as a city missionary. The following is the account of Oppenheimer's interview with the Board of Directors of the London City Mission:

2 August 1858

Oppenheimer

The Examg SubComm' reported that they had examined Joseph M. Oppenheimer of Palestine Place. This candidate offers himself for Dudley Street, if approved by the Comm'., at the request of the Revd. A. W. Thorold, who desires to have him as miss' there. He was originally a Jew at Frankfort on the Maine, But he was baptized 3 years since, & has been 4 years employed by the Jewish Converts Operative Institution.

(Palestine Place was the headquarters of the London Society for Promoting Christianity Amongst the Jews [LSPCJ], an Anglican society that was the largest by far of the British evangelical organizations concerned with proselytizing Jews. The Jewish Operative Institution had been established by the LSPCJ to provide employment for Jewish converts whose conversion had brought with it a loss of livelihood.) The LCM minute book makes further observations concerning Oppenheimer:

He is a single man, 26 years of age, & is a young man of some respectability & intelligence. His father was a shopkeeper, but he was educated, to gain his living as a teacher, especially of the ancient languages. The Subcomm. gave considerable time to the examⁿ of this Candidate. They were satisfied as to the soundness of his doctrinal views, & they believe him to be a true convert to Christianity, & sincerely desirous to bring others to the knowledge of Christ. They consider he may be useful in Dudley Street, under the Revd. A. W. Thorold, & they agree to recommend that he be sent to the Examrs. The testimonials of Oppenheimer were then read, after which he was called in & examd. by the Comm. . . . it was agreed that he be accepted as a miss' on the usual probation.[59]

Oppenheimer worked in the same district until he resigned from the mission in 1862 because of ill health.[60]

In a number of ways Oppenheimer was untypical of city missionaries. A well-educated, middle-class, German Jew would seem to have been an unlikely candidate to evangelize the Dudley Street district in a strongly Irish Roman Catholic area of St. Giles. (What was then Dudley Street is now the northern end of Shaftesbury Avenue.) While Oppenheimer himself may have been untypical, his views and his methods had all been adopted wholesale from the London evangelicals, and in some ways he may well reflect more clearly than others the version of Christianity that he had embraced.

In 1855 the *LCM Magazine* made the following observations about the district in which Oppenheimer was to serve:

Dudley-street and Monmouth-court are the entire district, which contains 95 visitable houses, 89 of which are shops, 4 publichouses, and 2 common lodginghouse. [sic] In these 95 houses live 697 families, of which 303 are Roman Catholic, 17 Jewish, and the remainder, with few exceptions, Infidels, sceptics, or mere nominal Christians. All these families, with the exception of 20, receive the missionary in his visitation.[61]

The agent responsible for the district in 1855 gave the following details about the occupations of the people in the district:

The occupations of the people are so varied that the whole scene may be looked upon as forming a little world in itself. The majority of the shopkeepers and those who occupy the kitchens are receivers of stolen goods, and also what is termed leaving-shops, or places where articles of too small a value to be received by the licensed pawnbrokers are left, by paying 3d. in the shilling interest for the loan of the money thus obtained. Mrs.—, the owner of one of these shops, has informed me that by far the larger proportion of money lent by her was borrowed for no other purpose than obtaining intoxicating drinks. Another section of the people, chiefly women, are employed in making soldiers' clothing, with regard to whom it has often struck me with considerable force, that if our brave armies in the East could hear the moans of the hungry, and listen to the bitter exclamations of the suffering thousands who are doomed to eke out their miserable existence in preparing the showy and comfortable garments they are wearing, it would tend to blight their boasted courage, and bring disappointment instead of victory in our contest. Another section of the people are employed in boot and shoe making, the majority of whom are what is termed translators. There is also a considerable number of bricklayers' labourers, costermongers, beggars, thieves, and fallen females.[62]

This section of the St. Giles parish had thus been under systematic visitation by LCM workers from at least 1853, five years before Oppenheimer began his work there.

Oppenheimer worked under the supervision of Reverend A. W. Thorold, the rector of St. Giles-in-the-Field. (Thorold was made bishop of Rochester by Disraeli in 1877.) His predecessor in the parish was Robert Bickersteth, one of the Evangelicals whom Lord Shaftesbury had been instrumental in having appointed to the episcopal bench (as bishop of Ripon) in 1856. Bickersteth, while at St. Giles, had supervised three curates, five Scripture readers, and seven city missionaries; thus Oppenheimer was likely to have been only one among a dozen lay workers whom Thorold supervised.[63] It was to Thorold that Oppenheimer's journal was submitted weekly. Stitched into the front of the journal are pages on which the agent was to record the statistics of his work: the number of visits and calls (the latter apparently being times when either no one was home or the agent was rejected), how often the Scriptures were read, how many tracts and Bibles were distributed, and so on. (See Illustration 8.) Inside the journal are lined pages on which the agent could record the details of his visits (Illustration 9). The journal reveals the systematic nature of the LCM system, with the agent being able to do the rounds of all his assigned families in a month.[64]

Oppenheimer's notes are of particular interest because they were only intended for the eyes of his supervisor and have not been edited in the way that published accounts were. He was particularly good at preserving oral history, which gives insights into the reception he received. The picture that emerges of his reception is that of a general willingness to listen to such a persistent proselytizer, if not to heed his message. The following are consecutive entries in his journal, which show the systematic approach used in visitation and the variety of address and response:

Dudley St.   September 1861

Sunday 1

Visited for five hours & a half in my district to day, out of the Sunday regular course of my visitation, had some very useful and interesting conversations with working men who I can't find at home any other day but Sunday, besides distributed tracts at the 7 Dials again, & have been permitted to say a few words to several whom I offered these tracts.

January MONTHLY SCHEDULE. 1862

District No. 126   Missionary Offenheimer

Superintendent Rev. A. W. Thorold   Residence 16 Bedford Sq.

Date	No. of visitable families.	No. of ditto visited and called on during the month.	Hours spent in domiciliary visitation.	Visits.	Calls.	Total of visits and calls.	Of which to the afflicted.	Meetings held.	Average number of attendants.	Tracts given away.	Copies of Scripture put into circulation.	Read the Scriptures.	Deaths of persons visited.	Ditto Visited by the Missionary only.	Interviews with Superintendent.	No. of children sent to schools.	No. of persons induced to attend.
1						Annual Meeting at Exeter Hall											
2	31	5	24	7	31	1				34	12						
3	38	6	29	4	38	2				32	1	14					
4	18	3	15	3	18	9				18	12						
5				See Journal													
6	31	5	27	4	31	1				22	9						
7	36	6	30	6	36					30	8						
8	32	6	24	8	32	2				27	10						
9	36	5	29	7	36	1				41	12						
10	30	5	25	8	33					32	8						
11	18	3	15	3	18	9				21	14		1				
12				See Journal													
13	29	6	23	6	29	2				27	10						
14	28	5	25	4	29	1				29	8						
15	32	6	29	7	36	1				35	12						
16	29	6	24	5	29					28	10						
17	31	5	26	6	32	2				34	11					2	
18	18	3	14	2	16	8				18	10	1					
19	16	3	12	4	16					38	6	1					
20	31	5	25	6	31	1				30	8						
21	30	6	28	4	30					32	12				1		
22	35	6	32	6	35	3				36	10						
23	28	5	24	4	28					26	9						
24				See Journal									1				
25																	
26	20	21	16	4	20					48	6						
27	30	5	27	6	39	2				28	11						
28	34	6	30	4	34	1				35	10						
29	31	5	29	5	34	1				34	12						
30	30	6	31	5	36	2				34	10						
31	22	3	18	4	22	1				26	10						
TOTAL	719	128	632	130	760	50				801	3	263				2	3

Illustration 8

A City Missionary's Compilation of Statistics

Workers with the London City Mission were required to report regularly to their superintendents and to provide the society with detailed statistics regarding their work. Stitched into their journals were these pages, which allowed them to quantify their work. Used with the permission of the Reverend G. C. Taylor, Rector of St. Giles-in-the-Fields, London.

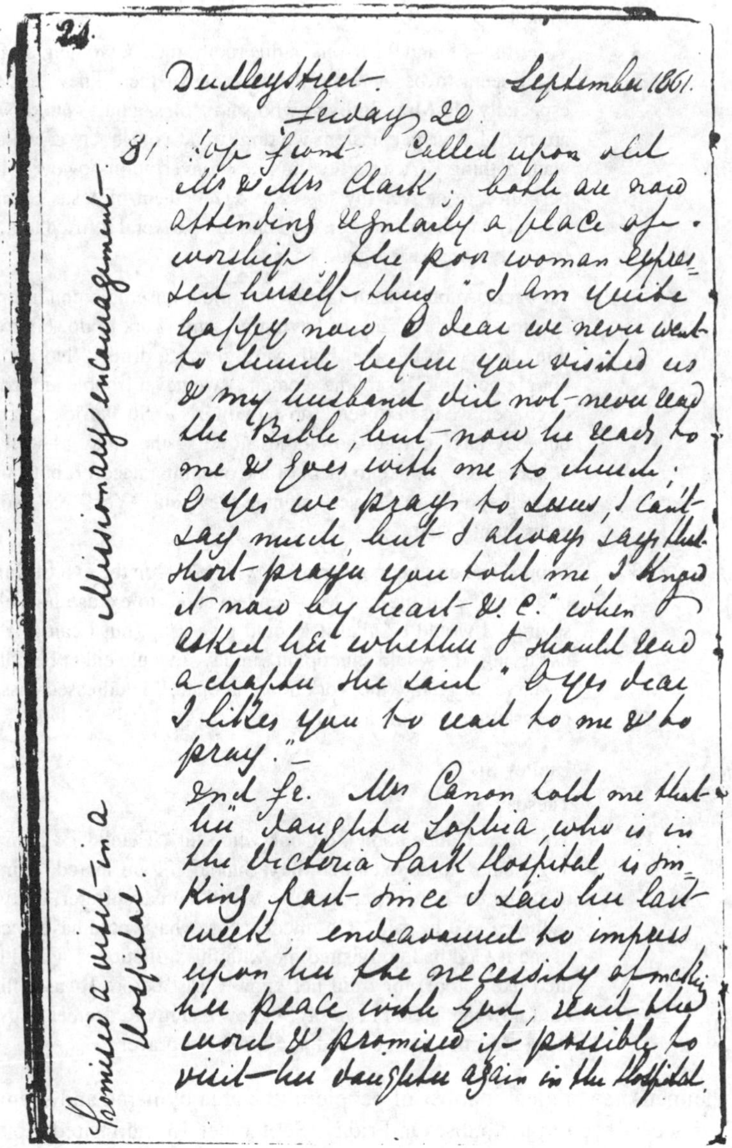

Dudley Street.   September 1861.
Friday 20.

31   ½ p. front   Called upon old
Mr & Mrs Clark : both are now
attending regularly a place of
worship. the poor woman expressed herself thus " I am quite
happy now, O dear we never went
to Church before you visited us
& my husband did not never read
the Bible, but now he reads to
me & goes with me to Church.
O yes we pray to Jesus, I can't
say much, but I always say that
short prayer you told me, I know
it now by heart &c." when I
asked her whether I should read
a chapter she said " O yes dear
I likes you to read to me & to
pray."
2nd fl.   Mrs Canon told me that
her daughter Sophia, who is in
the Victoria Park Hospital, is sin-
king fast since I saw her last
week, endeavoured to impress
upon her the necessity of making
her peace with God, read the
word & promised if possible to
visit her daughter again in the Hospital.

[margin note:] Missionary encouragement —

[margin note:] Promised a visit in a Hospital.

Illustration 9
A City Missionary's Journal

Each city missionary was required to keep a daily log on his visits in his district. This
is an extract from Joseph Oppenheimer's journal. Used with the permission of the Reverend G. C. Taylor, Rector of St. Giles-in-the-Fields, London.

Monday 2

8   Top front–; found 9 persons in this room, men & women, all Irish, & all seem to be at home there, some of them knew my face, especially old Mrs. Sullivan who said "bless you, You know we are not of your persuasion; we don't read your tracts & we don't want nothing." After a few minutes conversation however, I was permitted to deliver my message & tell them of Jesus Christ as the only Mediator between God and men; several refused to accept tracts, but we parted good friends.

8   1st back; Another Irish family in a most miserable condition; on account–; as they said, of having no army work to do, but everything looked to me as if both were given to drink. "No we have not got no Bible"; said the woman, "we never trouble any church or chapel; we used to send those two girls to St. Patrick's School, but they have not got no clothes now, so they may as well stay at home &c." Spoke to them of the one thing needful, but I might as well spoken to the very stones, they said "Yes" & "No" to everything I said.

10   Shop. I had another conversation with Mr.—on the evil of Sunday trading, like all the rest Mr.—endeavoured to excuse himself by saying "I would be glad if I could give it up, but I can't, it's no use trying, if I would shut up on Sunday, I would either be obliged to starve, or go into the work house at once." I addressed passages of Scripture and left a tract.

Dudley St.

Tuesday 3

13   Top back. Called upon old Cook who said "Thank God I am able to get out & to go to church, next Sunday if I am spared, & intend to attend the Lord's Supper"; he is still a great sufferer, but when I alluded to it he said "Oh my dear Sir, what would have become of me if God had not visited me with this affliction. I would have died like a fool, for I did not know Christ before I was afflicted but I now thank God I can say 'I know that my Redeemer lives.' " Read a portion of the word and offered a prayer.

Oppenheimer knew a great number of people in the area by name and seems to have had access even to the pubs. On Friday, September 13, he visited a public house at 58 Dudley Street:

58   Public house; distributed tracts at the bar of this Public house, to 4 men & 5 women, some of whom I knew to be from my district; however they were very civil & accepted the tracts. The Public Master who was standing at the bar accepted a tract likewise.

In examining Oppenheimer's diary, nine different categories of respondents to his efforts can be discerned: those overtly hostile; Roman Catholics; Jews;

"Nominal" Christians; "Infidels" and "Sceptics"; those Oppenheimer considered "indifferent"; Prostitutes; Sabbath breakers; positive respondents. The respondents within each group often raised similar objections to his approach, each of which are of peculiar interest. Thus we turn to an examination of how each of these groups were approached and how they responded.

Those Overtly Hostile

The most hostile reception Oppenheimer received usually came from Irishmen, who claimed to be staunch Roman Catholics, all the more fervent when fortified with dutch courage:

> September 22, 1861
>
> Dudley Street
>
> [19]   1st back. Another low Irish family, the husband named Lever [sp.?] was apparently the worse for liquor & when his wife opened the door & I went into the room he used the most filthy language towards the poor woman for letting me in; & told me he did not want any preaching & if I did not go at once he would be—if he did not give me something I would not like. Endeavoured to pacify him, but he became very excited so that I thought it expedient to leave the room.

> January 8, 1862
>
> Monmouth Court
>
> 6   2nd back; Was refused admittance by an Irish man who said "he was not of my persuasion"; I am a Catholic & a good one too & don't want to have nothing to do with you Bible Christians you are no good." I endeavoured to speak to him but did not succeed for he shut the door in my face.

Not all of the hostility was forthcoming from Irishmen. Oppenheimer normally identified the Irish on his district as such; the following rejection came from one who apparently was not of the emerald isle:

> 29 October 1861
>
> Monmouth Court
>
> 5   2nd back. Was refused admittance by a young man who told me to go to the—& not preach to him or he would let me know what his creed was, he went on thus whilst I endeavoured to speak to him & at last shut the door in my face, & I could hear him swear & curse whilst going down the stairs.

What is perhaps most surprising about the incidents of hostility is their infrequency. Such incidents seem to have happened to Oppenheimer about once a month at the most.

Roman Catholics

Although some of the strongest opposition that Oppenheimer encountered came from Roman Catholics, such hostility seems to have been very much the exception rather than the rule in his dealings with them. The most common Catholic response was simply to say to the agent, "I am not of your persuasion," hoping that the conversation would thereby be ended; however, the Catholics normally allowed the city missionary to have his say. The following is a fairly typical encounter with one of the more argumentative Irish Catholics:

> Tuesday 14 January 1862
>
> Dudley Street
>
> 19   top back; an Irishman did not seem best pleased with my visit at first, but after a few remarks entered into conversation when I found that he had read the Bible but only for the sake of argument. I endeavoured as much as possible to avoid controversy, but he insisted upon my answering him where the Protestant religion was before Luther and Henry VIII & when I told him that the religion of Jesus Christ was to be found in the Bible & that it was there before Luther as well as now, he said, "Well how is it then that you Bible christians all differ from one another but we don't profess to read the Bible & we have one church & one faith." I told him that there were differences of opinion in the Rom. Church as well, but that all Protestants agreed upon the Cardinal doctrines of the Bible, as an instance I read & explained to him part of the 3rd chapter to the Romans upon which all true Prots: agree; left a tract & promised to call again.

Oddly enough, even those Catholics who were forewarned by their priests about the dangers of listening to the Protestant agents usually allowed them to speak their minds. This is evident in the account of Oppenheimer's discussion with an Irish Catholic lady:

> Tuesday 29 October 1861
>
> Monmouth Court
>
> 6   2nd back, An old woman named Collyer said "You always come here & I told you the last time I was not of your persuasion; I am not one of your people & I never goes to any of your people for nothing at all & don't want to be visited. I know all you can tell me. Father Kelley bless his soul, is my priest & I knows him & he knows me, he is as good a soul as ever breathed & I will never listen to nobody else; Yes he told me of Jesus blessed be His name & his blessed mother & here, taking a Crucifix out of her pocket, he gave me that & told me never to part with it, which I never shall &c." Have been permitted to speak to her of Jesus as the only Mediator between God and men. No Scriptures.

Such an expression of popular Catholic piety would have pleased many of the proponents of the Ultramontane Catholic revival of the late 1840s and early 1850s, just as it might have scandalized English Catholics acquainted with the traditionally "rural and aristocratic world of genteel English Catholicism."[65] F. W. Faber, a Catholic renowned for his labors among the Irish poor, was able to draw heavily on his Evangelical past and freely confessed his debt to Nonconformity, which he felt appreciated "the Catholic view of excitement in things spiritual."[66] His phase as a High Church Anglican had convinced him that its dignified restraint would have little appeal among the poor, and he became endeared with the more emotive and enthusiastic strain in Ultramontane piety. Sheridan Gilley has pointed out that such Ultramontanism "too often found expression in Mariolatry and gross superstition"; yet Catholics like Faber were also willing to adopt Protestant tactics because of their "conviction that all religious methods were right and good which won souls lost in the spiritual destitution of the great English cities," a concern reinforced by the inroads made by Protestant workers like Oppenheimer.[67]

Jews

More cordial relations seem to have existed between Oppenheimer and the Jews in his district than with the Irish Catholics. He records no incidents in which he met open hostility, but rather had repeated contacts with several of them. There is no evidence that he ever referred to his own Jewish upbringing when proselytizing Jews, possibly feeling that such a confession would have rendered his task more difficult. Oppenheimer's approach to the Jews he visited illustrates the standard evangelical emphases in proselytizing them in the nineteenth century: an appeal to Jesus as the one who has fulfilled Old Testament expectations of the Messiah and the inconsistency of acknowledging him to have been merely a good man and an exemplary moral teacher while ignoring his claims to Messiahship. Oppenheimer never raises questions about the role that Jews would play in evangelical explanations of yet unfulfilled biblical prophecies, which has often been emphasized in the twentieth century by evangelicals. His conversation with one gentleman well illustrates his approach:

27 September 1861

Broad St.

23   Had another conversation with Mr. Angel (a Jew) was permitted to read to him again several old Test: prophecies relating to the Messiah & explained to him how each and all of them have had their litteral [sic] fulfilment in the person & work of Jesus of Nazareth & that "He" was the Light of the Gentiles & the glory of His People Israel. Mr. A. listened very attentively to all I read & said, but am sorry to say notwithstanding he calls himself a reformed Jew & entirely ignores the authority of the traditions of

the Rabbies [sic], yet he is as far from the Kingdom of heaven as
any of his more bigoted Jewish brethren. "I admire, he said, the
precepts & doctrines of the New Test: Jesus has been a great
benefactor to the human race, he was no doubt a great man, but
he was no more than other great men; if he had been God as well
as man he would have been able to convince the whole of the
Jews that he was the Messiah &c." We parted good friends & I
left him a tract on the Jewish subject.

As in his relationship with Roman Catholics, so too with Jews, Oppenheimer
was allowed repeated conversations about religious issues. One illustration of
this was his relationship with Mrs. Barnet, whom he visited in October 1861
and again in January 1862:

2 October 1861

Dudley Street

13   1st front. Old Mrs. Barnet, a Jewess, was very glad to see me
again & I have once more been permitted to speak to her of Jesus
of Nazareth as the only name given under heaven whereby we can
be saved. & that Jew or Gentile are all alike in the sight of Him
who is no respector of persons.

13 January 1862

13   2nd front. Called upon Mrs. Barnet, an old Jewess, who is always
very glad when I call, I urged upon her once more to accept Jesus
of Nazareth as the Messiah & explained to her several passages
from the old as well as the New Test: she listened attentively, but
said "Nobody knows who is right, we think we are & you think
you are, so nobody knows who is. & I am no scholar so I shall
die as I was born, a Jewess." I endeavoured to impress upon her
that the Bible is the only rule to be guided by & that God has
promised His Spirit, in answer to prayer, for to lead us into all
Truth. left a tract.

Oppenheimer's appeal to the Old Testament Scriptures might have been more
effective in terms of provoking debate when put to more religious Jews,
such as the Jews who were to emigrate to Britain from Eastern Europe later
in the nineteenth century. Many of the Jews in his district were from
Holland or Germany and were relatively indifferent to his religious arguments, as is borne out by this account of his encounter with a couple who kept
a shop:

6 January 1862

Dudley Street

85   Shop. A dutch Jew, did not seem best pleased with my visit at first, but after a few preliminary remarks he entered into conversation & I was permitted to speak to him of Jesus of Nazareth, as He who was provided to be the light of the Gentiles & the glory of his people Israel; I was listened to very attentively but found both Mr. & Mrs. Emanuel very indifferent to their own, as well as to any other religion. left a tract.

Nominal Christians

Evangelicals were not impressed with the habit of church going as a measurement of spiritual health. What they were anxious for was a wholehearted turning of one's life over to Christ, both for the forgiveness of sin and a life henceforth lived in daily reliance upon Christ as a personal friend and companion. The city missionary was encouraged to discern whether those professing to be Christians measured up to the evangelical understanding; did they in fact both believe and behave? Or did they rely on their own merits and acts of goodness to justify them before a God who insisted that only the sacrifice of his own Son was sufficient to atone for the heinousness of humanity's rebellion against the Divine Majesty? Those were doubly guilty who professed to be religious and yet insisted that their acceptance with God could be established on their own terms. They rejected God's loving offer of forgiveness and had the affrontery to substitute their own self-righteousness. Such was the condition of Mrs. Groves:

8 October 1861

Dudley St.

34   top front. Poor old Mrs. Groves is very much in trouble not having any work, she complained a great deal & I had some difficulty to avert the subject from things temporal to things spiritual, read the word and endeavoured to impress upon her to seek first the Kingdom of heaven &c. Mrs. G. is a regular attendant at church but is still far from the Kingdom of heaven.

That such entries are infrequent is understandable, given the disinclination of even the devout poor to attend church. They underline, however, an important aspect of evangelical attitudes toward church going.

Infidels and Skeptics

Almost as infrequent as the foregoing case was Oppenheimer's encountering open skepticism toward Christianity and a somewhat thought-out attack upon it.

The local skeptic in this case was a shopkeeper who seems to have had plenty of occasions to sharpen his arguments in debate with the city missionary:

> 17 October 1861
>
> Dudley Street
>
> 17   Shop. Mr. Vincy was glad to see me & I was again permitted to warn him to flee from the wrath to come. When I spoke of the fearful doom of those who neglect so great a salvation &c. he said "Now do you think that God punish [sic] all who don't believe what you call the gospel & if there is a hell do you think they will all go to hell; well you tell one you are sure of that because your Bible tells you so, but I tell you then that God must be very cruel & would act like a tyrant to sent [sic] to hell more than half the human race, what did he send them in the world for if it only to damn them.
>
> explained to him that God willeth not that any should perish in proof of wh. He gave his son to redeem them, so that like the fall was universal, redemption is universal, but men will not accept that provision freely made, hence they are under the curse of the law, entirely of their own choice.

As Hugh McLeod has pointed out, "confident dogmatism was not typical of the working class" in the nineteenth century. Religious eclecticism tended to be the more typical stance, something that irritated both the militant unbeliever and the ardent Christian.[68]

The Indifferent

Far more of the people whom Oppenheimer visited appear to have been simply indifferent to his message, rather than openly or thoughtfully hostile. What is perhaps most surprising in these cases is Oppenheimer's persistence and the willingness of those he addressed so frequently to hear him out. Some appear to have felt it necessary to justify their own actions to him:

> 6 September 1861
>
> Dudley Street
>
> 28   2nd back. Called upon Mrs. Terry who is still very indifferent to the things which make for Peace. "Poor people can't do what they ought, my husband & I work hard, and don't taste a drop of drink from one weeks end to another & we try to do our best to bring our children up well, they are all going to school; I know that all this won't save us, but there are plenty of people who go to church & all that–; but who are much worse than we are, we don't like to profess what we are not." Read & explained the 3rd chapter to the Roms & endeavoured to impress upon her the solemn truth "without holiness no man shall see the Lord."

Mrs. Terry's statement that "I know that all this won't save us" evidences her awareness of the missionary's line of argument about the futility of self-justification, although she insists on using that line of defense. Others seem to have listened to the missionary because he lent a sympathetic ear and liked to tell him their problems and complaints while remaining unmoved by his arguments. His consolation was obviously not always to their liking:

> 10 February 1862
>
> Dudley St.
>
> 32   1st front; found Mr. Blakehay in great distress on account of having lost all his little furniture for 22 shillings of Rent which he owed to his Landlord; Endeavoured to impress upon him that this world is not our home & that trials & troubles are sent for the purpose of bringing us to our senses & leading us nearer to God & I read & explained a portion of Scripture; but am sorry to say Mr. B. remained unmoved to all I said & read although he listened attentively.

From time to time, Oppenheimer endeavored to shake people out of their lethargy with a solemn rebuke. His stress generally was upon the love of God and his concern for people as miserably stationed in life as those he visited, but Oppenheimer could be moved to warn people "to flee from the wrath to come." Such was his tactic with one overly talkative lady:

> 4 September 1861
>
> Dudley St.
>
> 18   Kitchen. Called upon Ann Barry endeavoured to impress her with Divine truth, but she is so talketive [sic] about the things of time, & so indifferent about the one thing needful, that nothing seems to make any impression upon her, read the word & gave her a solemn warning.

Prostitutes

The Dudley Street District for which Oppenheimer was responsible included Monmouth Court, which seems to have been particularly resistant to his efforts. His task was made more difficult by the shifting nature of the population and the occupations that its inhabitants pursued, as the two consecutive entries demonstrate:

30 October 1861

Monmouth Court

9   Did not find a single person of those I visited last time [in this building], they all have left & the house is let out to new Tenants, the change I am sorry to say is not much for the better, I called at 6 rooms, but three refused me admittance, all Irish. 1st: floor back, I found a sick woman in most deplorable circumstances, spoke to her of Jesus & her immortal soul, she listened but with little interest; promised to procure her a letter for the Bloomsbury Dispensary.

10   This house is inhabited by all sorts of bad characters, prostitutes thiefs &c. but still I have been permitted to deliver my message in 3 rooms, the rest refused me admittance to day; There is not a Copy of Scripture amongst any of the 7 families; most are Irish.

Oppenheimer usually referred to prostitutes as ''unfortunates'' and was often able to overcome their initial hostility, gain a hearing, and learn about their backgrounds as is seen in the following:

6 January 1861

Monmouth Court

6   Second front; found two young girl [sic] in the room (unfortunates) they did not seem best pleased with my visit, but after a few minutes they seemed to be more inclined to listen & I was permitted to warn them to flee from the wrath to come; both are Country girls & neither can read; they told me that both their parents were dead & have no friends or relations in London.

Other visits to such women proved to be more fruitful. Again in Monmouth Court, Oppenheimer found:

28 October 1861

1   Monmouth Court. 2nd back two young girl [sic] (unfortunates) did at first seem not to be very favourable to my visit, but still were pretty civil, endeavoured to impress them with the terrors of the Lord &c. both listened attentively & one, the eldest seemed to be much affected & with tears in her eyes said, ''I know, Sir, I am ruining body & soul, but what shall I do, I have been seduced whilst in service & by decrees [sic] I have become what you see me now, I could not now get any place, my character & all is gone & I must put up with it there is no chance left &c.'' The poor girl seemed to feel what she said & I could not but feel with her; promised to see her again.

When the agent received a positive response to his pleadings and warnings, he went out of his way to assist in the reformation, as is evidenced in the following entry:

8 October 1861

> Went with a young girl, named McCarthy, to several Institution [sic] to get her in, but am sorry to say did not succeed in either. The poor girl is only 16 years old, has no parents or friends in England & unfortunately fell in with a girl of bad character who induced her to walk the streets with her, which she has done for the last three months & now as far as I can see she seems truly penitent & anxious to amend her life. I got her into the lodging house No. 75 Dudley St. for the present & hope by next week to get her into a Reformatory.

As will be discussed below, prostitution was a major concern of evangelicals in mid-Victorian Britain, and the efforts to rescue "fallen women" were largely directed by them.[69]

Sabbath Breakers

To the city missionary, Sunday trading was a flaunting of the revealed law of God and thus was something that he had to rebuke with the same forcefulness that he condemned prostitution and drunkenness. It is difficult for the twentieth-century reader to appreciate how seriously many nineteenth-century evangelicals viewed "the desecration of the Sabbath." The following entry is typical of the response that Oppenheimer received to his pleas:

18 September 1861

Dudley Street

> 77 Shop. Had another conversation with Mr. Riggs on the evil of Sunday trading & endeavoured to impress him with the exceeding sinfulness of this particular sin, but like on many previous occasions he pleaded "necessity" as an excuse & notwithstanding my convincing him of the fallacy, he persisted to say that he was not worse than other people, & was determined to give up Sunday trading altogether on some future day.

Others, however, were less receptive than Mr. Riggs and had to be told in no uncertain terms of the seriousness of their misdeeds:

27 September 1861

Broad St.

26   Shop. Had another conversation with Mr. Sullivan, an Irishman
        on the evil of Sunday trading, read a portion of Scripture, and
        endeavoured to impress upon him the exceeding sinfulness of sin
        and the reallity [sic] of that place, where the worm never dieth &
        the fire is never quenched; listed [sic] attentively but brought for-
        ward the miserable excuse that because others do it he is compelled
        to do the same. After my urgent pleading with him to flee from
        the wrath to come, I left him with that solemn warning "Be not
        deceived God is not mocked for what a man soweth that shall he
        also reap."

The city missionaries do seem to have had some impact in their areas, with the
City Mission's annual report regularly reporting on its agents' progress in this
regard. Undoubtedly there were numerous other factors at work influencing
Sunday closings, but the efforts of these lay agents is one that has seldom been
stressed in past discussion of Sabbatarianism by scholars of the movement.[70]

Positive Response

Considering the enormous amounts of time and effort that Oppenheimer ex-
pended, the results appear to have been rather discouraging. Given the ignorance
that he encountered, the anticlericalism ingrained in the poor, and the strong
class resentment of the upper classes who dominated and controlled the churches,
any attempt to win their allegiance was bound to be notoriously difficult. Such
difficulties that the evangelicals encountered, however, were undoubtedly mag-
nified by their penchant for rebuking. Although evangelical doctrine insisted that
a person's good works or moral life could not save him, their insistence upon
the keeping of a strict moral code seems to have led to confusion in the minds
of the poor. To many of their hearers, Christianity undoubtedly seemed more
like a stern ethical system that was far beyond the reach of the average mortal.
Later in the century, a city missionary summarized just such a view as typical
of the working-class understanding of what Christianity was all about: "These
people's idea of Christianity is 'Doing the best you can and doing nobody no
harm.' They appear to think that if they don't get to heaven, there was little
chance for anybody."[71] People may have listened and accepted tracts, but the
positive response appears to have been limited.

Such response as there was, Oppenheimer divided into two categories: those
"hopeful cases" in which people seemed to be on the verge of conversion, and
those who had made a commitment and needed strengthening in their faith.
Among those in the first category was Mr. Haig:

13 January 1862

Dudley St.

13   top front. Mr. Haig was glad to see me, & I can see a great change in him for the better; he seems now to be anxious for my visits & is very attentive to the word read & explained to him, whilst some time ago he would not even look at me, much less listen to the message. he told me to day that he reads his Bible every day & from the questions he put & the answers he gave me I have every reason to look upon him as a sincere & anxious inquirer after truth. May the Lord by His Spirit lead him into all truth, for His dear Son Jesus Christ's sake.

Another instance of this "hopeful" category can be seen in a young couple with whom Oppenheimer had had repeated contacts:

30 September 1861

Broad Street

27   top back. found a young couple who received me very kindly, found them very teachable & willing to listen to the glad tidings of salvation when I read & explained to them the 3rd chapt. of St. John. I dwelt more especially upon the necessity & nature of the New birth. the husband remarked "Yes I Know that if we would think more about it & remember what a awful thing it is to die unprepared, & to go to hell afterwards for ever, I am sure there would be more people living a better life as they now do [sic], but most of them don't Know their danger; it's as you say their heart is so bad & wicked that they live in sin & don't know the end of it; it's quite true but I know I have [not] thought quite as much as I ought about it myself, but I shall try to do so now &c." Promised to call again.

Occasionally, however, Oppenheimer met with great encouragement in his visitation. Such he found in the case of Mrs. Carla, whose simple faith helped him to persevere:

4 September 1861

Dudley St.

18   2nd back. Old Mrs. Carla is still very poorly, spoke to her of death & eternity when she said, "I trust in Christ & I prays to Him every day of my life; I know if I goes to heaven it's only for what Jesus has done for me. I am very poor you see but am thankful for ever so little, for I know I don't deserve nothing, I have got a bad heart, but I trust & pray to Jesus for I have nobody else to trust in; I read my Bible every day."

While Oppenheimer's most frequent contacts were with women and the elderly, who were more likely to be at home during the day, he also had some effect on whole families:

30 September 1861

Broad Street

27   1st. fl. front—Called upon Mrs. Herring who received me Kindly
         & told me that her husband wanted to see me & would be obliged
         if I would call upon him any day after 5 o'clock p.m. or on Sunday
         wh. I promised to do; read and explained a portion of Scripture
         and offered up a prayer. Mr & Mrs. H. attend St. Giles church
         & their children the Ragged school George st.

Undoubtedly the most encouraging case for this city missionary was the remarkable faith of the elderly Mr. Cook, a convert of Oppenheimer's, who was
referred to above:

13 January 1862

Dudley Street

13   top back; found poor old Cook in bed ill, but very happy & content
         in fact he never complained, although I know him to be very bad
         off, he told me to day that he is sure God will care for him "I
         like to keep out of the Workhouse as long as I can, he said, but
         if it is God's will that I should go in, I am willing; I can truly say
         that it was good for me to be afflicted, it has brought me to Jesus
         & I should be happy now even in the workhouse; I know he loves
         me & I never knew before as I do now what it is to have a Saviour,
         there is not anything like it—I would not change with a lord for
         I am as happy as if I was a King." Read the word & offered up
         prayer.

Such responses seem to have been few and far between, but they constituted for
a city missionary the reward which allowed him to persist in his often thankless
and rarely fruitful task.

Although the task was rarely fruitful, by the 1850s the mission of English
Christianity to the urban working classes had become an "urgent question,"
and as K. S. Inglis has demonstrated, it kept its central place in the concerns
of English Christians throughout the nineteenth century.[72] As Oppenheimer's
experience demonstrates, the Christians were up against a complex and difficult
situation, one which was largely the product of rapid industrialization. Methodism, which in the eighteenth century had succeeded (in Halévy's words) in
the "half-urban, half-rural" populations, was unable to repeat its successes
because the early industrial structures that had been so crucial to its growth were
gone.[73] The artisan classes, which in early industrial England had proven to be
the best recruiting ground for Evangelical Nonconformity, were associated with
preindustrial economic patterns and were losing their representation in the industrial work force.[74] Furthermore, evangelical Nonconformity was conscious
of its own upward social mobility, and many Nonconformists were acutely aware

of the distance between their new social standing and the environment in which they (or their parents) had often been recruited.

Horace Mann, in his remarks on the religious census of 1851, argued that the social structure of the sprawling industrial city made it virtually impossible to establish coherent communities that could support a church.[75] Joseph Oppenheimer's experience in St. Giles confirmed one aspect of this: it was difficult for a community to develop when so many people in his district were constantly on the move. This is not to say that working-class communities did not exist in the urban setting, but by their nature they tended to be hesitant about organized religion. As A. D. Gilbert has noted, such communities were of a "distinctive type, self-consciously 'working class' and unlike the older communities which had been based on a functional, albeit uneasy, integration of different classes. Organized religion, tending with an apparent inevitability in its denominational phase towards a middle class, professional leadership, has never been particularly welcome among them."[76] While small sects may succeed in fashioning such communities, and thereby sustain religious commitment, "the history of English religion from the late eighteenth century onwards has offered little evidence that [large-scale] religious associations can themselves provide the basis for fashioning communities out of an amorphous urban population, or of mobilising the particular kinds of communities which do emerge in urban contexts."[77]

As it came to be realized that recruits from the working classes could not be integrated into middle-class churches nor organized into their own churches with middle-class leadership, the City Mission workers were allowed to take on more and more pastoral roles within the communities they served. The same shift from an emphasis upon conversion to consolidation that occurred in evangelical Nonconformity took place here, too—the move from expansion to pastoral care had to come. Eventually the city missionaries would emerge as the foci of distinctly working-class communities in the mission halls of the latter part of the century.

7

Evangelism, Social Concern, and Social Control

In 1844 a young German writer made the following comments on the religious state of the English poor:

So short-sighted, so stupidly narrow-minded is the English bourgeoisie in its egotism, that it does not even take the trouble to impress upon the workers the morality of the day, which the bourgeoisie has patched together in its own interest for its own protection! Even this precautionary measure is too great an effort for the enfeebled and sluggish bourgeoisie. A time must come when it will repent its neglect, too late. But it has no right to complain that the workers know nothing of its system of morals, and do not act in accordance with it.[1]

This apparent unconcern for the morals of the English working class came as a surprise to Friedrich Engels; the self-interest of the bourgeoisie was not being properly served; religion was not being used as an effective instrument of social control. Engels later was to argue in *Socialism, Utopian and Scientific* that the British ruling classes were so terrified by the civil unrest of 1848 that they began to pour money into the Church.[2] Engels's assertions will be dealt with in this chapter along with questions raised by his views. What of evangelical motivation? Was it primarily an exercise in social control? Was it promoted as such? Or, did it arise out of a largely "other worldly" religious concern?

We begin by attempting to establish whether or not there was a consensus within evangelicalism on social policy, which may have affected their support for such aggressive evangelism. Kitson Clark has remarked on the difficulty of defining the issues and identifying the contestants in the debate on social and economic issues which raged in the 1840s:

This is partly because the policy of the economists is often summed up in the comprehensive phrase "*laissez-faire*," which presumably implies a policy in which government
interference was reduced to its barest essentials, but in fact this wish to limit government
activity was often promoted by historic traditions which had nothing to do with economic
thought. But confusion is also caused by the fact that it is not always clear which
economists taught the doctrines that are thought to be opposed to the claims of humanity.[3]

The popular understanding of what became known as "Political Economy" was
derived from the writings of the "classical economists," most notably Thomas
Malthus, James Mill, and David Ricardo. Concomitants with this view were an
emphasis on self-help and free contractualization.

The leading influence on Evangelicals in these matters was Thomas Chalmers,
who, following his understanding of Malthus, had steadfastly opposed the Poor
Law Amendment Act of 1834. Chalmers was joined in his advocacy by Baptist
Noel, but Chalmers did not extend his logic to the Corn Laws as Noel did.[4]
Also agreeing with Chalmers was the *Record*, which as early as 1828 supported
Chalmers's tough stand on Poor Law reform, opposing the current laws because
they interfered with the natural operation of social forces.[5] Stressing "Political
Economy's" individualism, the *Record* contended, "A man's position, in whatever class of society he may be placed, depends chiefly upon himself, under the
over-ruling providence of God—first, upon his natural abilities and education,
and next, and more especially, on his prudence, circumspection, and moral
qualities." The overarching purposes of God did not include a civil government
to provide for the necessitous:

From *suffering* we think it is not designed by God he should be saved. There is such a
constitution of things by the Almighty ruler of all, and so wakeful and merciful a providence over all his works, that from *starvation*, in all ordinary circumstances, he is
preserved.[6]

Like Chalmers, and unlike Noel, the *Record* supported the continuance of the
Corn Laws and was particularly upset with those of its opponents who made it
out to be a religious issue.[7] Such views lent themselves to caricatures of evangelicals as being cold and unfeeling, at least as regards the English poor. Their
concern for the oppressed abroad brought the repeated charge that they were
interfering busy-bodies who were only concerned with injustice abroad and not
cases which were on their own doorstep. (See Illustration 10.)

The middle ground in this debate within Evangelicalism was occupied by those
who held to the old form of Tory paternalism, based on an organic conception
of society, albeit hierarchically structured, and who yet were attracted by some
of the emphases of "Political Economy." The *Christian Observer* agreed with
what it understood to be the import of Chalmers's emphases, that "no encouragement should be given to waste, vice and improvidence" but it disagreed with
his view on the Poor Laws.[8] Similarly, John Bird Sumner, the leading Evangelical
ecclesiastic of the nineteenth century, who although he held to the teachings of

Illustration 10
Evangelicals and Social Concern

Evangelical philanthropy overseas was well known to the Victorian public and is here contrasted with an alleged lack of a similar concern for the English poor. The comparison conveniently ignored the tremendous work of evangelicals at the parish level and of leading figures like Lord Ashley (later Lord Shaftesbury). *The Penny Satirist*, July 15, 1843. By Permission of the British Library.

"Political Economy," tempered his devotion with the acknowledgment that the rich were to use "judicious expenditure" to relieve the sufferings of the poor and to correct social ills that produced poverty.[9]

There was, however, another group within Evangelicalism that has attracted little attention from historians, except for its efforts in defense of the establishment. A writer in 1844 claimed that "the nature and operation of the Christian Influence Society are very little known or understood," but acknowledged that its success "with its small committee and scanty funds, has been quite remarkable."[10] Organized in 1832 by a small group of Anglican laymen and clergy, it was designed to function as an Evangelical pressure group, influencing members of government and of the episcopacy, and attempting to affect the press as well, "in order to give a right direction to the public mind on the subject of Religion and Morals and the general state of Society."[11]

The society attracted much publicity from the 1838 lectures that it sponsored on church establishments, given by Thomas Chalmers. Although the society was originally formed to defend the Church from Dissenting attacks, it also sought to strengthen and purify the Church,[12] and especially addressed the questions of "church building, national education, the abolition of pluralities and non-residence, the safe and satisfactory commutation of tithes."[13] The Society solicited writers to address what its committee deemed to be important questions: impediments of Christian ministry,[14] the parochial system (for which they obtained Henry Wilberforce's pen),[15] theological education,[16] church extension, and schools for the poor.[17] In 1840 the committee was apparently behind the three thousand petitions that were presented to the House of Commons on the question of church extension.[18]

Two of the leading figures in the Christian Influence Society were Alexander Gordon, a wealthy Evangelical philanthropist and a long-time supporter of the LCM, and Robert Benton Seeley, one of the most important Evangelical publishers. Seeley was a close friend of Lord Ashley and worked with him on the matter of factory reform, and undoubtedly Lord Ashley was a key figure in the society.[19] Another significant ally was Charlotte Elizabeth. The mouthpiece of the society was the *Churchman's Monthly Review*, a periodical begun by Seeley in 1841 and theoretically designed to review theological works.[20] More often than not, the contributors wrote about subjects only vaguely related to the works that they were supposed to be reviewing. Like the *Record* the *Churchman's Monthly Review* was Calvinist in theology[21] and Conservative in politics;[22] unlike the *Record*, it was a strong advocate of historicist premillennialism.[23]

In all of the causes championed by the society during the 1830s it had been at one with the *Record*. In the early 1840s, however, the points of departure became very evident. The main issue was Political Economy, a policy that both the *Record* and Chalmers supported without extending its logic to the Corn Laws. The *Churchman's Monthly Review*, in vituperative language worthy of Alexander Haldane of the *Record*, vented its fury on the anti–Corn Law agitators who had influenced Baptist Noel to follow through the argument in his *Plea for the Poor*:

We believe that the modern race of writers, who assume to themselves the name of "Political Economists," are among the most mischievous of all the unclean things that "liberalism" has spawned. If we have never found cause to abhor these people before, we have assuredly abundant ground now, inasmuch as it is to *their* influence over the mind of an excellent man, that we owe the deplorable production now before us. [Noel's *Plea for the Poor*][24]

The blame for the popularity of Political Economy among Evangelicals was laid, not at the feet of J. B. Sumner, but at those of the Scottish divine:

If we remember rightly, even the present Bishop of Chester was led, in one of his earlier works, to rely upon the Malthusian theory. But the chief supporter of the system, in modern times, has doubtless been Dr. Chalmers. The Scottish divine is, unhappily, fully committed to a doctrine which is, in all its parts, in diametrical opposition to the word of God. He is a thorough "Political Economist." He opens his Treatise on that subject with a positive and unhesitating adhesion to the theory of Malthus; and. . . . All the monstrosities of the Malthusian system are unhesitatingly propounded; . . .
   . . . The misfortune is, that multitudes, having examined for themselves, and thoroughly appreciated his theological writings, are content to take his decisions on points of economy on trust. Such we must believe to be the case with the *Record* and the *Christian Observer*. For nothing can be more unreasoning than their adhesion.[25]

Arguing for the preservation of the "existing Corn Law solely *for the sake of the poor*,"[26] the journal attacked both the landowners and the manufacturers:

   While the landed proprietor is senselessly and wickedly driving the poor from his demesne,—the mill-owner eagerly invites them to him. Not that he wishes for the men, for our whole manufacturing system is an inversion of the order of nature. He requires only the poor children, whom he readily engages, leaving the parents to idleness and the beer-shop.[27]

Rejecting "free trade" as detrimental to the poor, the *Churchmen's Monthly Review* also doubted the long-term effectiveness of the other Evangelical response to the needs of the poor—district visiting:

Another class of persons [aside from the free-trade advocates], and very excellent and worthy persons, have recently exerted themselves, especially in the metropolis, to organize a system of district-visiting, whereby the poor shall be personally seen, and their wants ascertained, and, as far as possible, those wants supplied. The wish, the intention, is excellent. . . .
   This is all very good; and it is quite undeniable that it is a duty to visit the poor and distressed; and to give them, not alms only, but counsel and support in trouble; and that much good may be done in this way. But all this chiefly has reference to the mischiefs brought on the poor by *their own* misconduct; and even of this class of evils we can never expect to reach, with benefit, one fiftieth part.
   But of the evils inflicted on the poor by *others*—this plan of relief says nothing. It proposes no method of raising the wages of the shirt-makers above their miserable pittance

of 1¼d. or 1½d. each. A type-founder finds his wages reduced, by excessive competition, from 24s. to 12s. per week, and is thereby obliged to cram his whole family, like so many swine, into one miserable apartment, by night and by day, where eight persons of all ages, infect the air of a room nine feet by eleven, and for which shelter he must pay 3s. per week, or one-fourth of his whole earnings. The proposed district-visitor cannot do anything to improve this his condition. And so of fifty other miseries, now pressing with increased force on the poor, both in town and country. More than *alleviation* is necessary. Something must be done for a permanent *improvement*.[28]

In 1842 Seeley published a book outlining the economic philosophy of Michael Thomas Sadler, the Evangelical M.P. who was the first to champion factory reform.[29] Although the book was anonymous, Seeley himself was in fact the author.[30] In the work Seeley claimed that Sadler had effectively refuted Malthusian economics, and was horrified with the suggestion that the God who had commanded men to "be fruitful and multiply" would then seek to curb the natural increase of population by Malthusian devices of famine, war, and pestilence.[31] Acceptance of Political Economy logically implied a slur on the character of God. Following Sadler, Seeley proposed that allotments of land be rented to the poor on an annual basis, thereby giving the poor a means of self-support and an interest in the welfare of the community.

Another writer closely associated with the Christian Influence Society was Charlotte Elizabeth, who took up her pen to write a very popular novel entitled *Helen Fleetwood*, which, significantly, Seeley published. The story was of an orphan girl, raised by a poor pious Evangelical family, who was forced to take employment in a factory; because of the long hours and poor conditions she died a premature death. The eldest son of the family, who had planned to marry her, had avoided factory work by (significantly) taking a job as an agricultural laborer. His younger brother attempted to console him on her death:

"Well, I cannot deny that the factory system is one of the worst and cruellest things ever invented to pamper the rich at the expense of the poor. It fattens them and melts the flesh off our bones: it clothes them in grand raiment, and bids us shiver in our rags: it brings all indulgences within their reach, and kills the industrious creatures whose toil provides them: but even in the factory, Richard, God's own people are yet his care: he makes all things still work together for good to them. I say, and I don't say it in anger, but in grief, that the mill-work has shortened Helen's life—it has murdered her," he added, crimsoning with emotion: "and that will be declared at the judgment-seat, before all the angels of God, not only as to our Helen, but thousands and thousands more; and many a soul it has sealed up in sin, before casting the poor body into the grave."[32]

In the last line of the above quotation, Charlotte Elizabeth mentions a central concern of Evangelicals in dealing with the factory system: "many a soul it has sealed up in sin." She went on to elaborate on the effects of the environment:

Alas! many such a blight on young affections is daily falling through that most inhuman [factory] system, where no such Christian principle exists to sanctify the visitation. Many a young man sees the desire of his eyes taken away, as with a stroke; and while the vacancy in the mill is presently filled up from among the starving hundreds who press to barter their lives for bread, the bereaved bosom aches beneath the sense of a void that cannot be filled. Then comes the hour of sore temptation, when the ginshop, the low gambling-house, the licentious revel proffer their treacherous solace, and the house that should have been a sanctuary of wedded love becomes the filthy den of a heartless drunkard—the rendezvous of all that is vile—a habitation for devils.[33]

Class warfare was bound to be the result if the wealthy did not heed the warning:

Two classes, hitherto bound together by mutual interests and mutual respect, are daily becoming more opposed the one to the other. . . . If those who alone have power to do so refuse to listen, we cannot help it; but as we must all expect to be buried in the ruin they are bringing on the country, it is no less our duty to lift the voice of remonstrance, than it is theirs to regard that voice. If God gives over, alike the senators and the commercial classes among us to hardness of heart, we must bow beneath the trying dispensation: but one thing is certain—such hardness is of their own choosing; they can never cast off the responsibility that rests on them; and the curse that through their callousness smites the land, will lie, a fearful and an immoveable weight, upon their own guilty souls forever.[34]

The *Churchman's Monthly Review* was impressed; it both applauded and defended the book.[35]

In 1843 the Christian Influence Society solicited Charlotte Elizabeth's pen to produce a very popular book called *The Perils of the Nation*.[36] In its review of the work the *Churchman's Monthly Review* heartily approved of the author's attack on Political Economy and the denouncing of the sins of the rich as well as of the poor:

If then there has been want and misery, it is not and never has been the over-peopling of the island which is the real cause. Improvidence, sensuality, and ungodliness among the poor; luxury, and selfishness, and ungodliness among the rich, increased and fostered in their case by cold-hearted and unscriptural theories, these, and nothing but these, have been the true sources of the evil. The cure is to be found, not by ferreting, like moles, amidst the laws of arithmetical and geometrical progression, but by rooting out pride, and selfishness, and lust from their secret lurking-places within the hearts of our population.[37]

The attack was not limited to the unbelieving; Christians were especially in danger of becoming hard-hearted because of the influence of Political Economy. Speaking of the exploitation of the workers:

The poor people who are thus used as so many mere instruments of money-getting, have all of them *souls*! And, as we have already observed, there can be no surer way of closing up their ears against the truth, than by exhibiting, *especially on the part of professing Christians*—a hardness of spirit, a carelessness as to their temporal comfort and well-being. There is no room to doubt the melancholy fact, that a very large proportion of the working classes have imbibed an idea, that they are oppressed by those above them. To say that there is *no ground* for this belief, is unhappily impossible. Let our readers consider, each man for himself, how he may conduce towards the removal of this reproach. The gospel will hardly be preached with any success among the poor, until they can be made to believe that those who preach it, really care for their welfare, and sympathize with their sufferings.[38]

In a sequel, entitled *Remedies for National Evils*, also published by Seeley at the instigation of the Christian Influence Society,[39] solutions to the ills were suggested: parochial reorganization, church extension, religious education, improvement of laborers' dwellings, better sanitation, revised Poor Laws, Sabbatarian legislation. The anonymous author was R. B. Seeley.[40] This habit of writing anonymous works may be bothersome to historians trying to reconstruct the period, but it served an important function for people like Seeley and Charlotte Elizabeth: it allowed them to denounce Political Economy while working with anti–Corn Law supporters in fighting for factory reform;[41] it enabled them to attack positions that fellow Evangelicals held dear while cooperating with them in other enterprises. Seeley frequently contributed to the *Record*; Charlotte Elizabeth began editing the Protestant Association's magazine in 1841. It further enabled them to set up straw men in extreme positions and then appear the moderates in the debate. The latter appears to be the case in the *Churchman's Monthly Review*'s handling of Seeley's *Remedies*:

We have, indeed, to make a few slight exceptions in this tribute of hearty approbation. The statements of the author, in some cases, are, we think, too unguarded; and one or two of his quotations from other writers would have been better withheld. It is well and right to plead the cause of the poor against coldhearted and unfeeling theories; but to assert that "the charge against the workpeople of causing their own distress by their own improvidence is unfounded, and, being unfounded, is most unfeeling, cruel, and oppressive," is a statement that ought not to have been made, in such universal a form. ... Viewing the matter on a large scale, three-fourths of the miseries of the poor are perhaps due to their own improvidence, as one concurrent cause.

Even with this apparent criticism, however, the reviewer vindicates the position for which Seeley is arguing:

The admission, seen in its true light, rather increases than lessens our own responsibility. It is the guilt of the wealthy, that they have left the poor in such a state, and exposed to such influences, that habits of improvidence are their certain and natural result. What else could we expect in those who have no means of Christian instruction, no hope of permanently bettering their condition in life, but who have been either exposed, in towns, to a constant lottery of wages; or else, in rural districts, have been almost on the brink of starvation?[42]

The *Record* greeted the *Perils* and *Remedies* with a fierce attack, declaring them to contain *"exaggerated"* and *"dangerous"* statements, and feared that they would be used to incite the poor.[43] The danger, the *Churchman's Monthly Review* retorted, was in the opposite direction:

Does not the imputation of a "dangerous character" of writing rather attach to Chalmers, Malthus, and the *Record*, than to the *Perils* and the *Remedies*? These two last-named volumes are distinctly addressed to the rich. . . .

. . . If it would be injudicious and wrong to indulge, in tracts addressed to the poor, in diatribes on the luxury and self-indulgence of the rich, it must be equally wrong, and equally dangerous, to urge upon the rich—not their own duties—but the duties of the poor, and their short-comings in respect to those duties.[44]

Citing a passage from Chalmers in which he angrily denounced the poor for marrying and overpeopling the land without the prospect of being able to support their families, the *Churchman's Monthly Review* asked of the rich man reading it:

Is he not almost sure to close the volume with that sort of sigh which speaks a mind relieved of a burden, saying, "Ah! well, I see there is no cure for it. The poor creatures have their comfort in their own hands. If they will not help themselves, it is impossible for me to help them." And thus, by the advice of a sage in philosophy and a father in the church, he "shutteth up the bowels of compassion" towards his poor brother, and dreameth that he is doing right. Is there, then, no "danger" from *this* side of the question? Can the *Record* doubt that the result we have described has often followed from Dr. Chalmers' writings? Nay, can it feel quite assured that some such result may not have followed from its own essays, addressed, as they are, to the wealthy, and filled with assurances, that the sufferings of the poor are inevitable and necessary, and part of the plan of Divine Providence; and that most of their suffering arises from their own vice and indolence.[45]

Whatever validity there may have been in holding the poor responsible for their own poverty, the same statements, the *Churchman's Monthly Review* maintained, would have been equally

true in the days of Moses as well as in our days. Yet is seems to us that there is a perceptible difference in tone, between these passages [in the *Record*], and the general language of scripture when the poor are spoken of. It was "idleness and inconsideration" that led to poverty in the days of Moses as well as now:—yet the language of Moses is "Thou shalt surely give him, and thine heart shall *not be grieved* when thou givest." "Thou shalt open thine hand *wide* unto thy brother, to thy poor, and to thy needy in thy land."

We must add, too, that we feel convinced that these declarations, that destitution, "*in all ordinary cases*," arises from folly, idleness, or vice, are much too strong and general.[46]

This debate over the proper attitude toward the poor was not limited to the *Record* and the *Churchman's Monthly Review*. In 1842 the *Christian Guardian* in a series of articles on "Our Poorer Classes" had challenged the view that poverty was the fault of the poor, and the implication that the poor were more corrupt than their social superiors:

There are two opposite views generally taken by persons who are not acquainted, by personal observation, with the real character of the condition of the poor. The one regards them only as objects of compassion and sympathy,—the other as hopelessly vicious and degraded; and as if another and more corrupt nature belonged to them.[47]

Maintaining that all classes were equal in their fallenness, the *Guardian* developed an Evangelical apologetic for social action:

It is not that they exhibit a nature more radically evil than our own, but that they are placed in circumstances which more strongly and evidently develope [sic] their corruptions, and bring out more abundantly and into stronger light before others, proofs that "every imagination of the thoughts of man's heart is only evil continually."[48]

This led in turn to an acknowledgment that the environments in which the poor were forced to live were serious hindrances to the progress of evangelism and that Christians should seek their improvement.

Rather than being so concerned about the improvidence of the poor, the *Churchman's Monthly Review* warned fellow Evangelicals that they should be upset with the increasing materialism and covetousness within the Evangelical community. It accused the *Record* itself of unconsciously having "a slight bias" toward the "commercial spirit," which was prevalent in London, "which decides all questions, not by the rules of God's word, but by the probabilities of profit."[49] This aggressive materialism was taking its toll on societies concerned with evangelism:

A "making haste to be rich" has become fashionable among professing Christians. Take the list of the Committee of any of our Religious Societies,—that of the Bible Society,— the Church Missionary Society, or the City Mission. Look at the Committee of 1830 and of 1835, and compare it with the present Committee. You miss many names: some of these are dead, but *where are the others*? Have they become poor? No, but *they have become rich*!

Well, but the richer a Christian gets, the more *money*, and the more *time*, he has to spare. Why should not men who could give a £50 donation, and three hours attendance per week, in 1830, double their sacrifices, now, if their means are doubled?

There are many men whose means have increased *ten fold*, and who give less, *now*, than they did when they were moderately endowed.[50]

After citing numerous scriptural denunciations of covetousness, it asked, "Do our pulpits, do our religious societies in general, speak of the love of money in scriptural terms. Or, which is of more moment, do our preachers and writers warn their readers and hearers with apostolic vehemence and frequency?"[51] Unable to find an Evangelical minister noted for such rebukes, it cited W. F. Hook of Leeds, a leading High Churchman:

Too long have they [the rich] been permitted to usurp the chief seats in the synagogue, and because they give, to "oppress the Church:" too long has it been tolerated, in manufacturing districts especially, that by erecting churches for the rich, the pious poor should be compelled to become Methodists; finding among the Methodists that sympathy and brotherly affection which they dared not even look for in the gay assemblies which our churches too frequently are, where the man with a gold ring and goodly apparel and gay clothing virtually says, Stand thou there, or sit here under my footstool: too long have we permitted the rich to dictate to the poor, as if the souls of the poor only were in a state of danger, instead of the welfare of their own souls.[52]

In response to these criticisms the *Record*, while acknowledging that the poor had a legal right to relief, denied that the right was inherent or that it rested "upon the first principles of civil society, or on the essential principles of Christianity."[53] In meeting this position, the *Churchman's Monthly Review* reasoned to opposite conclusions, citing the example of Old Testament Israel. Just as Seeley had argued for the maintenance of an establishment on the basis of the corporate identity of Israel,[54] so the *Churchman's Monthly Review* derived social obligations as incumbent upon a Christian society:

In the first place, He settled every man upon a certain plot of ground, as his own landed estate.

In the next, He made this estate inalienable for ever, providing that if, from present exigencies, the owner parted with it for a time, it should constantly revert back to his family, every fiftieth year. In the third place, He prohibited the Israelites from taking interest of money from each other; and at the same time enjoined in the strongest terms, the free and ready loan of money, from the rich to the poor, *without interest.*[55]

Although the *Churchman's Monthly Review* did not mention the issue of church extension, the logic followed from the same vision of society: just as a Christian society could not leave church extension to the whims of voluntary giving, so it could not leave the responsibility of caring for the poor on such an unstable footing. In the first case both Chalmers and the *Record* agreed; in the matter of their attitudes toward the poor, people associated with the Christian Influence Society argued that the religious advocates of Political Economy fell short of the biblical view:

Now of all this, Malthus, Chalmers, and the *Record* would sweep away everything except the last; and touching that last, the voluntary almsgiving, which, among the greater part of the rich men of the world, is wholly neglected,—Mr. Malthus thus prescribes:

"If the hand of private charity be stretched forth in his relief," (the man who had committed the crime of an improvident marriage) "the interests of humanity imperiously require that it should be administered *very sparingly*. He should be taught to know that the laws of nature, which are *the laws of God*, had doomed him and his family *to starve*," "and that if he and his family were saved from suffering the *utmost extremities* of hunger, he would owe it to the pity of some kind benefactor, to whom he would be bound by the strongest ties of gratitude.[56]

The *Churchman's Monthly Review*, while agreeing that it was right to inculcate in the poor man (as well as in the rich) submission to laws and to his circumstances, it was not inconsistent "at the very same moment, to tell the legislature, or those above him, that those laws, or those circumstances, are cruel and demoralizing, and ought not to be continued."[57] Again the journal stressed that it had no fear of revolution, nor that its statements, as the *Record* charged, would be used to incite the poor:

Never was there a time in which wealth was more powerful, or better able to defend itself; or in which poverty was more patient or heart-broken. Our fears for the country are of a far different kind. . . . We cannot help thinking with apprehension of those threatenings which our Church causes to be continually read in our ears; "*For the oppression of the poor, for the sighing of the needy, now will I arise, saith the Lord, to save the children of the needy, and to break in pieces the oppressor.*"[58]

The controversy between the *Record* and the *Churchman's Monthly Review* served to promote discussion of Christian social responsibility and to focus attention on the *Perils* and *Remedies*.[59] The works were apparently also designed by the Christian Influence Society to lead to the formation of another Evangelical society to address the concerns raised. In January 1844 the *Churchman's Monthly Review* announced the forthcoming establishment of the Society for Improving the Conditions of the Labouring Classes (SICLC),[60] whose chief aims were: better housing for the poor, the extension of the allotment system, and the formation of loan societies.[61] (See Illustration 11.) The new organization was in fact the revamped Labourer's Friend Society, which had been founded in 1831 to replace the defunct Bettering Society of the Clapham Sect.[62] John Labouchere, a wealthy Evangelical philanthropist, served as treasurer of both the old and the new societies, and leading members of the Christian Influence Society were on the board of management of the SICLC.[63] The leading public figure in the new society was Lord Ashley, who had been active in the Labourer's Friend Society since 1842.[64]

Many Evangelicals did find it hard to accept Chalmers's and the *Record*'s thoroughgoing Political Economy as the committee and subscription lists of the Metropolitan Visiting and Relief Association demonstrate, and as both the *Christian Observer* and the *Christian Guardian* made clear.[65] It should therefore be evident that there was a wide divergence of opinion even among Anglican Evangelicals as to social policy, and on the part of many evangelicals there was a great deal of concern about such issues. This point needs to be underlined in view of assertions by leading historians to the contrary. For instance, K. S. Inglis in his work *Churches and the Working Classes in Victorian England* has maintained that

the crucial distinction within English Christianity on social questions was not denominational but doctrinal: it was evangelicalism, not Nonconformity, that offered a peculiar resistance to social radicalism. The sternest Christian opponents of reform were those

THE RENOVATED LODGING-HOUSE, CHARLES-STREET, DRURY-LANE.

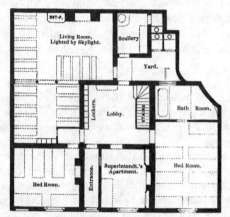

*Ground-Floor Plan of the Renovated Lodging-House, Charles-street, Drury-lane,
to accommodate 82 Single Men.*

NOTE—This House was formed out of three old Houses.

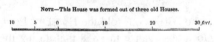

Illustration 11
Model Lodging Houses

From a work entitled *The Dwellings of the Labouring Classes*, published by the Society for Improving the Conditions of the Labouring Classes, London, 1853, p. 45, 2Δ. 929. Used with the permission of the Bodleian Library, Oxford.

who believed most completely that body and soul were antithetical, and that the duty of a Christian was to reject the world, not to sanctify it.[66]

Evangelicals may well have been opposed to social radicalism, but such opposition in large part arose out of a concern for the welfare of society, combined in many instances with a solicitous concern for the poor themselves. There was thus a wide divergence of opinion within Evangelicalism both as to the analysis of social problems and on the political solutions required. The strong pleading of the Christian Influence Society was reinforced during this period from yet another quarter: the LCM.

THE LONDON CITY MISSION: SENSITIZING ITS CONSTITUENCY TO THE PROBLEMS OF THE LONDON POOR

It is important to realize how Evangelical attitudes toward the urban poor were being molded by the evangelistic mission. Three factors can be seen as clear influences on the LCM: the problem of metropolitan sanitation, the lodgings of the poor, and the development of "ragged schools." Daily contact with the poor gave the city missionaries more than just a sympathetic concern for the unhealthy sanitary conditions of the London slums. R. W. Vanderkiste, who began working for the LCM in Clerkenwell in 1845, described the health problems he encountered:

On my first appointment to the district, in 1845, I was called upon to encounter a severe trial. I was seized with violent itchings between the joints, accompanied with redness. I appeared to have caught the itch. . . . I was careful, however, to keep away from my friends in a room by myself, and after a few days the intolerable itching went off. A large amount of itch existed on the district. . . . Bugs and fleas, and other vermin, however, abound, and have tormented me sadly. I have been compelled to submit my apparel to diurnal examination. Whilst visiting at night, I have sometimes seen numbers of bugs coursing over my clothes and hat, and have had much trouble to get rid of them. The stenches have sometimes been so bad that my mouth has filled with water, and I have been compelled to retreat.[67]

Robert Bickersteth, bishop of Ripon, told the House of Lords committee investigating popular religious observance in 1858 that during the five years he had served as rector of St. Giles-in-the-Fields (from 1851 to 1856) some nine or ten of his lay agents had suffered complete breakdowns in their health.[68] As early as 1838 the London City Mission Committee had to report:

some of the Missionaries have been seriously afflicted, as is to be expected from the crowded, and frequently infected, state of the houses of the poor. Three of them have suffered under Typhus Fever, and two of them have had the Small Pox, besides other cases of affliction. . . . In one case, the Small Pox spread in the family, and though the life of the father was spared, he had to weep over the loss of a beloved child through the ravages of that loathsome disease.[69]

Deaths of missionaries and their family members were reported throughout the 1840s and 1850s, with perhaps the worst instance being the death of three missionaries in a single week in 1856: one from smallpox and the two others from typhus.[70]

Such firsthand acquaintance with the conditions of the poor led the mission to publish extracts from its agents' journals, which graphically outlined the conditions they encountered. One such account was the following, made by a city missionary working in St. Giles in 1847:

As many as 20 persons sometimes live in one room, in addition to dogs, cats, and rabbits. The filth and stench of some of these rooms renders them hardly endurable, and expose their inmates to fever and disease. The wonder is, that they are not more frequent. Often has the missionary been overpowered, and obliged to retreat into New Oxford-street for air, and, although he has been but a few months on the district, his health has been more affected during that short time, than it has been for years previously; while the first missionary on the district lost his life through fever.[71]

Vanderkiste in his book spoke of the lower orders being "the flock of the slaughter" and urged the justice of rectifying the sanitation problem.[72] Such pleading by the city missionaries not only served to arouse middle-class evangelicals about the conditions of the slums; it also provided ammunition for Lord Ashley (later Lord Shaftesbury) in his parliamentary efforts to secure sanitary legislation for the metropolis.

The state of the lodgings of the poor was another factor pressing on the mission in its earliest years. In 1837, well before the parliamentary inquiries of the early 1840s began to raise the level of public awareness of the conditions of the slums, a city missionary reported, in a fashion typical of others throughout the period:

In some of the districts large numbers of families reside under ground in cellars. In many of these I have found, crowded together in one small room, as many as seven families, and in one instance thirty-eight families were residing under one roof. In such places I have often been shocked at the immorality and vice I have witnessed, though my surprize [sic] has immediately abated, when I reflected upon the way in which they were forced to live.[73]

In 1841 the *LCM Magazine* published an article that decried the miserable lodgings of the poor and attacked the squalor and poverty which was made worse by the subletting system. It warned that unless something was done, country youths migrating to the city would take "their ranks amongst the dangerous classes."[74]

Four years later the same publication, at the end of a detailed study of lodging houses, unleashed a blistering attack on the wealthy landlords who made exorbitant profits from their tenements while the poor lived in moral depravity that was caused in part by the overcrowded and unsanitary conditions.[75] So strong was the exposé that the LCM committee determined not to offend its constituency further "as different opinions had been expressed as to the propriety of publishing some of the more offensive evils connected with such places."[76]

A third concern of the LCM, and perhaps the one of which contemporaries were most aware, was its involvement in the establishment of schools for the poorest of the poor, the history of which has been recounted elsewhere.[77] Although it is not certain whether the city missionaries actually initiated the organization of the "ragged schools," they were among their earliest supporters, and by the mid–1840s the establishment of such schools was a standard feature of the LCM's activities in its districts.[78] A great asset to their house-to-house visitation, the city missionaries were usually involved only in the recruitment of the voluntary workers for these free schools; once a school was established they did not have to devote a great deal of time to its regular functioning.[79] These schools were particularly important in inducing the involvement of laymen in the social concerns of evangelicalism and were effective in winning the support of laymen who had previously stood aloof from other forms of pan-evangelical cooperation. (See Illustration 12.)

The most notable among these was Lord Ashley, that great and good eccentric, who was regarded as the leading Evangelical of the day. Ashley was a man of curious prejudices, and one of his more narrow ones was his dislike of Dissent. He had in fact voted against the repeal of the Test Acts in 1828, and his Parliamentary battles over the Ten Hours Bill had pitted him against Nonconformist mill owners, whom he regarded as "Jacobins of Commerce."[80] Openly associating with such religious Jacobins did not come easily. In 1842 Ashley turned down a request from the LCM to preside at its annual meeting, but the following winter he was delighted when he read an advertisement in the *Times* requesting assistance for a ragged school superintendent by a city missionary.[81] "I never read an advertisement with keener pleasure," Shaftesbury later recalled. "It answered exactly to what I had been looking and hoping for. I could not regard it as other than a direct answer to my frequent prayer."[82] Much of Ashley's concern for the poor and neglected undoubtedly arose from his own experience of a miserable childhood; once introduced to the workings of the City Mission through the ragged schools, he could not but embrace it as his own—in spite of the fact that it involved the countenancing of Dissenters.

THE IMPACT OF THE URBAN MISSION ON
EVANGELICAL SOCIAL VIEWS

The LCM thus did much to lead the way in attempting to inform, sensitize, and arouse evangelicals to the plight of the poor, stressing strongly the view that social ills were significant barriers to the progress of the Gospel:

Illustration 12
Ragged Schools

The posters on the walls of the workroom read "Thou God seest me" and "Thou shalt not Steal." They were silent reminders to students that those concerned with their vocational education were equally, if not more concerned, with their learning Christian morality. *Illustrated London News*, 23 (December 17, 1853):520.

There is a much more intimate connexion between the sanitary and the moral condition of the metropolis than may at first be supposed. We entertain no doubt, that if more could be done for the improvement of the physical and social condition of the poor of London, especial temptations to moral evil would be also removed, and powerful hindrances to the success of spiritual efforts for their benefit would be happily taken out of the way.[83]

In the debate within Evangelicalism regarding attitudes toward the poor, the LCM made it clear that it sided with the position argued by the *Christian Guardian*;[84] the poor were not at heart more immoral than the rich, or more criminal—their temptations were greater and their social conditions much more likely to lead to immorality and crime.[85]

By the mid–1840s, Evangelical writers were picking up the theme that the LCM had been rehearsing since 1837. The Reverend Charles Girdlestone's *Letters on the Unhealthy Condition of the Lower Class of Dwellings*, published in 1845, summarized in popular form the findings of several government inquiries into the conditions of the working classes. Although he argued that Evangelical involvement in social reform needed no further justification than the good it would effect, he acknowledged:

In truth, we have a further object; great moral and religious interests are, we believe, at stake. For the habits of life forced upon the poorer classes, to a great extent, by the faulty construction of their dwellings, are, not only most serious hindrances to the progress of true piety, but also most active incentives to the practices of gross immorality.[86]

This view received the strong support of the *Christian Observer*.[87]

Lord Ashley testified to the need for such publicity and to the LCM's effectiveness in providing it in his first public address on behalf of the mission in 1848:

I am here to bear my testimony to the very great debt which the public owes to you, and to your missionaries, for having developed to the world a state of things, of which nineteen-twentieths of the educated and easy part of this great metropolis were just as ignorant as they are of what is going on upon the left horn of the moon. Why, talk of journeying to Timbuctoo, or penetrating into the interior of New Holland! I will venture to say that your missionaries have made discoveries quite as curious, and to us ten times more interesting, than were ever made by all the travellers that have roamed over the habitable globe. They have proved to us that there are thousands and tens of thousands living in the courts and alleys of this great metropolis, in a condition disgusting to every sense, and ten times more fearful when contemplated in a spiritual aspect. For years and years these people continued to live and to multiply, and yet their existence was just as much unknown as are the inhabitants of many an undiscovered island at the present moment; and I dare say there may be, even in this present assembly, very many persons who may not know that within half an hour's walk of their own comfortable dwellings there are thousands and thousands of human beings who would furnish ten times more occupation for all their curiosity, all their intelligence, all their zeal, and all their prayers, than if they were to wander over the plains of Tartary, and the deserts of north and south Africa.

This is a state of things which has been brought to our knowledge by the exertions of the City Missionaries.[88]

Increasingly the mission saw its role as one of publicizing social ills which could then be addressed by other institutions or societies designed to deal with the needs.[89] Although unwilling to risk compromising its prime evangelistic goal,[90] the LCM could claim with much justice that it was productive of many social benefits.[91] While LCM agents (and Scripture readers) were forbidden to act as distributors of charity, they were instructed to inform local charities of needy cases,[92] thereby ensuring that medical advice and drugs, as well as financial relief were channeled to the poor.[93] Instances of city missionaries finding jobs for the unemployed, rescuing prostitutes, reforming drunkards, reconciling couples, and rehabilitating thieves are legion.

The evangelical mission to the urban poor was thus not only of sufficient magnitude to have an important impact upon the attitudes and habits of the urban poor, but it was also able to add a powerful voice to the evangelical chorus that pleaded for the removal of ills detrimental to human social and spiritual welfare. By striving to sensitize its middle-class constituency to the social problems of the poor, by involving them in attempts to alleviate suffering and injustice, and by facilitating the establishment of societies that attempted to demonstrate practical solutions to the problems, the LCM in particular made a significant contribution to the development of the evangelical social conscience which was to have such a profound effect on later Victorian Britain.[94]

EVANGELICALS AND SOCIAL CONTROL

In attempting to assess evangelical missions in terms of social control,[95] it is useful to follow the distinctions of E. A. Ross, between "ethical control" and "political control":

Such instruments of control as public opinion, suggestion, personal ideal, social religion, art and social valuation draw much of their strength from the primal moral feelings. They take their shape from sentiment rather than utility. They control men in many things which have little to do with the welfare of society regarded as a corporation. They are aimed to realize not merely a social order but what one might term a *moral* order. These we may call *ethical*.

On the other hand, law, belief, ceremony, education and illusion need not spring from ethical feelings at all. They are frequently the means deliberately chosen in order to reach certain ends. They are likely to come under the control of the organized few, and be used, whether for the corporate benefit or for class benefit, as the tools of policy. They may be termed *political* using the word "political" in its original sense of "pertaining to policy."[96]

There can be no doubt but that the evangelicals were desirous of "ethical control"—of the actions both of the poor and of the wealthy. What complicates the matter, however, is that evangelicals strongly asserted that Christians (and others) had a moral responsibility to "be subject to the higher powers" (Romans 13), and hence to some extent what one might label as a concern for "political control" was in their minds subsumed under the category of "ethical control."

Because Owenite socialism had included a distinctly religious view in its political creed, it had been an understandable object of evangelical concern. Chartism and other manifestations of social discontent during the 1840s presented evangelicals with a more blatantly political foe. Concern for "political control" did lend its weight both to evangelical concern for evangelism and for social reform. The LCM, as has been noted, expressed its anxiety for the improvement of social conditions so as to prevent country youths migrating to the city from taking "their ranks amongst the 'dangerous classes.' "[97] Evangelicals throughout the 1840s, however, were hardly agreed in their estimations of the actual threat facing society. One writer in the *Churchman's Monthly Review* in 1843 warned, "there are elements of ruin smoldering and increasing amongst the lower ranks of her [England's] own population, which might, any day, and almost within an hour's notice, bring the monarchy to the very verge of dissolution."[98] A year later, however, another writer in the same journal asserted that the wealthy were only too able to defend themselves and the poor too dispirited to revolt.[99]

Some speakers at the annual meetings of the LCM promoted the effectiveness of the mission as an agency of political control. One suggested, "the most effective police force London could have would just be 500 City Missionaries,"[100] a view strongly endorsed by another speaker.[101] In 1847 the political impact of the LCM was stressed by an Anglican rector who denounced equality as "a lie of Satan" and juxtaposed "the wholesome truths of the Gospel" against the growth of democratic feeling "which must destroy itself, but which presently makes this vast population as a mine at the base of society, ready to explode on any occasion, and throw the whole into disorder and confusion."[102]

Even Baptist Noel had at one time advocated a similar antirevolutionary apologetic. In his influential *State of the Metropolis Considered*, published in 1835, he had urged Blomfield to take leadership in sanctioning lay agency and in promoting evangelistic efforts; he concluded his appeal with the following:

You will have proved to the anarchist, who now rejoices in the deepening mass of those who look with hatred at the present order of society, that the Gospel, in spite of infidel and seditious excitation, is the parent of order and the safeguard of property; you will have given a deadly blow to the disorganizing and anti-social confederation which has for some years been acquiring strength in this city.[103]

Coleman has demonstrated that this antirevolutionary concern was one of the factors influencing the campaign for church extension in the late 1830s:

Men who saw hierarchy as the ordained structure of society and the influence of the resident landlord as the most effective form of social control believed this isolation of the urban lower classes to be not only unnatural but a primary cause of unrest.[104]

In 1841 the *Record* advocated support for evangelism for a blatantly political motive: it was the most effective way of combatting Chartism: "The efforts which are being made by the Pastoral-Aid Society as well as by Sunday Schools and other religious educational Institutions, furnish the readiest means present to us for immediately grappling with the evils of Chartism."[105] By the late 1830s, however, Baptist Noel emerged as the leading figure contending against this alliance of evangelicalism with the ruling powers. He warned the LCM that it should avoid any offers of government aid or the seeking of support in order to be a worldly agent of social control:

If Government lent you its aid, these poor persons, who are too much influenced by jealousy of Government, might suppose that this was some contrivance to keep them down, to contend against their "Charter," to fight against their rights, and would not see in it that which was alone to save their souls. They would scarcely believe in zeal, of which they themselves had no experience, and would be disposed to repel your agents, if there were in their minds the slightest connexion between them and the powers of this world.[106]

That just such an association was made by some is seen in the case of one city missionary seriously injured by the attack of an "infidel" who swore that he would "kill the devil, for he is only a Government spy."[107]

Evangelicals were quite convinced that their influence upon the poor had had a pacifying effect. Just prior to the large Chartist demonstration in London in 1848, Evangelicals were congratulating themselves for the impact that they felt that they had had on the working classes. The *Record* asked:

What would have been the state of this country at this moment if there had been no Bible Society, no Tract Society, no Pastoral-Aid Society, no City Mission, no Scripture-Readers' Society, no Ragged Schools; and no Ten Hours' Factory Bill?

Undoubtedly one of extreme peril. The working classes constitute, of necessity, so large a proportion of the physical strength of the population that, had they been left in neglect, ignorance, and irreligion, the opportunity afforded at the present moment to designing agitators would have been a fearful one.

Testimony of the great change already wrought by these various efforts for the amelioration of the condition of the poor, is heard on every side. There is no day that passes over without our hearing of this or that exclamation, of "Had these things happened ten years ago, the consequences would have been fearful."[108]

The newspaper cited as further proof the *Occasional Papers of the CP-AS* which reproduced letters from clergy to demonstrate "the important change already effected in various of our manufacturing districts," whereby "*patience* and *subordination*" were being learned by "the formerly *disaffected* and *violent* operative."[109] In a similar vein, Lord Ashley on March 21, 1848, recorded in his diary his thanksgiving "that the operatives of Lancashire and Yorkshire, suffering as they are, remain perfectly tranquil. Such, under God, is the fruit of many years of sympathy and generous legislation. In Manchester several thousands enrolled themselves as special constables."[110]

A similar effect was had in London. W. W. Champneys, perhaps the most effective Evangelical incumbent in London in ministering to the working class in the nineteenth century, testified to a government inquiry that the whole body of London coalwhippers came forward to act as special constables "on the occasion of the threatened outbreak of chartists" in 1848.[111] Champneys, a close friend of R. B. Seeley, was very likely a member of the Christian Influence Society and had gained the respect of the coalwhippers for his championing of legislation regulating their employment in 1845.[112] He continued to act on their behalf in the 1850s.

Lord Ashley, addressing the LCM Annual Meeting only a few weeks after the Chartist demonstration in London, put his view clearly:

I will not hesitate to say, it is my firm belief, that in the late confusion and difficulty which seemed to hang over this metropolis, the agency of the London City Mission, along with other bodies of a like character, did most materially contribute to keep the whole metropolis at peace. Large masses of this community have learned that they are really cared for, and that there are persons who make it their constant and unceasing business to consider their temporal and their eternal welfare. I do not believe that ten years ago this town could have withstood the mighty shock that came from the Continent.[113]

Ashley's view was also shared by the then home secretary, Sir George Grey, also an Evangelical.[114] Similar sentiments were echoed at the LCM meeting by Ashley's close friend Edward Bickersteth and by other speakers.[115] Even Baptist Noel agreed with this estimate of the evangelicals' impact upon the poor:

Various speakers, have adverted to the influence which the labours of this Society may have had in promoting the peace of this city, and preventing the shock which was recently experienced by it, from being more violent at the moment, and from having more fatal effects. I fully concur in the view that this Society has had a certain amount of influence in accomplishing that result, both because, as far as religion influences the mind of any man, it restrains him from criminality, and because, likewise, those 500,000 persons in this city who are continually visited by the agents of this Society, or the men who are the representatives of that half million, must have their feelings softened and their affections called forth by the unequivocal testimony of kindness which these visitations of mercy have given to them.

At the same time, however, he raised objections as to how the issue was handled:

But it would seem to me exceedingly unhappy, and even, I should say, most fatal to this Society, if it were to be supposed that this was the object of our labours. The object of the labours of this Society is not to be a sort of subsidiary moral police force, and to preserve the order of this community . . . if, instead of going forth to the masses of their fellow-citizens in this community with a wish to save their souls, they were to go with any subordinate object, I believe their force would be lost that moment, and their efforts paralyzed, and their spirit spoiled.[116]

Noel was most concerned that such a perceived object would prevent the city missionaries from reaching large sections of the working class community:

If it should be asserted among the Chartists or Socialists of this metropolis, that this Society exists, and calls forth the contributions of its members, because they wish to teach the miserable to be content with misery and famine, while themselves were supplied with all the comforts of life, it would steel the heart of every Chartist and Socialist against every missionary that might knock at his door. It is not, in fact, their object; and it ought not to be misapprehended by any of those to whom they go, that it is their object.[117]

Just as the LCM had been anxious that the direct involvement of their agents in social work would compromise their evangelistic mission, so Noel was concerned that the promotion of the society as an agent of "political control" would equally jeopardize the organization's prime function. It is noteworthy that the LCM never used its magazine to appeal for support for the mission as an anti-revolutionary organization. Such apologies were only made by individual clergymen and laymen at annual meetings of the society, none of whom were members of its committee. Furthermore, the LCM had no control over or foreknowledge of the speeches. The committee, which included Noel as a dominant figure, operated on a consensus and could never have agreed to such a course. In fact, the regulations of the society clearly instructed its agents to "Studiously avoid entering upon subjects of a political nature, as altogether foreign from the purpose of your visits."[118] Advocacy of evangelism as a means of "political control" was not popular within the broader Evangelical community; of all the Evangelical publications, only the *Record* had so promoted the cause.

Any attempt to use evangelism as a means of political control would seem to have been made more difficult by the pan-evangelical approach. Broadly based organizations like the LCM comprehended a wider range of political opinion than did the denominational societies. Indeed, of all the organizations that were concerned with urban evangelism, the one which came closest to advocating evangelism as a means of political control was the denominational District Visiting Society. From its inception in 1828, the DVS's committee had not hesitated to mix political and religious motives in its attempts to gain support for its efforts. In its first advertisement it had warned that the situation in St. Giles "gives to the noisy and vituperative eloquence of Mr. O'Connell and other agitators of Ireland its power."[119] Lord Lifford had made clear how much he valued the society as an agent of political control in 1830: "it must tend to diminish the risk attendant upon crowds of unemployed poor in a populous city,"[120] while the following year Lord Calthorpe cited the riots of the previous winter and urged that district visiting could calm such disorders.[121] Perhaps the most eloquent appeals for the society to foster political quiescence came from the clergy.[122] During the 1830s, however, some Evangelicals concluded that this emphasis had served to diminish the effectiveness of the district visitors and therefore jealously guarded such motives from creeping into the councils of the pan-evangelical societies. It is interesting that the leading Anglican proponent of interdenominational cooperation, Baptist Noel, was also the strongest voice in protest against those who sought to recommend evangelism as a means of political control.

Thus while the peace, order, and good government of society were important concerns of evangelicals, and although their numerous lay agents undoubtedly contributed to the maintenance of civil order in Victorian society, it would be wrong to elevate this concern to a place of undue importance. It does not appear to have been a factor contributing to the growing support for pan-evangelical evangelism. The LCM committee put the matter clearly itself when referring to the social benefits accruing from its work, comments that are equally applicable to suggestions about its usefulness as an agency of "political control":

Such benefits, great as they undoubtedly are, are yet only the incidental and indirect benefits of the Mission. Its great design is, to SAVE THE SOUL from everlasting ruin, and render it meet for everlasting bliss,— . . . The Committee are very desirous that nothing should unduly divert the attention of their missionaries from this primary object of their concern.[123]

While such evangelistic efforts were not promoted out of a desire for political control, were they regarded as such by the poor? It has been suggested that to many of them "an invitation to attend worship could seem like an incitement to betray their class. This was perceived by the [Anglican] clergyman [in 1881] who detected among working-class people a feeling 'that they compromise them-selves in some way by going to church.' "[124] According to such a view, the evangelical workers reinforced feelings of subordination among the poor, and hence they were rejected as emissaries of the upper classes. K. S. Inglis has maintained that to "the most articulate and class-conscious working men, the Christian missionary was a representative not only of a faith but of groups which were defending an unjust set of social arrangements."[125]

Such doctrinaire class consciousness sounds very plausible to twentieth-century historians and was the view expressed by a segment of the working class. There seems, however, to be little evidence that it was a very widespread view—at least in regards to the evangelical lay workers. The example Inglis cites is an Anglican minister whose social background and training would put him in a class far above the working classes and the evangelical workers. Charles Booth, writing toward the end of the century, made the following observation concerning popular attitudes toward the LCM workers:

The missionaries often remain many years on their beat, and, becoming well known and being honest and kindly people, their periodical visits are welcomed. . . .

The place these missionaries fill and the part they play are quite unique: their experiences are related with the conviction and *naivete* of a mediaeval saint. Not too far removed in social status from those they visit—father confessor at once and friend; themselves absolutely satisfied of the truth and sufficiency of the simple Gospel they preach; neither distrusted nor pandered to; instinctive in their horror of Rome and Romish ways, but with a good word for every Evangelical Church or Protestant sect—they are, more than all the rest, in tune with the sentiments of the people.[126]

The greatest problem that the workers faced was not hostility due to class consciousness; indeed, hostility seems to have been very much the exception. The real difficulty was religious indifference, something that in the twentieth century is not the peculiar characteristic of any single group in English society.

Part Three

The Advance of Pan-evangelical Missions

8

Setbacks and Advances for Pan-evangelicalism, 1846–1852

While the uproar over the Maynooth grant had done much to promote pan-evangelical unity in the mid–1840s, the great watershed for such progress was to come in the years between 1846 and the early 1850s. The climate for Anglican–Dissenting relations, however, was to deteriorate before it was to improve. The *Record*'s expectation that the Evangelical Alliance would serve as an umbrella organization under which evangelicals could unite in their opposition to Rome was disappointed. Not only did many Evangelicals reject it, but a leading Nonconformist minister in London opposed it on the basis that it glossed over vital differences and weakened the Nonconformists' distinctive witness.[1] The Dissenting minister thus inclined was John Campbell, a Scottish Congregationalist pastor who had long supported the LCM and had authored David Nasmith's biography.

By the mid–1840s Campbell's considerable journalistic talents had made him one of the most powerful figures in English Nonconformity. In January 1844 he had begun *The Christian Witness and Church Member's Magazine*, a monthly periodical whose circulation in its first year was more than double that of the long-established *Evangelical Magazine*.[2] From its commencement the *Christian Witness* was a fervent advocate of Voluntaryism, its motto being "Dissent from all Ecclesiastical Establishments." In the same year that the magazine was begun, Campbell became a founding member of the Anti-State Church Association[3] (which after 1853 was known as the Liberation Society[4]). In 1845 he would have nothing to do with the Central Anti-Maynooth Association, choosing to oppose the grant on a purely antiestablishment basis.[5] In part Campbell's opposition to the Evangelical Alliance stemmed from his view that any such co-operation with the establishment necessarily involved a compromise of the Voluntarist principle.[6]

In January 1846 Campbell launched the *Christian's Penny Magazine*. One of its first numbers included such a bitter attack on the Church of England[7] that the *Record* demanded that the Congregational Union dissociate itself from the magazine and from Campbell:

> We therefore implore the Congregational Union to separate themselves, OFFICIALLY, from Dr. Campbell and his magazine, to which, we may hope, they have inadvertently given their sanction. If they have not Christian vigour to do this—if they allow Dr. Campbell to drag them at his heels through the mire of his political Radicalism and Anti-State and Church Ultraism, they will be failing egregiously in their duty, and allowing, by their supineness, a cloud of darkness, confusion, and weakness, to settle down with increasing gloom over the church of Christ.[8]

The Methodist *Watchman* supported the *Record*'s demand, but Campbell was far from apologetic.[9] Andrew Hamilton, one of the three originators of the *Record*,[10] was so alarmed that he established a rival Anglican publication entitled the *Churchman's Monthly Penny Magazine*.[11] The *Record* gave it full support, confessing that it was anxious lest the Dissenting publication win over the "lower ranks" to Voluntaryism.[12]

The pan-evangelicalism fostered by the Central Anti-Maynooth Committee was also disintegrating. In July 1846 the *Churchman's Monthly Review* lamented that:

> Every election that has taken place within the last twelve months,—from that of Southwark down to that of Edinburgh, confirms us in these views. Nowhere has the protest against *any and every endowment of Popery*, been effectually maintained. Nowhere has there been seen, that union of parties—that earnestness upon this one point, which is essential to our success.[13]

With the Maynooth Grant accomplished, many Dissenting evangelicals returned to their former position, stressing their opposition to any and all endowments. The installation of a weak Whig Government in July 1846 produced a different situation. The new prime minister, Lord John Russell, urged state endowment for the Irish Catholic Church ("concurrent endowment") but was in too weak a position to introduce such legislation, the idea being anathema to the Voluntaries and the ultra-Protestants. Even the Irish Catholic bishops were opposed, fearful of losing their own independence.[14] Sir Culling Eardley Smith, a leading figure in both the Central Anti-Maynooth Committee and the Evangelical Alliance, feared that Russell's views might prevail. Thus in an 1846 by-election campaign, he attacked the Irish establishment and called for its reduction:

> It is detrimental to the honour of the Protestant faith—it is a gratuitous offence to the Romish population to maintain a sinecure ministry in any parish in Ireland. Policy, equity, and religion unite in this conclusion, to the justice of which Presbyterian Scotland will respond. . . .

But if upon the back of the Protestant Institution, there is to be erected a Romanist Establishment, what will remain for the Christians of this country but to unite for the abolition of the one in order to the prevention of the other?[15]

Significantly two leading anti-Catholic Evangelicals, Baptist Noel and Robert Daly, bishop of Cashel, were won over to Eardley Smith's position, arguing that "Rather than a national endowment of Popery, let us have no endowments at all."[16]

Anglican Evangelicals were divided about how to respond. The *Churchman's Monthly Review* urged continued pan-evangelical unity, as it felt that Churchmen "may look leniently on Sir Culling Smith's Voluntaryism believing that it will do little harm."[17] It was confident that "the standing of the Church Establishments of these kingdoms, ... would not be affected in the slightest degree by the return of a score of Voluntaries like Sir Culling Smith."[18] The *Record*, however, was smarting from the hostility of Dissenters like John Campbell; it also feared that other Anglicans might be won over to the nonendowment position.[19] By January 1847 the paper had come full circle and urged that Anglican and Dissenting attacks on Rome be mounted separately, whereas only thirteen months earlier it had maintained that Churchmen on their own would be ineffective in such a struggle.[20] In the months that followed, the gulf between the two groups widened. The educational proposals put forward by Lord John Russell[21] early in 1847 greatly angered Edward Baines, Jr.,[22] the evangelical editor of the *Leeds Mercury*, on three accounts: he opposed state aid to education; he viewed the scheme as an extension of the establishment principle to the realm of education;[23] and he reasoned that if the government was determined to intervene with state aid, then it should also be given to Roman Catholic schools. The logic of this was lost on the *Record*, which assailed both Baines and its former anti-Catholic ally, Sir Culling Eardley Smith.[24]

The Recordites were most upset, however, with Evangelicals who had voted for the Maynooth grant in Parliament. The *Churchman's Monthly Review* vented its rage following the "May meetings"[25] of 1846 at those Evangelicals who had saddled Britain with the "dual endowment" principle:

There is indeed enough to stir our deep indignation, in the practical treachery which the last year has enfolded to us. Noble lords and honourables compel us, one day, by their votes, to maintain five hundred teachers of idolatry, who shut the Bible out of Ireland, and pronounce God's curse on those who read it; and the next day they preside at meetings of Bible Societies, or tell us pitifully that the priests they have just compelled us to pay for, are starving and cursing the Protestant converts. What folly and madness! We marvel that meetings of Christian men can endure these contradictions; these moral griffins, the patrons, alike, of Bible-cursing Popery, and of Popery-cursed Bible Societies; who compel us to pay for the spread of poison through Ireland, and then describe to us, with sentimental compassion, the symptoms of the plague they have been spreading, when it has fully seized on its victims. .... There has been an accursed thing, a Babylonish vote, in the midst of the meetings of our Israel, and we cannot expect the blessing of

God to be continued, unless this flagrant and offensive contradiction be removed from the midst of us.[26]

This attack was aimed at Lord Sandon,[27] the Evangelical Tory M.P. for Liverpool; similar sentiments were expressed in the *Record* toward another Evangelical politician, Lord Robert Grosvenor, a Whig M.P.[28] With the approach of the 1847 general election the ultra-Protestants began to organize, and Sandon, realizing how unpopular he had made himself with his constituents, decided not to stand for office again.[29] As regards the approaching contest, Captain James E. Gordon urged fellow Protestants to support only candidates who would pledge themselves to repeal Catholic Emancipation.[30] While the *Record* thought the goal commendable, it advocated a more realistic course. It was aware that the No Popery cause had no home among the Whigs, Peelites, or the Protectionists and thus urged its readers to elect to "the next House of Commons a few men, if only ten or twelve, who shall be able to speak plain but unwelcome truths; and who will not shrink from speaking them."[31] The *Churchman's Monthly Review* was prepared to settle for less; it recommended the goal of electing "six or eight earnest, resolute Protestants" and did not care whether they were Churchmen or orthodox Dissenters, as long as they were "as resolute as Sir Culling Smith, or Mr. J. E. Gordon."[32]

The *Record*, like Sir Culling Eardley Smith but unlike the *Churchman's Monthly Review*, was greatly concerned that Roman Catholicism was going to be established in Ireland.[33] Its anxiety to defend the Irish establishment against Whig encroachments further alienated it from former Dissenting allies, but endeared it to the ultra-Protestants. In May 1845 Protestant Constitutionalists had formed the National Club, a group of Anglican clergy and laymen who sought to give direction and organizational expertise to the No Popery forces.[34] The day following the passage of the Maynooth Bill in the House of Lords, June 17, 1845, the club was strengthened by the secession of a number of leading ultra-Protestants from the Carlton Club; thereafter the National Club served as the London headquarters of the Protestant Association.[35] While leading Evangelical politicians were included in its ranks,[36] it declined to pronounce "on questions of 'high' or 'low' church."[37] The *Record* welcomed its activities in the election campaign.[38] The paper's interest was centred on four contests where the ultra-Protestants thought they had a reasonable chance of success.[39] The publication of a tri-weekly newspaper, *The Protestant Elector*, helped coordinate the effort, but much to their dismay, all four candidates were defeated. The campaign did succeed in eliciting pledges from many candidates not to make any more concessions to Rome, but these did not carry much weight; in 1848 Lord John Russell carried through with his promise to aid Roman Catholic schools.[40] The extreme Voluntaries had taken the same approach to the 1847 election as the ultra-Protestants, urging the election of their own candidates, disgusted as they were with Whig and Radical support for Maynooth. They were more successful than the ultra-Protestants. Professor Machin has estimated that "there were twenty-six members of the new parliament pledged to fight for the disconnection of Church and State, and a further sixty members who would resist all future attempts to extend the state endowment of religion."[41]

THE GORHAM CASE

The disappointing results of the No Popery cause in the 1847 elections were not the only factor contributing to the gloom in Evangelical circles in the late 1840s. The secession of Baptist Noel in 1848 over the question of baptism,[42] occasioned disappointment on the *Record*'s part, but no surprise.[43] Related to the question of baptism, but of immensely greater importance to the Evangelicals, was the refusal of the bishop of Exeter to institute the Reverend Cornelius Gorham to the living of Brampford Speke because of his views on infant baptism. Bishop Phillpotts's action provoked a long-term crisis for Evangelicals while they awaited a final ruling from the Judicial Committee of the Privy Council as to whether Gorham's understanding of baptismal regeneration would be declared to be tenable within the Church of England.[44] "Evangelicals, with their stress on moral regeneration and conversion, argued that the description of the baptized infant in the Anglican prayer book as 'regenerate' could mean only a conditional regeneration, a 'sign' which needed to be confirmed by the baptized individual's future acts and future faith."[45] Gorham's views on baptismal regeneration were very close to those of Evangelicals, and they regarded his case as their own.

Peter Toon has asserted that if the final decision in the Gorham case had been adverse, the Evangelical clergy would have seceded en masse.[46] Such a course had been recommended by one of the Exeter clergy in a letter to the *Record*.[47] The paper itself, however, did not commend such a course. It took strong issue with Baptist Noel's view that there was popular Anglican support for such a secession,[48] arguing that there was solid backing for the establishment as it stood, in proof of which it cited the testimony of the London correspondent of *The Witness*, the newspaper of the Scottish Free Church.[49] The *Record* also took great pains to counter Noel's critique of the establishment principle in his book *The Union of Church and State*,[50] and devoted no less than twelve articles to its refutation.[51]

When G. A. Denison, the examining chaplain to the bishop of Bath and Wells, rejected an Evangelical candidate for holy orders because of his views on baptismal regeneration, the *Record* demonstrated that it was willing to acquiesce in a situation similar to that which might have prevailed if the Gorham decision was unfavourable:

Some impatient persons may be inclined to argue, that this tyranny is intolerable, and that men are justified in leaving the Church, rather than submit to it. But few who can remember the state of things thirty years since, will adopt so hasty a conclusion. Even supposing there were six or eight dioceses in England from which Evangelical candidates were for the present excluded, that would still leave the far larger portion of the kingdom open to their choice. . . . the encouraging fact is, that there is not one-tenth of the difficulty existing now, in entering the Church, with Evangelical principles, and immediately obtaining a curacy, which there was, some thirty or forty years since.[52]

The announcement of Sir Herbert Fust's decision upholding Phillpotts's action caused the *Record* to depart from its wonted policy by speaking of the possibility that the Church "will very soon be rent in pieces,"[53] but it soon regained its composure and played down its significance:

All the Tractarians could gain by this decision, would be, the *nominal* establishment of an inoperative test. Inoperative at least in nine-tenths of the dioceses. For, if we could suppose that the Bishop of Exeter would himself apply his new rule generally, and that even one or two more bishops might be found to follow his example, *that*, we imagine would be the very *maximum* that even the Tractarians could expect from this decision.[54]

The uncertainty of the whole situation was, however, having a negative effect on Evangelical support for church extension and the building of new schools.[55] Part of the short-term strategy of Evangelicals was to establish new societies which were strictly Anglican, but the direction of which would remain in the hands of Evangelical laymen regardless of the final decision in the Gorham case. An example of this can be seen in the formation of the Church of England Metropolitan Training Institution in 1849. The new society involved many Evangelicals active in the pan-evangelical Home and Colonial School Society.[56]

Relations with Nonconformity were further strained, however, by the attempts made to use the Gorham case to further the ends of Voluntaryism. Sections of the Dissenting press promoted the prospect of a major disruption in the establishment. These predictions elicited strong attacks from the *Record*,[57] which again made its view clear; few would secede even if the judgment was unfavorable:

Most of us have reached the following conclusions;— . . .

That even should this reasonable anticipation [of the reversal of Fust's decision] be disappointed, our duty will be not to leave a Church, which . . . is the main bulwark and chief glory of the Reformation; but to operate, in the use of all legal means, for the removal of that, which our Reformers thought they had removed, and which, if interpreted then as now, would have brought them in guilty of annunciating as scriptural truth that which they abhorred as ruinous error.[58]

Aside from the single letter from the Exeter clergyman mentioned above, the letters from Evangelical clergy published in the *Record* up to the announcement of the Gorham judgment in 1850, were unanimous in favor of not seceding.[59] Edward Bickersteth, perhaps the most widely respected Evangelical cleric in England, wrote to the *Record* just before his death to plead:

Should the decision be adverse, my advice, as that of an elder brother, is, let no minister and no layman secede from our Church at present, but rather remain in it, and help faithful men in it, while there is any hope of remedying so great an evil, in their struggle to withstand error, and uphold the true faith of Christ in our Church.[60]

Even R. W. Dibdin, minister of West Street Episcopal Chapel in London, who had drawn down Blomfield's wrath upon himself in 1846 for taking part in a ceremony opening a Dissenting chapel,[61] informed the *Record* that he would have to be pushed out of the Church.[62]

The *Christian Observer* was also upset by Fust's decision in 1849 and feared an attempt to eject and exclude Evangelical clergy.[63] It was adamant, however, that there was to be no immediate secession if the decision was upheld:

One word on the subject of secession in case of an adverse judgment by the Court of Appeal. It has been somewhat curious to mark the exultation with which Tractarians and Dissenters have gloated over the prospect of a disruption of the Church; the aspect of some of the latter being more like that of birds of prey hovering over a battle field than that of Christian men anxious for the triumph of truth. We take leave to intimate to both parties that if they suppose that an adverse decision of the Court of Appeals would be taken as the final settlement of the question, and be followed by immediate secession, they are wholly mistaken in their calculations. . . . we trust that under such circumstances all those attached to the genuine Protestant doctrine of our Church would see the necessity of mutual conference, deliberation, and united action for the preservation of the truth in our Church, and avoid hastily committing themselves to any rash and isolate course of proceeding.[64]

Dissenters like John Campbell clearly hoped that the Gorham case would cause a disruption in the church:

The judgment of Sir Herbert Jenner Fust is an event of utmost moment, as it affects the Evangelical clergy. They are now deprived of their excuse in the course they have so long pursued. There is an end to their theological conundrum. How long will it be till these gentlemen shall see their true condition?[65]

While Campbell acknowledged that many Dissenters expected a disruption, he personally doubted very much that this would happen:

Reflecting men, who really know the clergy, will not be surprised if not one man should come out. With this view, how cold, prosaic, and uncharitable soever it may appear, our feelings and notions are quite in unison. . . . The Evangelical Clergy, supported as they are by the Evangelical bishops, who are not a whit more consistent than themselves, will cling to the Old Ship so long as there is a plank and a penny remaining . . . Of the clergy, then, we have no hope. and we almost despair of the laity.[66]

As the deadline for the final decision approached, the *Christian Observer* feared "as complete a disruption of the Church of England as that which we have so much reason to deplore in the Church of Scotland,"[67] and following the decision, argued that an unfavorable outcome "must have led to the present secession of many of the most faithful servants of the Church, and have constituted an invincible barrier against the entrance of many more such persons into it.''[68] Despite such dark threats, it would appear that a large secession would have been unlikely. A more plausible outcome would have been the secession of some Evangelicals in the Exeter diocese and in perhaps one or two other dioceses as well, with the great majority of the Evangelical clergy and laity remaining in their positions and mounting a strong national protest, while hoping that the test would remain inoperative. The Gorham decision did provoke a number of Tractarian clergy to go over to Rome, and the controversy served to make those who did remain in the Church of England even more unpopular.

The dispute over the Gorham case sharpened the Evangelicals' awareness of their Reformation heritage and served to underline their points of divergence from Catholic and Tractarian teaching. This was especially so in the case of the *Record*, which maintained time and again that it was illogical to suppose that the Calvinists who drafted the Thirty-Nine Articles would have intended the service of Baptism to be interpreted in such a way as to contradict their Reformed views:

The Reformers have unquestionably introduced the leading points of what is known as Calvinistic doctrine into the Seventeenth Article, and this system of belief is supported by the Ninth, the Tenth, and the Thirteenth Articles; and the idea that with such a faith the prayers for forgiveness,—the assurances that pardon and peace will follow amendment of life, such as occur in our services, are incongruous, is one of the most extraordinary misconceptions which ever issued from the Bench. If Sir H. J. Fust, after reading attentively the Seventeenth Article, shall say it is not Calvinistic, his judgment, in this respect, is in opposition to that of all Calvinistic persons.[69]

The Gorham controversy did much to exacerbate Evangelical–Tractarian hostility and increased Evangelical awareness of its Protestant distinctives. Furthermore, the confirmation of the Evangelicals' place in the Church of England was a significant blow to the Voluntaries' hopes for dismantling the establishment. With a new confidence with regards to their place in the established church and with a self-assertive attitude the Evangelicals could strengthen their ties with "orthodox Dissenters" while unconcerned about the taunts of High Churchmen.

The strengthening of such ties was greatly facilitated by John Campbell's reaction to the verdict in the Gorham case. Right up to the time that the Gorham decision was announced on March 9, 1850, the *Record* had been engaged in a running battle with Campbell, who in 1848 had begun yet another highly successful periodical, the *British Banner*, which he used ever so effectively in his antiestablishment campaign. As late as March 7 the *Record* was complaining of his attacks on the establishment in the *Christian's Penny Magazine*;[70] two months later it was applauding his dissociating of himself from Voluntaryism. Campbell had reassessed his support for the Anti-State Church Association once it was clear that all prospects for a disruption of the establishment had gone and it was evident that the Evangelicals were now more entrenched in the Church than ever. In the *Christian Witness* he gave his estimate that the Anti-State Church Association had been a complete failure politically, and at the same time had been spiritually injurious to the Christian church:

An ample experiment has now been made, and the result, in our judgment, has not been such as to furnish any solid reason for a continuance of the Association, but much to the contrary. It has, in our view, been a [sic] utter failure; there seems no rational ground whatever for believing, that it can, in any possible way, ever contribute to the accomplishment of the assigned object. . . .

. . . Your Organization is an utter failure. Your territory is but a speck in the map of Nonconformity. The mass of your own people are not with you. The Methodist million are dead against you. The countless myriads of the Church of England never even heard of your existence, and those who have, laugh you to scorn!"[71]

In laying down his arms in the antiestablishment struggle, Campbell did not abandon theoretical opposition to establishments. He did so in the hope that pan-evangelical unity and peace might promote spiritual renewal and lead to increased evangelism:

The importance we attach to separation [of church and state] is incalculable; but, to the revival and extension of true religion the importance we attach is infinite! All things considered, then, we think the great work of the day ought to be the REVIVAL OF RELIGION IN THE MIDST OF THE CHURCHES, AND ITS EXTENSION THROUGHOUT THE WHOLE LAND. . . . It therefore appears to us, that the time is come for suspending, if not altogether surrendering, all Organizations seeking the separation of Church and State by direct attacks, and for the combination of every element of power, spiritual, moral, physical, and pecuniary, that the Churches can command, in one grand effort for the revival of religion, and the multiplication of the means of Gospel diffusion in order to the salvation [sic] of our perishing countrymen.[72]

Campbell's action in renouncing political Voluntaryism deeply offended young Congregationalist leaders who succeeded in having the Congregational Union's official sanction removed from the *Christian Witness* and the *Christian's Penny Magazine*.[73] This move, however, did nothing to curtail Campbell's growing popular influence.

THE CHANGING CURRENTS IN EVANGELICAL ATTITUDES TO ROMAN CATHOLICS

The Gorham decision was announced in March 1850. In September of the same year Cardinal Wiseman was to provide evangelicals with one of the most effective incentives to pan-evangelical unity: "Papal Aggression." Before discussing the Cardinal's action and the public outcry that it aroused, it is important to appreciate how in the late 1840s and the early 1850s anti-Catholicism exerted itself as a leading influence on Evangelical thinking and evangelism. In part this was due to Maynooth, but other political and religious considerations were at play as well.

The concern for the salvation of Roman Catholic souls had long been a special factor shaping the evangelism of Anglican Evangelicals. To the Evangelicals the English heathens were at least open to the influence of the comprehensive parochial system of the established Church, which they had long hoped to capture for "vital religion." Roman Catholics were in a distinctly different category, however, as they were ensnared by the great "Mystery of Iniquity." Romanists were twice blind, spiritually dead in their trespasses and sins and yet deluded into thinking that the Church of Rome offered a way of escape. Evangelicals did not usually consign all Catholics to utter darkness, and often acknowledged that individual "Romanists" might be able to grope their way through the ignorance and superstitution fostered by the Church of Rome to a saving faith in Christ.[74] They were agreed, however, that it was the duty of all those who truly believed to forsake an apostate church, or in biblical parlance, "to come out from the midst of her" and to "forsake the unclean thing." Special aggressive efforts had long been in operation to liberate Catholics from their spiritual bondage.

English evangelical concern for the evangelization of Catholics was inseparably linked with the political and religious situation in Ireland. The Act of Union with Ireland in 1800 had served to heighten the English Protestant sense of responsibility for the evangelization of Irish Roman Catholics—a mission which would have both religious and political benefits. Desmond Bowen in his study of *The Protestant Crusade in Ireland, 1800–1870* has demonstrated how such a crusade was launched in 1822 by William Magee, the Evangelical archbishop of Dublin. The effort was remarkably effective both in winning converts to Protestantism and in destroying the religious calm which had prevailed in the first two decades of the nineteenth century in Ireland.[75]

As noted above, the Irish situation had long been the special concern of Anglican and Methodist evangelicals.[76] Evangelical concern for the Irish establishment was greatly enhanced by the fact that by 1830 Evangelicals had become "the most powerful single influence in the Church of Ireland;"[77] by mid-century they constituted the great majority of the Irish clergy.[78] Links between the English and Irish parties were strong: English Evangelicals frequently traveled and spoke in Ireland, and the Irish in turn had an impact in England—notably through Hugh McNeile, who was the first of a succession of Irish clergy at St. Jude's, Liverpool, and was a leading figure in Evangelical No Popery in Britain.

Another important link with Irish Evangelicalism was the influence of the Irish Church in the conversion of Charlotte Elizabeth. It was in fact the combination of the Voluntary Controversy and the attacks on her "beloved Church of Ireland" that caused the author to pull back from her drift away from the Church of England toward Dissent.[79] Her contribution to the anti-Catholic agitation was significant if one only considers the work of the *Christian Lady's*

Magazine and its incessant discussion of the Irish question; however, her considerable talents were further exercised in the cause when she became editor of the contentious *Protestant Magazine* in 1841, the mouthpiece of the Protestant Association.[80]

The Evangelical polemic sought both to stress the Protestant nature of the Church of England and to emphasize the unscriptural character of the Church of Rome, exposing its true identity as the Antichrist.[81] The aims of the former had been furthered in 1813 with the formation of the Prayer Book and Homily Society, which promoted the circulation of the Anglican Book of Common Prayer with the Thirty-nine Articles and the Homilies appended, a practice that was hitherto unknown.[82] By the 1840s the society had turned its attention to the reproduction of Reformation classics, including Fox's *Acts and Monuments*.[83] The society was regarded as an important weapon in the anti-Catholic arsenal of Evangelicalism. The strong pan-evangelical interest in missions at the turn of the nineteenth century had given rise to the oldest of the English evangelical societies operating in Ireland, the London Hibernian Society. Established on a pan-evangelical footing, the society had pioneered the use of full-time lay Scripture readers to visit Roman Catholic homes, and thereby set the pattern for missions to Catholics throughout the century.[84] Both the Hibernian Society and the Sunday School Society operated very successful schools in Ireland, which did much to arouse Evangelical hopes about the salvation of the Irish and to provoke Catholic hostility.

In 1823 James E. Gordon could write to Robert Peel, then the secretary for Ireland, and claim that these societies were "the two most powerful Institutions in the country, and contain the great bulk of the youth actually under instruction."[85] His request the following year that Peel consent to act as a vice president of the Hibernian Society was evidently declined.[86] Gordon's other letters to Peel in the 1820s reveal his contempt for Catholic claims to be concerned with the education of the Irish poor and his assertion that the Roman Catholic Church showed no anxiety about such education until the Protestant "scriptural" schools had provoked them to jealousy.[87] National attention was focused on both Gordon and Baptist Noel for their part in allegedly creating public disturbances in Ireland in the autumn of 1824. Sir Henry Parnell, M.P., had charged them with provoking Irish Roman Catholics in their role as delegates of the London Hibernian Society,[88] an accusation which was supported by Captain Maberley, M.P., who asserted, "Almost the whole of the south of Ireland had been converted into a scene of outrage and disorder, by the young crusaders who went from this country upon a Bible mission to Ireland."[89] Peel dismissed Parnell's accusation, saying that it was "perfectly ridiculous" for him to attribute "the alarm of Ireland to the missionary wanderings of captain Gordon and Mr. Noel (a laugh!)."[90]

Although the Hibernian Society was at the center of Evangelical concern for Irish Catholics in the 1820s, it suffered greatly from the Voluntary Controversy. Even the withdrawal of Dissenters from the society in 1841[91] was not able to halt the decline in support that the society experienced from the mid–1820s to the mid–1840s.[92] A rival to the London Hibernian Society had emerged in 1822 with the founding of the Anglican "Irish Society of London," a sister organization of the Irish Society of Dublin founded four years previously. The London Society also sought to evangelize the Irish poor living in London by means of circulating the Scriptures and the Book of Common Prayer in the Irish language and by establishing schools for immigrants. In 1830 it opened the Irish Episcopal Chapel in St. Giles under the pastoral care of Henry Beamish.[93] The significance of the efforts to evangelize Irish Roman Catholics in London for the broader Evangelical mission can be appreciated when one recalls that the first district visiting society in London was established in 1826 and designed to reach the poor of St. Giles.[94]

Evangelical activities regarding Roman Catholicism were orchestrated by two societies, both of which were founded by James E. Gordon: the British Society for Promoting the Religious Principles of the Reformation (known simply as the Reformation Society), begun in 1827; and the Protestant Association, organized in 1835.[95] The Reformation Society published the *British Protestant* but eschewed political issues, as it included evangelicals with very different views on the Irish question.[96] The Protestant Association with its *Protestant Magazine* was avowedly political. The public outcry over Maynooth did much to stimulate Evangelical concern for the evangelization of Roman Catholics in Ireland. Thus support for the renewal of the Protestant crusade in Ireland was especially appealing after 1845. The funds of the London Hibernian Society, which had been in decline to 1844, increased more than tenfold from that date to 1852.[97]

This rising concern for the evangelization of Roman Catholics had its impact on pan-evangelical societies like the LCM, an organization that itself had excellent anti-Catholic credentials. During the late 1830s, the LCM had stressed its effectiveness in terms of its ability to counter infidelity and "socialism," but by the 1840s the spotlight had been turned on its usefulness in checking the growing menaces of Tractarianism and of Romanism, with the latter function increasing in prominence in the last half of the decade. Contributing to this anti-Catholic concern was the Catholic resurgence experienced during the late 1840s and the adoption by Roman Catholics of evangelical methods to reach the poor. The LCM was particularly surprised by the willingness of a Catholic priest to adopt the practice of open-air preaching[98] and was concerned with the increased efforts by other priests who organized schools for Irish children.[99]

"PROTESTANT AGGRESSION": THE RESPONSE TO "PAPAL AGGRESSION"

The appointment in September 1850 of Cardinal Wiseman to be the head of the newly created Roman hierarchy in Britain with the title of archbishop of Westminster was a bold assertion of the strength of the Church of Rome and reflected the vigor of the Catholic revival on the continent. (See Illustration 13.) The Papal action was rendered even more unpopular to the British public by Wiseman's incautious letter of 1850.[100] The shock of this "Papal Aggression"

THE THIN END OF THE WEDGE.
DARING ATTEMPT TO BREAK INTO A CHURCH.

Illustration 13
"Catholic Aggression" of 1850

Punch 19 (1850):207.

BEWARE OF THE POPE!!

BIRT, Printer, 39, Great St. Andrew Street,
Seven Dials.

Have you heard what a row & a rumpus, oh! dear;
There is with the people now every-where,
Oh where shall we wander or where shall we stay,
The Pope is a coming get out of the way,
He his coming to England on Friday night sir,
With his Rubies, Cruc fix. Sceptre and Mitre,
His Faggots and Fires, Mould Candles and rope,
Oh! run and get out of the way of the Pope.

Wherever you wander, wherever you steer,
All old men and women are quaking with fear,
They are terribly frighened and cry out so queer,
The Pope is a coming, oh dear! oh dear!

Jack Russell and Nosey upon Guy Faux day,
Sent the Pope a long letter Prince Albert did say
To say if he dared land on England's ground,
The policemen should flog him all over the town,
And the Bishop of London will licence the boys,
To carry his effigy—making a noise,
singing up by the ladder and down by the rope,
Will you give us a penny to burn the old Pope?

If the Pope comes to London there'll be such a game
Archbishops of Shoreditch and Petticoat Lane,
Lord Bishops of Newgate mabe every day,
With Bishops of Wapping and Ratcliff Highway,
We will never be conquer'd come banish all pain,
We will never have fire or faggots again,
May this bother all end in a bottle of smoke,
Oh! England for ever and down with the Pope.

Two Parsons was talking and said in a joke,
That the ol D ke of Wellington wrote to the Pope
A tremendous long letter upon Gay Faux's day,
Saying, in Hyde Park on the seventh of May;
Where the people of England would play him a rig
And present to his Holiness such a big wig,
With a three farth ing rushlight to stick in his coat
Won't that be a jolly flare up for the Pope?

Oh Mother, cried Betty, the world's at an end,
Oh! save me from Pop ry, Mother,—Amen.
I heard my old grandmother's grandmother say,
She saw old Queen Mary burn ninety a day,
In the middle of Smithfield, oh! crikey, oh! dear,
I must not go out for I feel very queer,
They'll kill us and drown us, and eat us I fear
or the Pope is a coming oh, crike, ! oh, dear

Should the Pope come to England we'll pepper
his nob,
And tell all the Policemen to send him to q
We'll hiss him, and hoot him, and pelt him
eggs,
And send him to Rome upon his two wooden legs,
Why don't the old vagabond leave us alone?
We neither want him or his subjects of Rome,
If we catch him we'll flog him to his heart's content
Thirteen times a day in the middle of Lent.

Come, cheer up old woman, in sorrow don't mope,
We don't care a pin for the tinker or Pope,
Times are different now and so are peoples' ways
To what they was in my old grandmother's days
God save Prince Albert and long live the Queen,
And all the young lasses of Bethnal Green,
Cheer up like a brick, sing and banish all strife,
Since we don't care a fig for the Pope or his wife

Illustration 14
Popular Anti-Catholicism

Single handbill, no date. From the John Johnson Collection, Religion, Box 9. Used with
the permission of the Bodleian Library, Oxford.

did much to stir popular anti-Catholicism (see Illustration 14) and to spur Evangelical efforts to evangelize Roman Catholics. Hugh Stowell candidly confessed his delight with the various provocations:

> I had long wished that Rome might take some outrageous steps which must galvanize the torpid Protestantism of England. Such steps have surely been taken. If the Synod of Thurles, if the appointment of a (so-called) Cardinal Archbishop of Westminster, if the parcelling out of our country into Romish dioceses, if these things do not electrify us, then we are dead indeed. . . . Betrayed within and beleagured without, our Church must rouse herself. No time should be lost. Where is the Protestant Association? Where is the National Club? Addresses should be issued. Memorials to the Queen prepared. Petitions to Parliament got ready.[101]

The response of the LCM was twofold. At the suggestion of Lord Ashley it organized a special outreach to Roman Catholics in Bermondsey[102] and eventually established a Protestant Aggression Fund for the employment of agents in strongly Catholic areas.[103] It promoted the view that a united Protestant effort would be most effective in such evangelism:

> A friendly and harmonious combination of the members of different Protestant Churches is the best vantage ground from which Popery can be assailed—nay, forms of itself one of the most effective weapons that can be directed against it.[104]

Protestant disunity had been held up to ridicule by the Romanists in vindication of their claims of ecclesiastical superiority; Protestants must unite to evangelize Catholics effectively.

In another calculated response to "Papal Aggression" the LCM prepared an in-depth study of the City of Westminster, an area that had been of special interest since its formation.[105] The study was designed to stimulate evangelical concern for the locale for which the Cardinal had professed a special pastoral concern. The report on Westminster revealed the depths of Anglican disunity. City Mission workers had encountered some opposition to their efforts from Roman Catholics in the late 1830s, but in December 1850 the LCM confessed that its workers had experienced more difficulty from Tractarian opposition in the districts than from Catholics.[106] The LCM had been willing to counter Tractarian tactics with confrontation: one of its agents stationed himself outside of St. Barnabas, Pimlico, after a service and distributed anti-Tractarian and anti-Catholic tracts to the worshipers as they left.[107]

The evangelical efforts of the LCM were being thwarted in Westminster by Tractarian and Roman Catholic opposition. The LCM acknowledged in its report that while it would "gladly have kept back a reference to such a subject, except in a general manner, as we have done for years past,"[108] it now felt it necessary to expose the fact that "the professedly Protestant teaching which prevails in Westminster Proper . . . is essentially Romish in itself."[109] Nonconformist efforts to work in the area were frustrated by the effective exclusion of Dissenters from obtaining property to purchase or rent by the Dean and Chapter of Westminster Abbey, which owned a large portion of the land and which had inserted in rental agreements a clause prohibiting the lease of the same to Dissenters.[110] In the view of the mission, the Tractarians were paving the way for Roman advances:

> It is, we again repeat, extremely painful to us to refer, as we have done, to the efforts recently made in this part of the Church of England. But when the people are told it is "sin" in them to admit the missionaries; that they will "go headlong to hell" if they attend their meetings, or go to Dissenting chapels; that the doctrine taught by us is "a new-fangled doctrine," and the tracts we distribute, from the Religious Tract Society, wherever found, are burnt, or ordered to be burnt, we trust we shall not be blamed, if only in self-defence, for stating the good which has been effected by an agency so anathematized from day to day.
>
> Having stated these facts, we desire to leave the case of Westminster in the hands of our readers. Shall Cardinal Wiseman have its poor? Shall Popery win them over to its tyranny and follies? Shall semi-Popery in the more seducing garb of Protestantism?[111]

The secession of several of the Westminster clergy to Rome over the next year came as no surprise to the LCM.

In 1845 the attempt had been made to represent the anti-Maynooth campaign as mainly the opposition of Dissenters: the tactic in 1850 used to discount the opposition to "Papal Aggression" was to represent it chiefly as a Churchmen's affair.[112] The *Record* contended that this was a misrepresentation of the case promoted by the *Catholic Standard* and the *Dublin Evening Post*.[113] It did acknowledge that "Mr. Miall and his journal in London, and Mr. Bright and his at Manchester, warmly oppose all participation in the Protestant movement. But they are clearly in a minority, whether we look at the *mind* or at the masses of *Dissent*."[114] In proof of this view it cited the support of a host of Nonconformist leaders[115] and the statements of the *Evangelical Magazine*, the *Patriot*, the *British Banner*, and the *British Quarterly Review*.[116] Regardless of how one assesses the strength of the Dissenting protest, it is clear that the opposition to "Papal Aggression" did bring Anglican Evangelicals to seek the support of orthodox Dissenters. It is important to realize that there was a significant advance in pan-evangelical cooperation resulting from the opposition to "Papal Aggression."

The fact that the *Record* could point to Dr. John Campbell and his *British Banner* for support in the united Protestant crusade was perhaps the most significant new factor. Not only had Campbell ceased attacking the establishment, but he was also now willing to join in the pan-evangelical anti-Catholic coalition that he had shunned in 1845. The volumes of his *Christian Witness* prior to 1850 are remarkable for their relative lack of concern with No Popery when compared with other evangelical periodicals. It would appear that the "Papal Aggression" of 1850 did far more to affect Campbell's attitudes toward Catholicism than the Maynooth controversy. In December 1850 he warned the readers of the *Christian Witness*:

> The recent turn things have taken in relation to Popery will require that the Pens as well as the Pulpits of the Protestant Church, shall perform their part in the great conflict

with the powers of darkness now setting in, to an extent far exceeding anything known in our day, or in the days which immediately preceded it. Protestantism can no longer afford to stand merely on the defensive.[117]

His view of Catholicism involved a more radical critique than that to which most Evangelicals subscribed. According to Campbell, "Popery is a thing by itself; a system of falsehood; it is wholly independent of the grace of God. As the empire of darkness, it requires—it admits of no aids but those which are Satanic."[118]

Campbell's accession was an important boost to the pan-evangelical but non-political anti-Catholicism that had been nurtured in the period between 1845 and 1850 by the Evangelical Alliance and the Reformation Society. The *Record*'s 1847 suggestion that opposition to Catholic advances be handled on separate footings had largely been the method adopted. The Islington Protestant Institute was one such Evangelical society; its membership was strictly limited to Anglicans.[119] E. R. Norman is correct in saying that "There was no attempt at organization [against "Papal Aggression"] on a Protestant basis comparable to the great Central Anti-Maynooth Committee of 1845";[120] however, he fails to note that while there was no organization on the same scale, the Aggression did provoke the formation of the Protestant Alliance in 1851. Deliberately established to counter a Roman Catholic society organized to oppose the Ecclesiastical Titles Bill, the Alliance was pan-evangelical (unlike the Protestant Association) and unabashedly political (unlike the pan-evangelical Reformation Society) with the repeal of the Maynooth Bill as a central object. Interestingly enough, the earl of Roden, a leading member of the committee of the Protestant Alliance formed in 1851,[121] had attempted to form a similar organization with the same name in 1846 under his own chairmanship.[122] Apparently Anglican support had not been forthcoming at that time for a political alliance of Anglicans and Dissenters.

The Protestant Alliance received the unqualified approval of the *Record*[123] and proved itself a forum in which leading Evangelical clergy, who were previously unknown to pan-evangelicalism, warmly advocated the cause.[124] By the mid–1850s its funds had surpassed those of the Protestant Association, and the *Record* recalled that its formation had been a boon to the Church of England at the time,

as it greatly tended to pour oil on the troubled waters of denominational differences. It immediately and visibly mitigated the asperity of those feelings of hostility to the Church, which had arisen out of the Voluntary question, in the heat of which the old [Protestant] Association had been formed and nurtured.[125]

The anti-Maynooth campaign of 1845 had brought about a limited but important level of cooperation among evangelicals and had done much to increase Evangelical concern about the evangelization of the Roman Catholic population in Ireland and in England. The response to "Papal Aggression" in 1850 widened both the breadth of the pan-evangelical coalition against Rome and also the scope of the alliance.

While English evangelicals were responding to the actions of the Roman hierarchy in England, events in Ireland were greatly influencing Evangelical Anglican policy toward the evangelization of Roman Catholics. As discussed above, the Maynooth Grant had been a catalyst to Protestant evangelistic efforts in Ireland. This renewed campaign coincided with the great famine of 1845 to 1848, when Ireland experienced repeated failures of its potato crop. During the calamity, the Protestant clergy of the Irish establishment played important roles both in raising contributions for the relief and in the administration of the relief.[126] These activities brought Catholic charges of "souperism"—"the widely held belief that on the parish level it was the policy of the parson and his family to give relief aid only to those of the hungry people around them who were willing to surrender their traditional faith for a bowl of soup, stirabout or other pottage which would keep them alive."[127] For a time, the traditional loyalty of the Irish Catholic peasantry to the Church of Rome was weakened. The Reverend Alexander Dallas, a fiery English Evangelical who had been active in Ireland since 1843, was convinced by 1846 that Ireland was ready for a second Reformation. His appeal for funds in that year for a more vigorous proselytizing effort in Ireland was remarkably successful, and a committee headed by the duke of Manchester was organized to oversee the effort.[128] In 1849 the new venture was formally established as the Society for Irish Church Missions to Roman Catholics. The new mission very quickly upstaged the three long-established evangelical missions operating in Ireland,[129] and in 1852 its success provoked *The Nation*, an Irish Catholic newspaper, to raise the alarm:

There can no longer be any question that the systematised proselytism has met with an immense success in Connaught and Kerry. It is true that the altars of the Catholic Church have been deserted by thousands born and baptized in the ancient faith of Ireland. Travellers, who have recently visited the counties of Gallway and Mayo, report that the agents of that foul and abominable traffic are every day opening new schools of perversion, and are founding new churches for the accommodation of their purchased congregations. Witnesses more trustworthy than Sir Francis Head, Catholic Irishmen who grieved to behold the spread and success of the apostacy, tell us that the west of Ireland is deserting the ancient fold; and that a class of Protestants, more bigoted and anti-Irish, if possible, than the followers of the old Establishment, is grown up from the recreant peasantry and their children. How it is to be met and counteracted, is the problem. How is it to be arrested? is a solemn question, which priest and layman, which citizen and politician, should seriously consider. For our history tells us that the most persistent and formidable enemies to Catholicity, were the children of the first generation of Irishmen who joined the Established Church. Shall the soupers and tract-distributors accomplish the work which all the force of England for three hundred years, has been unable to effect?[130]

The *Record* delighted in such an admission and defended the establishment of the new organization against evangelicals who felt that the societies already in place were more attuned to the difficult Irish situation. The Irish Society of London, the *Record* maintained, had long been too timid, fearing that an aggressive attempt to evangelize Ireland would precipitate the destruction of the Irish establishment.[131] By the end of 1852 the Society for Irish Church Missions claimed that it had effected the conversion of 30,000 Roman Catholics in the past year, and confessed to being "embarrassed by its own extraordinary success." In support of this the *Record* cited the following:

The columns of the Ultramontane *Nation*, and the moans of the *Tablet* may be appealed to in proof of the hold which the Scriptures of truth are gaining upon the mind and heart of the Irish nation. According to the representations of the *Nation*, this Society is advancing fast towards the accomplishment in a few years, of what the power and persecution of England was unable to effect in nearly as many centuries. This admission, coming from such a source, is a sign of the times, far too significant and important to be neglected.[132]

Although the 1861 religious census of Ireland demonstrated that such Protestant optimism was unfounded, in the early 1850s the claims led Protestant societies to reexamine their efforts to reach the Irish poor in England.[133] By 1853 the Reformation Society had seven lay agents engaged in full-time evangelism to the London poor, men who had been specially trained in "the Controversy."[134] The work of the Reformation Society was deemed by some ultra-Protestants to be inadequate. The apparent susceptibility of the Irish Roman Catholics to the aggressive onslaughts of the Society for Irish Church Missions led James Gordon to propose the formation of a similar society for England. Gordon argued for a strictly Anglican agency to provide specially trained workers and stressed his view that the one million Roman Catholics in Britain were a threat to British society—that each one was in fact a Roman Catholic missionary.[135] In a strongly worded open letter to Gordon, Admiral Vernon Harcourt, the head of the Reformation Society, attacked him for trying a second time to strangle the society that Gordon had helped to found in 1827.[136] Notwithstanding these objections, the Society for English Church Missions to Roman Catholics was established in 1853 and was similar in design to the CP-AS. Aiming to use both lay and clerical agents it rejected the charges leveled against it:

With all the respect due to the Reformation Society for its faithful witness to Protestant and Evangelical truth, it never can, with its present mixed constitution, obtain from the clergy and bishops of the Church of England that amount of co-operation which is absolutely essential for a movement equal to the present crisis of Rome's aggression upon the civil and religious liberties of England.[137]

Unlike the formation of the CP-AS, the establishment of this society was not a deliberate rejection of pan-evangelicalism, but was more designed to enlist the cooperation of Anglicans who would have been unwilling to work with Dissenters in evangelistic efforts. A number of the leading figures in the new society were noted for their involvement in the LCM and other pan-evangelical organizations.[138]

The LCM, impressed with the success of the Irish Church Missions to Roman

Catholics, appealed to Alexander Dallas to help in the training of its agents to deal with Roman Catholics.[139] Special care was taken in the examination of applicants for work as city missionaries with preference being given to Irish Roman Catholic converts to Protestantism. The following is an excerpt from the minutes of the committee of the LCM in March 1851 and is typical of interviews with candidates at that time. It well illustrates the concerns of the Protestant mission:

The Examining Sub. Committee reported that they had examined William M. Hanlow of Douglas. This candidate is a single man & 30 years of age. He is by birth Irish, & was educated for the Romish priesthood—Doubts respecting the peculiar views of Popery came across his mind, & gained strength for 2 years, chiefly from reading the word of God, until at the end of that time he left the Church of Rome. But he considers that it was 2 years subsequent to this before he became a Protestant in spirit as well as in outward profession. This was about 3 years since. He was after that employed as Scripture reader, & master of a ragged school in Liverpool for 9 months, & subsequently for 1 year & 9 months at Douglas as Scripture reader. The Sub. Comm. regard him as a pious man & as well acquainted with the Scriptures. His manners are particularly pleasing, & they consider he will make an useful & acceptable missionary. He is well acquainted with the romish controversy & can speak Irish. But his last engagement has nevertheless been almost entirely among a Protestant population. They recommend that he be sent to the Examiners. The testimonials of Hanlow were then read, after which he was called, examined by the Comm. & on his withdrawal it was agreed that he be sent to the Examiners.[140]

By so selecting their agents, the LCM was able to conduct its crusade for the souls of the Irish poor with men far more suited to the slum dwellers than either the Anglican or Roman Catholic churches could provide. Sheridan Gilley has noted, "The Anglican Establishment was only in degree more foreign to the Celtic immigrant than the Roman Catholic Church in England, which in him confronted a manner of man remote from its experience. Its priests ministered to a devout gentry; they had now to serve a pious proletariat. The faith in England had survived in the country; the Irish flocked to the towns."[141] Not only were many of the LCM's recruits drawn from the Irish scene, but so also was the key weapon in their arsenal. LCM agents were armed with *A Handbook on the Romish Controversy*, a work by a Church of Ireland clergyman that in the second half of the century became the standard primer in the evangelization of Roman Catholics.[142]

It would appear that this Evangelical concern to evangelize the Irish poor in England was not greatly affected by fears of political insurrection among them. Much of the recent academic discussion of Victorian anti-Catholicism has centered on the growth of anti-Roman Catholic sentiment and the perceived political threat posed by the increasing numbers of Irish immigrants in England, as the Irish influx reached the proportions of a flood in the late 1840s during the Irish potato famine.[143] Gilley has commented:

The Irish in England do not significantly figure in the enormous specifically religious literature of Victorian anti-Catholicism. . . . No Popery polemicists searching the sins of the Scarlet Woman sought their materials in realms remote in time and place, in medieval Spain and the South Seas, rather than in the lean and ragged Irish beggar at their doors. There, in the Irish beggar, was proof in their own terms, of the blessings of the Reformation; there but for Henry VIII went they.[144]

Gilley does acknowledge that Scottish Calvinist No Popery was more concerned with the Irish presence than English No Popery, as the Irish influx into Scotland was proportionately greater than that into England.[145] He has also observed that "the fiercest denunciations of the Irish in England were penned by Scotsmen,"[146] notably the Reverend J. A. Wylie,[147] Catherine Sinclair, Alexander Haldane, Arthur Kinnaird, and John Cumming.[148]

Gilley's view would appear to be corroborated by further research. Only a few of the most extreme Protestants argued that the Irish were a serious political threat, candidates to replace the "socialists" and Chartists as the evangelicals' scapegoat. When Hugh McNeile (an Irishman) argued in his 1846 *Letter to Lord John Russell* that English Protestants had reason to fear a great persecution by Catholics, the *Churchman's Monthly Review* dismissed the suggestion and asked: "Now, can we wonder that worldly politicians should smile in utter disbelief and scorn, when we must admit the existence of a sort of incredulity in our own minds?" When John Cumming (a Scot) used the same sort of scare tactics at the LCM annual meeting in 1853, Baptist Noel put the view of the evangelical mainstream:

I do not, as my friend Dr. Cumming does, believe that they are so misled by their priests as to possess the most traitorous intentions, or that their aspirations are so wolfish that they would wish to plant a dagger in all our hearts. . . . It is neither by a fear of their force nor a fear of their progress—for they make next to none among the London population—they have hardly gained a convert among the lower classes.[149]

Similarly the *Churchman's Monthly Review*, while discounting Catholic political strength in England, acknowledged that Catholicism must be opposed: "We do not forget that Rome is despotic, cruel, and persecuting. She never was, and never will be, otherwise."[150]

Whatever their estimate of immediate Catholic political designs, Evangelicals were united in the view that the Irish poor, both in Ireland and in England, constituted Rome's soft "underbelly" and that evangelism of them was peculiarly and providentially adapted to the thwarting of Roman advances. A generalized fear of Catholicism combined with a perception of Roman weakness were two factors that occupied John Henry Newman's concern in his attempt to demonstrate the "Logical Inconsistency of the Protestant View" in 1851: "They coerce us while they can, lest they should not dare to coerce, when another twenty years has passed over our heads. 'Hit him, he's down!' this is the cry of the Ministry, the country gentlemen, the Establishment and Exeter Hall."[151]

THE DECLINE OF ANTI-CATHOLICISM AS A FACTOR IN EVANGELISM

It would appear, however, that while anti-Catholicism played a major role in opening up cooperation between Anglicans and Dissenters, it did not prove to be a sustaining motive for evangelistic efforts in the long term. The missions to Catholics in London were perhaps at the height of their effectiveness in 1853–1854 under the direction of Dr. Armstrong in Bermondsey,[152] but by 1857 want of funds was forcing the LCM to cut back its support, and in the following year the Society for English Church Missions to Roman Catholics failed.[153]

In part this decline was due to the difficulty of maintaining public interest in the political struggle. The initial storm over Wiseman's appointment and letter and the Protestant glee at the publication of an equally incautious letter from Lord John Russell to the bishop of Durham gave way to a protracted squabble over the Ecclesiastical Titles Bill, which sought to prohibit Roman Catholic use of the newly designated titles.[154] The *Record*, heartened by Russell's anti-Catholic and anti-Tractarian outburst, at first welcomed the bill, but as it was successively modified, the paper came to view the measure as "utterly contemptible."[155] Once the bill became law, it had little effect on the Catholic hierarchy and remained unenforced by the government.[156] By 1852 the *Christian Observer* was expressing doubts as to the effectiveness of evangelical attempts to obtain pledges from parliamentary candidates to vote against Maynooth and even wondered if Catholic priests might not receive a more repugnant education elsewhere, if the Irish college did not exist.[157] The *Record* was upset by such suggestions and concluded that the *Observer* was losing heart in the struggle simply because of the irritation caused by the campaign.[158] Despite evangelical success in electing members nominally pledged to oppose Maynooth, in 1853 the *Record* had to acknowledge that the promises had been more easily secured than the votes.[159]

Also contributing to the wane of political anti-Catholicism in the early 1850s was the awareness on the part of Evangelicals that their numerical strength in the House of Commons was declining. In 1850 the *Record* lamented the weakness of the Evangelical presence and looked forward with trepidation to the retirement of Sir Robert Inglis and the succession of Lord Ashley to his father's title.[160] The *Christian Observer* confirmed that the elections of 1852 had brought the very unhappy result that "whilst earnest religion has lost some few friends in the House of Commons, it has gained very few."[161] The political strength of the Evangelicals had been diminished by its paucity of legislators. In addition, the No Popery cause had not found a home in the Derby administration; indeed, the *Record* saw fit to warn the new government that it should not fulfill Tractarian hopes by ignoring the Evangelical party, as such a policy would not only anger staunchly conservative Evangelicals, but would also alienate sympathetic evangelical Dissenters.[162] Nor did it seem that the Evangelicals would turn to the Liberals, for despite Lord John Russell's outburst of anti-Catholic and anti-

Tractarian sentiment, his attitude "was really inconsistent with the principles of civil and religious liberty which the party was pledged to uphold."[163]

While these political factors contributed to the decline of political anti-Catholicism, its death knell was the outbreak of the Crimean War in 1854. The *Record* was only too well aware of what was happening. As early as January 1, 1855, it foresaw that the struggle in the Crimea would divert interest and sympathy away from the spiritual warfare being waged in Ireland:

> During several years past it was easy to see, by the tone of certain Irish newspapers, which are under the influence of the priests, that there was nothing more desired by the Pope's black-coated army in Ireland, than a WAR. While things remained quiet, and especially while the memory of the WISEMAN aggression was yet fresh, they could gain scarcely any ground. The rapid emigration of the peasantry weakened them; the success of the Irish Church Missions alarmed them; and, on looking round for some new resources, they saw nothing as likely to help them as a good stirring war.

The implications of Britain's alliance with Catholic France and the employment of Irish soldiers were not lost on the paper:

> If you send 10,000 Irish Romanists to fight England's battles, it is difficult to say that they shall not have some chaplains of their own creed, paid by the Government. Then a bevy of nuns and sisters of charity are sent out to the hospitals, and taught to write home pious letters, which are read from Protestant pulpits and praised by Protestant papers. Next, it is urged, that it is "ill-timed" to breathe a word against Popery while we are in alliance with a Roman Catholic Emperor, who sends out to our aid 100,000 Roman Catholic soldiers. Some Protestants propose to give up the commemoration of the Gun-powder Plot. The same sort of tolerance, silence, and mutual goodwill is inculcated on all sides, till it begins to be suggested, that all the ancient fear and dread of Popery ought to be given up, and everything Protestant be abandoned, or at least kept out of sight.[164]

The *Record*'s alarm was well founded. In the debate to repeal the Maynooth Grant in May 1855, one M.P. argued that the war made repeal unwise: " 'the worst enemies of England, even the Czar himself,' would only be pleased with a measure which would envenom Ireland and shake the loyalty of numerous Catholic troops."[165] Not only did the war contribute significantly to the waning of national interest in political anti-Catholicism, but it also slowed the giving to evangelistic efforts aimed at Roman Catholics.[166] As will be discussed below, evangelicals began to funnel funds into special evangelistic concerns related to the Crimean War (1854–1856) and then to the Indian Uprising (1857).[167]

In February 1856 the *Record* recognized that national interest in political anti-Catholicism was declining and called for the amalgamation of the Protestant Alliance and the Protestant Association, as both societies were experiencing financial difficulties, and especially in view of the fact that the latter was saddled with a large debt.[168] Such gloomy forecasts were a bit premature. The campaign to repeal the Maynooth Grant almost succeeded in Parliament three months later, but this was due more to the growth of Voluntarist strength than growth of No Popery's. The measure's sponsor bungled the affair, and when attempts were made to revive the effort in 1857, the campaign had lost its momentum.[169] These political factors undercut the appeal of anti-Catholicism and the support for evangelistic efforts to Roman Catholics. The poor economic climate of the mid–1850s undoubtedly also contributed to the decline. The diminishing effectiveness of such evangelistic efforts to Roman Catholics was also undoubtedly a factor, especially in face of the effective countermeasures taken by the Catholic hierarchy to prevent further Protestant inroads.[170] Sheridan Gilley has commented that "the Evangelicals forced the Roman Church to make proper spiritual provision for their poor and even armed it for the encounter"[171] while acknowledging that the Catholic response also "had purely Catholic and Ultramontane sources in the romantic and medieval ideas of monastic charity and holy poverty—and in the holy poverty of the Irish poor."[172]

The years 1846 to the early 1850s thus witnessed a major advance for pan-evangelicalism with positions being modified on both sides of the denominational divide. The failure of the Gorham case to result in a major schism contributed to Evangelical self-confidence and robbed Voluntaries of another issue with which they could taunt the Evangelicals. John Campbell's defection from the ranks of Voluntaryism also served to calm the waters of denominational strife. The pan-evangelical, anti–Roman Catholic coalition formed in 1845 had largely disintegrated by the 1847 elections, but the "Papal Aggression" of 1850 provided the opportunity for another pan-evangelical alliance against Rome. The furor that the "Aggression" aroused did much to stimulate Evangelical concern for the Irish poor in Ireland and in England and influenced the policies and actions of pan-evangelical societies like the LCM; however, the furor was short-lived and by the mid–1850s, evangelicals were turning their attention to devising new methods for use in fields other than the evangelization of Roman Catholics.

9

Specialization in Evangelism

The decade of the 1850s witnessed a great increase in specialized forms of evangelism designed to penetrate social, economic, occupational, and ethnic groupings. As the Church of England was much slower to adapt to social changes, these new ventures were pioneered by the innovating and more flexible pan-evangelical societies.

There are several factors that contributed to this penchant for specialization during the 1850s. One important factor was the publication of a national census of religious worship. Horace Mann, the registrar general, took responsibility for gathering and interpreting the statistics on religious worship in 1851. His report, which was not published until 1853, caused considerable distress among Anglicans, as it revealed that "about 40 per cent of churchgoers in England and over 75 per cent in Wales attended Nonconformist churches, while in Scotland about 60 per cent of Protestant worshippers attended the Free Church or Dissenting churches."[1] Dissenters were thus greatly heartened by the report, and weight was added to disestablishment.

The Victorian public was perhaps even more surprised by the fact that the survey revealed that only 7.26 million of the 17.92 million inhabitants of England and Wales had attended religious worship on the Sunday of the census.[2] The findings again focused evangelical attention on evangelism and on the need for interdenominational cooperation to win the working poor to the fold in much the same way as Baptist Noel's *State of the Metropolis* had done in 1835. The *Record*'s editor commented in September of 1854:

The late Census has done something towards opening the eyes of many to our true condition. It is well known that Protestant missionaries to the heathen are commonly more united than the Christian Churches or sects whose names they bear. The discovery, in plain numbers, of the heathenism at home has had one benefit, we think, in deepening the same spirit among British Christians. The instinctive thirst for closer union between pious Evangelical Churchmen and sound orthodox Dissenters, we are disposed to believe, was never so strong, since the time of the Revolution, as at the present hour. What steps can be taken to profit by this improved spirit, is a hard problem.[3]

The report had demonstrated conclusively that the church-building efforts had provided a great deal more accommodation for the poor. It was clear, however, that the poor were not taking advantage of the seats available, thus manifesting the folly of some of the earlier assumptions governing church extension.[4] The London City Mission (LCM) gave special prominence to the statistics contained in the census report and especially emphasized Mann's advocacy of lay agency.[5]

Mann's findings served to undermine confidence in the effectiveness of the traditional parochial system.[6] Lord Ashley, who in 1849 had had enough faith in it to procure for himself a place on the Parochial Subdivision Committee, had abandoned that confidence by the mid–1850s.[7] John Cale Miller, the leading Birmingham Evangelical, expressed the frustration felt by many. Although he acknowledged that he felt that the parochial system was fine on paper, it did not work in practice: "I find that to a very great extent the parochial system is absolutely non-existent. . . . We find our parishes so overgrown, that as to our talking of being shepherds of the people, it is a perfect absurdity. It is a theory; it is not a reality."[8] Miller acknowledged that he had been criticized for working with the LCM because it was a society that ignored ecclesiastical order, but he adopted a Wesleyan rather than a Simeonite attitude to the issue.[9] Rather than adhere strictly to the Anglican parochial system, many Evangelicals were preferring the comprehensive district system of the LCM, which was in effect, a pan-evangelical alternative to the traditional system and whose units were determined and directed by a lay committee rather than by ecclesiastical legislation and episcopal supervision.

In 1855 an open clash between Hugh Stowell, the Evangelical pope of Manchester, and Tractarian J.E.N. Molesworth highlighted Evangelical irregularity.[10] Stowell had officiated with Dissenting ministers at a YMCA meeting in Molesworth's parish without the vicar's permission. When the bishop of Manchester disavowed any authority to interfere in the matter, Molesworth complained to the *Guardian*.[11] The *Record*, with its characteristically acid tongue, dismissed the clergyman as a "little spiritual autocrat" who censured Evangelicals for their view that "they should sacrifice etiquette to the salvation of souls."[12]

The blurring of parochial boundaries was further abetted by the increasing mobility of operatives. A speaker at an 1853 clerical conference suggested that it was "necessary to deal with them as a distinct element in the social system."[13] One of the ways suggested for dealing with occupational groupings was "employee evangelism" whereby Evangelical employees were urged to take a benevolent interest in the spiritual state of their workers and to draw upon the help of the YMCA or the Church of England Young Men's Society in furthering this work.[14]

SPECIALIZED EVANGELISM

The employment of specialized forms of evangelism was not something new to the LCM, but the development of the size and level of sophistication of these forms of ministry is especially noticeable during the 1850s. By the end of the decade they accounted for a sizeable proportion of the society's funds and missionaries.[15] These agents can be divided into three different categories: workers among special ethnic or religious groups, missionaries to specific locations, and agents assigned to minister to occupational groupings. In 1858, 29 of the LCM's 350 paid agents worked in specialized areas:[16]

Agents to Ethnic and Religious Groups		Agents to Occupational Groups		Agents to Specific Locations	
Welsh	2	Soldiers	3	Public houses and coffee	
Asiatics	1	Cabmen	3	shops	2
Jews	1	Sailors	1	Homes of pensioners	2
Italians	1	Fire brigade workers	1	Hospitals	3
Germans	1	Police	2	Workhouses	1
Gypsies	1	Dock workers	2	Night houses	1
Total	7	Prostitutes	1	Total	9
		Total	13		

The *LCM Magazine* was employed in detailing the physical and social conditions of the different groups and in describing the spiritual conditions of each, effectively appealing to the consciences of Christians who had particular interests in any one group. Undoubtedly this eager solicitation of support by the LCM served to forestall the creation of smaller, less efficient societies that would have arisen to fill the gap. In at least one case the LCM took over the direction of a floundering evangelical society that was too small to continue in an effective manner the ministry that it had undertaken.[17]

Specialized ministries were especially needed if the evangelicals were to have any impact upon the large number of non-English-speaking immigrants in the capital. London's commercial and political importance as the focal point of the British Empire in the nineteenth century attracted many varied ethnic groups and the LCM played on the Victorian fascination with things foreign in its promotion of the society's work amongst these groups. Its magazine devoted whole issues to in-depth studies of the location, number, occupations, and religious habits of different minorities.[18] Besides their great concern for Irish Catholics in London, there was a particular concern for Welsh Protestants,[19] which stemmed in part from their tendency to abandon church going once they had emigrated to the metropolis.[20] The growing presence of immigrants from the Far East led the mission to appoint an agent in 1857 who was willing to learn "Hindoostanee" as the majority of his constituency appear to have been Muslims from India.[21]

The fact that the LCM had only one full-time agent engaged in Jewish evangelism hardly begins to reflect the peculiar concern that Anglican Evangelicals themselves felt for this group. Millenarianism had affected the urgency of Evangelical concern for foreign missions[22] and sharpened Evangelical anti-Catholicism,[23] but its influence over Evangelical activity was probably of greater importance when it came to the Jews. A firmly established plank of the millenarian creed was the restoration of the Jews to the land of Palestine,[24] a view which was maintained even by Charles Simeon.[25] Faber had argued that the Jews would be converted en masse to the Christian faith and would then in turn be the agents for the conversion of Gentiles; thus the conversion of the Jews was the key to world evangelization.[26]

Lord Ashley's effort in 1841 to secure the establishment of a bishopric in Jerusalem to serve Anglicans and German Protestants in the Middle East was closely linked with his millenarian views. Convinced that the British should protect the Jews in Palestine, he saw the bishopric as the first step toward their eventual return to the Middle East. Ashley viewed a letter by Palmerston to the Ottoman ruler urging "protection and encouragement" of the Jews, as "a prelude to the Antitype of the decree of Cyrus" (the Persian king who delivered the Jews from exile in Babylon—see Isaiah 45:1).[27] Of Palmerston's role in the Jerusalem bishopric Ashley recorded in his diary:

Palmerston has already been chosen by God to be an instrument of good to His ancient people; to do homage as it were to their inheritance, and to recognise their rights without believing in their destiny. And it seems he will yet do more. But though the motive be kind, it is not sound. I am forced to argue politically, financially, commercially; these considerations strike him home; but he weeps not like his Master over Jerusalem, nor prays that now, at last, she may put on her beautiful garments.[28]

Even Chevalier Bunsen, the evangelical German diplomat who acted on behalf of the king of Prussia in the matter of the joint Anglican–Lutheran bishopric, had Christian–Zionist motives. After an interview with Palmerston he recorded in his diary: "So the beginning is made, please God, for the restoration of Israel."[29] The leading influence on Lord Ashley in these matters was Edward Bickersteth, the prominent millenarian, who was his close friend and religious advisor.

Anglican enthusiasm for the proselytizing of Jews was not limited to the Evangelicals. Bishop Blomfield strongly supported the Jerusalem bishopric and "never tired of stressing the importance of preaching the Gospel to the Jews."[30] In 1843 one of his sermons in this regard was published under the title *God's Ancient People Not Cast Away*. Anglicans were far more enamored with millenarianism than were Dissenters, and this would seem to be a major reason why it was they who set the pattern in Jewish missions and Jewish evangelism in

Victorian Britain. The London Society for Promoting Christianity amongst the Jews (LSPCJ) had begun as an interdenominational agency in 1808 but had come under exclusive Anglican control by 1815. The enormous importance of this Anglican mission to Jews is attested to by the annual receipts of the LSPCJ, which made it one of the largest of the Evangelical societies, surpassing both the LCM and the CP-AS in revenue each year.[31] Nonconformists had no comparable organization. Given this perspective on Jewish evangelism, the LCM's single missionary to Jewish inhabitants of London appears to be a small effort indeed, but the great bulk of this sort of work was carried on by the LSPCJ itself.

This fascination with the Jews did have an effect on the approach that the city missionaries were urged to take in their evangelism. Edward Bickersteth personally exhorted the LCM workers to deal gently with the Jews on their districts:

> You will have to reason, also, with the Jews—that most interesting portion of the community. Treat the Jew tenderly; recollect he is the son of Abraham. Do not attack Leviticus, in order to exalt the Gospel; make Levi the precursor of Jesus, and Leviticus the pedestal for the lamp of the Gospel. Show that you love Aaron's rod, but that its bud has bloomed, and it has unfolded itself in the rose of Sharon.[32]

Such gentle but firm persuasion was used by Joseph Oppenheimer in his work as a city missionary in St. Giles (see chapter 6).

The second area of specialized ministry, the appointing of agents to visit locations where the poor congregated, demonstrates the flexibility of the mission's structure. It was able both to concentrate its efforts in domestic visitation and to approach the poor in places where their work would not distract them from listening to the agents: public houses, coffee shops (see Illustration 15), hospitals, work houses, common lodging houses, homes for pensioners, and night houses. Part of the reason for this approach stemmed from the concern that the workers involved in domestic visitation did not have sufficient access to men who were absent from their abodes during most hours of the agents' visitation.

The third strategy adopted, that of attempting to evangelize specific occupational groupings, was in part a response to the new conditions of industrial society. Instead of urging employers to take on the task of evangelizing their employees themselves, the LCM appealed to wealthy manufacturers for their support so that the LCM could evangelize both their workers and the district surrounding the place of employment. Perhaps the most successful at this was the Spitalfields and Bethnal Green auxiliary of the LCM which by 1850 was receiving over £1,000 annually from wealthy capitalists, including funds from evangelical brewers and silk manufacturers.[33]

The LCM's concern for the Metropolitan and City police forces testifies to the long-standing evangelical regard for and the significant evangelical presence within those institutions. Almost from the commencement of the Metropolitan

Illustration 15
The Coffee House

This is the sort of establishment frequented by City Mission workers charged with evangelizing the coffee houses. From Gustave Doré and Blanchard Jerrold, *London*, London, 1872, p. 141.

force the mission had taken a special interest in it,[34] and by 1858 three agents were involved in full-time work among the two forces.[35] Much of this concern for ministry to the police stemmed from the LCM's estimate of the importance of the establishment of the police forces "in the repression of crime in the metropolis, and in the social and moral well-being of our great city"[36] and from the much greater receptivity among the police to the religious ministrations of the LCM than among other social and occupational groupings.[37]

A distinct, but related concern, was evangelical interest in the British military, the history of which goes back at least to the Gordon riots in London in 1780. At that time the "highly immoral state of the soldiery" encamped in Hyde Park provoked evangelicals into organizing the Naval and Military Bible Society which circulated Bibles and Testaments among the armed forces.[38] The interdenominational nature of the society led some to fret that it was quietly promoting the "dreaded scourge" of Methodism among the troops. Fears about the political loyalty of the Methodists were particularly strong in upper-class circles at the turn of the nineteenth century.[39] In the 1820s attempts by the duke of York (in league with Archbishop Manners Sutton) to thwart the society's work were successfully opposed by a delegation to the duke that included Lord Rocksavage (later the marquess of Cholmondeley) and Captain James E. Gordon.[40] Such antievangelical sentiments were not uncommon in the military. Even the duke of Wellington, in a letter to the lord chancellor in 1820, requested special crown patronage for an army chaplain whose chief qualification was the following:

I will not detain your Lordship by enumerating his services; but I must say this for him, that, by his admirable conduct and good sense, I was enabled more than once to get the better of Methodism which had appeared among the soldiers, and once among the officers.[41]

The clergyman in question was soon rewarded with a comfortable crown appointment.[42]

This strident hostility toward evangelicalism in the military is all the more remarkable when one appreciates the dramatic changes that occurred later in the century in the attitudes of British society toward the army, and of the army toward evangelicalism. Olive Anderson has observed:

The gap between the "thin red 'eroes" of the end of the nineteenth century and the "brutal and licentious soldiery" of earlier generations is far too wide to be satisfactorily bridged by allusions to a growing admiration of Prussianism and the effects of prolonged non-involvement in European wars, or by discussions of the influence of Carlyle and Kingsley and the mid-Victorian cult of force.[43]

Much of the change, in her view, is attributable to the "novel development of missionary work among the troops during the [Crimean] War, and the encouraging interpretation which many letters and reports from the expeditionary force could be made to bear, which accustomed them to the idea that soldiers too had souls to be saved and would repay spiritual attentions."[44]

While the widespread popularity of such work may have been novel, the work itself was not. The establishment of a more decidedly evangelistic society than the Naval and Military Bible Society was effected in 1830. The pan-evangelical Soldiers' Friend Society was particularly concerned with ministering to the 4,000 household troops stationed in London. For a time it maintained a Soldier's Chapel in Westminster, but employed only one or two Scripture readers, as it suffered from a chronic lack of funds.[45] The LCM appointed its first agent to work with soldiers in 1849 and within four years had four men working among the troops and their families. These agents received almost all their support from their military constituency.[46] By the early 1850s the LCM's efforts had surpassed the accomplishments of the Soldiers' Friend Society in regard to the military.

Evangelicals had also developed societies specifically concerned with the British navy. The British and Foreign Seamen and Soldiers' Friend Society, begun in 1813, was primarily concerned with ministry to sailors, both military and nonmilitary. By 1830 it acknowledged that it was but one of seven societies established to promote religious instruction among sailors.[47] Its main support appears to have come from Dissenters. This society apparently united with a newly formed society in 1833 which had a similar title, the British and Foreign Sailors' Society. Organized on a pan-evangelical basis, it was able to attract the support of important Anglican laymen who had significant interests in shipping.[48] Two small Anglican societies operated to relieve the suffering of seamen and to convert them to Christianity, while a floating church was outfitted to attract sailors to worship in London's harbor by yet another Anglican society. (See Illustration 16.) The latter organization appears to have been superseded in 1844 by the Thames Church Mission, which sought to use a more comprehensive, aggressive form of evangelism with sailors and mariners, although again the pattern seems to have been one adopted from the example of Dissenters. The activities of no less than five rear admirals[49] and two admirals[50] on behalf of such evangelical societies in the 1840s and 1850s undoubtedly did much to promote interest in such missions. The fact that these senior naval officers were all Anglicans seems to have given Churchmen a decided advantage in soliciting support for this sort of ministry; however, the backing given to the LCM by Rear Admirals Harcourt, Waldegrave, and Parry aided the pan-evangelical cause in this sphere also. Indeed support for a pan-evangelical approach to naval missions continued a tradition in which Lord Gambier, an earlier admiral of the fleet, had participated.[51]

Evangelical sympathy with and admiration for the military grew steadily from the early 1840s. A number of factors were at work. Perhaps most important was the army's role in keeping the empire in good order, so that foreign mission work might continue apace, for such work was the primary task that God in his providence had entrusted to Britain. Protection of Protestant missions from pagan attack and from Popish aggression was expected. Thus the takeover of Tahiti

Illustration 16
Interior of the Sailor's Floating Church

by French forces in 1843 and their treatment of Queen Pomare, a convert of English missionaries, aroused a storm of protest in Britain. The subsequent arrest and imprisonment of an English missionary, Pritchard, further aggravated the situation and brought forth calls from evangelicals for armed British intervention, thus eliciting *Punch*'s sarcasm. (See Illustration 17.) In 1843 Lord Ashley was upset with Lord Aberdeen (the foreign minister) for his handling of the case ("a worthy man, but very timid and very slow. . . . a few words . . . would have saved the island from the French and upheld Protestant religion.")[52] In 1844, following a French apology (but not a withdrawal) he was angry with British acquiesence in the situation:

Grief and indignation cannot go beyond what I feel against the French aggressions in Tahiti. A peaceable and helpless people . . . are subjugated by savages and powerful Europeans, and inundated with bloodshed, devastation, profligacy, and crime. God gave the regeneration of this island to our people as a triumph of the Cross; and so it was a thing without parallel in the history of the Gospel. The missionaries made it Christian; they made it English in laws and Constitution. It had, by God's blessing, under their administration, everything but power and commerce. But, failing these, it has obtained no sympathies, and in the hour of danger, perhaps of extinction, finds not a single friend. . . . What a disgusting and cowardly attitude for England, thus to stand by and raise not a hand in defence of this merciful gift of Providence![53]

The Tahiti incident saw the evangelicals urging the British government to use the military to protect Protestant missions from Roman Catholic aggression. Lord Ashley was willing to make himself unpopular for his criticism of other aspects of British army activity, notably his condemnations of British actions in the Scinde in 1844.[54]

A second factor influencing evangelical attitudes to the army was their hope that they could commend their religious views to military leaders. While they might not convert them, they might at least lessen their hostility toward evangelicalism and thereby allow more effective evangelization to occur within the military establishment. In 1839 Rear Admiral Sir Jahleel Brenton's *The Hope of the Navy; or the True Source of Discipline and Efficiency* . . . argued in this vein.[55] Evangelicals not only made good soldiers and sailors, they made the best ones. Lord Robert Grosvenor used the same line of argument in public, reasoning that army discipline was promoted by "the principle that obedience should not be the result of the fear of punishment, but should spring from a sentiment of Christian duty."[56] By the late 1850s the theme of the suitability of evangelicalism to the military profession was often repeated: "Again and again Gough's order in an emergency during the Burmese campaign of 1825 was quoted with effect: 'Turn out the saints! Havelock never blunders and his men are never drunk!', and the motto, 'He who fears God most, fears men least' was repeated almost as often."[57]

A third consideration aiding the saints' assault on the British military was the support given by leading evangelical personalities. Fox Maule, a Scottish Liberal

Illustration 17
Evangelical Militarism

Punch mocks evangelical calls for British military intervention in Tahiti in 1844. The evangelicals were anxious to protect already established Protestant missions. *Punch* 7 (1844):105.

M.P. and an outspoken evangelical, was briefly secretary of war in 1846 and again occupied the same post from 1855–1858, during both the Crimean War and the Indian Uprising.[58] Along with the aforementioned admirals (including the explorer, Sir Edward Parry), Fox Maule was a willing candidate for religious propaganda. Such luminaries encouraged the lesser lights in the firmament to faithfulness and nursed the hope that the British military might be transformed from a sink of iniquity into a mighty pillar of Zion.

The most common means of changing popular views, however, was not through public meetings patronized by leading military figures. Too limited in scope, these could only be expected to enthuse the converted. The increasing number of biographies of evangelical military figures in the 1840s attests to the great faith the evangelicals placed in literature as a means of social and moral improvement.[59] The outbreak of the Crimean War in 1854 proved to be a stimulus to evangelical interest in the military and occasioned a significant change in both public attitudes toward religion in the army and of military attitudes toward religion. With the outbreak of hostilities, statements of unabashed militarism were made to the Soldiers' Friend Society by its clerical president, Dr. William March, honorary canon of Worcester Cathedral:

It had been supposed that religion was unsuited to a military life. He could never admit that, when he thought of the military men who feared God under the Old Testament dispensation or of the military men who had believed in Christ under the New Testament dispensation. No; religion made no cowards. (Cheers.) [Christians] . . . could look death in the face, because they believed in a Saviour who had purchased for them eternal life. It was delightful to be able to speak in such terms of men in the ranks as well as officers. One of the wounded privates was reported to have said to a bystander, "I have committed my soul to Jesus, and the only anxiety I now have is not to offend him." This was the Gospel, the pure Gospel, as described in the sacred Scriptures.[60]

In part, this vociferous defense of the military can be explained as a reaction to the publication of a pacifist statement by a group of evangelical Quakers, which the *Record* had felt necessary to refute earlier in the same year.[61]

Much more effective than Dr. Marsh's personal advocacy of the cause was the exceptional impact that a book written by his daughter was to have on the British public. Catherine Marsh's *Memorial of Captain Hedley Vicars, 97th Regiment* combined evangelical doctrine with a tale about military heroism in a Crimean setting. Standing squarely in the Puritan tradition of hagiography which nineteenth-century Anglican Evangelicals had sought to continue, *Hedley Vicars* stressed both a holy life, and of course, a happy death.[62] The work was indeed a "rare thing, a piece of religious propaganda sufficiently fresh and contemporary in form, and indirect in approach to achieve a wide and prolonged circulation" amounting "to something of a new departure in religious biography."[63] It sold "78,000 copies in its year of publication, compared with the 35,000 copies of *Bleak House*, sold between 1852 and 1853"[64] making Miss Marsh the "female

Dickens" of the evangelical world.[65] Within four years it had been translated into French, Italian, and German and underwent its last edition in 1916.[66]

As a result of its remarkable popularity, the book became "a classic 'textbook of the religious war party' in precisely the way the Peace Society had feared when it was first published."[67] Although *Hedley Vicars* was originally intended as an evangelistic tool, it popularized the somewhat novel idea that Christian zeal was not incompatible with good soldiering and the view that the British Army could and should be Christianized.[68] Lord Panmure (Fox Maule), still the secretary of war, spoke to a public meeting on the subject "Religion in the Army" in November, 1856 and argued that Catherine Marsh's biography of Vicars had convinced the British nation that "a man need not be a bad soldier because he is a good Christian. (Loud cheers). . . . The army is no longer that loose profession which it once was."[69]

The unparalleled identification of the British public with the hardships of the troops in the Crimea and the idealized notions for which they were fighting produced an immense emotional appeal that Catherine Marsh successfully exploited.[70] This same sort of emotional appeal was rekindled in the Indian Uprising of 1857 when British troops were popularly cast in the role of defenders of civilizing and Christianizing influences in the subcontinent. The suddenness and the ferocity of the revolt and the fact that British women and children had been the objects of attack aroused the nation to fury. Among many evangelicals these feelings were intensified "by their conviction that the Uprising was in reality a challenge to Christianity itself, which had been allowed as a divine punishment for official compromise with false religions."[71] In opposing the British army, the rebels were in effect defying Omnipotence to arms. Unwavering support for British control of India was expressed by the *Record* on the grounds that "India, as we firmly believe, has been given in a way the most unprecedented, [sic] by the God of Providence, to Britain in trust for the accomplishment of a glorious mission," which entailed the evangelization and civilizing of the subcontinent.[72] The paper was confident that "as the accomplishment of the designs of Providence is sure, until the end be nearer its culmination, our tenure of India is secure."[73] The *Record* tempered its support for the military suppression of the revolt by decrying the calls made in the British press for acts of vengeance against the Indian population.[74]

While the Uprising enhanced the careers of a number of military figures, it only produced one major national hero: Major-General Sir Henry Havelock, who died in the relief of Lucknow. Although from a middle-class background and long odious to his fellow officers because of his zealous evangelicalism, in the last six weeks of his life Havelock was transformed from a virtually unknown lieutenant into a national hero because he had "decisively castigated the rebels."[75] Posthumously promoted and knighted, it was Havelock's self-discipline and fearlessness that appealed to many as "his death occurred at a time when the educated classes were rapidly becoming enthusiastic about mid-seventeenth century puritanism, and about Cromwell and the Ironsides in particular. . . . In the 1850s it became increasingly common to praise 'true old Puritan conduct' while condemning 'Puritanic religion.' "[76] Much of this change was due to the writings of Carlyle.

Havelock himself was a Baptist, but one of notable ecumenical views, having helped establish the West Indian branch of the Evangelical Alliance, of which he became vice president.[77] His idolization by the British press and his canonization by British evangelicalism provided his biographers with a public hungry for works in the *Hedley Vicars* tradition. It also provided new enthusiasm for the army as a mission field. The organization that most benefited from this religious focus upon the military during the 1850s was the Soldiers' Friend Society which in 1856 was reorganized as the Soldiers' Friend and Scripture-readers' Society. In that year it had twenty-seven full-time agents at work among British troops, both at home and abroad.[78] Its restructuring enabled it to make more effective use of its enormously increased resources. Although it remained nondenominational, its governing body had a strong contingent of army officers, three-quarters of whom were Anglicans. This factor, along with the support of the chaplain-general of the day, G. R. Gleig, the care taken in selecting the Scripture-readers, and the requirement that its workers labor under the direction of the local chaplains or clergy officiating to the troops made the society more acceptable to military authorities.[79] Wesleyan Methodist concern for the military grew rapidly following the Crimean War with the Connexion's endeavors becoming a regular feature of Wesleyan home missionary efforts.[80] By 1862 the once despised Methodists were being given official army recognition, with recruits allowed to declare themselves as Wesleyans.[81] Other informal evangelistic efforts to reach the soldiers flourished in the late 1850s and early 1860s, much of the work carried on by women.[82]

If the religious public had adopted the army, the transformation that was taking place in military views of religion would seem to indicate that the army had done the adopting. The official position became that of "creating an almost ostentatiously Christian army," and moreover, "it was a *Christian* and not an Anglican army which became the object of official policy in these decisive years" after the Crimean War.[83] This de facto "Christianization" along denominational lines was accomplished piecemeal: the decision to maintain a substantial number of full-time chaplains in peacetime (1856); the placing of Anglican, Presbyterian, and Roman Catholic chaplains on equal footing, their numbers proportional to their denomination's strength among the troops (June 1858); and the commissioning of all full-time chaplains (November 1858).[84] Olive Anderson comments that "by the mid–1860s more complete provision certainly existed for the religious care of the troops than for either the town or the country population in general. Moreover, in making this provision the state had allowed the comparative position of the established church to be more effectively weakened than it had yet been in any comparable area of public life."[85] The pan-evangelical approach of societies like the LCM and, more particularly, the Soldiers' Friend and Scripture-readers' Society, made a significant contribution to the transformation of this aspect of British public life.

Evangelicals were eager not only to promote missions among those professions that they held in high regard—the police and the various branches of the military—but they were also concerned to reach those of less glamorous professions, such as the cabmen and fire brigade workers whose occupations left them with considerable free time in which they could converse with the LCM agents.[86] Other occupational groupings of perhaps more glamour but of less repute attracted the concern of evangelicals: the thieves (see Illustration 18) and the prostitutes of London.

All LCM agents were brought into daily contact with prostitutes, and within a few months of the mission's founding, it had considered adopting special means of reaching them.[87] The "seeking and saving" of such women was a central concern of nineteenth-century evangelicals, and much of the impetus came from religious women who were willing to risk their reputations, respectability, and at times their own safety in pursuit of wandering females.[88] The LCM, however, had declined to employ women and hoped that its male workers would refer repentant prostitutes to the homes and asylums run by evangelicals.[89] In the early 1840s evangelical interest was again focused on the problem with the publication of a series of *Lectures on Female Prostitution* by Dr. Ralph Wardlaw, a leading Scottish evangelical.[90] The mission made clear that its sense of moral outrage was more directed at the "great men and debauched nobility" who frequented the brothels than with the prostitutes themselves.[91] In fact, this view seems to have been characteristic of evangelical attitudes and was certainly shared by many of the female reformers who "welcomed drunken whores into their homes but swore 'never to receive . . . any man, whatever his rank may be, who is known to be a profligate.' "[92] Prostitution, it was felt, affected women more profoundly than men.

In 1842 the *LCM Magazine* provided its readers with detailed accounts of the operations of the profession in the metropolis,[93] and much to the chagrin of the Dean and Chapter of Westminster it pointed out that twenty-four of the twenty-seven houses on its almonry property were houses of ill fame.[94] An interesting study by a city missionary appointed to work among the estimated 2,000 to 3,000 "fallen women" in Marylebone revealed that applications for "rescue" were chiefly received from older women fearful for their health, instead of from among the majority aged sixteen to twenty.[95] The agent's work was aided by the women directing the brothels, who were eager to encourage religious visitation when their charges were ill, in the hope that "an inmate so useless to herself should be persuaded to return home to her friends, or to enter an asylum."[96]

As has been seen in the case of Joseph Oppenheimer, it was not unusual for a lay agent to establish cordial relations with prostitutes in his district. R. W. Vanderkiste described one "wretched place" where he was regularly welcomed:

CONFERENCE WITH THIEVES.
LORD ASHLEY (SHAFTESBURY), AND MR. JACKSON.

Illustration 18
A Thieves' Conference

One city missionary established a close relationship with the common thieves in his neighborhood and arranged for Lord Ashley to meet with them privately. Like journalist Henry Mayhew, Ashley owed much of his knowledge of the London poor to his association with city missionaries. From John Weylland, *These Fifty Years*, London, 1884 opposite p. 154, 1330 e. 7. Used with the permission of the Bodleian Library, Oxford.

This den of infamy was situated in W—H—C—, T— Street. It consisted of one small room on the ground floor, and parties might well be excused for remaining dubious, as to whether so small an area could have been so replete with pestiferous moral influence to the neighborhood, as this place unequivocally has been.

He also explained the key to his access with these women and detailed the manner in which he dealt with them:

The fact is, I appeared to have a great influence *given* me over the proprietor of this wretched place and others, in consequence, perhaps, of attention I had paid to one of their companions, who died in a very dreadful manner. They appeared to retain so grateful a sense of these attentions, that they could not insult me. It constituted one of the strangest sights in the wide world, to see me enter this place at night, sometimes alone—on one occasion my companion was ordered away; it was said to him, "You go, or else perhaps you'll have a knife put into you. He (me) may stop"—disturbing all kinds of wickedness, and merely saying "I've come to read to you." Standing there in the midst of ferocious and horrible characters, reading the Scriptures, and explaining portions concerning our Lord and Saviour Jesus Christ, heaven and hell, and a prostitute holding the candle next to me. This young woman has since abandoned her evil course of life. Then would follow some discussion; one would say, "I don't believe there's no hell—it's in your heart, mister." Then some prostitute would burst out into indecent profanity, would be *sworn* at until she was quiet. Then I would go down on my knees in the midst of them and pray, waiting to see if the Spirit of God would act, (and the Spirit of God *did* act).[97]

Such stories did much to arouse evangelical concern for the prostitutes and encouraged their hopes that the rescue mission could be successful. Prostitution, as one historian has suggested, may have seized the English imagination at mid-century through Henry Mayhew's articles in the *Morning Chronicle* in late 1849 and early 1850, but the evangelical imagination had already been captivated by the phenomenon through the publicity given it by the LCM.[98] (Mayhew, as has been noted, was himself indebted to the city missionaries for his knowledge of the London of which he wrote.) While public concern, and especially the female public's concern, caught up with evangelical interest in the 1850s, it was the evangelicals who dominated the outreach to "fallen females" throughout the century. The great innovation of this period was the development of "rescue work," which sought to remove the prostitutes from their habitual haunts, and women roamed the streets and even visited brothels to seek the lost sheep.[99] In 1859 a number of evangelicals associated with the LCM promoted an outreach to prostitutes which became known as the "Midnight Meetings movement" whereby large numbers of women were invited to attend free meals in designated restaurants late at night, following which a sermon implored the prodigals to take the proffered assistance of a place in a "home" or asylum.[100] These meetings attracted considerable attention in both the religious and secular press, and the pattern was quickly adopted in other cities throughout Britain. This sort of approach remained popular throughout the country, but it was not regarded by all women rescue workers as an effective substitute for the visiting of brothels themselves.[101]

The LCM's willingness to become involved in so many different forms of evangelism to so many varied groups was part of its genius; it was far more sensitive to the needs of the British working class and much more able to adapt to those needs than was the Anglican church and its parochial system. Furthermore, this flexibility allowed a single society to coordinate ministries to various spheres of endeavor that otherwise would have been met by smaller, less efficient, and poorly coordinated societies.

The increasing sophistication of the LCM as shown in its branching into so many different areas of specialization in the 1850s was also reflected in attempts to broaden its basis of support throughout Great Britain. In 1852 the mission appointed a part-time and then a full-time traveling agent to organize and sustain country associations. Compared with the seventeen full-time traveling agents of the Church Missionary Society or even the six employed by the Church Pastoral-Aid Society, these efforts by the LCM appear to be small indeed; however, they were apparently very effective and significantly raised the proportion of the LCM's support that came from areas outside London.[102] In pleading for the assistance of the provinces, the mission was able to argue that there was a special responsibility incumbent upon the areas that had contributed so largely to the rapid migration into London during the first half of the century.[103]

The LCM's flexibility, its willingness to adapt to changing social conditions, and its remarkable ability to enlist a broad support base had made it the pacesetter in evangelical missions in Britain. When the society considered that a new evangelistic approach was beyond the scope of its own ministry (such as the Midnight Meetings movement), it encouraged concerned evangelicals to establish a pan-evangelical organization to coordinate the effort and instructed its agents to cooperate freely with the new movement. The rising evangelical concern with female prostitution in the 1840s revealed one important area within the mission's proper scope that it had failed to develop. The prostitution issue aroused female sympathies, and it was widely felt that women were the most effective in befriending and aiding prostitutes. One writer put the female view well when she wrote: "a woman's hand in its gentleness can alone reach those whom *men* have taught to distrust them."[104]

THE NEWCOMER: THE RANYARD BIBLE MISSION

As early as 1836 the LCM Committee had agreed in principle that "the employment of a judicious and experienced Female Agency was greatly needed and might prove of essential service in attaining the object of the Mission especially amongst women of bad character."[105] At the same time, however, the committee declined to apportion any of its funds to such an object and suggested that the lady who had recommended their employment form an auxiliary to provide the funds for their maintenance. In the following year, Baptist Noel urged that the ladies occupy themselves with visiting their neighbors and in raising subscriptions for the organization.[106] Women were important donors and key fund raisers for evangelical organizations. F. K. Prochaska has commented, "The evangelicals . . . were particularly adept at extracting money from women. They were not only relatively open to women socially, but they also worked harder than anyone else. This combination of zeal and organizational flexibility triggered the rapid expansion of female contributions in their charities."[107] Female support was especially important to the City Mission. The subscription lists of the LCM in 1838 reveal that 38 percent of its subscribers were female, and that figure rose throughout the century (to 42 percent in 1870 and to 57 percent in 1901).[108]

In spite of strong female support, the LCM stopped short of employing women. The hesitancy to allow women to act as city missionaries in the 1830s likely stemmed in part from the danger to their health. Another compelling explanation may be drawn from the experience of district visiting: Victorian men hesitated to perform work that was associated with women. Whatever the reason for the LCM policy, the issue was not raised again in the LCM committee for formal discussion until 1860, although women constituted about one-third of the agents used by the provincial Town Missionary Society.[109] The LCM's failure to move into this area left the field wide open for others.

The pioneer of a new movement to evangelize poor working-class women was Ellen H. Ranyard (1810–1879), who in 1857 founded the London Bible and Domestic Female Mission, or as it came to be known, the Ranyard Bible Mission (RBM). Long active in canvassing for the British and Foreign Bible Society, Ranyard began publishing a monthly periodical in 1857 entitled *The Book and Its Mission*, which was designed to promote the worldwide operations of the Bible Society. Convinced of the importance of circulating the Bible among poor women, Ranyard determined to employ their peers of distinguished piety to sell them Bibles. She had been particularly impressed by the stress upon "native agency" in foreign missions[110] and acknowledged the influence of Pastor Theodor Fliedner at Kaiserswerth in Prussia who effectively used deaconesses in a similar work.[111] (Fliedner himself had been directly influenced by Elizabeth Fry. His work had a great impact on another English woman, Florence Nightingale, who spent several months at Kaiserswerth in 1851.[112]) Aiding Ranyard in the establishment of her organization was the change in mid-Victorian attitudes toward women, hastened by the example of Nightingale's nurses in the Crimean War. Their full-time employment in other spheres of Christian ministry was being promoted at this time as well.[113]

Initially the new work was prosecuted by independent local committees and publicized by Ranyard in *The Book and Its Mission*. Not until June 1859 was the Mission properly organized and a governing committee set up. Progress from this date was truly astounding, with the number of full-time "Bible-women" employed jumping from 35 to 137 from November 1859 to November 1860.[114] Leading lay figures on the committee were Lord Shaftesbury and Arthur Kinnaird,

M.P., along with two representatives of the Bible Society. The leading clerical figure was Arthur W. Thorold, rector of St. Giles-in-the-Field, the clergyman who supervised the work of Joseph Oppenheimer (see Chapter 6). (Thorold later became bishop of Rochester.[115]) Although the society was pan-evangelical, it was clearly dominated by Anglicans, for the most part by Anglicans who were also active in the LCM.

Great impetus was given to the new mission not only by the greatly increased funds that the new committee was able to solicit, but also by the agreement of the British and Foreign Bible Society (BFBS) to provide the Bible women with free grants of Bibles and Testaments. The mission was permitted by the BFBS to use the proceeds from their sale to pay the salaries of the workers.[116] As the women so employed were only paid ten shillings per week, the RBM was soon able to employ a number of agents equal to about half the LCM's staff. By 1867 Ranyard's mission was paying its workers about £32 per year, "a figure which, though modest, compared favourably with moulding wax flowers or the lower forms of domestic servants."[117]

The LCM for its part appreciated the new mission's desire to circulate the Scriptures and its strong emphasis upon the promotion of self-help. It noted, however, that the city missionaries were not permitted to sell any materials nor were they equipped to help teach women how to perform domestic and household duties as the Bible women did. The LCM did take strong exception to passages in a book by Ranyard though,[118] particularly to one portion that asserted that the city missionary was of a social standing so far elevated above the very poor as to be ineffective in evangelizing them.[119]

The largest of the pan-evangelical societies to emerge in London since the formation of the LCM, the RBM's spectacular growth owed much to the toil and cultivation of an evangelical constituency by the LCM. The RBM's novel approach captured the attention and support of middle-class evangelicals and effectively mobilized lay men and women of widely differing social backgrounds in the task of evangelizing the poor. In so doing, the mission was effecting a coalition of social classes that urban Anglican parishes fondly desired but for the most part experienced only as a dream of bygone rural harmony. In large part the coalition consisted of middle-class Anglican ladies who supervised poor Nonconformist Bible women.[120] In fact, a large proportion of the Anglican superintendents were "either the wives, daughters or sisters of clergy of the Church of England."[121] One measure of the mission's success can be seen in the organizing of a parallel High Church Anglican organization, the Parochial Mission Women, which freely acknowledged its indebtedness to its evangelical forerunner.[122]

Adopting the LCM pattern of geographically defined districts, each with its local superintendent, the RBM agents canvassed the areas trying to induce women to purchase Bibles. Ranyard was adamant about this procedure, which was a clear point of departure from LCM policy: "it is not enough to read or speak the message without leading to the *purchase* of the Book, for *this involves* the seeking on the part of the purchaser. It enlists her in the effort to raise herself."[123] Once a sale had been made, the purchaser was invited to meet with others of her peers in the agent's poor abode, where in the words of Ranyard, "Being alone together they talked freely; and in one or two things they were all agreed. They all had bad husbands, and they could not go to public worship for want of clothes."[124] It was in this setting that various methods of self-improvement were discussed and advice given on a host of domestic matters. Along with this self-help emphasis there was a strong stress on the importance of teetotalism as "these, with a kind and sober wife, and tidy children, *tended to make good husbands*."[125]

The third step in the outreach to these women was for the Bible woman to induce her charges to accompany her to a society-run "Mission-room" "easy of access, and not too light or large for the very ragged and wretched," where they could be taught by "a SISTER IN CHRIST of any grade."[126] The ultimate goal was their participation in the life of a local congregation, but the key to the whole approach was that of personal contact:

the degraded must be sought and individualized *with more earnest sympathy*. They can no longer be dealt with in masses . . . women in small groups must come under the influence of their sister-women one by one, and we may *select of the people to mend themselves*, as we may *help them to help themselves*.[127]

Ranyard continued to expand her organization in creative ways and has been credited with establishing "the first corps of paid social workers in England."[128] In 1868 she arranged for the training of poor women as itinerant nurses in the wards of Guy's Hospital. Ranyard called them her "Bible-nurses." Armed with Florence Nightingale's *Notes on Nursing* and their Bibles, they soon became well known as evangelist-nurses in London's slums giving "medicines and solace to patients with ailments ranging from bedsores to 'sloughs of despond'."[129] One of the earliest examples of district nursing in London, this aspect of the RBM has been praised as "a gallant pioneering achievement."[130]

The similarities between the LCM and the RBM are striking. Not only were they alike in approach and structure, but those who directed the work of the missions and those to whom the missions were directed also clearly overlapped. Both managed effectively to combine middle- and upper middle-class Anglican money and skills with a poorer, predominantly Nonconformist agency. While the RBM was the largest of the new evangelistic societies begun in the 1850s, there were others whose inspiration and organization were more clearly bequeathed by the City Mission.

THE OPEN AIR MISSION: AN OLD METHOD FOR NEW FOES

During the first half of the nineteenth century the practice of open-air preaching seems to have been the almost exclusive preserve of the Methodists.[131] Baptist

Noel's commendation of the practice in his 1835 *State of the Metropolis Considered* did not find favor with the *Christian Observer*, which argued that neither the British temperament nor climate were suited to the practice; furthermore, Irvingite use of it had demonstrated that "such a plan was not for edification."[132] Its employment was urged upon the clergy of the capital in an anonymous work published in 1849, but not until 1850 was Anglican interest aroused by a Cambridgeshire clergyman who had used the means to address up to 2,000 people in his parish at one time.[133] He advocated its use in a series of articles in the *Christian Guardian*.[134] Hugh McNeile and his Evangelical coterie in Liverpool apparently adopted the practice in 1850 as well.

Interestingly enough, it would appear that it was not the effective use of this means by Nonconformists which caused Anglican Evangelicals to reconsider their attitude toward the practice; rather it was its employment by infidel preachers and Mormon missionaries. W. W. Champneys had suggested to the LCM in 1849 that it employ some especially effective missionaries "to reply to infidel preachers on the Sunday in Victoria Park," a recommendation that was deemed "inexpedient" by the committee.[135] The atheistic and anticlerical stance of these speakers and their continued taunts greatly vexed Evangelicals as letters to the editor of the *Record* in the early 1850s reveal.[136] It was felt by many that the only effective way of meeting them was to challenge them on their own ground.

Evangelical concern about the growth of Mormonism in Great Britain had been increasing steadily from the early 1840s with the *Record* keeping its readers informed on the progress of the sect in America.[137] By 1850 the paper confessed to having received numerous requests to recommend books written to counter Mormonism.[138] The wholesale adoption of evangelical methods such as tract distribution and open-air preaching is perhaps most easily explained by the claim that many of the Mormon converts came out of a Primitive Methodist background. By 1852 a city missionary was complaining that the Mormons were leaving "their tracts on every part of my district,"[139] while a year later another testified that "Mormonism, Swedenborgianism, Irvingism (so called), and Roman Catholicism" were the chief topics of religious inquiry among the poor.[140] The 1853 Annual Report of the LCM decried the prevalence of "the absurd and blasphemous system of Mormonism" and reported that "there are very few of the 300 districts occupied by the Mission in which strenuous efforts have not been made to propagate its lies."[141] Lectures against the new faith were organized and a book written by one of the LCM agents was published.[142] Curiously, the followers of the American millenarian, William Miller, failed to attract much of a following in Britain. They were greatly outnumbered by the Mormons and were often confused with them.[143]

The founders of the inter-denominational Open-Air Mission, begun in 1853, attributed much of their concern for its commencement to the example of the Mormons and infidels. In 1856 the *Christian Observer* cited the *First Annual Report of the Open-Air Mission* and pointed out that the society vindicated its mission by pointing to "the lectures of Mormonites and Infidels," coupling this with "the just remark, that 'the question is not, whether we are to begin its use (that of open-air preaching), but whether we will leave such a powerful engine wholly to our adversaries.' "[144] The new organization sought to employ laymen on a part-time basis to preach at selected locations throughout the metropolis at various times during the week. Two of the leading men in the society were Alexander Haldane, the key figure in the *Record*, and William Dugmore, another Recordite lawyer. Only after the publication of the results of the 1851 census in 1854 did the LCM venture to allow some of its own agents to take part in open-air preaching, feeling that the recommendation of the practice by Horace Mann had helped to prepare the public mind for its acceptance.[145] The mission persevered in its course despite occasions of personal violence being directed against its agents, and the practice soon became a regular function of the society's workers.[146] (See Illustration 19 for an example of hostility toward the new society.)

A measure of the change that had occurred in Evangelical thinking between 1836 and 1856 can be seen in the attitude of the *Christian Observer*: not only was it now willing to countenance open-air preaching, but it was also prepared to sanction its practice by laymen:

Let it be the work of Presbyters, where they may be had. But where, as in London and other cities, and in densely peopled districts, the number of the clergy is insufficient to do this as well as the other work of their ministry, let laymen be encouraged, not forbidden, to speak to the people, and to endeavour to teach them the truth as it is in Jesus.[147]

At this time, the only Anglican society in London that was willing to use open-air preaching was the Islington Church Home Mission, an organization established in 1855 by the Evangelical clergy of that parish.[148] By this time even Bishop Blomfield was willing to commend the practice when performed by clergymen.[149]

In part the Evangelical openness to the use of lay agency in what had long been a closely guarded preserve of the clergy stemmed from the growing appreciation of anticlericalism among the working classes. The *Christian Observer* emphasized this in an article, "The Working Men of London": "The fact is, that many of the working-men have got the idea firmly fixed in their minds, that the 'parsons' only preach a certain set of doctrines because it is their profession, their business, to do so."[150] Horace Mann was to argue to a similar conclusion in his analysis of the religious census.

THE LECTURE MOVEMENT

In order to overcome this hostility against religious instruction evangelicals developed a less direct evangelistic approach, one that was designed to appeal to the higher classes of working men and artisans by offering them lectures on secular topics, such as history, science, and archaeology. It was hoped that these

Open Air Preaching!

WHAT a bustle is now made about this! Yea there is a *Home Missionary Society* formed expressly for it, but not upon that *plan* that Christ and his Disciples acted. which was, '*freely ye have received--freely give*.' O no! there is cause to believe they are *paid* for it, because money is given to *support* it; if they were not, money would not be required, as there is no *rent* to pay for *open air*. Well if the harvest is really great, it cannot be said the *labourers* are *few*, for they *swarm* like *caterpillers* in all directions of the metropolis, on sunday mornings in particular, and confine their labours to the common and lower order of society. Why do this? are they more wicked than the rich? if not, why *neglect them*? the cause is plain, any one may guess it! but I ask of *what use* is their *preaching*, seeing what *they set forth*, is *not calculated* to inform the judgment and reform the practise of men. It is only framed to work on the tender feelings, to excite both hope and fear about imaginary matters, which all equivocal points and mystical notions are, and they only urge the necessity to believe these. Now there is strict propriety in styling their process *preaching*! for it is not teaching in any sense of the word, because the subject matter generally *cannot be understood* for *want of evidence* to *prove it true*; yet, behold how many are led away with the *illusion*. But the *preaching* of Jesus was the reverse of this, that was, strictly *teaching*—how widely different was his process!—he appealed to the conscience and judgment, through the senses, by referring to natural things; for it is said, he taught in parables, and without a parable spake he not; and all the parables are evidently framed upon natural things. I could easy produce many more cases to prove this, but this paper will not admit of doing so. Let me therefore advise every one (who may read this) to search the 'History of Jesus,' not merely read it in the common way, but deliberately examine every part strictly, and you will perceive his whole end and aim was to improve the condition of man, by shewing him that sincere principles and uniform virtuous practice, was alone necessary to make him happy in the present, and prepare him for future state of happiness. The only point of faith that he pressed was, believing Him to be the *Messiah*; in short, whoever takes the name of *Christian*, should take *Christ* for their *pattern* in all things, and *reject all others*, beside *him*, even the mystical *Paul*, and all other mystics too, both ancient and modern, and *follow Christ*, or they are not his disciples. I will add the caution he gave, and there with close, "*Beware of False Prophets*."—**E. B.**

Note.—All Priestcraft, Religion, and State Politics are only a legion of Juggling Tricks.

Illustration 19
"Infidel" Opposition to Open-Air Preaching

The writer of this handbill displays a remarkable acquaintance with biblical phraseology while at the same time being anticlerical and opposed to orthodox Christianity. His work attests to the widespread influence of the preachers who "swarm like caterpillars in all directions in the metropolis . . . and confine their labours to the common and lower order of society." From the John Johnson Collection, Religion, Box 27. Used with the permission of the Bodleian Library, Oxford.

lectures would be used "to lodge some one Christian truth in their minds, demonstrating it . . . and so rebuilding, by slow and cautious steps, the edifice which infidelity has nearly succeeded in levelling with the ground."[151] In so doing, the evangelicals hoped to win a hearing from the often highly skilled, self-improving artisans who came to London to complete their training. It was from the ranks of such young craftsmen that some of "the most articulate and politically influential working men" were drawn.[152] These lodgers were without homes of their own and they were generally unwelcome at their lodgings except to sleep and thus frequented drinking places for meals and recreation.[153] Given evangelical support for the temperance movement and for attempts to restrict Sunday travel, entertainment, and shopping, it is understandable that radical working-class opposition to evangelicalism was drawn from this group. It was hoped that the lectures would win a hearing for evangelical views through an appeal to the workers' desire for self-improvement.

Evangelical efforts in this regard were promoted on an organized basis by the Working Men's Educational Union (WMEU) formed in 1852. Like the Open-Air Mission, its leading backers were laymen well known for their involvement in the LCM and other evangelistic enterprises. The new society met with what the *Record* described as "astounding" success,[154] while the *Christian Observer* hailed it as "one of the best and most promising plans" for the evangelization of the working classes.[155] The movement quickly spread to cities throughout England, Scotland, and northern Ireland.

The WMEU prepared numerous series of lectures for the use of speakers and also furnished large pictures for the purpose of illustrating the talks.[156] These "wall sheets" were made of cloth (in order to avoid the paper duty), and as they could be folded, they were easily portable for display in village halls throughout Britain. The earliest illustrated lectures were on Nineveh and Assyria (thirty diagrams); the solar system (twenty-three diagrams); Eastern habitations— a series on the manners and customs of nations mentioned in Scripture (ten diagrams); Human physiology in relation to health (ten diagrams); the Catacombs at Rome and the early Christians (twenty-one diagrams—see Illustration 20); and Paganism and its practices (six diagrams). By 1860 the society was able to provide a list of some 500 topics ranging from natural science to details of life in the most distant British colony, all of them illustrated for the benefit of speaker and audience.[157]

In the first year of the new society's operation, attendance at the lectures numbered over 120,000, and the success of the new scheme led its promoters to outfit a permanent lecture room for twice-daily lectures. Aware of the desire of the lodging class for self-improvement through reading and the wisdom of offering an alternative to the pub, the building was also fitted with a library and a reading room. Evidence of the impact of the scheme can be seen in the opposition it stirred up in the "infidel press" as quoted in the *Record*:

The Infidel portion of the press is not blind to the probable effect of the KING WILLIAM-STREET ROOMS, in attracting and softening the working classes. They cannot afford to

GLADIATORIAL COMBATS, FROM POMPEII.

THE DYING GLADIATOR.

Illustration 20
Working Men's Educational Union

These wall posters were used to illustrate a lecture on the catacombs at Rome. From Benjamin Scott, *Catacombs at Rome*, London, 1860, opposite p. 34, 246 g. 52. Used with the permission of the Bodleian Library, Oxford.

leave the effort to itself;—already they are warning the working men of London against it.

Lloyd's Weekly London Newspaper, edited by DOUGLAS JERROLD, is one shade lower and more mischievous than the *Weekly Dispatch*. This paper could not let a single week pass without an attack on the Lectures in King William-street. The warfare was commenced as follows;—

"Lord Shaftesbury and his friends appear to have some notion of being able to insinuate scraps of Evangelicalism into the minds of working men, *sandwich-like*, between comic anecdotes and showy pictures. At Charing-cross the worker is inveigled into a *sermon* by the promise of amusement, and finds merely the chatter of Exeter Hall."[158]

In spite of such opposition, this sort of lecture appears to have been remarkably popular throughout the 1850s.[159]

The Lecture Movement invites comparison with both the YMCA and the Mechanics' Institutes, the latter being a form of evening school for adults. The origin of the evening schools was pre-Victorian, and they had a significant influence on the mainstream of Victorian adult education. David Nasmith, the LCM's founder, had been involved in the first such institute while a teenager in Glasgow in the late 1810s. It was not until the 1840s, however, that the Mechanics' Institutes Movement really got off the ground. Their aim was the diffusion of "useful knowledge" along with the promotion of the twin virtues of self-help and mutual improvement. They included a strongly moral element and received the warm support of evangelical Dissenters like Samuel Morley and the Baines family of Leeds; however, more often than not, the religious impetus behind them was not evangelical. Two of the leading figures in the movement were the Reverend Henry Solly, a Unitarian minister, and F. D. Maurice, who was known for his theological liberalism and his Christian Socialism.[160] Clyde Binfield has observed how close the similarities were between the Mechanics' Institute and the YMCA: both shared the same emphases on self-help and mutual improvement, and both appealed to the same sort of young man—"rather carefully lowest middle-class."[161] The Lecture Movement aimed at the same group, hoping to use the lecture approach without appearing as overtly evangelistic as the YMCA.

While the new evangelistic societies that emerged in the 1850s (the Ranyard Bible Mission, the Open-Air Mission and the Working Men's Educational Union) varied greatly in the methods that they employed in evangelism, important similarities do exist. Lord Shaftesbury was the most prominent figure in each,[162] and the key positions of treasurer in each society were filled by wealthy Anglican laymen, each of whom had long been associated with Shaftesbury in other evangelistic efforts.[163] The fact that all three of these pan-evangelical societies received strong support from the *Record* and the fact that they were effectively under the control and direction of Anglicans was not coincidental; both were due to the domination of the Shaftesbury-Haldane group of laymen in the new societies. The increasing specialization in evangelistic methods thus served to promote the formation of new societies established on interdenominational footings. The cause of pan-evangelicalism was further advanced by the need for more innovative approaches to an increasingly urban society whose poor were disaffected with church going and with other more traditional means of winning their loyalty.

The rapid growth of the LCM and of the new evangelistic societies during the 1850s stands in marked contrast to the Anglican Scripture Readers' Association (SRA), which until 1850 had experienced a growth rate comparable to that of the LCM. (See Appendixes A and B.) During the 1850s the SRA's receipts fluctuated between £8,000 and £10,000, and its level of support peaked in the mid–1860s, while the LCM continued to expand throughout the century.[164] (See Appendix C.) Unable to specialize or to establish a national basis of support as the LCM had, the SRA was severely restricted in its operations. The challenge to the pan-evangelical societies of a strictly Anglican approach to urban evangelism had been greatly impeded by the increasing specialization. The triumph of the pan-evangelical approach to home missions was becoming evident.

10

New Incentives to Pan-evangelical Unity

The 1850s appeared to many to be the heyday of Anglican Evangelicalism. The confidence and assertiveness of the Evangelicals had been bolstered by the Gorham judgment in 1850. Secure in their beloved establishment, the Evangelicals were in a position to forge new links with both orthodox Nonconformity and with other parties within the Church's pale. Their new mood reflected the broader social trends of Victorian society at mid-century resulting from increased prosperity and relative social peace.

The increasing numbers of Evangelical clergy served to strengthen the party's position. The growth of Evangelical influence was perhaps most remarkable in London, where the ecclesiastical landscape had been significantly altered by their ascendancy. In 1855 the *Christian Observer* could rejoice:

No part of England [during the eighteenth century] was more overrun by the race of "high and dry" preachers than the city of London. Indeed, the very term "high and dry" is said to have a metropolitan origin, and to belong by emphasis to one of its clergy. But what a change has come over the scene! The principal parishes, especially in the north of London, are in the hands of some of the most distinguished and energetic ministers of the day.[1]

A year later the same journal reported that the previous decade had witnessed a rapid increase in the numbers and influence of Evangelical clergy, and it doubted whether the party had ever been so strong in the history of the Church of England. After citing as evidence the growth of support for the CMS and the CP-AS and the increase in Evangelical clergy particularly in Manchester and East Kent, the writer continued:

But nowhere has this change been more remarkable than in London. Contrast its present position with those days not long passed away, when persons were obliged to flock from all parts of London to St. John's, Bedford Row, as the only place they knew in which the great evangelical truths of the Gospel were habitually and powerfully preached; and who can rise from such a contrast without the exclamation, "What hath God wrought!" Without attempting to notice the important changes made prior to the year 1845, we find that within the last decade many of the largest and most important parishes have been placed under the parochial care of a better and abler evangelical clergy. There would be no difficulty in drawing up a list of at least forty such parishes, containing an aggregate population of little less than half a million. Nor are they to be found merely in densely-peopled, poor districts, but many of them are amongst the most influential rectories in London. Indeed St. Paul's Cathedral itself has experienced as great a change as any of our churches, and is becoming, through God's great mercy, a radiating point for evangelical truth through the City.[2]

According to the writer "by far the greater amount" of the recently bestowed London patronage was in the hands of the Crown. This claim, although exaggerated, has some basis in fact.[3]

If clerical strength was rapidly increasing, it would appear that lay strength was even outstripping it. The laity's support for the growing number of local associations of both the CMS and the CP-AS is impressive and is clearly attested to by the burgeoning budgets of the organizations.[4] By 1858 another contributor to the *Observer* could assert that "while the Evangelical clergy are still numerically inferior to the rest, yet the majority of the people who attend Church at all are found in their congregations—."[5]

SABBATARIANISM AND EVANGELISM

During the early 1850s evangelicals of all denominations had united in the campaign against "Papal Aggression." By 1854 the anti-Catholic cause had given way in prominence to another evangelical concern: Sabbatarianism. It has been noted that "although the English Sunday is often considered as a manifestation of the Nonconformist conscience," it was in fact Anglican Evangelicals who took the legislative lead in attempting to enact Sabbatarian legislation.[6] They were the ones responsible for the establishment of the pan-evangelical Lord's Day Observance Society (LDOS) in 1831, urging upon Evangelicals a course of action long repudiated by the Clapham Sect.[7] Original Dissenting hesitancy over involvement in the LDOS was due to two factors: the asperity of the Voluntary Controversy in the 1830s, and the LDOS's strong emphasis upon "national responsibility," which the Dissenters found difficult to harmonize with their views on civil and religious liberty.[8] It was thus the lot of the *Record* to hold high the Sabbatarian standard during the 1830s. In the early 1840s Henry Blunt claimed for it the distinction of having put a stop to Sunday Cabinet dinners and councils and an end to the Speaker's Sunday dinners.[9] Such agitation was despised by many and caricatured as hypocritical. (See Illustration 21.)

It is not without significance that the leadership of the English Sabbatarian movement was strongly influenced by expatriate Scots,[10] for their Scottish Calvinistic background both strengthened concern for the issue and increased the likelihood of a pan-evangelical coalition on the matter:

In the Calvinistic churches, where particular stress was laid on the unity of the Old and New Testaments, the stringent pattern of Mosaic sabbatarianism was often copied as closely as possible. In spite of the emphasis usually placed upon Methodism in the Evangelical revival, the Anglican Evangelicals and the evangelical Dissenters were the representatives of the awakening who were more likely to take a part in public affairs. And they were essentially Calvinistic and Puritan. So the interest in Sunday observance rose with the tide of revival.[11]

It is important to appreciate the link between Sabbatarianism and evangelism, for many evangelicals viewed Sabbath keeping not only as a means of grace for Christians but also a means of grace to the unbeliever and hence saw it as "an important instrument of evangelism. If the non-Christian kept Sunday he was putting himself in a position where he might hear God's word to him. Conversely, if he did not use Sunday in this manner, it became an opportunity for evil."[12]

The LCM had thus been long active in promoting the Sabbatarian cause: the committee sponsored a petition to Parliament to oppose the Sunday opening of the British Museum and other public buildings in 1840, and its missionaries regularly denounced Sabbath breaking as a sin as grievous as theft, fornication, and murder.[13] The mission worked in concert with Sabbatarian organizations like the Sunday Baking Abolition Society in attempts to prevent specific trades from functioning on the day of rest[14] and kept its constituency regularly informed of the state of the metropolis's Sabbaths[15] and of its own success in ameliorating them.[16]

Sabbatarianism received some renewed vigor in the late 1840s with its advocacy by the Hon. Arthur Kinnaird, another Evangelical Scottish M.P., and by Lord Ashley. In 1850 it achieved a short-lived victory. Sunday postal deliveries were withdrawn but soon reinstated by Parliament.[17] Not until the mid–1850s, however, did it assume the center of the stage in evangelical concerns. (See Illustration 22.) Apparent threats to established Sabbath practice were central to this renewed interest. Attempts by Henry Mayhew, M.P., to procure the opening of the Crystal Palace to the working classes on Sundays caused them great alarm. Evangelicals, whose sense of propriety had been deeply offended by the refusal of the directors of the Crystal Palace to remove nude statuary from its grounds, were incensed with the proposal to open the Crystal Palace on Sundays and did all within their power to oppose the idea. This opposition was sustained throughout 1853 and 1854 and was orchestrated by the LDOS. In 1853 the LCM used its network of agents to circulate tens of thousands of copies of tracts opposing the palace's opening on Sundays.[18] Continuing aid and comfort were given to the cause by papers like the *Record* despite the vociferous opposition of the popular press.[19]

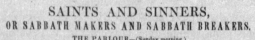

Illustration 21

The Rich, the Poor, and the Sabbath

Anti-Sabbatarian polemics emphasized the view that the Sabbath was a day of leisure for the rich, enjoyed by them at the expense of the poor. Above, Sir Dogberry Doubleface lectures his newsman for working on Sunday, while his servants in the kitchen (below) complain of the work required for their master's family to have a day of rest. *The Penny Satirist*, April 18, 1840. By Permission of the British Library.

Puritan. "VERILY, BROTHER ASHLEY—BETWEEN YOU AND ME, AND THE **POST**—WE HAVE MADE A NICE MESS OF IT."

Illustration 22
Lord Ashley and the Post Office

In 1850 the Sabbatarians achieved a short-lived victory, stopping the delivery of mail on Sundays for a brief period. The stoppage pleased the Post Office workers but was resented by many as an inconvenience to the general public. *Punch* 19 (1850):5.

Sir Joshua Walmsley, the M.P. who represented the radical and secular National Sunday League, introduced a bill in March 1855 to open the British Museum and the National Gallery after morning services. The *Record*'s response is instructive as to how deeply serious many evangelicals were about this matter:

The adoption of the principle of this Motion would be a more portentous calamity to England, and a greater blow to her greatness, than if her army had actually perished to a man upon the shores of the Crimea, and not one had been left to tell the disastrous tale. . . . While God is with us, doing as He will in heaven above and in the earth beneath, we may look at the issue of these earthly wars undismayed at any temporary defeats; but if God leave us, leave us to our pride, our carnal folly and philosophy, leave us to show before the world another warning instance of a nation exalted to heaven, but now for its sins brought down to hell, then, indeed, may we write Ichabod on our greatness, and expect to see the sun of Britain go down even in its zenith in shame and degradation.[20]

The overwhelming defeat of the motion (235 to 48) is an indication of the Sabbatarians' power in Parliament, an influence that was disproportionate to their popular appeal. "Let the people choose!" was a motto frequently on the lips of the anti-Sabbatarians. In a host of crusades, however, the evangelicals had been able to refine their weapons of moral warfare. They were quite prepared to do battle for the Sabbath rest and could deluge members of the House of Commons with petitions "whose number bore little relation to the intensity of public feeling on the issues" and which "could be turned on or off like a tap."[21]

The Sabbatarians were headed for disaster. Anxious to restrict pub opening hours on Sundays, they had combined with the United Kingdom Alliance (formed in 1853) to procure the passage of "the Wilson-Patten Act, which closed English drinking places on Sunday between 2.30 P.M. and 6 P.M. and after 10 P.M."[22] This legislation caused a great deal of inconvenience and provoked much resentment among respectable Londoners who were accustomed to week-end excursions to the outer suburbs, where they patronized recreation grounds which were often controlled by the publicans. The two leading defense organizations of the publicans declined to protest the Wilson-Patten Act, fearing the Sabbatarians' anger at a time when they faced the threat of a free trade in intoxicants.[23] Popular agitation against the act persisted throughout the winter of 1854–1855.

THE SUNDAY TRADING RIOTS OF 1855

It was against this background that a group of tradespeople requested a prominent Evangelical, the Whig member of Parliament for Middlesex, Lord Robert Grosvenor, to introduce a Sunday Trading Bill.[24] In this instance there was a broader support base than the religious public; shop assistants who worked extraordinarily long hours stood to benefit from it, as did large shop owners who lost business by remaining closed. Another group pleased with it were the "smaller tradesmen whose rivals stayed open [and] found respectability expensive, and wanted the state to ease their path to virtue."[25] The progress of

Grosvenor's measure in April 1855 was aided by the absence of three leading anti-Sabbatarians from the new house[26] and by the announcement by Sir George Grey that the Whig government was willing to endorse the legislation.[27] The bill prohibited all Sunday trading in London with the exception of meat and fish sold before 9 A.M. and newspapers and cooked food sold before 10 A.M. The restrictions were particularly onerous for the poor. They were not normally paid until Saturday evening and were therefore unable to store up food supplies for the weekend. Furthermore, they "could not keep food fresh in their unsanitary homes: hence they depended on the flourishing Sunday trade of small food shops and stalls."[28] Despite popular confusion over the matter, Grosvenor's measure made no attempt to restrict Sunday drinking times. When the bill reached the amendment stage on June 14, 1855, it was clear that it had considerable support among members.[29]

Within a few days the whole situation changed. The measure had aroused the long-standing hostility of the London radicals to evangelicalism. On June 15 the *Times* came out strongly against the bill, and posters appeared throughout London calling for a public demonstration against it in Hyde Park on the afternoon of Sunday, June 24.[30] Karl Marx, who was one of the observers of the protest, "held that at least 200,000 people attended."[31] The crowd was noisy but peaceful, and the following week more posters materialized announcing another gathering on the following Sunday. This groundswell of opposition from the *Times*, the popular press, and the Sunday crowd led Sir George Grey to retreat from his original position, and he denied that the government "were at all responsible" for the measure.[32] Grey had further cause to worry; the French government informed him secretly during the week before the proposed second demonstration that its intelligence sources had discovered that Chartists would try to exploit the July 1 demonstration and would launch an uprising in which French refugees would play a part.[33] Grey, the same Evangelical cabinet minister who had been responsible for public order during the Chartist upheavals of 1848, ordered 600 police officers to be on duty in the park.

The second demonstration was banned by the police; yet, in spite of this, the *Times* estimated that nearly 150,000 people congregated in the park on Sunday, July 1.[34] Under considerable provocation the police decided to assert their authority and clear the congested carriageway. Using their truncheons, they tried to bring the crowd under control and arrested seventy-two people in the riot that ensued.[35] Many of those present were young, and most had traveled some distance to the park, the most likely source of "the most determined rioters" being the "Hounsditch area of East London, home of so many of the Sunday Markets threatened by Lord Robert's Bill."[36]

To a public unaware of the government's fears of an uprising, the police actions seemed at the very least to be overzealous. Monday's papers vigorously protested police brutality, and both Grosvenor and Grey came under harsh press criticism for their conduct.[37] The immediate upshot was that Lord Robert withdrew his Sunday Trading Bill, complaining that he had been "mobbed and

bullied" into capitulating.[38] The *Record*, however, expressed its disappointment
with Grosvenor's decision to back down on the measure.[39]

The Hyde Park demonstration had begun with an air of festivity; its violent
end seemed unnecessary and senseless. Yet, as Brian Harrison has pointed out:

to assume that a festive atmosphere is incompatible with political danger would be to
distinguish too sharply between moods of festivity and protest. The very term "riot"
was only in the process of losing its ancient associations with excessive enjoyment, and
if events in Hyde Park on 24 June resembled a saturnalia rather than a reforming demonstration,
this shows that the government had every reason to be alarmed. For the festive mood *is* the
revolutionary mood, the mood prevailing at St. Petersburg in October 1905; Tocqueville heard
"more jokes than cries" uttered by the Paris crowd in February 1848.[40]

Even after Grosvenor had withdrawn his bill (and thus withdrew from public
life), the riots continued. On Sunday, July 8, the rioters "were probably led by
East End radicals anxious to take vengeance on the police."[41] They expressed
their anger by turning into the fashionable Belgravia district where they broke
749 window panes. On the subsequent Sabbath the demonstration was much
smaller and dissipated with some pilfering and hooliganism.

The demonstrations on the first two Sundays were well financed and organized,
with foreign émigrés prominent as instigators. As the events occurred during the
Crimean War, some feared that Russian gold was behind the effort.[42] The demonstrations were probably financed and organized by less sinister plotters: likely
a combination of East End Sunday traders in league with beer-selling interests.
The drink sellers had both money and experience—and recent experience at
that—having succeeded in breaking up prohibitionist meetings in Dudley, Birmingham, and Bristol only a few months earlier.[43] Brian Harrison has also
observed that the conspirators were aided by the convergence of several factors
in their promotion of the riots: an unduly hot July (June and July being the
favorite months for English insurrections), hunger (the East End of London had
experienced a bread riot in February, and wheat prices were even higher by
June), and the ingrained "Cockney hatred of the police."[44]

Playing into the hands of the London radicals was the convenient occurrence
that it was an aristocrat who had introduced the offensive legislation into Parliament—and an Evangelical at that. Lord Robert was caricatured by the *Reynolds's Newspaper* on July 1 as " 'a perfect type of his order' 'bigoted, insolent,
obstinate, and tyrannical.' "[45] In fact, many aristocrats were anti-Sabbatarian,
and indeed, antievangelical. Lord Shaftesbury was ever conscious that his religious views qualified him as a social leper among his peers. ("My popularity,"
he noted in his diary, "such as it is, lies with a portion of the 'great un-
washed.' "[46]) Furthermore, Sabbatarians saw themselves as "defending employees' leisure time against employers' rapacity."[47] The movement flourished
because of "a genuine coincidence of interest between evangelicals and working
men afraid of being exploited."[48] Thus support for the legislation cut across

class divisions. Many working men, however, were irked by the fact that gentle-men's clubs "had long been exempted from licensing restrictions on the dubious principle that they were 'homes from home.' "[49] (See Illustration 23.) Thus the violence of the protest had thrived "however mistakenly in this instance, on the belief that there was one law for the rich and another for the poor."[50]

The London newspapers attempted to minimize the significance of the dis-turbances and to downplay any impression of class conflict. The *Times* was particularly concerned that the July 1 demonstrators had misdirected their wrath toward innocent Hyde Park promenaders with taunts of "Go to Church!" The real culprits, in its view, were not the upper classes:

The upper classes of England are not Puritans, but members of the church of England. They do not regard harmless recreation on Sunday in the light of sin, still less so the necessary purchases of the poor. The strict Sabbatarians upon the Scotch model must be sought among the middle classes, at Exeter-hall, among the Dissenters.[51]

The *Times* was close to the mark. The activities of the evangelicals can best be understood in terms of culture conflict, rather than class conflict. Unintentionally the Sabbatarians forced hostile working men into an alliance with other social classes. Thus, in their Sabbatarian campaign, as in their temperance and animal cruelty concerns, their reforming movements "helped to ensure that members of any one social class were cross-pressured in such a way that the social structure was shielded from violent change; contemporary England was thus 'sewn together by its inner conflicts.' "[52]

Exactly what the Hyde Park demonstrators had been protesting remained a matter of debate throughout the century: temperance reformers insisted that the disturbances were over Sunday trading rules, not the issue of Sunday closing hours of pubs; Sabbatarians blamed the hostility on the Wilson-Patten Act of 1854. On either count, the discredit fell on one of the twin darlings of the evangelicals, and they, and not the aristocracy, came to bear the brunt of the discredit. Oddly enough, the evangelicals had been divided over Lord Robert's proposal; the more extreme Sabbatarians in the Lord's Day Observance Society had not approved of the measure in the first place, as it "had not been based on purely religious considerations, and had actually legalized some degree of Sunday trading."[53]

The Sunday Trading Riots provide interesting insights into changing attitudes toward violence in mid-Victorian England. Harrison has noted that the police were uneasy in Hyde Park in part because they were anxious to replace the cutlass with the truncheon in the process of maintaining order:

Public opinion, largely under Evangelical influence, was becoming increasingly sensitive to violence of any kind; a few years before, far greater violence might have been displayed against the rioters without arousing protest. Shaftesbury noted in 1867 that no minister would now dare to use "the fire of the Military" against civil disturbances like those at Bristol in 1831.[54]

THE CLUB.

Just a Sandwich and a Nice Glass of Hock and Seltzer Water.

THE ROADSIDE INN.

A Mouthful of Dust and a Pull at the Pump.

Illustration 23
A Home Away from Home

The private clubs of the wealthy were exempted from Sabbatarian legislation which affected the drinking establishments of the poor, on the grounds that the former were "homes away from home." In the two scenes above, Lord Grosvenor is seen taking refreshment at his private club on the left, while in the other, he stands in front of an inn, denying the same treatment to the poor. *Punch* 29 (July 1855):6–7.

The impact of plebian violence on the political process is also revealing. Just over a month after the riots, Henry Berkeley, "Liberal Member of Parliament for Bristol, illegitimate son of the fifth earl of Berkeley, and arch-enemy of Evangelicalism" succeeded in repealing the year-old Wilson-Patten Act.[55] The effect of the riots was thus to arouse the anti-Sabbatarian forces to arms; the marquess of Clanricarde claimed in the House of Commons that petitions signed by 440,000 had been received requesting repeal.[56] The riots and the ensuing clamor thus reinforced "Victorian reluctance to impose temperance legislation on London" and led to the reversal of legislation that affected not only London, but the whole country. Lord Shaftesbury was appalled by the reversal, viewing it as "a base truckling to popularity and fear."[57] In the longer term, by revealing to the temperance reformers their political weakness, it taught them the need "for that aggressive electoral and parliamentary temperance policy later pursued with such success" by the United Kingdom Alliance.[58]

If Lord Robert's proposals had brought to light the disunity of the saints and the apparent weakness of the Sabbatarian forces, subsequent events were to demonstrate their capacity for renewed vigor. In 1855 Palmerston "allowed Sir Benjamin Hall, the Commissioner of Works, to arrange for military bands to play in London parks on Sunday afternoons. By May 1856 the Horse Guards band was playing in Kensington Gardens, the band of the Second Life Guards in Regent's Park, and a third military band in Victoria Park. It was estimated that on Sunday, May 4, 1856, 140,000 people, a tenth of the population of London north of the Thames, gathered in the parks to hear the bands."[59] A tug-of-war between pro- and anti-Sabbatarian forces did much to strengthen pan-evangelical cooperation, with the Evangelical Alliance putting itself forward to lead the battle.[60] Evangelical cooperation on the issue was further strengthened by the formation of the Metropolitan Committee for Promoting the Observance of the Lord's Day late in 1855.[61] This new organization was specifically concerned with stopping the Sunday performances of the regimental bands.

Opposition to this popular government innovation was led by Edward Baines, Jr.[62] To the Victorian public, the Baines name was synonymous with respectable evangelical Nonconformity.[63] Edward Baines, Sr., was a leading Congregationalist and an M.P.,[64] although his oldest son, Matthew (also an M.P.), had become an Anglican Evangelical.[65] Clyde Binfield had observed that to men like the Baines, social progress depended upon personal initiative, and thus if the challenges of an industrializing and increasingly urban society were to be met, then individual self-control had to be emphasized and practiced.[66] In the mind of Edward Baines the younger, martial music was not conducive to self-mastery. He thus produced a pamphlet attacking the bands:

The strains of martial music cause the pulse to bound, and fire the imagination, and they are wholly out of accordance with the sacred repose of the Sabbath. It is, however, their fascination which here constitutes their chief danger. Crowds are sure to follow them; and among these crowds, arrayed in their Sunday finery, thousands of young girls and young men, with no more than the average amount of vanity and weakness, will be brought into circumstances of extreme peril.

The linking of Sabbatarian concern with efforts to evangelize the working classes was then made clear by Baines:

At these places, I fear, thousands of Sunday scholars will first learn to desert the school and the place of worship, and to enter on the downward path of folly and vice. The danger may be scoffed at by thoughtless persons; but is there any Christian father or mother who would willingly let their children or servants attend such scenes? Is there any Sunday-school teacher who would not feel that the scholars were lost to the school, and to the sanctuary, when they had begun to frequent the military performances in the parks?[67]

Significant for the progress of pan-evangelicalism was the fact that Baines's considerable energies were now being used to gain a common objective; in the early 1840s Baines, as the editor of the *Leeds Mercury* had been a leading figure in opposing Sir James Graham's Factory Education Act which Evangelicals had so strongly supported.[68] Now he was working closely with those he had once so strenuously opposed.

Sabbatarian pressure was so powerfully and skillfully applied that Palmerston, while acknowledging that he considered the playing of the military bands to be "innocent recreation," admitted that the Sabbatarian clamor had forced him to capitulate. Both the prime minister and the queen were in favor of the bands, but Palmerston cited a letter in Parliament from the Evangelical archbishop of Canterbury, J. B. Sumner, which he alleged, had been instrumental in his backing down.[69] In fact, the archbishop had been requested by Palmerston "publicly to demand concession to the sabbatarians" so that he might retreat without loss of face.[70] Hence the archbishop took the brunt of the blame for an action most vociferously demanded by Dissenters and Scottish Presbyterians. The prevention of scores of thousands of Londoners from passing their Sunday afternoons listening to the bands was no mean feat, and the *Record* rejoiced in so grand a victory. (See Illustration 24.) It was particularly pleased that evangelicals were learning their fundamental political lesson that "in unity there is strength."[71] The *Times* in a leading editorial acknowledged and disparaged the triumph:

So Exeter-hall has triumphed, and the working population of this metropolis is driven back to the publichouse. The PRIMATE and Mr. BAINES, with their well-organized army of Sabbatarians, have silenced the bands, cleared the Parks, and set the tap once more flowing. Their zeal has its reward.[72]

THE RELIGIOUS WORSHIP BILL

Sabbatarianism was not the only political issue related to evangelism on which evangelicals found themselves being drawn toward each other in the 1850s. In

THE GREAT EXETER HALL TRIUMPH.

First Publican. "IT'S ALL RIGHT, BILL—THEY'VE BIN AN' STOPPED THE BANDS PLAYING IN THE PARKS!"

Second Do. "WELL DONE OUR SIDE—WE WIN—WE SHOULD HAVE SHUT UP SHOP ELSE. SO 'ERE'S THE HARCHBISHOP'S JOLLY GOOD 'ELTH!"

Illustration 24
The Bands Are Silenced

Two publicans rejoice that the evangelicals have succeeded in stopping the Sunday bands which were depriving them of customers. Note the *Record* newspaper in the right of the picture (upside down). *Punch* 30 (May 1856):210.

1855 the Hon. Arthur Kinnaird introduced into the Commons and Lord Shaftesbury into the Lords a religious worship bill, which sought to abolish the compulsory registration of Dissenting places of worship and to dispense with the law limiting to twenty the number who could attend unsanctioned religious meetings. As such measures were clearly consistent with Whig principles, government support could be anticipated. The *Record* gladly endorsed the legislation, interpreting it not as a blow to the establishment principle, but as serving to promote episcopacy by discouraging secessions.[73] Anglican Evangelicals had long been vexed by the law; it was recalled that William Wilberforce had often kept a servant posted at the door of his lounge to keep a count of the number of attenders at informal religious gatherings.

The LCM was particularly concerned with this legislation, as it regarded the small cottage meetings which it held in its districts as essential "stepping stones" for the poor in their progress toward full participation in public worship. When in 1850 a provincial laborer was successfuly prosecuted for allowing an unlicensed meeting in his home, the mission published an article entitled "The Injury which Obsolete Laws, Unrepealed, Inflict on Religious Societies." Aside from the impracticality of observing the law, the LCM pointed out that it clearly could not register rooms in connection with the Church of England and had no desire to injure its pan-evangelical constitution by consenting to have them registered as Dissenting places of worship. The only other option that the LCM understood was open to it at the time was "that a religious Society should 500 times each week act in direct infringement of the law of the land," something that was not deemed to be "altogether desirable."[74]

Great was the *Record*'s anger when Bishop Wilberforce and Lord Derby succeeded in steering the bill into committee where, with Derby's casting vote as chairman, they managed to set aside Shaftesbury's proposals and to draft a measure to their own liking. The *Times* chided Lord Derby and Bishop Wilberforce for their hesitancy to repeal obsolete and unfair legislation that had succeeded in driving so many people into Dissent. It also suggested, however, that Evangelicals like Shaftesbury enjoyed the prosecution of illegal meetings:

They who remain in the Church are also actually affected. There are those who set the law at defiance, who preach and pray themselves in public, upon all manner of pretences, of course innocent enough, but who are taught rather to plume themselves on the notion that they are defying the law. That evidently is Lord SHAFTESBURY's tone. He is rather pleased than otherwise at the thought that he and his legionaries of the City Mission and other similar societies are so many religious Arabs, pitching their tents anywhere, and despising the orthodox dwellers in consecrated walls. Such a feeling is very natural under the circumstances, though rather too braggart for our taste. But it is a positive evil that it should be encouraged, and that great numbers of zealous men should start with the sentiment of spiritual defiance, and that in this mood of mind they should form the religious faith and habits of large bodies of poor, uneducated people.[75]

When Lord Derby's committee finally produced its own proposal for a religious worship bill, it was acutely evident that its drafters were lacking in political acumen. Alarmed that Evangelical laymen might attempt to establish congregations of their own while at the same time professing attachment to the Church of England, the bill proposed bringing the religious activities of the laity under the control of the clergy. Lord Derby argued in support of the bill that:

At present it is doubtful whether any layman is capable of assisting the clergyman of the parish, even though with his consent and by his authority, in visiting the sick and holding meetings for the purpose of religious worship; but this Bill provides that for the future no penalty shall attach to any layman performing these duties with the concurrence of the clergyman of the parish in which he labours.[76]

If the clergy refused such permission, laymen could appeal to the bishop of the diocese to override his veto.[77] The ensuing debate saw Lord Shaftesbury launch an attack on what he regarded as an attempt to increase episcopal power and to destroy pan-evangelical cooperation in evangelism. He especially attacked Bishop Blomfield, who had been one of the episcopal members of the committee that framed the bill:

I have gained what I wanted. I have shown that the noble Earl [Derby] and the right rev. Prelates [Wilberforce and Blomfield] are afraid of having the facts disclosed. The services held by the agents of the London City Mission are as completely religious services as can be held in any church or chapel, and I must express my regret that that society, notwithstanding the good it has accomplished, has never received that countenance from the Bishop of the diocess [sic] which it might have anticipated. On the contrary, I believe the right rev. Prelate is extremely hostile to the London City Mission, and I therefore regard with much suspicion this clause, which was introduced into the Bill by the Committee of which he was a member, for it is obvious that, if the clause is brought into operation, it will extinguish altogether the efforts of the City Mission.[78]

In his defense Blomfield noted that he could hardly be expected to support a society whose constitution he did not approve of and cited Charles Simeon on the dangers of irregularity.[79] Archbishop Sumner made it clear that he could not endorse the use of unsanctioned lay agency, as such would be a direct violation of the Twenty-third Article.[80] Bishop Wilberforce joined the fray with an attack on Shaftesbury, also basing his opposition to the earl's views on his subscription to the Thirty-nine Articles.[81] Lord Derby hastily withdrew his measure once the archbishop had voiced his discontent with it, and through the whole exercise had only succeeded in confirming himself in the role of chief villain in the Evangelicals' eyes.

Fearing further attempts to interfere with Shaftesbury's design of abolishing the restrictive legislation, evangelicals organized a public protest which involved leading Anglican and Dissenting ministers, including the Methodist leader, Jabez

Bunting.[82] A public meeting was convened and the *Record* remonstrated with the bishops in predictable tones:

We hope that the Bishops will take warning, and not try to rouse the tempest, of which one of the speakers at the Meeting of yesterday spoke, which will sweep through the country, when once it is understood that the Bench of Bishops are resolved to "warm into venomous life" those torpid penalties which have too long been the disgrace of the statute-book.[83]

Shaftesbury, working in conjunction with the archbishop, modified his bill, so that it only claimed protection for private dwellings in which more than twenty persons gathered.[84] During the debate over Derby's measure, Lord Broughan had brought to the attention of the Lords that the 1812 Act (42 Geo. III), commonly known as "Lord Sidmouth's Act," already allowed for the possibility of registering buildings simply as "Protestant" places of worship, thereby obviating problems for pan-evangelical meeting places such as Exeter Hall.[85]

The informal religious services which the City Mission conducted in the slums of London were to become an increasingly important aspect of their outreach throughout the rest of the century, developing the basis of what Jeffrey Cox has called the "Mission hall movement." In the 1830s and 1840s the city missionaries had been expected to hold their weekly meetings in the homes of the poor who offered them or in a school room lent by a sympathetic clergyman.[86] Through the 1850s the LCM insisted that it would not spend money erecting permanent meeting places; such venues appear only to have been acquired later in the century. The emergence of such halls "was itself a formal recognition of the middle-class character of ordinary Sunday churchgoing,"[87] and although the LCM insisted that its workers were not to "assume the office of the ministry" it is clear that they often did.[88] The *LCM Annual Report* of 1860 gives a lengthy but highly informative description of their roles, and one can appreciate that the mission hall was the next step in consolidating their numerous functions:

It should be known by the supporters of the Mission, that many of the missionaries are themselves the centres of usefulness in a district, which is otherwise almost wholly unattended to, and have themselves originated a most extensive machinery for usefulness, no part of which would have existed but for them. In many cases they have their schools, which they have themselves founded, and the management of which they superintend— schools not unfrequently for Sunday and for week-day, for children and for adults. They have their different social meetings, Bible classes, expository services, and the like, often largely attended, almost every evening of the week; they have their penny banks, placed under responsible management independent of themselves, through each of which hundreds of pounds pass annually; they have their sick funds, their mothers' meetings, their tea-meetings, their baby-linen fund, and their annual treats. They have their lectures, their magic lanterns, and the like. They have their staff of private friends, often those benefited by their labours, who do much in voluntary visitation, to strengthen their hands.

They have their libraries, and their stock of tracts and books for special cases. And many of them have their open-air services on the Sunday, at which attendance is often very large.[89]

Other more social occasions were also being organized by the city missionaries:

In no previous year has it been so common, as in the last, for the missionaries themselves to take out the people of the district which they visit, for a summer's excursion. In this they have often had help sent to them, but in many cases the poor have borne their own expenses, and have themselves requested the missionary to superintend all the arrangements.[90]

In many cases, the city missionaries were in effect pastors to a slum church of their own, and the consolidation of these congregations in mission halls later in the century was the effective acknowledgment of this. In spite of all these extra activities, the mission did not relax its requirement that its agents spend thirty-six hours a week in door-to-door visitation. It is not surprising, therefore, that for weeks in succession during the spring of 1860, between fifty and sixty of the city missionaries were under medical care and had to work reduced hours.[91]

THE FIGHT AGAINST "NEOLOGY"

While the two political issues of Sabbatarianism and the Religious Worship Bill were working to unite evangelicals who were particularly concerned with working-class evangelism in the mid–1850s, other broader theological concerns were forcing evangelicals together in a defensive alliance. The emergence of theological liberalism, or "Neology" as its detractors labeled it, did much to provoke such a combination. In 1853 the *Record*, with the approbation of the *Christian Observer*,[92] joined in the campaign to procure the dismissal of F. D. Maurice from his chair at King's College, London.[93] The *Record* happily welcomed the support of members of other churches, such as Dr. Candlish, whose published lectures attacked Maurice's theology.[94] Benjamin Jowett's theological views were criticized in the *Christian Observer* in 1855,[95] and the *Record* fiercely assailed his appointment as regius professor of Greek at Oxford.[96] The paper made it clear that in its view this struggle was of much more import than wrestling with Tractarianism or with Roman Catholicism:

If this Neological School takes deep root in Oxford, wounds far more ruinous and fatal will be inflicted upon our Church than those which the parti-coloured followers of NEWMAN and PUSEY have occasioned. Compared with these philosophical subtleties the depths of Jesuitism are child's-play. The end of the latter is superstition, through which, and out of which, and in which, poor dark souls may peradventure grope their way to Christ, salvation, and heaven; but the end of those abominable, sceptical, Neological subtleties is doubt, darkness, and a cold, helpless, naked Infidelity, out of which and in which there can be no salvation![97]

In the Rivulet Controversy which tore apart English Congregationalism in 1856,[98] the *Record* gave its strong backing to Dr. John Campbell in his bitter attacks on a Congregational hymnbook in which he discerned the thread of German rationalism.[99] Conservative evangelicals were increasingly being forced into each other's arms in a defense of what they understood to be fundamental to their faith.

These controversies need to be seen in the broader European context, for it would seem that during the mid–1850s a vexatious spirit of strife had settled on much of the continent's religious life. Both Irish and French Catholicism were experiencing deep divisions, and Protestantism in England hardly fared better.[100] Archdeacon Denison seemed determined to provoke a fight with his superiors by preaching the doctrine of the Real Presence in the elements of Holy Communion in 1853–1854. Apparently anxious to be prosecuted, a neighboring Evangelical incumbent finally obliged. Archbishop Sumner proceeded against Denison only when forced to by the Court of Queen's Bench.[101] At the same time, Evangelicals waged war on the Broad Churchmen. Wesleyans were still attempting to recover from their mid-century split, and Presbyterians were suffering from their own internal controversies. In view of all these disheartening divisions, the *Record* in 1856 saw a special need for evangelical unity:

> These features of the times should teach many lessons, but perhaps the first and plainest is the duty of promoting, by all possible means, love and union among all true servants of Christ. We know that in their case the essential elements for a firm and solid union of heart and judgment do exist. . . . In proportion to the visible disorder and confusion of secular and ecclesiastical politics will be the moral power of every genuine manifestation of union and love among the disciples of Christ. The light will shine more conspicuously because of the darkness that surrounds it.[102]

The following year the *Record* expressed its view that a significant new alliance had been formed:

> The external differences between Church and Dissent are losing much of their absorbing attraction, but the battle about essential saving truth is becoming fiercer. We discern a wide line of demarcation between those Dissenters who are represented by Dr. CAMPBELL and the *British Standard*, and those who rally round the Rev. Mr. Miall, M.P., and the Radical *Nonconformist*. Dr. CAMPBELL shows that, compared with the great cardinal truths of the Gospel, he has no longer any sympathy with anti-State Church principles. Mr. MIALL, on the contrary, throws his shield over Dr. DAVIDSON and the assailants of inspiration, and holds forth as exclusive bigots those who dwell on the evils of departing from the great truths of the Gospel.[103]

In this alliance of theological conservatives the *Record* reckoned the *Wesleyan Watchman* as a worthy ally but was less pleased with the "uncertain sound" emitted by both the *Patriot* and the *Wesleyan Times*.

The bitterness of such internecine warfare among professing Christians undoubtedly did much to disillusion Victorians as to the validity of Christianity. In 1853 W. J. Conybeare had warned in his article on church parties in the *Edinburgh Review* that such divisions promoted skepticism: "these unnatural hostilities must cease, if we are ever to re-convert the pagans of the factory, or the pantheists of the forum. . . . The true battle is . . . between Faith and Atheism."[104] Such warnings went unheeded, undoubtedly much to the discredit of the Christian cause, particularly among the literate working classes.

EVANGELICALS AND THE WHIG PARTY

While Evangelicals were distancing themselves from theological liberalism they were drawing toward political liberalism, or at least many of them were finding themselves more comfortable with the Whig party. The Tories under Peel at one time had the strong support of Anglican Evanglicals, but the party had repeatedly disappointed them; the Tory failure to sponsor church extension measures, its record on the Church of Scotland and Irish education, the enacting of the Dissenters' Chapels Bill, and the Maynooth legislation all contributed to their disillusionment. This disaffection had led to an attempt to elect ultra-Protestants to Parliament in 1847. Its failure led many Evangelicals to be more concerned with individual candidates' positions vis-à-vis the No Popery question than with their party affiliation.[105]

In 1852 the *Record* expressed the fear that the new Derby government would be anti-Evangelical, influenced by High Churchmen like Phillpotts against the appointment of Evangelical bishops,[106] thus maintaining what it referred to as the standard policy of the "good old Tory times" when

the Evangelical body was a proscribed race. It was not even thought worth while to examine into their political principles . . . they were regarded as Methodistical and fanatical men, flighty and dangerous, whose religion had too close an affinity to that of the political Puritans, who, in a bye-gone age, had overthrown the constitution of Britain, to be cherished in the present times. Nay, that they should be tolerated, was considered more than their deserts.[107]

In the same year the *Christian Observer* spoke of the preceding four years of Whig rule in favorable terms,[108] while the *Record* viewed the Whig dispensation of Church patronage as a mixed blessing:

Instead of pulling down the Established Church, the tendency of the Liberal school, of late, has been to lend an impartial patronage to all religions, and to make the State the common drynurse of all creeds and parties, however opposed to each other.[109]

Lord Aberdeen's government, which succeeded Lord Derby's in December 1852, was a curious combination of High Church Peelites and Erastian Whigs under the leadership of a Presbyterian prime minister.[110] It was probably the *Record* that labeled Aberdeen a "popishly-inclined-puseyite-presbyterian,"[111] but his appointment of the first Tractarian bishop (W. K. Hamilton to Salisbury in 1854) came only after "much restless thought" and was balanced by his elevation of one uncontroversial Evangelical to another see (John Jackson to Lincoln).[112] The Aberdeen administration, however, did much to frustrate Evangelical No Popery.[113]

Shaftesbury at first despaired when Lord Palmerston became the Whig premier in 1855; he expected that his wife's brother, William Cowper, would be able to exert more influence than himself on the Cowpers' stepfather.[114] Cowper, an ex-Evangelical convert to Broad Churchmanship, was detested by his noble brother-in-law, who regarded Cowper as a "Mephistopheles, who is ever at Palmerston's elbow."[115] The new prime minister's understanding of ecclesiastical affairs was, in Shaftesbury's eyes, somewhat limited. In a letter to his wife he confided his estimate:

He does not know, in theology, Moses from Sidney Smith. The vicar of Romsey, where he goes to Church, is the only clergyman he ever spoke to; and, as for the wants, the feelings, the views, the hopes and fears, of the country, and particularly of the religious part of it, they are as strange to him as the interior of Japan. Why, it was only a short time ago that he heard, for the first time, of the grand heresy of Puseyites and Tractarians![116]

These limitations, however, were to be turned to the earl's advantage as Palmerston proved to be quite willing to take his advice on the appointment of bishops and during his first period as premier (1855–1858) did much to redress the balance caused by the paucity of Evangelical members of the episcopate. Samuel Wilberforce (bishop of Oxford) despised such "wicked appointments," but the direction of Palmerston's choices was to change only slightly after Gladstone entered Palmerston's second administration in 1859. Evangelicals continued to be appointed to the episcopal bench: Dr. J. C. Wigram became bishop of Rochester, and Samuel Waldegrave went to Carlisle in 1860; Francis Jeune became bishop of Peterborough in 1864.[117]

During the 1850s, however, the Whigs were helpful in uniting evangelicals, particularly with their support on the issues of Sabbatarianism and the Religious Worship Bill. Sensitive to Sabbatarian pressure, Palmerston had given way and discontinued the Sunday bands; on the Religious Worship Bill, Lord Derby had personally alienated the Evangelicals. Thus Palmerston's appointing of Evangelical bishops would appear to have been the most important, but not the sole, factor inducing Evangelicals to support his government. Despite fears expressed in the popular press that the Prime Minister was strengthening Sabbatarian and anti-Maynooth forces, Palmerston persisted in his course.[118] The *Record*, in explaining why it laid so much emphasis on the importance of Palmerston's appointments, argued that they would serve to conciliate Dissenters:

A few more such appointments as have just been made would be more effectual than volumes of controversy to abate the bitterness of dislike on the part of the great majority of Nonconformists, and to restore no small number of them to direct communion with a Church in which the Gospel is honoured while order and reverence are maintained.[119]

The role in strengthening Evangelicalism at a time of crisis was, however, also given prominence:

With the Church of England the necessity is the more imperative from the doctrinal ambiguities to which we have already alluded.... The more pronounced schools of theological opinion, the Tractarian, the Broad Church, and the Evangelical, are ever advancing in weight and influence; and it may be safely said that that party which will pervade the Episcopate most extensively with its own leaven will determine for good or evil the fortunes of the Church of England. A greater service to Protestant truth cannot therefore be conceived than the appointment of true-hearted men to our ecclesiastical dignities.[120]

The appointments in themselves not only strengthened Evangelicalism but also the fact that the men who were chosen as bishops were Whig sympathizers who would work well with Nonconformists served to promote the pan-evangelical cause. Bishops Bickersteth (Ripon), Pelham (Norwich), and Villiers (Carlisle) were all life-long Whig/Liberals who had worked with the LCM while parochial clergymen in London.[121] Bishop Tait, although not an Evangelical, was another Palmerston appointee who gave the LCM his tacit support.

The significance of the Evangelical–Whig alignment was not lost on Lord Derby, who, during the 1857 election campaign showed signs of being particularly irked by the popularity that Palmerston had gained. Derby "took no pains to conceal his mortification" with the epithet "Palmerston–man of God."[122] The *Record* bitterly denounced Derby as anti-Evangelical[123] and defended Palmerston, praising the fact that he had given satisfaction on the Sabbatarian question, particularly by his refusal to endorse legislation affecting the Lord's Day.[124] The paper was indignant with the *Saturday Review*'s accusation that the *Record* was the clerical journal that had coined the epithet alluded to by Derby.[125] At the same time the *Record* was discriminating in its support of the Whigs: radicals like Sir Benjamin Hall and Sir Joshua Walmsley (the anti-Sabbatarian menace) were not to be countenanced.[126] Once the election was over, the *Record* estimated that the appointments had had much to do with "handing over twenty or twenty-five seats for the counties to the supporters of the present administration."[127] "There never was," maintained the paper, "a purer or a more sincere or disinterested feeling than that which led multitudes to exclaim, in the course of the last three weeks, 'Though I am a Conservative, I cannot vote *against Lord Palmerston.*' "[128]

One might be inclined to discount the *Record*'s opinion as being unrepresentative of Evangelicalism, given the close friendship between Shaftesbury and Alexander Haldane. Evidence that the Evangelical mainstream was drifting in the Whig direction is also found in the more cautious *Christian Observer*. It claimed that it had "no wish to send our Clergy Quixoting in the field of

Electioneering conflict," but it recommended a specifically political course of action to Anglican clergy: "they are furnished with large means of influence on the consciences of their parishioners, and we are persuaded that they may freely employ them, in the present case, in order to keep in Lord Palmerston and keep out Lord Derby."[129] This unabashed Evangelical delight with Palmerston undoubtedly contributed to his attaining a comfortable majority in the general election, and was "a moderate success for evangelicalism against the high church party."[130] It also represented a major political shift for the predominately Conservative Evangelical constituency and made cooperation with orthodox Dissenters much less politically vexatious than it had been in the 1830s and 1840s.

By the late 1850s, therefore, evangelicals were no longer in opposing political camps, as both Anglican Evangelicals and moderate Dissenters were content with the same Whig administration. One of the greatest divides between Anglican and Nonconformist evangelicals had been bridged. With Anglican fears of disestablishment receding, those who were championing the cause were tarnished in evangelical eyes with the brush of "Neology"; hence, a common cause among evangelicals was inducing them more and more toward cooperation: the defense of "the faith once delivered." Specific political issues related to evangelism, such as Sabbatarianism and the Religious Worship Bill, were providing new platforms on which evangelicals could work together in harmony, while the former arena of anti-Catholicism declined in national importance.

The confusion of the political scene and the relative peace among evangelicals did see the decade out. The 1859 election found Lord Derby's Conservative party strengthened by the blessing of Cardinal Wiseman and the support of Irish Catholics; yet, the Conservatives were not strong enough to retain power. Lord John Russell's outburst over Catholic Aggression in 1850 had damaged the Whigs. Party loyalties, however, were only temporarily blurred.

The damage done to the Whigs would be repaired by Gladstone at the expense of Evangelical support. The disestablishment campaign, which was only in "incubation" in the 1850s, would eventually help him to accomplish that.[131] In 1856, three years before Gladstone's emergence as a Whig, he was seen by Anglican Evangelicals as a dreadful foe. In that year, the *Record* warned Evangelicals, "the Evangelical body have not a more dangerous enemy, nor the Tractarian, or Popishly affected party, a more zealous, intriguing and powerful friend."[132] In the long run, as the architect of Irish disestablishment in the late 1860s, it was Gladstone who was to reverse Palmerston's policy of "resting on evangelical approval and paying little attention to the claims of Dissent."[133] Gladstone, the High Churchman so despised by many Anglican Evangelicals, was soon "to clear party confusion by driving Conservative Establishmentarians to find leadership in their own party" and thus undid the odd alliance which Palmerston had been able to forge.[134]

11

Bishop Tait's Episcopacy, 1856–1860: Further Advances for Pan-evangelical Evangelism

Bishop Blomfield's disapproval of the use of a paid lay agency and his opposition to pan-evangelical organizations such as the LCM had made the pursuit of an ecumenical approach to evangelism very difficult in the 1830s. It was not, in fact, until 1842 that a London rector even dared openly to advocate the LCM's activities in a public meeting, and even the bishop's sanctioning of the SRA had been under duress.[1] Blomfield's passive opposition to the LCM, acknowledged by him in 1838,[2] slowly diminished, and shortly before his death "he even recommended [to several of] the clergy to apply to the Society for its help, allowing them in making the application to say that they did it with his sanction."[3] Such is a measure of the success of a pan-evangelical approach to evangelism in breaking down the denominational barriers and in increasing cooperation between Anglicans and Nonconformists.

During his twenty-eight-year episcopacy Blomfield's relations with the Evangelicals had been less than smooth, but he had appreciated the dedication and evangelistic zeal of the Evangelical clergy and had appointed them freely within the diocese. The bishop had, however, kept aloof from Evangelical organizations, long hesitating to join the CMS and never giving his countenance to the CP-AS. In the important Gorham case he had sided with Bishop Phillpotts, and when the Privy Council's decision was adverse, he was not prepared to acquiesce in it. He devoted the principal part of his 1850 *Charge* to the refutation of Gorham's doctrinal views, which he considered "transgressed the bounds of latitude, which has been allowed or tolerated, ever since the Reformation."[4]

The situation at the commencement of Tait's episcopacy in London in 1856 thus contrasted sharply with that which his predecessor had encountered almost three decades earlier. The Evangelicals were by now an important group both among Tait's clergy and laity, and many had strong, well-established links with

Nonconformity. Tait's elevation to the bishopric, moreover, generally pleased them; although regarded as a Broad Churchman,[5] Tait was in Shaftesbury's view "the mildest among them."[6] His willingness to act as a Vice President of the interdenominational Bible Society and his embracing of the CMS endeared him to the Evangelicals. Early in his episcopate the new diocesan made clear the breadth of his churchmanship with his appointment on the one hand of Arthur P. Stanley, a noted Broad Churchman, as an examining chaplain, and on the other, his endorsement of the YMCA.[7] His firm stance against the innovations of ritualists in his 1858 *Charge* also pleased the Evangelicals and the general public. In the same year Tait himself organized and addressed a joint meeting of all the SRA and LCM workers, thereby demonstrating his willingness to support already existing evangelistic organizations, however constituted, and his eagerness to cooperate with Dissenters whenever feasible.[8]

At a national level this same trend was accelerating among Evangelicals. Hugh McNeile, who had so fiercely attacked Dissenters in the 1830s and who had been in the forefront of opposition to the Evangelical Alliance in the mid–1840s, well exemplifies this change. In 1858 he made public inquiries as to the feasibility of joining the Evangelical Alliance he had once so opposed.[9] Of the triumvirate of Evangelical clergy renowned for their leadership in the No Popery crusade (Close, McNeile, and Stowell), McNeile was apparently the last to move toward cooperation with Nonconformists.[10]

Two new situations were to emerge during the first few years of Tait's oversight of the London diocese that were to test the limits of pan-evangelical cooperation in evangelism. The first was related to the issue of preaching, a means of grace which Evangelicals had long held in high regard—their detractors said too high— but in the early 1850s complaints were growing about the ineffectiveness of much Evangelical use of it. The Reverend John Hampden Gurney, a leading figure in the SRA and a highly respected Evangelical incumbent, complained in print in 1852 of "*a want of freedom in the pulpit*," that Evangelical preaching had been forced to fit too narrow a mold:

We are cramped and fettered by the supposed necessity of excluding from Sunday ex-hortations what fastidious hearers will think too secular; language is to be chosen which shall suit the refined taste of the few, not that which best suits men doing the rough work of life, and used to plain-speaking everywhere else; . . . Too much deference is paid to the little knot of religious critics, who acquit and condemn with reference to their own likings; while the crowd of common hearers, who are bigoted to no school of doctrine, but wish to hear about plain things in plain English, are held too cheap.[11]

One might suppose that Evangelicalism's strongly middle-class constituency was being catered to while the masses were unaffected. The following year Lord Shaftesbury cautioned that if the clergy were to have any impact on the working classes, they had to adopt a new style of preaching. It had to be "adapted to their tastes and apprehensions, and formed more on the primitive model of the early Christian preachers."[12] Other critics suggested that the Evangelicals were having little impact upon their middle-class listeners. The *Clerical Journal* was less gracious and more specific than Lord Shaftesbury. It argued that the Anglican Evangelicals

have unconsciously stereotyped a monotonous form, which has become a practical model, for what is denominated, in the phrase of a Puritanic school, "preaching Christ with simplicity." It may be described as consisting of "The Apostle, in the preceding verses," &c. then, a firstly, a secondly, and a thirdly, with a melancholy and uniform cadence, called an improvement. Add to this a stock of stale quotations, the use of well-known texts, sundry blows directed at the Pope, and backhanded hits at the Tractarians, together with hysterical raptures shouted over the glorious Reformation—and we are describing a large number of discourses, which those who do not admire are branded by the *Record*, and similar prints, as Rationalists, worldlings, and men who are puffed up with intellectual pride.[13]

Sadly enough for the state of Evangelical preaching, even the *Record* acknowledged that there was "some room for the critical censure."[14]

Working-class receptivity to sermons suited to their tastes had been clearly demonstrated by the reception given in 1854 to a nineteen-year-old Baptist preacher from Cambridgeshire. Within a few months of his arrival in the metropolis Charles Haddon Spurgeon was deemed the city's most powerful preacher and soon was addressing crowds of 5,000 to 6,000 twice each Sunday. His special services at Crystal Palace drew upwards of 25,000.[15] (See Illustration 25.) Hoping that the use of an unconsecrated building would help to attract the working classes, the Evangelical Alliance in 1855 began special Sunday evening services in Exeter Hall.

The increasing willingness of Evangelicals to adopt evangelistic practices long associated with Nonconformity is seen in what appears to be the first evangelistic mission run by Anglicans in 1856. These missions centered on a protracted series of religious meetings each night of the week, lasting for one or two weeks.[16] By 1857 Anglican incumbents were organizing such missions in their own churches and employed the talents of well-known Evangelical speakers such as J. C. Miller, Hugh McNeile, and J. C. Ryle in the evangelist's role.[17] The *Record* was particularly enthused about their suitability in reaching the unchurched, provided that the meetings were held at a convenient time, had adequate publicity, sufficient accommodation, and a judiciously chosen speaker. "Mr. SPURGEON," the editor maintained, "is not the only living preacher who can instruct the working classes, or arrest their attention."[18]

Aware that there were, however, many whose class consciousness would never allow them to darken the door of a church, the Evangelicals were also eager to make use of buildings for preaching purposes that were not associated with the Church of England. When the series of special services sponsored by the Evangelical Alliance was completed, the cause was apparently taken up by a uniquely Anglican organization.[19] Vehement opposition was immediately encountered:

Illustration 25
Spurgeon at Crystal Palace

Charles Haddon Spurgeon drew some of the largest crowds of his preaching career at Crystal Palace, some upwards of 25,000 people. London had not known such a phenomenon since the ministries of Whitefield and Wesley. *Illustrated London News* 31 (October 17, 1857):400.

There is a chorus, it seems, of censure, pity, and sorrow for the grievous irregularity of a Gospel preached by bishops, deans, and canons in a place so profane and impure as Exeter Hall! The *Guardian* is incensed, the *John Bull* is indignant, the *Union* is furious, and the neutral *Clerical Journal* is plaintive and dolorous at the enormity of these episcopal misdoings.[20]

When the initial series was completed, however, it was announced that they had gained a new ally. Bishop Tait had agreed to act as their patron.[21] The second series, however, came to an abrupt halt in November 1857 when the Reverend A. G. Edouart, incumbent of St. Michael's, Burleigh Street, the Strand, reversed his earlier approval of the meetings. On the grounds that Exeter Hall fell within his parish, he declared the meetings prohibited, arguing that they did not in fact attract the working classes but only emptied the surrounding churches of their regular attendants. Edouart was not alone in this view; even as eminent an evangelical as John Campbell expressed similar doubts in private.[22]

In an attempt to remedy the situation Shaftesbury introduced a "Bill for further Securing the Liberty of Religious Worship" into the House of Lords in December 1857. This bill would have allowed a clergyman like Edouart to prohibit Anglican clergymen from participating in meetings in his parish of which he disapproved, provided that he was supported in his opposition by his bishop.[23] The proposed measure immediately encountered the strong opposition of Bishop Wilberforce, and after extended debate Shaftesbury agreed to delay its consideration.[24]

Obviously hoping to harness the Evangelicals' zeal for the benefit of the greater Anglican communion, Bishop Tait organized a new society, which was responsible for organizing special services in metropolitan churches and for appointing clerical missionaries in London.[25] In promoting such a "church home mission" the bishop was following the recommendation of a committee of the bench of bishops made earlier the same year.[26] The alliance was broad enough to include Evangelicals of the stamp of Champneys, Thomas Dale, and William Cadman; Broad Churchmen like William Cowper; and Tractarians of the stature of Bryan King. This bold attempt to combine such unlikely Anglican strains in the same effort was vehemently attacked by the *Record*. The paper was puzzled as to how so many leading Evangelicals could be a party to mixing truth and error:

Here we have some of the most faithful heralds of the pure Gospel of JESUS CHRIST linked together with others who preach "another gospel:" the Rev. Dr. M'NEILE with the Rev. W. SCOTT, of Hoxton, the Bishop of CARLISLE [H. M. Villiers] with the Rev. FREDERICK MAURICE. Never during Bishop BLOMFIELD'S vacillating Episcopate do we remember so glaring an attempt to confound truth and error in one Babel of confusion. But what better could we have expected from "the mixed multitude" whose names appear on the list of the Committee of the Diocesan Home Mission?[27]

The *Record* was later to make clear that it discerned the hand of its archenemy, Bishop Wilberforce, behind such efforts:

For some years past there has been in certain quarters a deep design to fuse High Church
and Low Church, Sacramentarian and Evangelical, into one confused mass; and that the
plan of purposely linking together preachers holding opposite opinions on fundamental
questions has been one of the favourite tactics visible in the diocese of Oxford.[28]

Evangelicals, however, were not alone in their opposition to the new Diocesan
Home Mission. Archdeacon Hale wrote to Bishop Tait protesting the fact that
his name had been published as one of the diocesan's nominees for the Committee
of the Mission when he knew nothing of the new society. Hale's disconcert,
however, went deeper than the matter of the bishop's indiscretion. In another
letter he clarified the reasons for his opposition to the new society: "it will
undermine the authority of the Diocesan and substitute in its place a Committee
of Clergy and Laity; so that within the course of a few years the Church at home
will be under the charge of Church Missionary Committees, as is the case with
the Church abroad."[29]

Archdeacon Hale had little to fear from the new mission. Strictly limited by
its constitution to the employment of clergymen as roving evangelists, it never
attracted the enthusiastic support of the Evangelical community. At the same
time it is worth noting that by 1860 it employed six full-time clerical missionaries
who were all of a conservative enough stamp to be deemed worthy of the *Record*'s
approval.[30] Set apart to fulfill their ministry, the agents concentrated on reaching
the unchurched in the parishes of the north and east of London, provided local
incumbents approved of their activities. The agents widely employed open-air
preaching and some worked in closest conjunction with Evangelical clergy like
W. W. Champneys.[31] It would appear that the organization became more and
more a uniformly Evangelical one with the withdrawal of people like Bryan
King from its committee. The setting up of such an organization is testimony
to the widespread belief in the inadequacy of the parochial system to reach the
urban poor by the late 1850s.

As it was Edouart's prohibition of the special services in Exeter Hall which
had given Tait the opportunity to establish the Diocesan Home Mission initially
so disapproved of by the *Record*, Shaftesbury pressed on with his attempt to
find a legislative solution to the problem. Although confident of widespread lay
support, Shaftesbury was at length forced to acknowledge that both the clergy
and the bench of bishops were adamant against his measure, and hence he
withdrew it.[32] In its place Archbishop Sumner proposed another bill but this was
unsatisfactory to many Evangelicals with Shaftesbury arguing that it gave too
much power to the bishops.[33] Eventually the failure to reach a legislative compromise and increasing Evangelical unease about the course pursued by the
London Diocesan Home Mission led a group of Evangelicals to adopt the plan
advocated from the beginning of the dispute by the *Record* for dealing with
Edouart: ignore him.[34] Regardless of their views on the propriety of the Home
Mission, many Evangelicals were convinced that the meetings held in churches
were themselves of limited effectiveness. The names of a number of Evangelical

clergy were published for a series of meetings to be held in Exeter Hall, and Bishop Tait was informed by the committee responsible that the clergymen would be preaching without using the liturgy.[35] When Edouart appealed to him to prohibit the services, the bishop declined, saying that the matter would have to be decided by a diocesan court if the incumbent wished to proceed.[36] In the face of episcopal intransigence Edouart decided to capitulate and threw the responsibility for the continuation of the services on to the shoulders of his diocesan.[37] Henceforth many Evangelical clergy seem to have had no compunction about participating in unsanctioned preaching services, and in 1859 the reorganization of the special services on a pan-evangelical footing seems to have caused no stir.[38]

One innovation that did create a furor was the decision to hold religious services in theaters. As the Evangelicals had long been the leading opponents of theaters and associated as they were in the public's mind with vulgar and lewd entertainment, it was a bold move indeed to propose that such locales be hired as preaching venues. The practice was not welcomed by all evangelicals, none of whom would have thought it proper to be seen in a theater on any other day of the week.[39] The strongest denunciations of the services came, however, from the floor of the House of Lords. Lord Dungannon, an old-style "high and dry" Irishman, as well known for his anti-Catholicism as for his anti-Evangelical sentiments,[40] decried such meetings in that they lowered the dignity of religious worship and were often accompanied by scenes of rowdy behavior.[41]

Archbishop Sumner made his position clear: the approval of the bishops had not been sought, nor did they at any time consider their commencement proper or expedient, but at the same time they were not prepared to interfere.[42] Bishop Tait was more approving and said that he was glad that the laymen had begun the movement without seeking episcopal sanction, as it was an experiment too doubtful of success to have merited it.[43] Such measures were necessary, Tait reasoned, in view of the fact that "No idea seemed more deeply ingrained in the minds of many officials of our parishes than that the abject poor had no right to be accommodated in our churches."[44] The strongest and most spirited defense of the movement came, predictably, from Lord Shaftesbury. In a well-prepared and well-received speech to the Lords he refuted Dungannon's assertions of rowdy scenes and dealt with the Irish peer's concern for the dignity of Anglican worship. Theater services were the only means by which many of the anticlerical and antiestablishment poor could be wooed to faith.[45]

Thus in the first five years of Bishop Tait's episcopacy his clergy had come to experience a much greater measure of freedom in the use of preaching to evangelize the London poor. Tait's personal willingness to make use of open-air preaching had been a great encouragement to them. Furthermore, he had not prohibited his clergy from cooperating with Nonconformists or in using buildings in parishes where incumbents were opposed to their ministry. The Evangelicals were delighted with the new opportunities open to them.

THE IRISH REVIVAL AND EVANGELICAL UNITY

Toward the end of the decade a second important movement served to promote greater interdenominational cooperation. To a limited extent, united prayer meetings in connection with the 1857–1858 Indian Uprising had served to prepare evangelicals for what was to come.[46] The belief was gaining ground among evangelicals that pan-evangelical unity was the necessary precondition for a spiritual awakening. The emphasis had been strongly stressed in the revival that began in the United States in 1858 and soon spread to Britain.

American-style revivalism per se had not risen much higher in the estimation of Anglican Evangelicals since the 1830s, and the association of Charles G. Finney with Dr. John Campbell of London did nothing to allay Anglican fears during the 1840s that revivalism might be used in an effort to subvert the Anglican establishment.[47] During Finney's first preaching tour in Britain in 1849 he was totally ignored by the *Christian Observer* and the *Record* despite his protracted revival campaign in London. J. W. White states, but unfortunately does not document the fact, that a contingent of Anglican clergy attended Finney's meetings and that after questioning him most left

convinced of the genuineness of the work, and determined to begin it in their own parishes, since Finney had earnestly assured them that a professional revivalist was not required for the launching of a revival. A typical response was that of one of the rectors present: the Rev. Hugh Allen, who travelled through his parish to establish twenty different prayer groups on Finney's pattern. All of these met regularly and some daily and during the winter of 1850–51, Allen reckoned that 1,500 of his parishioners professed conversion.[48]

It should be noted that Allen was an Irishman educated at Trinity College, Dublin, the same institution that turned out another London clergyman, Richard Burgess, also known for his propensity for irregular ministrations.[49]

The cautious, hesitant response given to reports of the American revival by the *Record* was perhaps the most positive thing it had managed to write about American revivalism in over three decades, the last notice apparently having been given in 1846 of an American revivalist in Birmingham whose meetings presented "a scene of the most manic-like description which can possibly be conceived."[50] The paper was impressed by the lack of displays of emotion in the American movement, and in a thinly veiled reference to its dislike of Finney's advocacy of the promotion of revivals by specially contrived means, the *Record* stated, "We are led to regard this movement with greater hope, because it has been wrought by ordinary means."[51] Directly modeled on the American pattern, pan-evangelical prayer meetings were begun on weekdays in Exeter Hall.[52]

The *Record*, however, continued its deliberate policy of ignoring Finney and was singularly silent on the American revivalist's second tour of England in 1858–1860. Neither his techniques nor his Arminianism nor his emphasis upon a conversion experience endeared him to Evangelicals. The paper, however, was willing to give the lead to Anglican Evangelicals; it urged support for the expectation of a revival and commended the prayer meetings organized by the Evangelical Alliance.[53] At the end of 1858 it confessed some disappointment with the result but cautioned patience. In March 1859 it published its first reports of religious stirrings in Wales and Scotland.[54] But for a few localized rumblings in Yorkshire and the West of England,[55] the *Record*'s reporting indicates that the revival was largely limited to Ireland, Scotland, and Wales.[56]

The progress of the revival in Ireland was followed closely by the *Record* and well reported in the secular press. Manifestations of apparent religious hysteria attracted a great deal of attention and censure, but even the *Times* was prepared to overlook the extravagances and generally approved of the movement at first:

These miraculous impressions and violent effects are said, however, to be the exceptions, the main result of the movement being increased seriousness of the ordinary kind, crowded attendance at places of worship, and a general apparent awakening of religious feeling.

Furthermore, the newspaper had no fears that similar excesses could ever overtake an Anglican congregation in England, and well appreciated the different attitudes toward conversion that Evangelicals had long maintained:

It must be remembered that the Dissenters have a different standard of conversion from that of the Church. Our sects, and especially the Methodists, look upon "conversion" as a sudden thing; they do not recognize gradual conversion, taking place insensibly in the course of time, as the result of slow ordinary influences; individuals indeed may think this "conversion," but the popular creed only acknowledges the other kind. . . . A Church of England congregation could never become a scene of this demonstrative sort, because if it were addressed ever so effectively and powerfully, if the preacher were not a Canon of Westminster, but an angel from Heaven, its standard of conversion does not allow suddenness, or therefore give room to the action of sympathy. Three thousand of them might be undergoing conversion at once, and nobody would *see* anything; it would all be as noiseless and as invisible as thought itself. The glacierlike movement would not attract the slightest attention, and the whole mass would go out of church looking very much the same as when they went in, because the process in their case is long and steady, takes its time, does not hurry itself, and has no tangible and sensible climax. There is no fear, then, that either St. Paul's or Westminster Abbey will ever witness, after the most "awakening" succession of sermons in the naves, such effects as these.[57]

For once the *Record* gave an approving nod to a *Times* editorial.[58]

The protracted coverage given the revival by the *Times'* Irish correspondent was quite hostile and undoubtedly did much to prejudice English opinion against the movement.[59] His work elicited letters of protest from *Times* readers but to no avail.[60] In November 1859 the *Times* reprinted charges first made in the *Northern Whig* that the areas where the revival was strongest had simultaneously experienced an increase in drunkenness and other social evils,[61] objections that the *Record* considered serious enough to counter.[62] Out of concern, several leading English Evangelicals toured Ireland and reported favorably on its progress.[63] The *Record* was convinced that for the most part, the press was being very partial and prejudiced in its treatment of the revival:

The *animus* which delights in crying down such a work as this, and in mercilessly exposing every questionable feature of it, while all that can recommend it is coolly thrust aside, is one of the worst symptoms of the heart's rebellion against the things of God.[64]

Even more significant for an appreciation of Evangelical attitudes was the favorable treatment given the revival by the *Christian Observer*.[65] After remarking on the depth of changes wrought in society and the breadth of the constituency affected by the revival, the journal did acknowledge some shortcomings:

With more regret than surprise we have to add, that no small amount of mere excitement, arising from the contagion of sympathy—pure fanaticism, if the reader prefer the term—mingles with all this; and, as far as it extends, disfigures and disgraces the work. . . . They remind us of the extravagances of early Methodism. And yet, with all their extravagance, who will now deny that those revivals were signally the work of God? When the wood, and hay, and stubble perished, what a mighty work remained! The foundations of society were shaken, and the results are evident to this day in the altered mind and morals of England.[66]

The magazine, particularly pleased to see Irish prelates and clergymen engaged in assisting the movement, expressed its satisfaction with the estimate of Presbyterian leaders "when they tell us that, on the whole, the work, though marred with some infirmities, is substantially, in their judgment, the work of God."[67]

In a subsequent study of religious revivals the view forming the bedrock of Evangelical ecclesiology was plainly put: "The normal state of the church of Christ in this fallen world, is that of languor and decay, a 'settling upon the lees.' "[68] Given this pessimistic view, the excesses of the revival could be overlooked quite easily. The author admitted the genuineness of religious revivals and enumerated six scriptural distinctives of such movements. He was able to discern all of them in the Irish awakening. The writer was greatly concerned with the possibly spurious and deliberate promotion of experience, again likely in reaction to Finney's emphases:

There is also a strong disposition in the minds of some persons, unduly to encourage, at these seasons, physical excitement, and to look upon these manifestations as conclusive evidences of the Spirit's work. Some sections of the Methodists are obviously predisposed to pursue this course. Their cast of mind and religious tenets encourage it.[69]

Arguing in a directly opposite direction, the view was presented that "All hasty decisions as to conversion are dangerous. We find very few sudden conversions recorded in the word of God."[70]

While the author acknowledged that the real effects of the revival would only be appreciated in the long term, he was prepared to conclude, "A good and great and genuine work is going forward, which Satan is attempting to mar by counterfeits," and the *Christian Observer* appealed for efforts to encourage a revival of piety in the Church of England, especially directing its address to the clergy:

That there is ample scope for such a revival, all must admit. Something, it is true, has been done by the special services, which have been carried on in our cathedrals and parish churches, and in the open air; but we fear that few permanent results have followed. . . . Prayer meetings have been established in the metropolis, but they have been thinly attended. We clearly want a revival of genuine piety. This revival ought to begin with the clergy.[71]

Especially important for the progress of pan-evangelicalism was the fact that this journal, representative of the mainstream of English Evangelicalism, countenanced prayer meetings with Nonconformists:

We would also urge the importance of establishing special meetings for prayer. It must be left to the judgment and discretion of each, whether these meetings should be open to different denominations of Christians, or confined to members of our own church. Where these meetings have been wisely and prudently conducted, they have proved a great blessing to the neighborhoods in which they have been held.[72]

In yet a third notice of the Irish revival in the following issue, the question of hysteria-induced manifestations and the problem of press criticism were dealt with. The importance of the clergy was again emphasized:

It may be well for the clergy to consider whether some special services might not be begun with advantage. . . . It is a grave question what part the clergy should take. If they hang back, they may incur the charge of lukewarmness; and where dissenters have taken up the cause of Revivals, this will certainly be the case. We think they should be careful how they commit themselves to any demonstration they may afterwards be unable to controul. [sic] Yet on the other hand, the work, if it be of God, ought not to be slighted, much less discouraged.[73]

This remarkably open attitude of the *Christian Observer* to the revival and to the issue of pan-evangelical cooperation was likely the result of a change of editors. John W. Cunningham,[74] the elderly vicar of Harrow, had taken over the direction of the publication in 1850 at the age of seventy and did not relinquish control until 1858.[75] A leading spokesman in the 1820s and 1830s for the accommodating policy of the moderate Simeonite clergy, Cunningham represented the views of those who had long been wary of too close an affinity on the part of Evangelicals with Dissent, fearing that such ties would endanger Evangelical attempts to gain ground within the establishment.[76] His successor, J. B. Marsden, was a Birmingham incumbent who reflected the concern of those post-Simeonite clergy who willingly sacrificed a strict measure of ecclesiastical order in favor of the more effective pan-evangelical approach to evangelism.[77] Marsden likely owed his pan-evangelical inclinations to the influence of J. C. Miller, the leading Evangelical in Birmingham, and a person renowned for his cooperation with Dissent.

In spite of the generally approving attitudes toward the revival maintained by both the *Christian Observer* and the *Record*, the harsh press criticism took its toll on Evangelical clergy. Perturbed by the distrust that this fostered, a group of twenty-eight London clergymen issued a cautious but approving statement and established a conference of clergy to promote prayer and action.[78] At the Islington Clerical Conference in 1860, Daniel Wilson made it clear that the desire to promote the revival was having a positive impact upon evangelical unity:

A third point which he would mention was the increased spirit of unity and love prevailing among the different denominations of Christians. He was aware that he was here trenching on delicate ground, and he did not desire that any of his brethren should alter their opinions because he and others took a different view. He would, however, remark that in his own parish there had been, for nine months past, weekly prayer-meetings at which Christians of different denominations united together, not for exposition, not for exhortation, but simply for the reading of the Bible, the offering of prayer, and the singing of praises to God; and he believed there were some present who could testify that these Meetings had been truly profitable to their own souls. Such Meetings were now being held at Freemasons' Hall, and other places; and, whatever difficulties there might be in connexion with them, one thing, at all events, was clear, namely, that they had a tendency to promote a spirit of mutual forbearance, sympathy, and love.[79]

While Wilson did not argue about the merits of the revival taking place in Ireland, Scotland, and Wales, he did imply that evangelical unity was important for the spiritual health of congregations. Significantly, Wilson maintained that England was, in its own quiet way, undergoing a spiritual renewal:

He could only mention one other point, and that was the vast awakening that was now witnessed among dead souls. He was not referring to Ireland, Scotland, and Wales. He believed many present would bear him out in saying that there was in our neighborhood a spirit of inquiry, a desire to gather together for edification, and a real genuine awakening of dead souls, and conversion of hard hearts, such as had not been seen at any previous period.[80]

Other speakers at the conference were clearly concerned about taking advantage of the prevailing spiritual climate. J. C. Ryle, the well-known Evangelical spokesman who was later to become the first bishop of Liverpool, addressed the meeting on the means of promoting a revival among the clergy, the course that had been urged by the *Christian Observer*. W. W. Champneys lectured on home missions, and H. J. Lumsden spoke on the role of the Holy Spirit in prayer and on the tendency of Christian union to foster the "spirit of supplication."[81] Thus the response of Anglicans to the Irish revival was certainly not as hesitant as some historians have made out. It was cautiously endorsed by a number of leading Evangelical clergy and by both the major Evangelical publications. It is undoubtedly true that many individual Anglican clergy did hold back, but it would be a mistake to allow even the reception given to the revival to be taken as an accurate indication of Evangelical willingness to cooperate with Nonconformity. Given the tradition of distrust of American revivalism and Evangelical anxiety to dissociate itself from the excesses of Methodism, the caution is not remarkable. For Anglican Evangelicals the prospect of working with Dissenters in organizations like the LCM was one thing; promoting a free-wheeling and potentially volatile revival movement was quite another.

Thus the depth and degree of pan-evangelical cooperation in this period should not be obscured by any negative Anglican assessments of the 1859–1860 revival. In the first five years of Bishop Tait's episcopate two great strides had been taken along the path to a fuller evangelical common ground. More freedom in joint pulpit ministry was being exercised, and a shared concern to do all in their power to evangelize the poor through their combined strength was serving to deepen mutual understanding and to promote unity among Christians of different traditions. By 1860 many Anglican clerics and laymen were willing to work alongside Dissenters in the difficult task of evangelism, something that only three decades before would have been unthinkable.

A very different view of this period has been advanced by A. D. Gilbert, who has maintained that by the 1830s and 1840s popular ecumenism among evangelicals was dead, a view that fits well his sociologically oriented interpretation, which emphasizes Church-Chapel rivalry during this period.[82] Such rivalry of course existed, and it may well have led to an emphasis upon consolidation and a neglect of outreach on the part of denominations, but that is only part of the story. Denominational ecumenism may have been declining, but popular ecumenism was alive and well as is evidenced by the rapid growth of the budgets of the large pan-evangelical societies. It is clear that in home missions interdenominational organizations were winning the day. By the late 1850s a great deal more cooperation was occurring at the local level between Anglican Evangelicals and Nonconformists than had ever before been the case in the history of English Protestantism.

Epilogue

The Significance of the Evangelical Urban Mission

> For the social and political historian the Oxford Movement is of much less moment than Evangelicalism because, while the Oxford Movement's influence was clear and strong enough within the Anglican communion, Evangelicalism mattered enormously outside as well as inside the Church of England, and outside the religious world altogether. Historians of British society and culture in the nineteenth century all, I think, agree that Evangelicalism was in some ways responsible for some of its dominant characteristics. What we are not so sure about is exactly how far its influence reached and how it got there.[1]
>
> —Geoffrey Best

This book has largely been about how evangelical influence "got there," and how in getting there it affected the relations between Anglican and Dissenting evangelicals. It has not been the contention of this work that all or even the great majority of Anglican Evangelicals were converted to pan-evangelicalism by 1860. What has been demonstrated is that a sizable proportion of the Evangelical incumbents in London were willing to cooperate in interdenominational societies like the LCM by that date, and that the influential Evangelical Anglican periodicals supported such involvement, as did a number of the leading Evangelical clergy and bishops. No evidence has been found to support Jeffrey Cox's assertion that "Those Anglicans who participated in the L.C.M. were in many cases on the ideological fringes, not merely of Anglicanism, but of Anglican Evangelicalism."[2] Though not an Evangelical himself, Bishop Tait followed their example by his own endorsement of the LCM and by his appropriation of evangelistic techniques that the evangelicals had fashioned. Once this interdenominational tradition was established, it continued.

It is somewhat surprising that this union of evangelicals went completely unmentioned in W. R. Ward's *Religion and Society in England 1790–1850*, a major study on denominationalism. The fact that such cooperation significantly increased in the early 1840s runs directly contrary to Professor Ward's view that the intense denominationalism of the 1830s was mitigated only much later, once it had surrendered "its own main function when the steam went out of English social tension after 1850."[3] Cooperation began earlier than Ward suggests, in part because social tensions among some evangelicals were reduced by a common opposition to Tractarianism, Maynooth, and Papal Aggression. Out of a more positive concern, however, evangelicals were able to go against powerful pressures and transcended religious, social, and economic barriers in order to accomplish their cherished evangelistic mission. The catholicity of the lay and clerical supporters of the London City Mission represents an aspect of Victorian evangelicalism that is often ignored by historians and demonstrates a liberality of spirit rare to that age.

PAN-EVANGELICALISM AND VICTORIAN EVANGELICALISM

The evangelical fraternity that developed in interdenominational societies like the London City Mission found some ground for joint action in the 1859–1860 revival, and it was to play an important role in the subsequent development of Victorian evangelicalism. It provides part of the background to the Keswick Convention, which began in 1875. Keswick was indebted to the Wesleyan Holiness tradition and, more directly, to American preachers of combined Methodist and Quaker stock who popularized "Higher Christian Life" concepts in Britain in the 1870s.[4] Such views did not sit well with Evangelical Anglican leaders like J. C. Ryle (the leading Evangelical clergyman of the last quarter of the nineteenth century and the first bishop of Liverpool). Being a staunch Calvinist, Ryle felt that the early architects of Keswick's theology did not have a biblical conception of sin and were far too fuzzy in their theology. Being a man of certitudes, he made his own views clear in no uncertain terms.[5] By the 1880s, however, the Keswick Movement had effectively been taken over by men like Ryle who were able to establish it in its milder second phase in which the perfectionist inclinations were deliberately toned down.[6] Such a takeover by Anglicans would not have been possible in the 1820s because of the self-distancing of Anglican Evangelicals from Nonconformity. Indeed, Keswick's very existence was deeply indebted to the interdenominational approach, which the urban mission had fostered.

The new evangelical fraternity was also to affect Anglican Evangelicals' attitudes toward American revivalism. Fears in Anglican circles that American revivalists might be used to further the cause of disestablishment seem to have receded by the 1870s, thereby making them more open to the efforts of Dwight L. Moody than they had been to those of Charles Finney. John Kent has argued in his work, *Holding the Fort*, that it was Moody's visits of 1873 and 1882 "which thoroughly mixed up Anglican Evangelicals with others of the same ethos."[7]

This mingling also had an important effect on the Anglican Evangelicals' approach to foreign missions. Since the beginning of the Church Missionary Society in 1799, the Evangelicals had strongly supported their own denominational missions, which were under the party's control. The early Anglican willingness to back the interdenominational London Mission Society had faded early in the nineteenth century, and the LMS quickly became a Congregationalist body. By 1860, however, organizations like the LCM had demonstrated to Evangelicals that effective home missions could be carried out on an interdenominational basis. Some Anglican Evangelicals were by then willing to extend the principle to foreign missions and their support for nondenominational faith missions such as the China Inland Mission was important to their success and established a tradition of interdenominationalism in foreign missions, which is still carried on by Anglican Evangelicals.[8]

PAN-EVANGELICALISM AND POLITICS

In political terms, the evangelicals were much stronger in 1860 than they had been in 1828. In the 1850s Anglican Evangelicals had enjoyed "a belated worldly ascendancy," thanks in large measure to Palmerston.[9] Nonconformist evangelicals also were flexing their political muscles. Fortunately for the pan-evangelical cause, in the 1830s the architects of societies like the London City Mission had put them beyond the reach of those who might have wanted to use them in disestablishment warfare, which heated up again in the late 1860s. Palmerston's wooing of Anglican Evangelicals was to be undone by Gladstone, whom the Evangelicals distrusted because of his Tractarian sentiments and who was to anger them because of his support for the disestablishment of the Church of Ireland. J. C. Ryle expressed his frustration with the Liberals in a tract in 1868 entitled *Strike: But Hear!* In it he explained that he had campaigned vigorously against Gladstone: "Tory politics were not my reason. I am not a Tory, and never was: if I have any politics I am a Liberal. But I am not a politician: as a clergyman I have abstained on principle from voting at any election. This time I did vote on principle."[10] Thus the alliance in which Anglican Evangelicals had found themselves in 1857 was in ruins. Disraeli was enabled to play on fears that the established Church was again in danger, and Gladstone was left with the odd coalition of Tractarian, Roman Catholic, and Nonconformist supporters, which made it difficult for him to arrive at any coherent ecclesiastical policy.[11]

The concern that the Evangelicals had for the establishment principle is remarkable and deserves further comment. As has been seen, it was the Clapham Sect that nurtured a strong attachment among Evangelicals to the Church of England, hopeful that such a course would earn them the highest blessings and preferments that the establishment could offer. Hence they stressed the need to respect the parochial system and to defer to bishops. Such a concern intensified during the 1790s, as the Claphamites endeavored to persuade skeptical High Churchmen that they were not Jacobins in disguise. It was only in the 1830s, however, that some Evangelicals began to hammer out a theological, rather than a purely pragmatic justification of establishments. This apology stressed the Protestant nature of the Thirty-Nine Articles as the great summation of Protestant doctrine. This the British government was pledged to uphold. In 1844 Lord Ashley grew tired, even nauseated, with Peel's attempts to urge pragmatic arguments in defense of the Church of Ireland. In his diary he remarked, "If the Church is defensible on those grounds only, I, for one, will vote against it."[12] Ashley freely acknowledged the weight of the arguments of the Church's detractors: "The Church, in fact, is assailable on twenty points, defensible only on one, and that is, that it testifies and teaches the truth. This ground the Peel Ministry will never take."[13]

Even in the 1860s the anti-Catholicism of the Anglican Evangelicals was closely linked to their support for the English establishment. They did not simply fear losing some peculiar advantage over Dissent; rather they trembled because they believed that disestablishment would inevitably lead to the overthrow of Protestantism and the triumph of persecuting Rome. The prophets of the 1820s who had cautioned that Catholic emancipation was but the thin end of the secularist's wedge seemed to have been vindicated. Thus Ryle was convinced that the disestablishment of the Irish Church was but a stepping stone to the destruction of the English and that "the disestablishment of the English Church would, sooner or later, bring the whole country under the power of Popery. Dissenters would be gagged and crushed by the Pope as well as Churchmen. I wish," Ryle insisted, "to keep up the Church of England for the common good of all English Protestants."[14]

The Anglican Evangelicals became some of the strongest supporters of the establishment principle, and it is hard to imagine how the Church of England could have survived the century as an establishment without their strong commitment to "the Church as by law established." The same sort of arguments as those worked out by Evangelicals in the 1830s can be found in Ryle's pamphlet of 1868, but are best expressed in T. R. Birks's *Church and State*, which was published in 1869.[15] If the reform of the Irish Church in 1833 had led the early Tractarians to espouse disestablishment, it was the failure of Catholic emancipation to pacify Ireland which induced the Evangelicals to follow the opposite course. These two conservative movements reacted in opposite ways to the growing threat of political liberalism. The Evangelicals feared it most, for they saw it as the death knell of Britain as a distinctly Protestant nation. To them it appeared that Rome was going to triumph by using the cloak of political liberalism. Thus the Evangelicals, rather than advocating the spiritual independence of the church, reasserted their support for the Protestant establishment.

Outside the immediate political arena, the pan-evangelical mission had other effects. Its influence on national institutions was perhaps no more striking than in its impact upon the British army. The very institution that in the early nine-

teenth century had discriminated so blatantly against Methodists, shed its Anglican bias and made an effort to deal even-handedly with various denominational
groups. It consciously sought to be less Anglican, while at the same time it
fostered the image of being a distinctly "Christian" army. In part this change
was due to the great concern that the religious public demonstrated toward the
army during the Crimean War and the Indian Uprising, and also to the popularity
of the efforts of interdenominational groups like the Soldiers' Friend and Army
Scripture-readers' Association.

THE URBAN MISSION AND THE CHURCH OF ENGLAND

The Evangelical mission to the urban poor had its impact upon the Evangelical
party within the establishment and upon the Church as a whole. The parochial
system had been weighed in the balances by Evangelical laymen in the 1820s
and found wanting. Although these laymen were strongly Erastian, their views
differed sharply from those associated with the Clapham Sect, who had given
leadership to the Evangelical group for several decades. By the late 1820s Evangelical laymen were taking the lead and forming institutions like the District
Visiting Society, which simply ignored ecclesiastical boundaries, in order that
the poor might be evangelized. This abandonment of ecclesiastical decorum
bothered them little, because, although they were attached to the establishment,
they were convinced that clerical pretensions could not be allowed to take prec-
edence over the evangelization of the poor. By the mid–1840s a good portion
of the Evangelical clergy in London had followed suit and were willing to work
with an interdenominational agency that effectively substituted its own parochial
system for that of the Church of England. This represented an enormous shift
away from the consensus that the Clapham Sect had nurtured. In effect, it was
an admission of defeat. The hopes that Charles Simeon and William Wilberforce
had fostered of capturing the Church from within for "Vital Religion" had been
abandoned.

The sanctioning of lay agency was another area in which the Church of England
was affected by the urban mission. The formation of the Scripture Readers'
Association in 1844 was a bold step taken by Evangelical laymen who were
insistent that the Church had to stengthen the hand of Anglican clergy in the
crowded slums, and were determined that such an agency would be established,
with or without episcopal approval. High Churchmen like Bishop Phillpotts were
never reconciled to the scheme, and Tractarian clergy continued to hold such
workers in disdain.[16] The acceptance that such lay workers received, however,
made the work of groups like the Church Army in the 1880s much easier for
Anglicans to accept. The Church Army should not be understood simply as a
reaction against the Salvation Army, although it in many ways resembled it.
Anglican laymen had been working in urban evangelism for forty years under
episcopal sanction in connection with the numerous Scripture Readers' Societies;
the Church Army was another expression of a long-standing concern on the part

of some Anglicans to evangelize the working classes. Thus the evangelical mission forced Anglicans to broaden their concept of "the ministry" and afforded hundreds of earnest Anglican laymen lifelong opportunities to minister, opportunities that would have otherwise been denied them within the Church of England.

Presuppositions underlying much of the Victorian concern for church extension were also called into question by the experience gained from the urban mission. By the mid–1840s it was becoming abundantly clear that the mere provision of more accommodation was not going to resolve the dilemma that slum incumbents faced. Resistance to church attendance among the working classes was strong and what is surprising is the assumption that many Victorian churchmen seem to have made that a church that had for so long and so effectively excluded the poor (pew rents being a fairly effective means) could expect them to return to the fold with the erection of a church nearby. Clearly, part of Bishop Blomfield's willingness to allow the Scripture Readers' Association to function within his diocese was due to his realization that the newly constructed Bethnal Green churches were not the successes he had anticipated.

In other ways the Church of England had been profoundly influenced by the evangelical mission to the working classes. It led Anglicans to use evangelistic means that had not previously been acceptable to them, thus contributing life and vigor to the mainstream of the Anglican communion itself. The closing lines of a letter from Benjamin Jowett, the master of Balliol College, Oxford, to Bishop Tait in 1862 indicate that the contribution was not universally welcomed. Jowett's parting gibe to Tait was: "I heard a person ask of you the other day, 'Why does he not take up the Ecclesiastical Commission or the London Endowed Charities & set them to rights; that would be of more real use than preaching to cabmen.' "[17]

THE URBAN MISSION AND VICTORIAN EVANGELICALISM

The urban mission demonstrates how important lay initiative was to Victorian evangelicalism. The Second Evangelical Awakening (1785–1825) greatly influenced the English middle classes, creating followers concerned to reach those who had fallen between the cracks in the parochial system. Lay initiative was one of the great strengths of evangelicalism, enabling the evangelicals to organize voluntary bodies, which were far more flexible and adaptable than traditional ecclesiastical ones and which could command greater resources and mobilize more volunteers than any clergyman had at his disposal.

Of course, there were problems with such an approach: some of the societies were overlapping, and a number were poorly run. To a certain extent these difficulties were mitigated by people like Lord Shaftesbury, who patronized innumerable societies, always satisfying himself that those he supported were efficient and effective. In many cases High Churchmen opposed such evangelical societies, arguing that they undermined the corporate nature of the church and encouraged a sort of maverick individualism. Certainly the lay involvement did come at a price, but it was one that the evangelicals were prepared to pay. The boldness and creativity of the laymen were part of the reward, and both are certainly remarkable, especially in the field of evangelism; the formation of the Ranyard Bible Mission and the Working Men's Educational Union in the 1850s are testimonies to these. The increasing sophistication of the London City Mission's approach is also witness to the same in its allocation of workers to various ethnic communities, occupational groups, and locations where working people congregated.

The urban mission in turn had its impact upon evangelicalism. It did so by revealing to Victorian evangelicals the extent of the gross religious ignorance that prevailed among the urban poor. Horace Mann's religious census may have shocked many church-going Englishmen, but it should not have come as any surprise to the readers of the *City Mission Magazine* or the *Scripture Readers' Journal*. Mann echoed a theme that evangelicals had been playing for well over a decade. More than expose the extent of spiritual destitution, however, the urban mission focused attention on the more glaring aspects of Victorian slum life and sensitized its constituency to numerous social problems.

THE URBAN MISSION AND ITS IMPACT ON THE WORKING CLASSES

The process of educating the English middle classes about the gross religious ignorance of the poor caused many to hanker for a romanticized medieval past when all classes were united by a common faith, when squire and peasant were bound together by the cords of Christian love. Often the idealization involved an appeal to a distinctly rural or village setting, to a small unit in which religion served as an important cohesive force. This reasoning thus reinforced the view that industrialization and urbanization were key factors in the alienation of the urban poor from organized religion. The situation was not, however, as new as it appeared. Keith Thomas has shown that even in the Elizabethan age, when it was a criminal offense for a man to be absent from Church on a Sunday, "many of the poorest classes never became regular church-goers."[18] And throughout the sixteenth and seventeenth centuries many of those who did attend "went with considerable reluctance . . . [and] a certain proportion remained throughout their lives utterly ignorant of the elementary tenets of Christian dogma."[19] The sixteenth- and seventeenth-century Puritans often assumed that such was a hangover from Popery, something that would be corrected by a preaching ministry. The situation was not remedied, however, and the problem did not go away. What the evangelicals were encountering in the urban slums of the nineteenth century was not simply a situation of religious ignorance created by the Industrial Revolution, although many of them believed that to be the case. The problem had, in Keith Thomas's words, "always been there."[20] It is in light of this that one must evaluate the impact of the evangelicals.

While the evangelical workers were effective to a degree as proselytizers, they did not have the impact they desired. Although the evangelicals did not succeed in converting large numbers of the poor to their version of Christianity, there can be little doubt that their mission to the urban poor had a significant effect upon the development of popular religion in the nineteenth century. In 1903 the bishop of Rochester labeled English popular religion "diffusive Christianity": a rather eclectic blend of impressions and hopes about a superior being, who was seen as a kindly Father Christmas. Jeffrey Cox has described the components of this "diffusive Christianity":

A general belief in God, a conviction that this God was both just and benevolent although remote from everyday concerns, a certain confidence that "good people" would be taken care of in the life to come, and a belief that the Bible was a uniquely worthwhile book and that children in particular should be exposed to its teachings.[21]

By the end of the century evangelicals were up against a popular religion that they had helped to mold but they certainly did not want to own. There were two aspects of "diffusive Christianity" that the evangelical mission had done a great deal to reinforce: the emphasis upon Scripture and the concern that children be exposed to it. Certainly evangelicals were dismayed with the central tenet of this syncretistic faith: that " 'good people' would be taken care of in the life to come" simply because of their own moral strivings. Such was a misplaced confidence that ignored the person and work of Christ and made his sacrifice meaningless. Yet for all the evangelicals' hesitancy about "diffusive Christianity," even here their influence is evident. Keith Thomas has suggested that popular religion did not necessarily change significantly between the sixteenth and the nineteenth century.[22] Yet, to the extent that it did change in the nineteenth century, it would appear to have moved closer to recognizably Christian beliefs, rather than farther away.

In this regard, it is significant that complaints about total religious ignorance that the city missionaries had voiced in the 1830s and 1840s were rare later in the century. Joseph Oppenheimer's diary entry for October 29, 1861, is noteworthy in this regard, not because it was common, but because after at least eight years of systematic visitation in the area, it was so unusual:

>29 October 1861
>
>Monmouth Court
>
>#6   top front; induced a poor woman to send her girl 11 years old to St. Giles Ragged School, the poor girl has never been to school & is as ignorant of the name of Jesus as if brought up amongst the heathen.

By the end of the century the evangelical complaint was not that the people were irreligious. One Baptist minister complained that in his area of London, people were anything but; rather they had been "sodden by the gospel, and not saved by it."[23] And many of the late Victorian poor continued to insist upon thinking of themselves as Christians, even if their definition of that faith varied widely from a recognizably orthodox one.[24] By and large, they also insisted upon maintaining the ritual rites of passage that the sacrament of baptism, a church wedding, and a church funeral provided. Even in modern Britain the habits remain. Many otherwise irreligious people still consider it "unlucky" not to be baptized.[25]

In the nineteenth century, respectability and a vague concept of luck may have been important in the maintenance of such rituals, but undoubtedly the regular visitation of the evangelical agents served to reinforce such concerns among those most responsible for the religious affairs of a working-class home: the wives.[26] Particularly effective in this regard was the Ranyard Bible Mission which was staffed by working-class women and geared to reaching their peers. The Ranyard Mission, like the other evangelical societies, was aware of the difficulty in overcoming working-class discomfort in the confines of any church.

During the last quarter of the century such efforts focused on the mission halls, which had slowly grown in importance as centers for reaching those who would never darken the door of a church. They certainly became a very important part of the machinery by which evangelicalism "got there" and were built by city missions, by concerned individuals, denominations, and nondenominational societies and congregations. At the end of the century, Charles Booth observed, "we find London dotted over with buildings devoted to this work. In the poorer parts especially, in almost every street, there is a mission; they are more numerous than schools or churches, and only less numerous than public-houses."[27] All this sort of work, whether Anglican or Nonconformist or independent was "interwoven with that of the Society known as the 'London City Mission.' "[28] Regardless of who carried out the work, it was essentially the same:

> The amount of work done from these shabby centres is, however, in the aggregate enormous. In character it differs little. All the missions, of whatever description, or denomination, or lack of denomination, take up very similar ground. They set out to preach the Gospel, to teach and train the children, to influence and guide the mothers, to visit the homes and relieve poverty. They bring help in sickness and comfort in distress. They all seek to inculcate temperance, and most aim at being centres of social relaxation and enjoyment, while underlying all is the desire to lead man to God. And all alike acknowledge that if this is not accomplished nothing is accomplished. The heart must be touched.[29]

The mission hall movement was a clear admission that the churches were the preserve of the middle classes and the fact that such halls were far more widespread in the United Kingdom than they ever were in North America undoubtedly reflects the strength of the British class structure.[30] The city missions eventually experienced the same sort of metamorphosis that had affected evangelical Nonconformity by mid-century: in the long run they had to shift from their overwhelming concern with conversion and emphasize consolidation or pastoral care.

Booth commented that "A [city] missionary who had a hall in which he regularly preaches on Sunday evening, tends to gather around him a body of supporters, and then with their aid to develop the work along ordinary mission lines."[31] Although they were never allowed to abandon their visiting roles, they eventually came to function as working-class pastors for the flocks they had gathered.

Undoubtedly the city missions and the enormous evangelical effort they represent were an important means by which evangelicalism affected Victorian social relations. Arguably, the moral, philanthropic, and religious crusades of the evangelicals were important factors in overcoming the isolation of social classes and in shielding society from violent change. At the same time they promoted peaceful change. For instance, for middle-class women such campaigns provided "the lever which they used to open the doors closed to them in other spheres"[32] and gave them the political training that was later to be used in the suffrage movement.[33]

Yet in the long run, the evangelicals' impact upon the working class was not what they had desired. "Diffusive Christianity" was a far cry from the evangelical version of the faith. Should the whole exercise be viewed then as a failure? By evangelical standards it should. But the aim of the movement was nothing less than the conversion of an entire social class that was largely indifferent to organized religion. If judged by such a standard, almost anything Victorian Christians did must be viewed as a failure.[34] While the evangelical mission did not achieve its goal, it certainly was not a failure. When one appreciates the size of their urban mission, its pervasive character, its often superb organization (and important at times its lack thereof), as well as its remarkable duration, one could make a case for its being the most influential religious crusade to affect the Victorian working classes.

The very fact that such an enormous attempt was made by evangelicals to reach the poor was, at the very least, a vindication of their consistency. One critic of Victorian evangelicals commented in 1861, in words designed primarily to bury them:

the Evangelical party is redeemed by the working of its parishes. It is to its credit that it is foremost in united schemes of charity: it is to its credit, to some extent, that foreign missions have so increased and spread. But that which saves it from wreck, which atones for its arbitrary social maxims, which partly conceals its obnoxious polemic organization, is the fact that the Evangelical clergy, as a body, are indefatigable in ministerial duties, and devoted, heart and soul, to the manifold labours of Christian love. The school, the savings bank, the refuge, all the engines of parochial usefulness, find in them, for the most part, hearty supporters and friends. There is a positive literature of parish machinery. . . . But when the history of the Evangelical party is written, it will be told of them, that with narrow-mindedness and mistaken traditions, with little intellectual acquirements and ill-directed zeal against their brothers in the Church, they yet worked manfully in the pestilent and heathen by-ways of our cities, and preached the gospel to the poor.[35]

Appendix A

Annual Incomes (in Pounds) of Leading London Evangelistic Societies, 1835–1860

Year ending	LCM	SRA	Year ending	LCM	SRA	RBM
1836	2,714		1848	16,147	4,316	
1837	3,107		1849	19,069	5,882	
1838	3,887		1850	20,320	6,063	
1839	4,820		1851	23,053	8,465	
1840	3,897		1852	23,216	7,624	
1841	4,831		1853	26,481	8,618	
1842	5,534		1854	27,484	8,890	
1843	6,754		1855	30,706	8,924	
1844	8,800		1856	32,398	9,747	
1845	9,571	3,488	1857	30,693	9,261	
1846	11,715	3,692	1858	32,230	9,384	
1847	13,934	3,384	1859	35,798	10,352	1,699
			1860	35,573	9,529	6,077

Appendix B

Numbers of Agents Employed by the Three Leading London Evangelistic Societies, 1835–1860

Year Ending	London City Mission	Scripture Readers' Association	Year ending	London City Mission	Scripture Readers' Association	Ranyard Bible Mission
1836	40		1848	201	87	
1837	63		1849	214	91	
1838	42		1850	242	98	
1839	50		1851	232	106	
1840	58		1852	270	116	
1841	63		1853	300	125	
1842	61		1854	327	127	
1843	82		1855	328	121	
1844	101		1856	320	120	
1845	121	33	1857	329	122	
1846	152	50	1858	350	110	
1847	186	81	1859	362	115	37
			1860	375	119	134

Appendix C

Annual Incomes of Leading London Evangelistic Societies, 1865–1900

Year Ending	London City Mission		Scripture Readers' Association		Ranyard Bible Mission	
	Receipts	Agents	Receipts	Agents	Receipts	Agents
1865	40,041	395	12,589	n.a.	11,100	209
1870	40,616	375	12,020	n.a.	11,743	222
1875	44,047	437	10,254	n.a.	11,523	203
1880	46,990	447	11,202	n.a.	9,713	166
1885	50,195	461	12,312	126	9,199*	159*
1890	54,129	500	10,339	134	n.a.	n.a.
1895	48,754	477	11,500	125	n.a.	n.a.
1900	40,607	458	9,274	n.a.	n.a.	n.a.

Symbols:

* - Figures are for 1883.

n.a. - Figures are not available.

Note: The above figures are for the amounts received in donations to the general funds of the societies. In the case of the Ranyard Mission the income was augmented significantly by the sales of Bibles. It should also be noted in regard to the Ranyard Mission that in 1868 it began to employ 'Mission Nurses' as well as 'Bible women.'

Appendix D

Below is a listing of the occupations of the LCM workers in 1849 classified according to Hobsbawm's categories.

Priest of Church of Rome	1	General Shopkeeper	1
Undergraduate of Corpus Christi College, Cambridge	1	Musician in 56th Regiment	1
		Officer in the Corporation of the City of London	1
Student of St. Bee's College	1	Public Lecturer on Scientific Subjects	1
Alamode Beef Shop, keeper of	1	Salesman	1
		Schoolmasters	24
Artist	1	Shipbroker	1
Bookseller	1	Silk Manufacturer	1
Botanist	1	Surgeon	1
Clerks, Mercantile	2	Teachers in schools	2
Clerk, Lawyer's	1	Tobacco Manufacturer	1
Coal Merchant	1	Travellers	2

Total 48

CATEGORY B
Workers classified by Hobsbawm in occupations "known to be aristocratic, or to contain a high proportion of aristocrats":

Block Printer	1	Curriers	3
Coachmaker	1	Print Cutter	1
Compositors	5		

Total 11

CATEGORY C
Workers classified by Hobsbawm in occupations "containing an aristocracy, but also many depressed workers":

Bakers	2		
Brushmaker	1	Carvers and Gilders	3
Builders, Bricklayers &c	5	Tailors	10
Cabinet-makers	2		

Total 23

CATEGORY D
From working class - below "aristocracy of working class"

Brewer	1	Pattern and Clog Maker	1
Butcher	1	Perfumer	1
Cabmen	2	Porters	2
Carpenters	5	Saddlers	2
Coachsmiths	2	Sealing-wax Maker	1
Confectioners	2	Shoemaker	11
Corn-chandlers	2	Shopmen	3
Farmers &c	7	Silk Weavers	6
Fellmonger	1	Silversmith	1
Gardeners	4	Stage Coachman	1
Greengrocer	1	Table-cover Printer	1
Grocers	4	Tobacconist	1
Hairdresser	1	Tobacco-pipe maker	1
Ironfounder	1	Waiter at Hotel	1
Labourer in Gas Works	1	Warehousemen	3
Linendrapers	4	Wheelwright	1
Miller	1	Woolcomber	1
Miner	1	Woolstapler	1
Painters, Plumbers &c	9	Woollen Cloth-worker	1
Paperhanger	1	Wove Spinner	1
		Writer and Grainer	1

Total 93

CATEGORY E
Unclassified:

Bird Fancier	1	Other servants	4
Servants, Steward	1	Soldiers	2
" Butlers	2		

Total 10

CATEGORY F
Unclassifiable:

Ministers of the Gospel	3
Catechist of Church Missionary Society	1
Missionary of Wesleyan Missionary Society	1
Missionary of London Missionary Society	1
Catechist of London Society for Promoting Christianity amongst the Jews	1
Missionaries of Home Missionary Society	2
Missionaries of Town Missionary and Scripture Readers Society	3
Paid Agent of Christian Instruction Society	1
Readers of Scripture Readers Association	2
Scripture Readers, employed by Clergymen privately	5
Irish Scripture Readers	4
Lay Agent of Cork Pastoral Aid Society	1
Colporteurs of British and Foreign Bible Society	2
Temperance Society Agents	2

Total 29

Summary

48	Category A: workers from lower middle class or above
11	Category B: from "aristocracy of working class"
23	Category C: from groups known to contain some members of aristocracy
93	Category D: from below "aristocracy of working class"
10	Category E: unclassified
29	Category F: Unclassifiable

214 total number of agents

Appendix E

London City Mission
Instructions to Missionaries
1858

1. Visit the inhabitants of the district assigned you for the purpose of bringing them to an acquaintance with salvation, through our Lord Jesus Christ, and of doing them good by every means in your power.

2. Read a portion of the Scriptures, and offer prayer, if practicable, in every house or room you visit; if impracticable, introduce into your conversation as much of the Scriptures as possible, and see that the terms used are understood. In reading or speaking, let those portions that bear on the depravity of man, justification by faith alone, the necessity of a change of heart and of holiness of life, ever hold a prominent place.

3. Inculcate upon all persons the duty of searching the Scriptures as a revelation from God, and as the standard by which they will be judged at the last day.

4. Urge upon all persons you visit the necessity of attending the public worship of God. If they are neglecting it, point out to them the especial importance and duty of their attending the ministry of the Gospel. Specify no particular church or chapel, leaving to those you visit the selection of the place most accordant with their own views, provided that in that place the great doctrines of the Reformation are faithfully taught.

5. Inculcate upon parents the duty of training up their children in the way they should go, and the propriety of procuring for them week-day and Sunday-school instruction. Point out, as occasion may require, their relative duties, and faithfully but prudently reprove open vice, such as swearing, intemperance, and the profanation of the Sabbath.

6. See that those persons who have not the Scriptures are supplied with them.

7. Endeavour to hold two meetings every week in different parts of your district for the purpose of reading the Scriptures, exhortation, and prayer. Let those exercises be brief, the whole service not exceeding one hour, and do not undertake more than two meetings a week without the permission of the Committee.

8. Circulate no tract or book in your district which has not been approved and recommended by the Committee.

9. Avoid all unnecessary controversy upon religious subjects. Do not interfere with the peculiar tenets of any individual respecting Church government. Carefully avoid all topics of an irritating tendency, and seek by a simple manifestation of the truth to commend yourself to every man's conscience.

10. Studiously avoid entering upon subjects of a political nature, as altogether foreign from the purpose of your visit.

11. Devote yourself entirely to the objects of the mission, and abstain from all secular employment. Spend 36 hours every week in visiting from house to house, exclusive of meetings and other engagements. Give yourself to the study of the Scriptures and to prayer.

12. Write the journal of your daily proceedings with the strictest accuracy as to facts and circumstances, and submit it once a week to the superintendent of the district for his inspection.

13. Conduct yourself in such a manner as will prove to all persons that you are in earnest in seeking their spiritual welfare. Be humble, courteous, and affectionate. Constantly realise your own obligations to the Saviour. Go to your district in a spirit of prayer, and with an earnest desire that every person you visit may be brought to a saving knowledge of the Lord Jesus Christ. Your work is awfully important; you have to deal with immortal souls, many of whom may never hear the Gospel but from you, and whose eternal condition may be determined by the reception or rejection of the message which you deliver to them. Be courageous, be faithful; keep the Lord Jesus continually before your own mind, and commend Him and his great salvation to the people. Be watchful and exemplary in every part of your conduct, public and private. "Owe no man any thing." Go forth daily to your work with your heart lifted up to God, for the assistance and direction of his Holy Spirit, and relying upon his promise for that wisdom and strength which all your adversaries shall not be able to gainsay or resist. Let the glory of God and the salvation of souls be your chief, your only end.

Scripture Readers' Association
Instructions for Scripture Readers
1858

1. You are to visit in your district from house to house, for the purpose of reading the Scriptures to the poor, accompanying such reading with plain remarks, pointing their attention to the Saviour of whom they testify.

2. Remember that your principal object must be to call attention to the Scriptures, strongly urging upon their authority the sin of neglecting them, setting them forth as the only infallible rule of faith and practice, as able "to make men wise unto salvation, through faith which is in Christ Jesus."

3. You are strictly prohibited from carrying about with you, for the purpose of reading to the people, or of distributing among them, any book or publication but the Scriptures of the Old and New Testament, and the book of Common Prayer; and such small books and tracts as may be sanctioned by the Committee of the Scripture Readers' Association, and by the Incumbent; taking care to avoid, as much as possible, all controversy.

4. You are strictly prohibited from preaching, either in houses or elsewhere.

5. Urge upon all persons you visit the duty of attending the public worship of God in the church; inculcate upon parents the duty of presenting their children for baptism, of training them up in the way that they should go, and of procuring for them week-day and Sunday-school instruction. In any particular case which seems to call for the visit of the parochial clergyman, report it forthwith to him.

6. The amount of time which can be devoted to visiting the houses of the district in rotation, for the purpose of reading the Scriptures to the inhabitants, may vary according to circumstances, of which the clergyman of the parish or district will judge: but those who have engaged their whole time to the work of Scripture reading, shall in no case employ less of it than six hours a day, or thirty-six hours a week, in reading the Scriptures from house to house. Less, however, will be of course expected from those who engage themselves only for partial employment.

7. You are directed to keep this regular journal of each day's proceedings, noting carefully the parties visited, and mentioning the portions of Scripture read by you on each occasion. You must not suffer the preparation of the journal to interfere with your more important duties. Let it be a plain narration of facts, briefly but accurately stated. Trust as little as possible to memory, but, at farthest, note the transactions of each day before the close of the next. Your journal must at all times be open to the inspection of the clergyman of your district, and must be deposited with him at the end of three months, and it will be finally retained by him after having been transmitted to the Committee for their information.

8. Let it be your constant endeavour to adorn the doctrine of God your Saviour by your life and conversation; and to this end be diligent in the study of Holy Scripture; attend on all the ordinances and means of grace; and cultivate a spirit of prayer.

General Directions for Keeping a Journal

1. Never omit to fill up your journal each day after the cessation of your active labours.

2. Write the date on the first line of the page; the name of the street, lane, or court visited, on the second; the number of the house in the margin.

3. Leave a line between every separate narrative; and if several incidents be mentioned, leave a line between each incident.

4. On no account tear a leaf out of the journal; if any error occurs, cancel the page by running the pen across it.

5. Leave your journal with the clergyman every Saturday evening when you call to leave your report paper.

6. Let your journal take the form of a narrative of the day's proceedings. State everything that occurs and conceal nothing. Mention where you were well received and where

rejected. State briefly the several subjects of your conversation, mention the passages of Scripture read, and record the effect which your visit appeared to have produced.

Source *Parliamentary Papers, 1857–8*, 9, "Deficiency of the Means of Spiritual Instruction," Select Committee, House of Lords, Report, pp. 575–6.

Notes

INTRODUCTION

1. See J. E. Orr, *The Second Evangelical Awakening in Britain*, London, 1949; J. W. Bready, *Lord Shaftesbury and Social-Industrial Progress*, London, 1933 and *England Before and After Wesley*, London, 1938.

2. K. S. Inglis, *Churches and the Working Classes in Victorian England*, London, 1963, p. 1.

3. For a survey of recent works dealing with the Halévy thesis, see Elissa S. Itzkin, "The Halévy Thesis—A Working Hypothesis? English Revivalism: Antidote for Revolution and Radicalism 1789–1815," *Church History* 44(1975):47–56.

4. A. D. Gilbert, *Religion and Society in Industrial England: Church, Chapel and Social Change, 1740–1914*, London, 1976, pp. 51 and 30.

5. E. J. Hobsbawm, *Labouring Men: Studies in the History of Labour*, London, 1964.

6. Gilbert, *Religion and Society*, p. vii.

7. Ibid., pp. 83–93.

8. W. R. Ward, *Religion and Society in England 1790–1850*, New York, 1973, p. 6.

9. G. Kitson Clark, *The Making of Victorian Britain*, London, 1962, p. 23.

10. Geoffrey Best, "Evangelicalism and the Victorians," in *The Victorian Crisis of Faith*, ed. Anthony Symondson, London, 1970, p. 54.

11. Gilbert, *Religion and Society*, p. 135.

12. A recent study of the work of ritualists, Broad Churchmen and Evangelicals in East London makes the same point. See D. B. McIlhiney, "A Gentleman in Every Slum: Church of England Missions in East London, 1837–1914," Ph.D. thesis, Princeton University, 1977.

13. K. S. Inglis, *Churches and the Working Classes in Victorian England*, p. 21.

14. K. S. Inglis, "English Churches and the working classes, 1880–1900, with an introductory survey of tendencies earlier in the century," D.Phil. thesis, Oxford University, 1956.

15. John Kent, book review in *English Historical Review* 65(1980):427.

16. Gordon Read and David Jebson, *A Voice in the City*, Liverpool, 1979, p. 18.

17. See chapter 6, n.8.

18. W. E. Gladstone, *Gleanings of Past Years*, 8 vols., London, 1879, 7:213. Cited by W. J. Clyde Ervine, "Anglican Evangelical Clergy, 1797–1837," Ph.D. thesis, Cambridge University, 1979, p. 192.

19. *Bodley Mss.*: Add. Ms.c. 290, Bodleian Library, Oxford.

CHAPTER 1: The Divided Evangelicals

1. Owen Chadwick, *The Victorian Church*, London, 1966, 1:5.

2. See Owen Chadwick's lengthy introduction to *The Mind of the Oxford Movement*, London, 1960.

3. This point has been made by Thomas Laqueur. See his review of Alan D. Gilbert, *Religion and Society in Industrial England: Church, Chapel and Social Change*, London, 1976, in *American Historical Review* 82(1977):637–638.

4. Owen Chadwick, *The Victorian Church*, 1:34.

5. Ibid., 1:26.

6. Ibid., 1:35.

7. W. B. Sprague, *Letters From Europe*, New York, 1828, p. 86.

8. Nancy Murray, "The Influence of the French Revolution on the Church of England and Its Rivals, 1789–1802," D.Phil. thesis, Oxford University, 1975, p. 5.

9. W. R. Ward, *Religion and Society in England 1790–1850*, New York, 1973, p. 52.

10. W. B. Sprague, *Letters from Europe*, pp. 85–86.

11. Murray, "French Revolution," p. 5.

12. W. J. Clyde Ervine, "Anglican Evangelical Clergy, 1797–1837," Ph.D. thesis, Cambridge University, 1979, p. 2.

13. For a study of Simeon's Trust, see Wesley Balda, "Simeon's 'Protestant Papists': A Sampling of Moderate Evangelicalism Within the Church of England 1839–1865," *Fides et Historia* 11 (Fall-Winter, 1983):55–67.

14. A. W. Brown, *Recollections of the Conversation Parties of the Rev. Charles Simeon*, London, 1863, p. 224. Cited by R. H. Martin, "The Pan-Evangelical Impulse, 1790–1830," D.Phil. thesis, Oxford University, 1974, p. 28. Simeon's view of Dissent was repeated by other prominent Evangelicals writing in the 1820s and 1830s. An examination of private letters written in the 1830s and 1840s by Henry Budd, a leading Evangelical clergyman, reveals continual lamenting over evangelical disunity, especially in the face of rising Tractarianism; he regarded it, however, as the problem of the Dissenters, who should return to the Church of England, the "constituted channel" of God's truth. He personally found "silence and distant courtesy the best mode of dealing" with his neighboring ministers. Budd's stance appears to have been typical of many Evangelical incumbents in London. See Henry Budd, *Infant Baptism*, London, 1827, pp. 282–283; Charles Bridges, *The Christian Ministry*, London, 1830, p. 114; and E. Bickersteth, *The Christian Student*, 3d ed., London, 1832, p. 291. For Budd's personal views, see Letter from Henry Budd to the Reverend C. J. Bird, February 11, 1834, in

Memoir of Budd, London, 1855, p. 500; and Letter from H. Budd to C. J. Bird, June 28, 1838, Ibid., p. 538.

15. J. H. Philpot, *The Seceders*, London, 1964, p. 80. The Irvingites, the Plymouth Brethren, and the High Calvinist followers of Henry Bulteel, a former fellow of Exeter College, Oxford, had all served to draw away small numbers who otherwise might have been influential as Evangelicals.

16. *Christian Observer* (June 1843):350.

17. Ashton Oxenden, in his popular work *The Pastoral Office*, cautioned fellow Evangelical clerics: "To be always dwelling on the Church's authority, and the Church's superior excellence, in the pulpit, is certainly neither politic nor scriptural. It will repel, rather than attract; it will weary, rather than persuade. In our zeal, too, to make proselytes from Dissent, we may neglect the great end for which we are sent—namely, to win souls to Christ." As Oxenden wrote in 1857, it is clear that a significant section within Evangelicalism long remained steadfastly opposed to pan-evangelical cooperation. That Oxenden also felt it necessary to rebuke some of his brethren for the pharisaical party spirit which had descended on a section of Evangelicalism is indicative of the narrowness and isolation of some of the Evangelical clergy in the late 1850s. Ashton Oxenden, *The Pastoral Office*, London, 1857, pp. 230–231 and pp. 240–245.

18. Martin, "The Pan-Evangelical Impulse, 1790–1830," p. 368.

19. Martin writes: "For all its carefully planned and well-publicized equality, the pan-evangelical societies . . . were in reality always dominated by the Anglicans who on a number of occasions . . . imposed their system on docile Dissenters who blindly submitted." Ibid., p. 369.

20. Various factors were reinforcing Methodist conservatism. Among them were the question of the control of Sunday Schools, attitudes to revivalism, government distrust, political radicalism and economic and administrative problems. See David Hempton, *Methodism and Politics in British Society 1750–1850*, London, 1984, pp. 55–115.

21. Ervine, p. 253.

22. Ibid., p. 306.

23. J. H. Stewart, *Thoughts on the Importance of Special Prayer for the General Outpouring of the Spirit*, London, 1821. Cited by Ervine, p. 253.

24. J.F.C. Harrison, *The Second Coming: Popular Millenarianism, 1780–1850*, London, 1979, p. 7.

25. Ervine, p. 258.

26. Ibid., p. 254.

27. Ibid., p. 267.

28. See I. S. Rennie, "Evangelicalism and English Public Life," Ph.D. thesis, University of Toronto, 1962, p. 116; John Wolffe, "Protestant Societies and Anti-Catholic Agitation in Great Britain, 1829–1860," D.Phil. thesis, Oxford University, 1984, p. 43; and D. Hempton, *Methodism and Politics*, p. 136.

29. Hempton, p. 136.

30. G.I.T. Machin, *Politics and the Churches of Great Britain, 1832–1868*, Oxford, 1977, p. 31. See also D. Hempton, *Methodism and Politics*, p. 136.

31. Wolffe, "Protestant Societies and Anti-Catholic Agitation," p. 42.

32. *Record*, July 12, 1830. Cited by Wolffe, "Protestant Societies and Anti-Catholic Agitation," p. 63.

33. Rennie, "Evangelicalism and English Public Life," p. 77.

34. *Record*, Dec. 29, 1853.

35. The suggestion that such a paper should be established was first made by James Evans, a wealthy English philanthropist who had lived in Edinburgh for some time. Evans was able to interest two other Evangelical friends in the project: Andrew Hamilton, an Edinburgh friend who had moved to London in 1824; and John Stuckey Reynolds, a senior figure in the Treasury.

36. See *Dictionary of National Biography* and Charles Hole, *Life of Phelps*, London, 1871, 2:13.

37. Two other figures became regular contributors: one was a clergyman who eventually became a bishop (probably Daniel Wilson, second Bishop of Calcutta); and a layman (probably Captain James Edward Gordon). Another figure who would appear to have been in the "Recordite" inner circle was Abel Smith Sr., a wealthy Tory M.P. and philanthropist. It was he who had induced Andrew Hamilton to move to London in the mid–1820s. Smith's Scottish connections, however, did not end there; his brother-in-law was Captain James Edward Gordon. See *Recollections of the late Andrew Hamilton reprinted from the 'Record' Newspaper*, London, 1854.

38. Wolffe, pp. 63–64.

39. Ervine, pp. 306–307.

40. Ibid., p. 308.

41. Ibid.

42. I. S. Rennie, "Evangelicalism and English Public Life," p. 87.

43. *Fraser's Magazine*, 18(1838):330.

44. Hempton, *Methodism and Politics*, p. 128.

45. Ibid.

46. Machin, p. 46.

47. Rennie, "Evangelicalism and English Public Life," p. 111.

48. Ibid.

49. *Record*, July 29, 1828.

50. *Record*, June 11, 1829.

51. *Record*, Oct. 18, 1830.

52. Machin, p. 39.

53. C. J. Blomfield, *Charge to the Clergy*, London, 1834, p. 2.

54. See Thomas Binney, *Dissent Not Schism*, London, 1835 and Charles Lushington, *A Remonstrance Addressed to the Bishop of London on the sanction given in his late charge to the Clergy of that Diocese, to the Calumnies against the Dissenters*, London, 1834.

55. *Record*, Jan. 23, 1840 and Dec. 3, 1846.

56. *Evangelical Magazine* n.s. 12(Feb. 1834):62.

57. Evangelical clergy apparently often did lose converts to Dissent; a clergyman wrote in the *Christian Guardian* in 1830: "If they [the Evangelical clergy] look around their congregations for the fruits of their ministry, for those whom it has pleased God to awaken and convert through their instrumentality, how often are they pained to miss them from their places, and to hear that they have been prevailed upon to join other communions." *Christian Guardian* (January 1830):16.

58. *Evangelical Magazine* n.s. 12(April 1834):154.

59. James' *Christian Fellowship or Church Member's Guide* was published in 1822 and had subsequently undergone a harsh critique in the Evangelical *British Review*, causing James to modify and clarify some of his statements in later editions. In 1829 a reprint of the *British Review*'s critique was published for free distribution, but James again

abstained from a direct reply for the sake of interdenominational peace. In 1830, when the Evangelical publishing house of Seeley and Sons came out with an expanded version of the same article entitled *The Church of England and Dissent*, James broke his silence. In reply he wrote *Dissent and the Church of England*, in which he tried to refute Evangelical attempts to use his earlier work as evidence of the inferior quality of Nonconformist Christianity. See *British Review and London Critical Journal*, 23 (1825):200–229 and J. A. James, *Dissent and the Church of England*, London, 1831, p. iii.

60. *Evangelical Magazine*, n.s. 11 (August 1833):357.

61. "A Plea for the Restoration of Confidence and Co-operation Between Pious Churchmen and Dissenters," *Evangelical Magazine* n.s. 17 (Supplement 1839):643.

62. *Evangelical Magazine* (April 1834):153–154.

63. *Record*, Oct. 18, 1830.

64. See Owen Chadwick, *The Victorian Church*, London, 1966, 1:73–74 and *Record*, Nov. 4, 1841.

65. Rennie, p. 29.

66. See William Warburton, *The Alliance between Church and State, or the necessity and equity of an Established religion and a Test Law*, 1736 and N. Sykes, *Church and State in England in the Eighteenth Century*, p. 322, cited by G.I.T. Machin, *Politics and the Churches of Great Britain, 1832–1868*, Oxford, 1977, p. 4.

67. *Christian Guardian* (1824):385–386. Cited by Rennie, p. 29.

68. Rennie, p. 29.

69. Ibid.

70. Ibid., pp. 113–114.

71. *Christian Guardian* (1829):110.

72. Rennie, pp. 122–123.

73. *Evangelical Magazine*, n.s. 11 (August 1833):357.

74. Seeley published Irving's works until 1828. Haldane had been allied with Irving in the Apocrypha Controversy.

75. R. B. Seeley, *Essays on the Church*, London, 1834.

76. Seeley, *Essays*, p. 104.

77. Letter from Edward Bickersteth to Mr. Baker, February 13, 1837. *Bickersteth MS Papers*, Bodleian Library, Oxford, box 25, notebook 1.

78. Seeley, *Essays*, pp. 32–33.

79. Ibid., p. 33.

80. Ibid., pp. 41–44.

81. *Record*, July 23, 1838.

82. Geoffrey Best, "The Protestant Constitution and Its Supporters, 1800–1829," *Transactions of the Royal Historical Society*, 5th ser., 8 (1958):116.

83. *Record*, July 23, 1838.

84. Best, "Protestant Constitution," p. 114.

85. D. Wilson, "Introduction" in Richard Baxter, *Reformed Pastor*, ed. William Brown, Glasgow, 1829, p. xx.

86. In his diary he recorded a prayer of thanks on the anniversary of the St. Bartholomew's Day Massacre: "Blessed be Thy providence that the murder of Protestants (at Paris Aug. 24, 1572) is not now to be dreaded in our Protestant country! —but that peace and protecting laws prevail. May England never lose her Protestant spirit and Protestant Character." Bishop Wilson Diary, August 24, 1845, *Bodley MSS.*, Bodleian Library, Oxford.

87. G. H. Sumner, *Life of Charles R. Sumner*, London, 1876, pp. 162–163.

88. Machin, p. 76.

89. *Record*, July 23, 1838.

90. For examples see the following publications of Nonconformist pamphleteer John Search: *What? and Who says it? An Exposition of the Statement that the Established Church "destroys more souls than it Saves,"* 2d ed., London, 1834; *Strike, but Hear: A Correspondence between the Compiler of "What and Who Says It?" and the Editor of the Christian Observer*; London, 1838; and *John Search's Last Words*, London, 1839. Two significant publications by Thomas Binney also added fuel to the fire: *An Address on Laying the first stone of the New King's Weigh-House Chapel*, London, 1834; and *The Ultimate Object of the Evangelical Dissenters Avowed and Advocated; a Sermon Preached at the King's Weigh-House Chapel*, London, 1834.

91. *Churchman's Monthly Review and Chronicle* (September 1844):671.

92. R. Wardlaw, *National Church Establishments Examined: A Course of Lectures, delivered in London in 1839*, London, 1839.

93. Hugh McNeile, *Lectures on the Church of England*, London, 1840.

94. G. Redford, *Christianity Against Coercion*, London, 1840.

95. *Record*, July 9, 1835.

96. *Record*, May 21, 1838. Ashley was its president and Farquhar its treasurer.

97. Machin, p. 40.

98. Ibid.

99. Rennie, p. 108.

100. Henry Phillpotts, "The Roman Catholic Oath," *Publications of the Protestant Association*, vol. 1, pamphlet 12, (London, 1839).

101. Rennie, p. v.

102. R. W. Dale, *The Life and Letters of J. A. James: Including an Unfinished Autobiography*, London, 1861, 2d. ed., p. 585.

103. Letter from J. A. James to W. Sprague, December 15, 1828. Quoted in Dale, *Life of James*, p. 251.

104. Letter from J. A. James to W. Sprague, April 13, 1831. Quoted in Dale, p. 263.

105. *Record*, Oct. 18, 1830.

106. Letter from J. A. James to Dr. Patton, March 13, 1834. Quoted in Dale, p. 339.

107. A. D. Gilbert, *Religion and Society in Industrial England: Church, Chapel and Social Change*, London, 1976, p. 27.

108. Ibid., p. 94.

CHAPTER 2: Evangelicalism in Flux

1. I am indebted to Dr. John Walsh of Jesus College, Oxford, for his assistance with the question of religious experience and for allowing me to read his unpublished manuscript "The Moderate Calvinism of the Early Evangelicals."

2. "Letter to a Friend on Growth in Grace," *Christian Guardian* (October 1828):369–372.

3. The Western Schism men of 1816 and Henry Bulteel, the leader of the 1831 Oxford secessionists, were all hyper-Calvinist Antinomians who had been influenced by Hawker's teachings. For details on the Western Schism see H. H. Rowdon, "Secession from the Established Church in the Early Nineteenth Century," *Vox Evangelica* 3 (1964):81. Also disruptive to Anglican Evangelicals were the efforts of eccentrics like

William Huntingdon, a Nonconformist minister who succeeded in creating havoc in thriving Anglican congregations, including that of Rowland Hill in London. I am indebted to Dr. Rennie for information on the connection of the Western Schism men with Dr. Hawker. For his influence over Bulteel see Rowdon, "Secession," p. 81.

4. The swing of the pendulum toward a more subjective emphasis appears to have gained ground about 1810 among the Clapham Sect. According to Samuel Garratt, a leading Evangelical cleric, John Venn became the leading spokesman for the subjective view. He also suggested, in his *Personal Reflections*, that this view led to a disparaging of the Reformation classic, *Luther on the Galatians*, and a promotion of Jonathan Edwards's *On the Religious Affections*. "The joyful assurance of salvation," wrote Garratt, "was changed into a tone of doubt, as the expression ran, 'as to my interest in Christ.' To doubt, in that sense was gradually . . . thought the best proof of being a Christian, and the subjective in religion, the feelings and emotions, very much took the place of the objective belief in Christ and His work." Given this heritage, one can better appreciate why so many of the children of the Clapham Sect were attracted to the romanticism embodied in the Oxford Movement, and indeed, why, as Yngve Brilioth observed, so many who made the trek to Rome later in the century, had begun their pilgrimage at Clapham. See Evelyn Garratt, *Life and Personal Reflections of Samuel Garratt*, London, 1908, p. 201, and Yngve Brilioth, *The Anglican Revival: Studies in the Oxford Movement*, London, 1933, p. 123.

5. E. Garratt, *Life of Garratt*, p. 207.

6. *Record*, Feb. 6, 1837.

7. Ibid.

8. For an account of the Socinian Test Controversy, see I. S. Rennie, "Evangelicalism and English Public Life," Ph.D. thesis, University of Toronto, 1962, pp. 67f.

9. T. Chalmers, *Chalmers' Works*, vol. 14:108–109, Glasgow, 1849.

10. E. P. Thompson, *The Making of the English Working Class*, New York, 1965, pp. 116–119.

11. J.F.C. Harrison, *The Second Coming: Popular Millenarianism, 1780–1850*, London, 1979.

12. R. A. Soloway, *Prelates and People*, London, 1969, p. 34.

13. Ibid., pp. 38–42.

14. Thomas R. Birks, *Memoir of the Rev. Edward Bickersteth*, 2 vols., London, 1852, 2:43.

15. Bickersteth's formulation of the premillennial view was only one of several variations. For a discussion of this and other interpretations of biblical eschatology, see chapter 4.

16. Birks, *Memoir of Bickersteth*, 2:44.

17. Letter from Edward Bickersteth to ?, December 1835, *Bickersteth MSS*, Bodleian Library, Oxford, box 25, notebook 1.

18. Letter from Edward Bickersteth to E. Hankinson, 10 March, 1836, *Bickersteth MSS*, box 25, notebook 1.

19. See W. R. Ward, "Short Notices," in *English Historical Review* 86 (1971):632–633, and R. A. Soloway, *Prelates and People*, p. 267.

20. *Christian Observer* (April 1828):275.

21. *Christian Observer* (August 1828):473–481.

22. *Christian Observer* (March 1829):187.

23. W. B. Sprague, *Letters from Europe*, New York, 1828, p. 90.

24. *Record*, Aug. 4, 1831.

25. Daniel Wilson, "Introductory Essay," in *The Reformed Pastor*, Richard Baxter, ed. William Brown, Glasgow, 1829, p. xxx.

26. Ibid., p. xxix.

27. Letter from Edward Bickersteth to W. B. Sprague (?), August 18, 1832, *Bickersteth MSS*, box 25, notebook 1.

28. *Congregational Magazine*, n.s. 3 (1827):477.

29. Bickersteth to Sprague.

30. W. B. Sprague, *Lectures on Revivals of Religion*, Albany, New York, 1832.

31. John Hill Diary, January 8, 1834, p. 103, *MSS St. Edmund Hall*, Bodleian Library, Oxford.

32. See chapter 1.

33. Hill Diary.

34. Charles Bridges (1794–1869) was a well-known Evangelical clergyman and author.

35. Hill Diary.

36. Richard Yates, *The Church in Danger*, London, 1815, pp. 36ff.

37. Brian I. Coleman, "Anglican Church Extension, c. 1800–1860 with Special Reference to London," Ph.D. thesis, Cambridge University, 1967, p. 42.

38. W. J. Clyde Ervine, "Anglican Evangelical Clergy, 1797–1837," Ph.D. thesis, Cambridge University, 1979, pp. 198–200.

39. Soloway, *Prelates and People*, pp. 316–348.

40. *Congregational Magazine*, n.s. 1 (February 1837):77.

41. Ibid.

42. *Record*, Feb. 14, 1831.

43. *Record*, Sept. 10, 1835.

44. *Record*, March 15, 1832.

45. T. Chalmers, *Christian and Civic Economy of Large Towns*, Glasgow, 1821.

46. H. D. Rack, "Domestic Visitation: A Chapter in Early Nineteenth Century Evangelism," *Journal of Ecclesiastical History* 24 (October 1973):359, n.4.

47. Ervine, "Anglican Evangelical Clergy," p. 202.

48. J. B. Sumner, *Primary Visitation Charge*, London, 1829, p. 25.

49. *Record*, Sept. 26, 1828.

50. Ibid.

51. *Record*, Nov. 20, 1828.

52. Those closely associated with the *Record* included John Bridges, a lawyer, and John Stuckey Reynolds, a wealthy public servant and later a banker.

53. F. K. Prochaska, *Women and Philanthrophy in Nineteenth-Century England*, Oxford, 1980, pp. 98–99.

54. Charles Foster, *An Errand of Mercy, the Evangelical United Front, 1790–1837*, Chapel Hill, N.C., 1960, p. 62.

55. Letter from Edward Bickersteth to his parents, December 24, 1810. Quoted in T. R. Birks, *Memoir of Bickersteth*, 2d ed., London, 1852, 1:173.

56. Letter from Edward Bickersteth to his parents, December 21, 1810. Ibid., p. 171.

57. Wilson, Introduction to *Reformed Pastor*, p. xli.

58. Ibid., pp. xliii-xliv.

59. *Record*, Jan. 10, 1833.

60. *Fourth Annual Report of the GSPDV*, London, 1832, pp. 44–45.

61. *Record*, June 8, 1829.

62. Christian Instruction Society, *A Statement on the Awful Profanation of the Lord's Day*, London, 1829, p. 6.

63. *Record*, May 14, 1834.

64. *Record*, Aug. 18, 1834.

65. *Record*, May 21, 1835.

66. *Record*, April 16, 1829.

67. *Record*, June 6, 1829.

68. *Fourth Annual Report of the GSPDV*, London, 1832, p. 42.

69. C. J. Blomfield, quoted in *District Visitor's Handbook*, London, 1840, p. 27.

70. Rennie, "Evangelicalism and English Public Life," pp. 80–81.

71. See J. B. Sumner, *Charge to the Clergy*, London, 1829, p. 25, and *Record*, May 23, 1831.

72. *Record*, April 29, 1833.

73. *Christian Observer*, (Nov. 1832):736–737.

74. Birks, *Memoir of Bickersteth*, 1:167.

75. *British Critic and Quarterly Theological Review*, (October 1840):350–358.

76. Hugh Stowell's speech to the GSPDV, *Record*, May 15, 1834.

77. Prochaska, *Women and Philanthropy*, p. 110.

78. Ibid., pp. 117–125.

79. *Record*, May 24, 1830.

80. *Record*, May 13, 1833. According to H. D. Rack, CIS visitation peaked at about 60,000 families in the early 1840s. H. D. Rack, "Domestic Visitation," *Journal of Ecclesiastical History* 24 (October 1973):367.

81. *Record*, Dec. 15, 1828.

82. See the speech of the Reverend Baptist Noel in *Record*, June 8, 1828.

83. This was an expression used by one of the speakers at an annual meeting of the GSPDV. *Record*, May 21, 1835.

84. Prochaska, *Women and Philanthropy*, p. 116.

85. See *Record*, Nov. 20, 1828 and Dec. 15, 1828.

86. *Record*, May 16, 1836.

87. *Record*, April 29, 1833.

88. For a discussion of such organizations as thrift clubs later in the century see Jeffrey Cox, *The Churches in a Secular Society: Lambeth, 1870–1930*, New York, 1982, p. 64.

89. *LCM Minutes*, July 30, 1835.

90. Metropolitan Visiting and Relief Association. For a discussion of the Metropolitan Visiting and Relief Association, see Coleman, "Anglican Church Extension," pp. 279–295; and J. C. Pringle, *Social Work of the London Churches*, London, 1937, pp. 188 f. Neither Coleman nor Pringle acknowledges the existence of the GSPDV nor do they realize that three of the new Association's founding trustees were Evangelicals.

91. Sampson Low, *The Charities of London*, London, 1850, pp. 127–128. Cited by Prochaska, *Women and Philanthropy*, p. 104.

92. Cox, *Churches in a Secular Society*, pp. 73–76.

93. Ibid., p. 201.

94. Letter from John S. Reynolds to David Nasmith quoted in *LCM Minutes*, July 30, 1835.

95. *Record*, Sept. 12, Sept. 16, and Dec. 26, 1833, and Jan. 27, 1834.

96. *Record*, Nov. 19, 1839. This letter is signed "D. C." and was probably written by Dandeson Coates, who was active in the Church Missionary Society and who emerged as a key figure in the CP-AS.

97. *Record*, Dec. 3, 1835. See the letter by "F. S." For the identification of "F. S." as Frederic Sandoz see E. J. Speck, *Sketch of the Church Pastoral-Aid Society*, London, 1881, p. 1.

98. John Weylland, *These Fifty Years*, London, 1884, p. 34, and John Garwood, *The Claims of the LCM on Members of the Church of England*, London, 1836, p. 19.

99. *Record*, Dec. 21, 1835.

100. *Record*, Feb. 13, 1837. Letter from a CP-AS committee member.

101. *Record*, Dec. 31, 1837. See "D. C.'s" letter.

102. *Record*, Jan. 3, 1836. See the letter from "F. S." Sandoz's defense against this criticism was that his proposal was not as restricted as the critic had imagined. The society hoped to work with the sanction of the clergy but did "not necessarily exclude the eventual occupation of other stations according to its means."

103. Letter from Frederic Sandoz to Bishop Blomfield, n.d., quoted in Speck, *Sketch of the CP-AS*, p. 21, cited by Coleman, "Anglican Church Extension," p. 122, n. 109.

104. "Member of the CP-AS Committee," *Record*, Feb. 13, 1837.

105. Speck, *Sketch of the CP-AS*, p. 15.

106. *Record*, Feb. 13, 1837.

107. Ibid.

108. Speck, *Sketch of the CP-AS*, pp. 11–12. An example of this clerical pressure can be seen in a letter from Edward Bickersteth to his friend Lord Ashley: Letter from Edward Bickersteth to Lord Ashley, February 7, 1837, *Bickersteth MSS*, box 25, notebook 1.

109. Letter from George Atkinson to the Editor of the *Record*, July 7, 1836, *Record*, July 14, 1836.

CHAPTER 3: New Approaches

1. See John Campbell, *Memoirs of David Nasmith: His Labours and Travels in Great Britain, France, the United States and Canada*, London, 1844, and John Clyde G. Binfield, *George Williams and the Young Men's Christian Association*, London, 1973, chapter 7.

2. John M. Weylland, *These Fifty Years*, London, 1884, p. 15.

3. *Record*, March 19 and March 30, 1835.

4. B. W. Noel quoting Thomas Chalmers in *State of the Metropolis*, London, 1835, p. 29.

5. *Christian Observer* (April 1835):225–226.

6. Noel, *The State of the Metropolis*, p. 13.

7. Ibid., pp. 13–26.

8. B. I. Coleman, "Anglican Church Extension, c. 1800–1860, with Special Reference to London," Ph.D. thesis, Cambridge University, 1967, p. 117.

9. Noel, *State of the Metropolis*, p. 52.

10. Campbell, *Memoirs of Nasmith*, p. 310.

11. Letter from Baptist W. Noel to David Nasmith, April 28, 1835. Quoted in J. Campbell, *Memoirs of Nasmith*, pp. 303–304.

12. *LCM Minutes*, June 8, 1835.

13. Charles Buxton, *Life of Thomas Fowell Buxton*, London, 1848, p. 4.

14. Ibid., p. 35.

15. W. J. Clyde Ervine, "Anglican Evangelical Clergy," Ph.D. thesis, Cambridge University, 1979, chapter 6.

16. G.F.A. Best, "The Whigs and the Church Establishment in the Age of Grey and Holland," *History* 45 (1960):107.

17. Ibid., p. 114.

18. Ibid., p. 107.

19. Ibid., p. 104.

20. Letter from Francis Noel to Baptist W. Noel, May 22, 1823, *Noel Family Collection*, Leicestershire Record Office, *MSS* DE 1787/1/77.

21. His eldest brother became the first earl of Gainsborough; his father-in-law was Sir George Grey, a leading Evangelical Whig M.P.

22. I am indebted to D. W. Bebbington's article, "The Life of Baptist Noel: Its Setting and Significance," *Baptist Quarterly*, n.s. 34 (Autumn 1964):406, nn. 9 and 15. See B. W. Noel, *Notes of a Short Tour through the Midland Counties of Ireland in the Summer of 1836*, London, 1837; B. W. Noel, *A Plea for the Poor*, London, 1841; and B. W. Noel, *The Catholic Claims: A Letter to the Lord Bishop of Cashel*, London, 1845.

23. Among these were Sir George Grey, the Hon. Arthur Kinnaird and William Evans, all of whom were Evangelical Liberal M.P.s.

24. *LCM Magazine* (January 1840):1.

25. See *First Report of the LCM*, 2d ed., London, 1835, p. 13, and *Second Report of the LCM*, London, 1836, p. 30.

26. *LCM Magazine* (January 1849):15.

27. A. P. Stanley, *Memoirs of Edward and Catherine Stanley*, London, 1879, p. 74.

28. *Record*, May 13, 1845, and May 3, 1848.

29. Stanley, *Memoirs of Stanley*, p. 74.

30. Ibid., p. 77, and *Record*, May 22, 1847.

31. Campbell, *Memoirs of Nasmith*, p. 325.

32. It was first mentioned in a MCM advertisement in *Record*, Sept. 10, 1835. See also *Record*, Nov. 30 and Dec. 3, 1835.

33. *Record*, Dec. 14, 1835.

34. *Record*, July 28, 1882. Cited by M. Hennell, *Sons of the Prophets*, London, 1979, p. 13.

35. John M. Weylland, *Round the Tower*, London, 1875, p. 11.

36. See chapter 1, n. 35.

37. *LCM Minutes*, Dec. 30, 1835.

38. Letter from J. S. Reynolds to David Nasmith, n.d., quoted in *LCM Minutes*, July 30, 1835.

39. *Christian Guardian* (June 1834):235, and *Record*, March 26, 1840, and March 22, 1847.

40. *LCM Minutes*, Nov. 25, 1835, and Campbell, *Memoirs of Nasmith*, p. 325.

41. Robert and James Haldane may well have had more influence on the Recordites on this issue at this time than they did on Alexander Haldane. Both had made their presence felt on the Continent and in England. See I. S. Rennie, "Evangelicalism and English Public Life," Ph.D. thesis, University of Toronto, 1962, pp. 39f.

42. *Record*, Dec. 14, 1855.

43. Ibid.

44. Ibid.

45. *Christian Guardian* (February 1836):79.

46. Ibid.

47. *Christian Observer* (April 1836):251.

48. *Christian Observer* (May 1836):257.

49. Ibid., p. 259.

50. Campbell, *Memoirs of Nasmith*, p. 317.

51. For her advocacy of the LCM see *Christian Lady's Magazine* 7 (1837):180.

52. Evelyn Garratt, *Life and Personal Reflections of Samuel Garratt*, London, 1908, p. 208.

53. Rennie, "Evangelicals and Public Life," pp. 45f.

54. See "Liberalism," *Christian Lady's Magazine* 7 (1837):463, and her attack of Baptist Noel's *Tour of Ireland* in *Christian Lady's Magazine* 7 (1837):464–469.

55. *LCM Magazine* (June 1836):65.

56. *LCM Magazine* (November 1837):176.

57. *LCM Magazine* (January 1839):42, and *LCM Magazine* (June 1841):96.

58. John Garwood, *Claims of the London City Mission*, London, 1836, p. 19.

59. *LCM Magazine* (June 1836):65.

60. Garwood, *Claims of the London City Mission*, p. 19.

61. *LCM Magazine* (January 1836):4.

62. Garwood, *Claims of the London City Mission*, p. 5.

63. Letter from Bishop Blomfield to the Bishop of Nova Scotia, April 19, 1845, *Fulham Palace MSS.*, Lambeth Palace Library, London, fiche 376, f.218.

64. *LCM Magazine* (Feb. 1836):16.

65. H. D. Rack, "Domestic Visitation: A Chapter in Early Nineteenth Century Evangelism," *Journal of Ecclesiastical History* 24 (October 1973):360, n.2.

66. *LCM Minutes*, Dec. 30, 1835; Feb. 2 and March 1, 1836.

67. *LCM Minutes*, March 8, 1837.

68. Letter from B. W. Noel to David Nasmith, March 8, 1837, quoted in Campbell, *Memoirs of Nasmith*, pp. 339–340.

69. *LCM Minutes*, March 17, 1837.

70. *Record*, Sept. 1, 1836.

71. Campbell, *Memoirs of Nasmith*, p. iv.

72. *First Report of the LCM*, London, 1835, p. 4.

73. *Record*, Feb. 26, 1828.

74. *Record*, Oct. 25, 1830, and Feb. 13, 1834.

75. Letter from "C.S.P." to the editor of the *Record*, April 5, 1837.

76. Letter from John Garwood and Robert Ainslie to the editor of the *Record*, April 26, 1837, *Record*, April 27, 1837.

77. *Record*, April 29, 1837.

78. See letter by "C.S.P." in *Record*, Sept. 14, 1837.

79. See letter by "C.S.P." in *Record*, June 19, 1837.

80. Ibid.

81. *Record*, Oct. 26, 1837.

82. Elizabeth Jay, *The Religion of the Heart*, Oxford, 1979, p. 25.

83. Ibid., p. 26.

84. Jeffrey Cox, *The English Churches in a Secular Society: Lambeth, 1870–1930*, New York, 1982, p. 135.

85. Ibid., pp. 134–135.

86. F. K. Brown, *Fathers of the Victorians*, p. 155, cited by Nancy U. Murray, "The Influence of the French Revolution on the Church of England and its Rivals," D.Phil. thesis, Oxford University, 1975, p. 260.

87. *Fourth Annual Report of the LCM*, London, 1839, p. 2.

88. Ibid.

89. *Christian Observer* (May 1836):259.

90. *LCM Magazine* (Jan. 1839):23.

91. Ibid., pp. 22–23.

92. Ibid., p. 24.

93. *LCM Magazine* (Sept. 1846):202.

94. *LCM Magazine* (Jan. 1839):26.

95. *LCM Minutes*, Oct. 29, 1838.

96. *LCM Minutes*, Nov. 15, 1838.

97. *LCM Minutes*, Dec. 4, 1838.

98. *LCM Minutes*, Dec. 4, 1838, and *LCM Magazine* (January 1839):4.

99. Letter from Bishop Blomfield to John Garwood, February 9, 1839, *Fulham Palace MSS.*, book 353, ff.21 and 22.

100. *LCM Minutes*, Dec. 24, 1838, and Jan. 1, 1839.

101. Letter from Bishop Blomfield to John Garwood, January 8, 1839, *Blomfield MSS.*, book 352, fol. 83–84; and letter from Bishop Blomfield to R. Hankinson, January 8, 1839, *Blomfield MSS.*, book 353.

102. Letter from Bishop Blomfield to John Garwood, February 9, 1839, *Blomfield MSS.*, book 353, fol. 21–22.

103. *Record*, May 21, 1838.

104. *Record*, Dec. 17, 1838.

105. *Record*, Jan. 28, 1839.

106. *Record*, Feb. 4, 1839.

107. Ibid.

108. Ibid.

109. *Record*, Feb. 11, 1839.

110. *Record*, Dec. 12, 1839.

111. Apparently many Dissenting ministers were dissuaded from signing the Remonstrance. Even the moderate *Evangelical Magazine* feared to recommend it. See *Evangelical Magazine* (supplement) 17 (1839):642–644.

112. John Walsh, "Methodism and the Mob in the Eighteenth Century," in *Studies in Church History*, ed. G. J. Cumming and Derek Baker, vol. 8, Cambridge, 1972, pp. 219–223.

113. Edward Royle, *Radical Politics*, London, 1971, p. 29.

114. *LCM Minutes*, Aug. 15, 1842.

115. *Record*, May 27, 1841.

116. *Fourth Annual Report of the GSPDV*, London, 1832, p. 45.

117. R. Younge, *The Drunkard's Character*, 1638, quoted in Keith Thomas, *Religion and the Decline of Magic*, New York, 1971, p. 17.

118. *An Address to the Public from the Society for the Suppression of Vice*, London, 1803, part ii, p. 61 Cited by R. W. Malcolmson, *Popular Recreations in English Society*, Cambridge, 1973, p. 150.

119. Robert C. Dillon, *A Sermon on the Evils of Fairs in General and of Bartholomew*

Fair in Particular, London, 1839, p. 132. Cited by Malcolmson, *Popular Recreations*, p. 103.

120. *LCM Magazine* (Oct. 1839):172.

121. Ibid.

122. *LCM Magazine* (Aug. 1839):140.

123. Ibid., pp. 140–141.

124. *Morning Herald*, July 11, 1839. Quoted in *LCM Magazine* (Oct. 1839):146–147.

125. The *LCM Magazine* printed the new legislation in full for its readers. *LCM Magazine* (Sept. 1839):157–160.

126. *LCM Magazine* (July 1840):110.

127. *LCM Magazine* (Aug. 1840):123.

128. *LCM Magazine* (Oct. 1839):175.

129. *LCM Magazine* (Aug. 1840):126.

130. *LCM Magazine* (April 1841):62–63; (May 1841):77–79; (Aug. 1841):129–132; (Sept. 1841):151–152; (Oct. 1841):160–164; and (Oct. 1842):177–178.

131. *Times*, Aug. 15, 1842. Quoted in *LCM Magazine* (Oct. 1842):179–181.

132. For an example of this see *LCM Magazine* (Oct. 1840):177. In this case the LCM involved the local vicar in opposing the Camberwell Fair.

133. A title given to Close by Geoffrey Berwick in "Close of Cheltenham," *Theology* 39 (July-December 1939):270–285.

134. Francis Close, *The Evil Consequences of Attending the Race Course Exposed*, 3d ed., London, 1827, p. 13.

135. For pamphlets supporting Close see: "Scrutator," *The Races Condemned, as Contrary to Christianity, in a Reply to Vindex*, Cheltenham, 1827; "A Peasant," *The First Part of Falsehood Exposed; or, the Reprover Reproved; A Poetical Epistle to Vindex* . . . , 2d ed., Cheltenham, 1827; "A Peasant," *The Second Part of Falsehood Exposed;* . . . , 2d. ed., Cheltenham, 1827. For a view opposing Close see: "Phillippus," *The Spiritual Quixote, Geoffrey Wildgoose, in Cheltenham: Or, a Dis-Course on a Race-Course*, 3d ed., Cheltenham, 1827.

136. *LCM Minutes*, April 30, 1838.

137. *LCM Minutes*, May 21, 1838.

138. *LCM Magazine* (Oct. 1842):188.

139. *LCM Magazine* (Oct. 1842):189.

140. Clarke, *Recreations of the People: Real and Imaginary*, London, 1858, p. 10.

141. *Record*, Sept. 17, 1829.

142. *Record*, Aug. 8, 1833.

143. *LCM Minutes*, Oct. 14 and 21, 1839.

144. Mr. Witham, "Report of the Court of Sessions, Clerkenwell, Oct. 20, 1842," reprinted in *LCM Magazine* (Nov. 1842):199.

145. David Hempton, *Methodism and Politics in British Society 1750–1850*, London, 1984, p. 29.

146. Clarke, *Recreations of the People*, p. 5.

147. Brian Harrison, "Religion and Recreation in Nineteenth Century England," *Past and Present*, no. 38 (Dec. 1967):98.

148. Cox, *English Churches in a Secular Society*, p. 153. For a full discussion of the Nonconformist conscience see David W. Bebbington, *Nonconformist Conscience*, London, 1982.

149. R. A. Soloway, *Prelates and People*, London, 1969, p. 256.

150. *LCM Fourth Annual Report*, London, 1839, p. 12.

151. Royle, *Radical Politics*, p. 21.

152. Its full title was "The Society for Giving Effect to His Majesty's Proclamation against Vice and Immorality" and was founded in 1787 by Wilberforce.

153. Royle, *Radical Politics*, p. 29.

154. W. V. Holmes in *The Republican*, May 17, 1822, quoted by E. Royle, *The Infidel Tradition*, London, 1976, pp. 134–135.

155. Royle, *Infidel Tradition*, p. xvi.

156. Robert Owen, cited by Royle, *Radical Politics*, p. 38.

157. Soloway, *Prelates and People*, p. 262.

158. Royle, *Infidel Tradition*, p. 42.

159. Ibid., p. 43.

160. Soloway, *Prelates and People*, p. 258.

161. Ibid., pp. 262–263.

162. Royle, *Infidel Tradition*, p. 44.

163. T. H. Hudson, *Christian Socialism Explained and Enforced, and compared with Infidel Fellowship, especially as pronounced by Robert Owen, Esq., and his Disciples*, London, 1839. See also *Evangelical Magazine* 18 (Feb. 1840):71–72.

164. *LCM Magazine* (June 1839):108.

165. Ibid., p. 103.

166. Edward Bickersteth, *Signs of the Times in the East*, London, 1845, p. 72.

167. Edward Bickersteth, *The Divine Warning to the Church*, London, 1842, p. 9.

168. Ibid., p. 10.

169. Francis Close, *A Sermon to Chartists*, London, 1839. Both Close and Hugh McNeile were "outspoken critics of Chartism and Socialism." Royle, *Radical Politics*, p. 8.

170. *Christian Observer* (Feb. 1840):125.

171. *Congregational Magazine*, n.s. 4 (Feb. 1840):135.

172. Weylland, *These Fifty Years*, p. 47.

173. *Lectures Against Socialism. Delivered Under the Direction of the Committee of the London City Mission*, London, 1840.

174. *Christian Observer* (May 1840):319.

175. G.I.T. Machin, *Politics and the Churches in Great Britain 1832–1868*, Oxford, 1977, p. 14.

176. *LCM Magazine* (June 1839):114.

177. Ibid., p. 115.

178. *LCM Magazine* (Aug. 1839):135.

179. For a copy of the tract that they distributed, see *LCM Magazine* (Dec. 1839):198–207.

180. *LCM Minutes*, March 7, 1842.

181. W. R. Ward, *Religion and Society in England 1790–1850*, London, 1972, p. 103.

182. A. D. Gilbert, *Religion and Society in Industrial England*, London, 1976, p. 156.

183. Ibid., p. 145.

184. Ibid., p. 157.

185. Ibid., pp. 187–203.

186. D. Hempton, *Methodism and Politics*, p. 14.

187. Ibid., p. 110.

CHAPTER 4: Issues of Church and State

1. G.I.T. Machin, *Politics and the Churches in Great Britain: 1832–1868*, Oxford, 1977, pp. 53–71.

2. Norman Gash, *Sir Robert Peel*, London, 1972, p. 103.

3. G.S.R. Kitson Clark, *The Making of Victorian England*, London, 1962, p. 156.

4. Olive J. Brose, *Church and Parliament: The Reshaping of the Church of England, 1828–1860*, London, 1959, p. 34.

5. Ibid., p. 39.

6. Robert H. Eden (1789–1841), 2d Baron Henley, married Peel's sister, Harriet, in 1824. Although an Anglican, he acted as chairman of public meetings of the Christian Instruction Society and supported the LCM financially.

7. See Ian S. Rennie, "Evangelicalism and English Public Life," Ph.D. thesis, University of Toronto, 1962, pp. 292–300; *Christian Observer* (March 1837):172.

8. Machin, *Politics and the Churches*, p. 149.

9. See P. J. Welch, "Blomfield and Peel: a Study in Co-operation between Church and State, 1841–1846," *Journal of Ecclesiastical History* 12 (1961):71, and Edwin Hodder, *Life and Work of the Seventh Earl of Shaftesbury*, 2 vols., London, 1887, 1:342.

10. *Record*, Aug. 8, 1836.

11. *Christian Lady's Magazine* 8 (1837):344.

12. Baptist W. Noel, *A Letter to the Right Honourable Lord Melbourne on Church Extension*, London, 1839.

13. *Christian Guardian* (Jan. 1840):25–32.

14. For a full report on this meeting, see *A Corrected Report of the Speeches Delivered at a Public Meeting in Behalf of Church Extension*, London, 1839. The only copy of this that the writer was able to find is in the pamphlet collection of Pusey House, Oxford, Ref. 2803 PA 99(10).

15. Sir Culling Eardley (Smith) (1805–1863) was the son of Sir Culling Smith by Charlotte Elizabeth, daughter of Lord Eardley. He adopted the name Eardley in 1829. He was briefly a liberal M.P. in 1830.

16. *Record*, March 23, 1840.

17. *Hansard*, n.s. 157, col. 312, Speech of Sir Robert Inglis in the House of Commons debate on June 30, 1840.

18. John Venn was the son of John Venn of the Clapham Sect and brother of Henry Venn of the CMS. He was long-time vicar of St. Peter's, Hereford.

19. Inglis, col. 304–305, speech in House of Commons, June 30, 1840.

20. Ibid., col. 321.

21. *Hansard*, n.s. 157, col. 358–360.

22. *Record*, July 6, 1840.

23. *Christian Observer* (August 1840):511.

24. *Christian Guardian* (December 1840):479.

25. Letter from Walter A. Shirley to "A Friend Abroad," June 23, 1841, quoted in A. A. Shirley, *Memoir and Letters of Bishop Shirley*, London, 1849, p. 318. Shirley himself was to benefit from this Whig patronage in his appointment as Bishop of Sodor and Man in 1846.

26. B. I. Coleman, "Anglican Church Extension, c. 1800–1860, with Special Reference to London," Ph.D. thesis, Cambridge University, 1967, p. 127.

27. *Record*, July 15, 1841.

28. *Churchman's Monthly Review* (1841):454.

29. British Museum, *Gladstone MSS.*, 44,355, ff. 184 and 188.

30. Letter from Robert Benton Seeley to Lord Ashley, September 2, 1841, British Museum, *Peel MSS.*, 40,483, f. 18.

31. Seeley also used his influence to secure the appointment of Evangelical Thomas Dale to a canonry of St. Paul's on the grounds that the Tory government should please "those among the people who are best worth pleasing." Letter from R. B. Seeley to Lord ?, September 4, 1843, British Museum, *Peel MSS.*, 40,533,f. 27.

32. Gash, *Sir Robert Peel*, p. 395.

33. Ibid., p. 304.

34. Ibid., p. 342.

35. Sir Robert Peel to Sir James Graham, December 22, 1842, cited in Charles Stuart Parker, *Sir Robert Peel from His Private Letters*, 3 vols., London, 1899, 2:551.

36. *Hansard*, n.s. 157, col. 335f, speech of H. G. Ward in the House of Commons debate on June 30, 1840.

37. Gash, *Sir Robert Peel*, p. 402.

38. Machin, *Politics and the Churches*, p. 152.

39. *Christian Observer* (April 1843):256.

40. Machin, *Politics and the Churches*, p. 152.

41. David Hempton, *Methodism and Politics in British Society 1750–1850*, London, 1984, p. 165.

42. Ibid., p. 169.

43. Ibid., p. 183.

44. John Prest, *Politics in the Age of Cobden*, Basingstoke, 1977, p. 77.

45. *Christian Observer* (June 1843):384.

46. Letter from Sir Robert Peel to Rt. Hon. Henry Hobhouse, January 21, 1843, quoted in Parker, *Peel*, 2:563.

47. *Christian Observer* (April 1843):256.

48. *Record*, May 6, 1843.

49. *Christian Observer* (June 1843):383.

50. By "1847 metropolitan Middlesex had received only £1,090 of the £30,000 which the Act gave the [Ecclesiastical] Commission to distribute." Coleman, "Anglican Church Extension," p. 113.

51. *Record*, Aug. 5, 1843.

52. *Christian Observer* (July 1843):448.

53. See chapter 3.

54. Machin, *Politics and the Churches*, p. 112.

55. Ibid., p. 141.

56. Quoted in ibid., p. 136.

57. *Record*, May 18, 1840.

58. *Record*, July 21, 1842.

59. *Record*, April 20 and May 18, 1843.

60. *Record*, July 3, 1843.

61. Machin, *Politics and the Churches*, p. 145.

62. *Record*, May 29, 1843.

63. *Record*, Nov. 2, 1843.

64. *Christian Observer* (Oct. 1843):638, and *Record*, July 3, 1843.

65. *Record*, Jan. 1 and Jan. 15, 1844.

66. *Record*, Feb. 22, 1844.

67. See chapters 1 and 2.

68. *Record*, Dec. 11, 1843.

69. *Record*, Jan. 29, 1844.

70. *Record*, Jan. 29, 1844.

71. For the background to this dispute see Rennie, "Evangelicalism and English Public Life," pp. 268–269.

72. Hempton, *Methodism and Politics*, p. 95.

73. *Record*, March 18, 1844.

74. Letter from James Edward Gordon to Sir Robert Peel, February 4, 1835, British Museum, *Peel MSS.*, 40,413, f. 140.

75. Letter from the same to the same, June 5, 1844, British Museum, *Peel MSS.*, 40,546, f. 127.

76. *Record*, June 24, 1844.

77. *Christian Observer* (May 1844):320; (July 1844):447–448; and (Aug. 1844):511–512.

78. *Christian Observer* (Oct. 1844):640.

79. *Record*, July 25, 1844.

80. *Record*, March 13, 1845.

81. *Christian Observer* (April 1845):251.

82. Gash, *Peel*, p. 393.

83. Ibid., p. 413.

84. G.I.T. Machin, "The Maynooth Grant, the Dissenters and Disestablishment, 1845–1847," *English Historical Review* 82 (1967):61.

85. John Wolffe, "Protestant Societies and Anti-Catholic Agitation in Great Britain, 1829–1860," D.Phil. thesis, Oxford University, 1984, p. 64–65.

86. *Record*, Feb. 6, 1845.

87. See Edward Norman, *Anti-Catholicism in Victorian England*, (London, 1968), p. 25 and D. Hempton, *Methodism and Politics*, p. 194.

88. *Eclectic Review* (April 1845):67 quoted in Machin, "The Maynooth Grant," p. 67.

89. *Record*, April 24, 1845. McNeile was one of three Evangelical clergymen who had national reputations for their anti-Catholic agitation. The two others were Hugh Stowell of Manchester and Francis Close of Cheltenham.

90. *Record*, March 17, 1845.

91. Quoted in Machin, *Politics and the Churches*, p. 171.

92. See *Christian Observer* (May 1845):320 and *Christian Observer* (June 1845):384.

93. *Record*, March 27, 1845.

94. Culling Eardley, *The Romanism of Italy*, London, 1845. See *Churchman's Monthly Review* (July 1846):532.

95. Machin, "The Maynooth Grant," pp. 66–67.

96. Ibid., p. 66.

97. See *Congregational Magazine*, n.s. 3 (Aug. 1839):504–509; and (Sept. 1839):578–580.

98. D. N. Hempton has argued that Methodist anti-Catholicism came primarily from two sources: the first was the legacy that Wesley as a High Church Tory bequeathed to his followers; the second was as a result of Methodist missionary activity in Ireland.

D. N. Hempton, "Methodism and Anti-Catholic Politics 1800–1846," Ph.D. thesis, St. Andrew's University, 1977.

99. *Congregational Magazine* (April 1839):263.

100. Ibid., p. 264.

101. *Congregational Magazine*, n.s. 3 (Oct. 1839):668.

102. *Congregational Magazine*, n.s. 6 (Aug. 1842):557 and n.s. 8 (Jan. 1844):13.

103. *Congregational Magazine*, n.s. 9 (May 1845):397.

104. Machin, "The Maynooth Grant," p. 70.

105. Ibid.

106. Letter from Sir Robert Peel to John Wilson Croker, April 22, 1845, quoted in C. S. Parker, *Sir Robert Peel*, 3:175.

107. *Record*, May 29, 1845.

108. *Record*, May 29 and June 2, 1845.

109. *Record*, June 9, 1845.

110. Letter from Sir Robert Peel to H. L. Bulwer, May 12, 1845, Peel is quoting Inglis. Quoted in Parker, *Sir Robert Peel*, 3:177.

111. Ibid.

112. *Record*, June 16, 1845.

113. *Record*, June 16 and June 23, 1845.

114. *Record*, Aug. 7, 1845.

115. *Record*, Aug. 11, 1845.

116. *Record*, Oct. 6, 1845. For a discussion of Wesleyan Methodist involvement in the Alliance, see D. Hempton, *Methodism and Politics*, pp. 195–6.

117. *Record*, Nov. 3, 1845. For such an assertion see the letter from "A Layman."

118. *Christian Observer* (Dec. 1845):739.

119. Ibid., p. 743.

120. Ibid., p. 748.

121. Ibid., p. 749.

122. Ibid.

123. *Free Church Magazine* 3 (May 1846):132.

124. *Christian Observer* (Dec. 1845):759.

125. *Record*, April 27, 1844.

126. *Record*, Sept. 16 and 19, 1844.

127. *Record*, Sept. 19, 1844.

128. *LCM Magazine* (June 1844):90.

129. J. W. Massie, *The Evangelical Alliance: Its Origin and Development*, London, 1847, p. 88.

130. Ibid., p. 111.

131. Hall had been the travelling secretary of the interdenominational Reformation Society (*Christian Guardian* [Nov. 1849]:526–527) and had worked with both the LCM (*Record*, Feb. 8, 1838) and the Interdenominational Town Missionary Society. (*Record*, May 20, 1844).

132. Peter Hall, *Reasons for declining an Invitation from the Anti-Maynooth Committee to attend . . . a Conference of Protestants . . . to be held in Liverpool . . . in a letter to Sir C. E. Smith*, London, 1845.

133. J. B. Marsden, *Memoir of Stowell*, London, 1868, p. 116.

134. *Record*, Feb. 5, 1845.

135. *Record*, Dec. 22, 1845. No copy of this sermon seems to have survived.

136. Ibid.

137. Letter from J. W. Brooks to the editor of the *Record*, December 26, 1845, published in *Record*, Dec. 29, 1845.

138. See chapter 2.

139. Ernest Sandeen, *The Roots of Fundamentalism*, London, 1970, p. 39.

140. Ian S. Rennie, "Nineteenth Century Roots of Contemporary Prophetic Interpretation," in *Dreams, Visions and Oracles*, eds. Carl E. Amerding and W. Ward Gasque, Grand Rapids, Mich., 1977, p. 44.

141. Sandeen, *Roots of Fundamentalism*, p. 60.

142. *Record*, April 27, 1848, and Feb. 7, 1853. This point is against Elizabeth Jay who asserts that the Recordites were characterized by their "apocalyptic fervour and zealous espousal of premillennialist doctrine." E. Jay, *Religion of the Heart*, Oxford, 1979, p. 23.

143. Sandeen, *Roots of Fundamentalism*, p. 23.

144. *Christian Observer* (Feb. 1843):80–85; (April 1843):204–207; (July 1843):385–393; (Oct. 1843):577–581.

145. T. R. Birks, *The Religious Condition of Christendom*, ed. E. Steane, London, 1857, part 2, pp. 64–65.

146. James Grant, *The End of All Things*, 2d ed., London, 1866, 2:92. Cited by Sandeen, *Roots of Fundamentalism*, p. 25.

147. *Christian Observer* (March 1844):138–139 and (Jan. 1845):15.

148. Sandeen was apparently only able to locate one of these volumes (p. 25). The British Museum Catalogue unfortunately does not list the works under the names of each contributor. The Bodleian Library, Oxford, does have a number of the works. They are, in chronological order: E. Bickersteth, ed., *The Second Coming, the Judgment, and the Kingdom of Christ . . .* , London, 1843; (no volume was published in 1844); T. R. Birks, ed., *The Hope of the Apostolic Church*, London, 1845; Alexander R. C. Dallas, ed., *Lift Up Your Heads*, London, 1848; James Haldane Stewart, ed., *The Priest Upon His Throne*, London, 1849; W. Dalton, ed., *God's Dealings with Israel*, London, 1850; Edward Auriol, ed., *Popish Darkness and Millennial Light*, London, 1851; W. R. Fremantle, ed., *Present Times and Future Prospects*, London, 1854; H. M. Villiers, ed., *The Titles of Christ Viewed Prophetically*, London, 1857; and Emilius Bayley, ed., *The Signs of the Times*, London, 1858.

149. Sandeen, *Roots of Fundamentalism*, pp. 18–22.

150. Grant, *The End of All Things*, 2:95–96.

151. Sandeen, *Roots of Fundamentalism*, p. 22, n. 37.

152. Ibid., p. 22.

153. *Christian Observer* (Sept. 1844):537.

154. *Christian Observer* (Jan. 1845):15.

155. J. H. Frere, *The Harvest of the Earth Prior to the Vintage of Wrath, Considered as Symbolical of the Evangelical Alliance*, London, 1846. Cited by Sandeen, *Roots of Fundamentalism*, p. 60.

156. J. H. Frere, *The Great Continental Revolution Marking the Expiration of the Times of the Gentiles . . .* , London, 1848, p. 6.

157. Edward Hoare, *The Time of the End*, London, 1846, p. 42.

158. Ibid., p. 51.

159. Sandeen, *Roots of Fundamentalism*, p. 17.

160. Ibid., p. 14.

161. G.S.R. Kitson Clark, "The Repeal of the Corn Laws and the Politics of the Forties," *Economic History Review*, 2d series, 4, no. 1 (1951):5.

162. Ibid.

163. Ibid.

164. *Christian Observer* (Sept. 1841):572–573.

165. Clark, "Corn Laws," p. 5.

166. *Record*, May 9, 1842.

167. *Christian Observer* (Feb. 1846):148.

168. Baptist W. Noel, *A Plea for the Poor, Showing how the Proposed Repeal of the Existing Corn Laws will Affect the Interest of the Working Classes*, London, 1841, p. 6.

169. See the British Museum's Catalogue listings under Noel. The Anti-Corn Law League was so pleased with the pamphlet that it published selections from it in 1842.

170. *Record*, Feb. 28, 1842.

171. *Christian Observer* (1841):572–573.

172. *A Quaker Journal: being the Diary and Reminiscences of William Lucas of Hitchin (1804–1861), a member of the Society of Friends*, eds. G. E. Bryand and G. P. Baker, London, 1934, 1:362. Cited by D. Bebbington, "Baptist Noel," *Baptist Quarterly Review* 24 (1972):394.

173. Bebbington, "Baptist Noel," p. 394.

174. *Record*, March 7, 1842.

175. Gash, *Peel*, chapter 11.

176. Ibid., p. 607.

177. *Churchman's Monthly Review* (July 1846):538.

CHAPTER 5: The Scripture Readers' Association

1. *Christian Guardian* (Feb. 1830):67–70. See Evelyn Garratt, *Life and Personal Reflections of Samuel Garratt*, London, 1908, p. 240.

2. Garratt, *Life of Garratt*, p. 239. Blomfield instructed his clergy to offer the prayer for the church militant even when there was no communion.

3. Peter Toon, "The Evangelical Response to Tractarian Teaching," D.Phil. thesis, Oxford University, 1977, pp. 61 ff.

4. Letter from R. B. Seeley to Sir Robert Peel, September 7, 1843, British Museum *MSS.*, 40,533, ff. 29–32.

5. Letter from Edward Bickersteth to Bishop [Blomfield?], November 28, 1843, *Bickersteth MSS.*, box 25, notebook 2.

6. Garratt, *Life of Garratt*, p. 248.

7. K. S. Inglis, *Churches and the Working Classes in Victorian England*, London, 1963, p. 6.

8. Ibid., p. 8.

9. See chapter 3.

10. *Christian Guardian* (May 1839):196–197 and (Sept. 1840):357–358.

11. Letter from Bishop Blomfield to Baptist W. Noel, October 29, 1845, *Fulham Palace MSS.*, fiche 86, f. 262.

12. Bishop Wilson Diary, August 27, 1845, *Bodley MSS*.

13. B. I. Coleman, "Anglican Church Extension, c. 1800–1860 with Special Reference to London," Ph.D. thesis, Cambridge University, 1967, p. 175.

14. P. J. Welch, "Difficulties of Church Extension in Victorian London," *Church Quarterly Review* 166 (1965):306.

15. *Christian Observer* (Jan. 1843):59–60.

16. *Record*, Aug. 22, 1853.

17. Letter from "A Poor Incumbent" to the editor of the *Record*, n.d., published in *Record*, Sept. 8, 1853.

18. Ibid.

19. *Christian Guardian* (May 1839):197, and Bishop Wilson Diary, September 4, 1845, *Bodley MSS.* Bodleian Library, Oxford.

20. Coleman, "Anglican Church Extension," p. 152, n. 223.

21. *Record*, May 6, 1843.

22. *Record*, Jan. 12, 1846.

23. *Record*, Jan. 22 and Feb. 2, 1846.

24. *LCM Minutes*, September 11, 1843.

25. Robert Hanbury (1796–1884) was a cousin of Sir T. F. Buxton and a partner in the family brewing firm of Truman, Buxton and Hanbury.

26. Coleman, "Anglican Church Extension," p. 182.

27. Letter from Bishop Blomfield to the Bishop of Nova Scotia, April 19, 1845, *Fulham Palace MSS.*, fiche 376, f. 218. Cited by Coleman, "Anglican Church Extension," p. 187.

28. *Record*, Nov. 30, 1843.

29. Bishop Blomfield to the Bishop of Nova Scotia, April 19, 1845.

30. See Henry Phillpotts, *Letter to the venerable archdeacons of the Diocese of Exeter on the proposed Office of Scripture Readers*, London, 1847.

31. These included J. Coghlan of St. James the Great and E. W. Relton of St. Bartholomew's.

32. See Letters to the editor of the *Times* by "Monitor," in May 6, 1844 edition, p. 5; "A Lover of the Church," in May 13, 1844, p. 3; and "A Parochial Clergyman," in May 15, 1844, p. 7.

33. *Record*, June 3, 1847.

34. *Correspondence from the "Record" related to the Establishment of a Scripture Readers' Society*, London, 1845, p. 1.

35. *LCM Magazine* (Feb. 1849).

36. *Quarterly Educational Magazine* 1 (January 1848):48–49.

37. See *Record*, July 27, 1843, and *Church of England Young Men's Society For Aiding Missions at Home and Abroad, First Annual Report*, London, 1845, p. 6.

38. *Young Men's Society for Aiding Missions . . . First Annual Report*, p. 11.

39. See Appendix A.

40. *Sixteenth Annual Report of the Church of England Young Men's Society*, London, 1860.

41. *Young Men's Magazine and Monthly Record of Christian Young Men's Society* 1 (1844):194.

42. See *Young Men's Magazine* 1 (1837):14; 2 (1838):187–189; 3 (1839):108 and 177.

43. J. Clyde Binfield, *George Williams and the YMCA: A Study in Victorian Social Attitudes*, London, 1973, p. 113.

44. R.C.L. Bevan and George Hitchcock worked with both organizations.

45. Binfield, *George Williams*, p. 44.

46. Ibid., p. 86.

47. Ibid., pp. 73–74, and John Kent, *Holding the Fort: Studies in Victorian Revivalism*, London, 1978, p. 104.

48. *Christian Observer* (June 1843):347.

49. Ibid., p. 348.

50. *Record*, June 12, 1843.

51. A. D. Gilbert, *Religion and Society in Industrial England*, London, 1976, p. 139.

52. Ibid., p. 141.

53. Ibid., p. 147.

54. *Record*, Oct. 31, 1842.

55. *Record*, Nov. 14, 1842.

56. Ibid.

57. *Record*, Nov. 30, 1843.

58. Only one such case has been found by this writer; see *LCM Magazine* (Oct. 1856):255.

59. Nine of the forty-eight leading Evangelicals identified by the *Times* in 1844 supported the LCM in that year. By 1850, seventeen of the forty-eight did. A similar result is found when one considers the figures of those who can clearly be identified as Evangelical clergy in the diocese in 1844: 15 of 106 supported the LCM; by 1850, 35 of 104 in the smaller Diocese of London worked with the mission.

60. *Record*, April 10, 1845.

61. *LCM Magazine* (July 1850):163.

62. See "D. C.'s" letter to the Editor of the *Record*, Aug. 25, 1845.

63. The Reverend Dr. Bryth's speech to the LCM annual meeting in *LCM Magazine* (1842):123.

64. *LCM Minutes*, Nov. 18, 1844.

65. *LCM Magazine* (June 1846):149.

66. *LCM Magazine* (Feb. 1849):30.

67. *LCM Magazine* (August 1846):182–187.

68. *LCM Magazine* (June 1850):170 and (Oct. 1850):242.

69. *LCM Magazine* (Sept. 1849):179.

CHAPTER 6: From Door to Door

1. The 1837 reorganization of the LCM had led to a sharp cutback in agents.

2. *9th Annual Report of the LCM*, London, 1844, p. 29.

3. *11th Annual Report of LCM* in *LCM Magazine* (June 1846):116, and *9th Report of the SRA* in *Scripture Reader's Journal* (May 1853):53.

4. *LCM 15th Report* in *LCM Magazine* (June 1850):128, and *Scripture Reader's Journal* (May 1853):53. There were then 242 LCM workers and 98 SRA workers.

5. *LCM 25th Report* in *LCM Magazine* (June 1860), and *SRA 16th Annual Report* in *Scripture Reader's Journal* (May 1860):417.

6. They were employed by the Ranyard Bible Mission. See chapter 9.

7. *LCM Magazine* (July 1851):172. Church of England clergy accounted for 834 and the others for 441 ministers.

8. The largest of these was the pan-evangelical City and Town Missionary Society founded by David Nasmith in 1837. It changed its name to the "British and Town Mission Society" in 1842 and then again in 1844 to the "Town Missionary and Scripture Readers'

Society." By 1862 this society had 155 agents, a third of whom were women. See *Town and Village Mission Record* (Jan. 1852 and June 1852) and *City and Town Mission Magazine* (May 1862):52 and (May 1864):53. By the late 1850s many Anglican dioceses had their own Scripture Readers' Associations for the employment of lay agents among the poor. See Robert Bickersteth, *A Charge Delivered to the Clergy of the Diocese of Ripon*, London, 1861, pp. 21–22.

9. See A. D. Gilbert, *Religion and Society in Industrial England*, London, 1976, p. 136. Even in 1850 the CP-AS provided grants for only ninety-one lay assistants in the whole of Britain. Less than a dozen of these were employed in the Dioceses of London and Winchester. *Appendix, CP-AS Annual Report for 1850*, London, 1850, p. 11.

10. *LCM Magazine* (July 1849):135–137.

11. Henry Pelling, *Popular Politics and Society in Late Victorian Britain*, London, 1968, p. 37.

12. E. J. Hobsbawm, "The Labour Aristocracy in 19th Century Britain," in *Democracy and the Labour Movement*, ed. John Saville, London, 1954, pp. 201–239.

13. Pelling, *Popular Politics and Society*, p. 61. See H. Seton-Watson, *Pattern of Communist Revolution*, London, 1953, p. 341 for comments regarding the concept in an international context. (Cited by Pelling.)

14. I am indebted to Dr. Graeme Wynn of the University of British Columbia for his help on this difficult and controversial subject of attempting to classify these workers.

15. Hugh McLeod, "Class, Community and Region," *A Sociological Yearbook of Religion in Britain*, vol. 6, 1973, p. 34.

16. *Scripture Readers' Journal* (1851):94.

17. *LCM Magazine* (June 1847):132.

18. Charles Clayton, CP-AS Secretary from 1845–1851, frequently visited the LCM offices. See Charles Clayton Diary, February 9, 1846, August 8, 1846, and November 5, 1846. *Gonville and Caius College MSS.*, Cambridge.

19. Brian Harrison, "The Sunday Trading Riots of 1855," *The Historical Journal* 8, no. 2 (1965):243.

20. *LCM Minutes*, Aug. 26, 1835.

21. See *LCM Magazine* (July 1850):173; *LCM Minutes*, March 31, 1851, for the Board of Health inquiry; Ibid. May 11, 1857, for Lord Charles Russell's request regarding metropolitan sanitation. As early as February 1843 Ashley was prepared to use LCM statistics in Parliament. Lord Ashley, *Moral and Religious Education of the Working Classes, the Speech of Lord Ashley, M.P., in the House of Commons*, London, 1843, p. 38.

22. *LCM Magazine* (Jan. 1850):19. Mayhew acknowledged the assistance of Mr. Richard Knight of the City Mission in his work. See Henry Mayhew, *London Labour and the London Poor;...*, London, 1851, p. iv.

23. *LCM Magazine* (June 1847):101.

24. John M. Weylland, *Valiant for Truth: Being the Autobiography of J. M. Weylland*, London, 1899, p. 39.

25. These include: R. W. Vanderkiste, *Notes and Narratives of a Six Years' Mission, principally among the Dens of London*, London, 1852; and J. M. Weylland's three works: *Round the Tower; or, the Story of the London City Mission*, London, 1875; *These Fifty Years, being the Jubilee Volume of the London City Mission*, London, 1884; and *Valiant for Truth*.

26. *LCM Magazine* (June 1855):136 cited by Harrison, "Sunday Trading Riots," p. 243.

27. Vanderkiste, *Narrative of a Six Years' Mission*, p. 35.

28. Ibid.

29. Ibid., pp. 40–41.

30. Ibid., pp. 36–38.

31. Ibid., pp. 33–34.

32. Jeffrey Cox, *English Churches in a Secular Society*, New York, 1982, p. 97.

33. Ibid., p. 98.

34. Vanderkiste, *Narrative of a Six Years' Mission*, p. 34.

35. For versions of this prayer see: W. J. Thoms, "Chaucer's night-spell," *Folk-Lore Record* 1 (1878), and W. D. Macray, "Lancashire superstitions in the sixteenth and seventeenth centuries," *Local Gleanings Relating to Lancashire & Chesire* 1 (1875–1876). Cited by K. Thomas, *Religion and the Decline of Magic*, New York, 1971, p. 181, n.2.

36. R. Tressell, *The Ragged Trousered Philanthropists*, London, 1965, p. 141. Cited by Hugh McLeod, "Class, Community and Region," *A Sociological Yearbook of Religion in Britain*, vol. 6, 1973, p. 61, n.6.

37. Testimony of William W. Champneys, *Parliamentary Papers, 1857–8*, 9, "Deficiency of the Means of Spiritual Instruction," Select Committee, House of Lords: Report, p. 127.

38. Hugh McLeod, "Class, Community and Region," p. 35.

39. Testimony of William Cadman, *Parliamentary Papers, 1857–8*, 9, "Deficiency of the Means of Spiritual Instruction," Select Committee, House of Lords: Report, p. 13.

40. The Reverend J. Colbourne, ibid., p. 13.

41. Vanderkiste, *Narrative of a Six Years' Mission*, pp. 119–120.

42. Ibid., pp. 120–121.

43. Ibid., p. 121.

44. *Fifth Annual Report of the SRA*, Quoted in *LCM Magazine* (Feb. 1850):25.

45. Ibid.

46. *Illustrated London News*, May 22, 1847. Cited by R. W. Vanderkiste, *Notes and Narratives of a Six Year Mission*, London, 1852, p. 5.

47. *LCM Magazine* (June 1855):132.

48. The Reverend J. Colbourne, *Parliamentary Papers, 1857–8*, "Deficiency of the Means of Spiritual Instruction," p. 46.

49. *Dictionary of National Biography*.

50. G. R. Balleine, *History of the Evangelical Party in the Church of England*, London, 1932 edition, p. 237.

51. Religious Census returns for St. Mary's, Whitechapel (Home Office 129/5/1/2). It would appear that the numbers of "Sunday scholars" in the Returns were estimates. There were reportedly 390 in the morning, 390 again in the afternoon, and 180 in the evening. Another table in the report indicates that Champneys himself estimated the average attendance as follows: morning adults, 1,250, afternoon adults at 430, and evening adults at 1,350. I am indebted to Dr. John Wolffe of the University of York, England, for his assistance in searching these records for me.

52. *Parliamentary Papers, 1857–8*, 9, "Deficiency of the Means of Spiritual Instruction," Select Committee, House of Lords: Report, p. 124.

53. Ibid., p. 125.

54. Ibid., p. 133.

55. Ibid., p. 128.

56. Ecclesiastical Census Returns (H.O. 129/22/4/1/1). In contrast, the Reverend John Lyons, the perpetual curate of St. Mark's, Whitechapel, declined to work with the LCM and preached to a meager congregation. St. Mark's had sittings for 1,000 but had a total morning congregation of 260 (including 80 Sunday scholars) and an evening service of 200 adults. St. Mark's was consecrated in 1839. Ecclesiastical Census Returns (H.O. 129/22/6/1/2).

57. *Parliamentary Papers, 1857–8*, "Deficiency of the Means of Spiritual Instruction," p. 145.

58. Balleine, *Evangelical Party*, p. 238.

59. *LCM Minutes*, August 2, 1858.

60. *LCM Minutes*, May 26, 1862.

61. *LCM Magazine* (Dec. 1855):283.

62. *LCM Magazine* (Dec. 1855):283–284.

63. Testimony of Robert Bickersteth, *Parliamentary Papers, 1857–8*, 9, "Deficiency of the Means of Spiritual Instruction," Select Committee, House of Lords: Report, pp. 184–185.

64. For an instance of this, Mr. Cook of 13 Dudley Street, top back, was visited on September 3, and then again on October 2, 1861, in the regular course of Oppenheimer's visiting.

65. Sheridan Gilley, "Catholic Faith of the Irish Slums, London, 1840–1870," in *The Victorian City: Images and Realities*, 2 vols., eds. H. J. Dyos and Michael Wolff, London, 1973, p. 837.

66. Ibid., p. 839.

67. Ibid.

68. Hugh McLeod, "The Dechristianisation of the Working Class in Western Europe (1850–1900)," *Social Compass*, 27, no. 2–3 (1980):194.

69. See chapter 9.

70. The important role played by organizations like the LCM is given no attention in John Wigley's recent work on *The Rise and Fall of the Victorian Sunday*, Manchester, 1980.

71. Quoted in Hugh McLeod, *Class and Religion in the Late Victorian City*, London, 1974, pp. 49–50.

72. K. S. Inglis, *Churches and the Working Classes in Victorian England*, London, 1963, p. 118.

73. Gilbert, *Religion and Society in Industrial England*, p. 114.

74. Ibid., p. 147.

75. Horace Mann, *Report on the Census of Religious Worship*, p. cxxvii, cited by Gilbert, *Religion and Society in Industrial England*, p. 113. For discussion of this question, see R. A. Nisbet, *The Quest for Community*, Toronto, 1953, pp. 50–4, 179–180, 244, and E. R. Wickham, *Church and People in an Industrial City*, London, 1957, pp. 237, 262.

76. Gilbert, *Religion and Society in Industrial England*, p. 114.

77. Ibid.

CHAPTER 7: Evangelism and Social Control

1. Friedrich Engels, *The Condition of the Working-Class in England in 1844*, London, 1892, p. 114.

2. K. S. Inglis, *The Churches and the Working Classes in Victorian London*, London, 1963, pp. 325.

3. G.S.R. Kitson Clark, *Churchmen and the Condition of England*, London, 1973, p. 290.

4. *Christian Observer* (June 1841):379, and (Aug. 1841):459–466.

5. *Record*, Dec. 4, 1828.

6. *Record*, Aug. 29, 1844.

7. *Record*, July 28, 1842. For its position on the Corn Laws see *Record*, Aug. 9, 1841.

8. *Christian Observer* (Aug. 1841):466.

9. J. B. Sumner, *A Treatise on the Records of Creation*, London, 1816, 2:86. Cited by E. R. Norman, *Church and Society in England, 1770–1970*, Oxford, 1978, p. 47.

10. *Churchman's Monthly Review* (Sept. 1844):671.

11. *Sixth Annual Report of the Christian Influence Society*, quoted in *Christian Observer* (Oct. 1838):655.

12. *Christian Observer* (Oct. 1838):654.

13. Ibid.

14. William Nicholson and William Roberts, *The Call Upon the Church, Considered in Two Essays*, London, 1838.

15. Henry W. Wilberforce, *The Parochial System: an appeal to English Churchmen*, London, 1838.

16. Charles Perry, *Clerical Education, considered with Especial Reference to the Universities*, London, 1841.

17. Thomas Page, *Letter to the Rt. Hon. Lord Ashley on the Present Defective State of National Education*, London, 1843. See *The Churchman* (April 1843):279.

18. *Churchman's Monthly Review* (Sept. 1844):672.

19. Letter from Robert Benton Seeley to Dr. S. L. Gifford, editor of *The Standard*, n.d., *MS. Eng. Lett.*, C 56, fol. 19, Bodleian Library, Oxford. In this letter, Seeley, who frequently contributed to *The Standard*, appealed on Lord Ashley's behalf for Gifford to moderate his sweeping attacks on Corn Law repealers, as some were working with Ashley on the Ten Hour Questions.

20. The *Churchman's Monthly Review* ceased in 1847 following the loss of two of its leading contributors—probably through the death of Charlotte Elizabeth and the appointment of Charles Perry as bishop of Melbourne. *Churchman's Monthly Review* (Sept. 1847):727.

21. *Churchman's Monthly Review* (May 1844):445–457.

22. *Churchman's Monthly Review* (August 1841):445–457.

23. *Churchman's Monthly Review* (Dec. 1845):931–945. See also chapter 4.

24. *Churchman's Monthly Review* (Sept. 1841):521.

25. *Churchman's Monthly Review* (Aug. 1842):578–579.

26. *Churchman's Monthly Review* (Sept. 1841):523.

27. *Churchman's Monthly Review* (Oct. 1841):588.

28. *Churchman's Monthly Review* (Jan. 1844):63.

29. R. B. Seeley, *Memoirs of the Life and Writings of Michael Thomas Sadler*, London, 1842.

30. *Publisher's Circular* (1886):602.

31. *Churchman's Monthly Review* (April 1842):298.

32. Charlotte Elizabeth [Tonna], *Helen Fleetwood*, London, 1841, p. 392–393.

33. Ibid., pp. 393–394.

34. Ibid., p. 395.

35. *Churchman's Monthly Review* (March 1841):165–167.

36. *Record*, Aug. 3, 1843, and *Publisher's Circular* (1886):602.

37. *Churchman's Monthly Review* (April 1844):359.

38. *Churchman's Monthly Review* (April 1843):391.

39. *Churchman's Monthly Review* (Sept. 1844):674.

40. See *Publishers' Circular* (1886):602, and *Churchman's Monthly Review* (Nov. 1844):841.

41. See chapter 4.

42. *Churchman's Monthly Review* (April 1844):353.

43. *Record*, Sept. 12, 1844, cited in *Churchman's Monthly Review* (Sept. 1844):674.

44. *Churchman's Monthly Review* (Sept. 1844):679.

45. Ibid., p. 680.

46. Ibid., p. 690.

47. *Christian Guardian* (April 1842):155.

48. Ibid., p. 156.

49. *Churchman's Monthly Review* (Sept. 1844):674.

50. *Churchman's Monthly Review* (Oct. 1845):738.

51. *Churchman's Monthly Review* (Sept. 1844):696.

52. Ibid., p. 697.

53. *Record*, Oct. 17, 1844, cited in *Churchman's Monthly Review* (Oct. 1844):771.

54. See chapter 1.

55. *Churchman's Monthly Review* (Oct. 1844):771–772.

56. Ibid., p. 772.

57. Ibid., p. 778.

58. Ibid., p. 788.

59. See Thomas Chalmers's blistering attack on the author of the two books (he incorrectly assumed that they had been written by one person) in *North British Review* 3 (Nov. 1844):1–52. For Seeley's reply, see *Churchman's Monthly Review* (Nov. 1844):840–866.

60. *Churchman's Monthly Review* (Jan. 1844):60–70.

61. *Christian Guardian* (June 1844):239.

62. *Labourer's Friend Magazine* (1836):109.

63. *Labourer's Friend Magazine*, n.s. 1 (June 1844):30.

64. Edwin Hodder, *Life and Work of the Seventh Earl of Shaftesbury*, 2 vols., London, 1887, 2:154. Hodder's account of the origins of this society is incorrect.

65. *Record*, Dec. 18, 1843.

66. K. S. Inglis, *The Churches and the Working Classes in Victorian London*, London, 1963, p. 304.

67. R. W. Vanderkiste, *Narrative of a Six Years' Mission*, London, 1852, pp. 48–50.

68. *Parliamentary Papers, 1857–8*, 9, Deficiency of the Means of Spiritual Instruction, Select Committee, House of Lords: Report, p. 187.

69. *LCM Third Annual Report*, London, 1838, p. 5.

70. *LCM Minutes*, July 28, 1856. For other examples, see *LCM Magazine* (Nov. 1847):242 for the death of the first St. Giles missionary from fever; Ibid., (June 1849):110 for the death of two missionaries from fever and one from a recurrent cold; Ibid. (Aug. 1849):156 for the death of Mr. Henry Clark from Asiatic cholera; Ibid., (Oct. 1849):199 f.

for the death of another missionary from cholera and the deaths among families of missionaries, including two children of one missionary.

71. *LCM Magazine* (Nov. 1847):242–3.

72. Vanderkiste, *Six Years' Mission*, p. 45.

73. *LCM Second Annual Report*, London, 1837, p. 2.

74. *LCM Magazine* (Aug. 1841):129.

75. *LCM Magazine* (Aug. 1845):170–185.

76. *LCM Minutes*, August 25, 1845.

77. J. K. Heasman, *Evangelicals in Action*, London, 1963, chapter 5, pp. 69–87.

78. See *Quarterly Review* (Dec. 1846):130–131.

79. *LCM Fifteenth Annual Report* in *LCM Magazine* (June 1850):144.

80. Clyde Binfield, *George Williams of the YMCA*, London, 1973, p. 228.

81. *LCM Minutes*, April 4, 1842. Ashley declined the invitation to preside at the LCM's annual meeting.

82. Hodder, *Shaftesbury*, 1:482.

83. *LCM Magazine* (April 1848):75.

84. See pp. 159–160.

85. *LCM Magazine* (Feb. 1850):26–27.

86. Charles Girdlestone, *Unhealthy Condition of Lower Class of Dwellings*, London, 1845, cited in *Christian Observer* (Nov. 1845):701.

87. *Christian Observer* (Nov. 1845):701.

88. *LCM Thirteenth Annual Report* in *LCM Magazine* (June 1848):126.

89. *LCM Magazine* (Feb. 1850):26.

90. *LCM Magazine* (June 1846):121.

91. Ibid., p. 118.

92. *LCM Minutes*, April 2, 1839.

93. See *LCM Magazine* (April 1840):55–57 and (May 1840):80.

94. J. K. Heasman, *Evangelicals in Action*, London, 1963.

95. Perhaps the best discussion of this issue is in A. P. Donajgrodzki, ed., *Social Control in Nineteenth Century Britain*, London, 1977.

96. E. A. Ross, *Social Control: A Survey of the Foundations of Order*, New York, 1929, cited by Donajgrodzki, *Social Control*, p. 10.

97. See p. 165.

98. *Churchman's Monthly Review* (May 1843):377.

99. *Churchman's Monthly Review* (Oct. 1844):789.

100. *LCM Magazine* (June 1845):124.

101. Ibid., p. 138.

102. *LCM Magazine* (June 1847):117.

103. Baptist Noel, *State of the Metropolis*, London, 1835, p. 70.

104. B. I. Coleman, "Anglican Church Extension, c. 1800–1860, with Special Reference to London," Ph.D. thesis, Cambridge University, 1967, p. 93.

105. *Record*, Jan. 4, 1841.

106. *LCM Magazine* (June 1847):121.

107. *LCM Magazine* (June 1851):120.

108. *Record*, March 30, 1848.

109. *Record*, March 30, 1848.

110. Hodder, *Shaftesbury*, 2:241.

111. See Champneys's testimony in *Select Committee of the House of Lords on the*

Coalwhipper Act; together with the Proceedings of the Committee, Minutes of Evidence, Appendix and Index, vol. 12, 1857, p. 75.

112. *Dictionary of National Biography*, s.v., R. B. Seeley.

113. *LCM Magazine* (June 1848):127–128.

114. Lord Shaftesbury, introduction to *Round the Tower; or the Story of the LCM*, by J. M. Weylland, London, 1875, p. vii.

115. *LCM Thirteenth Annual Report* in *LCM Magazine* (June 1848):128–129.

116. Ibid., p. 137.

117. Ibid., p. 138.

118. *LCM Magazine* (Nov. 1849):230.

119. *Record*, Sept. 26, 1828.

120. *Record*, May 24, 1830.

121. *Record*, May 23, 1831.

122. See Hugh Stowell's speech to the DVS in *Record*, May 15, 1834.

123. *LCM Eleventh Annual Report* in *LCM Magazine* (June 1846):121.

124. *Church Congress Report* (1881), p. 215, cited by Inglis, *Churches and the Working Classes*, p. 215.

125. Inglis, *Churches and the Working Classes*, p. 335.

126. Charles Booth, *Life and Labour of the People in London*, London, 1902. Third Series, vol. 7:289–290.

CHAPTER 8: Setbacks and Advances

1. Albert Peel, *These Hundred Years: A History of the Congregational Union of England and Wales, 1831–1931*, London, 1931, p. 147.

2. The *Christian Witness*'s circulation averaged 33,783 per month in 1844 (*Christian Witness* 1 [1844]:v) while the *Evangelical Magazine*, established in 1793 had a circulation of about 16,000 in 1845. See *Congregational Magazine* (Jan. 1846):58.

3. *Christian Witness* 7 (1850):216.

4. The full name of the organization after 1853 was the Society for the Liberation of Religion from State Patronage and Control.

5. *Christian Witness* 2 (May 1845):231 and 233.

6. *Christian Witness* 3 (August 1846):369–376.

7. *Christian Witness* 3 (February 1846):81.

8. *Record*, Jan. 12, 1846, quoted in *Christian Witness* 3 (February 1846):81.

9. *Record*, Jan. 14, 1846, quoted in *Christian Witness* 3 (February 1846):81.

10. See chapter 1, no.35

11. *Record*, Dec. 29, 1853.

12. *Record*, May 10, 1847. By 1847 the Anglican magazine was selling about 112,000 copies per month, about 10,000 ahead of its rival.

13. *Churchman's Monthly Review* (July 1846):537.

14. G.I.T. Machin, *Politics and the Churches in Great Britain 1832–1868*, Oxford, 1977, pp. 181–182.

15. C. E. Smith, *A Statement to the Electors of Edinburgh*, Edinburgh, 1846, quoted in *Churchman's Monthly Review* (July 1846):529.

16. *Churchman's Monthly Review* (July 1846):534. Robert Daly (1783–1872), Bishop of Cashel and Waterford, was an eminent leader of the Evangelical section of the Church of Ireland.

17. *Churchman's Monthly Review* (July 1846):537.

18. Ibid.

19. *Record*, April 12, 1847.

20. *Record*, Dec. 8, 1845, and Jan. 4, 1847.

21. See John Prest, *Lord John Russell*, London, 1972, pp. 256–257.

22. Edward Baines, Jr. (1801–1890) was M.P. for Leeds, 1859–1874 and was eventually knighted. He was well known as a leading temperance figure.

23. *Record*, April 12, 1847.

24. Ibid.

25. Most evangelical societies held their annual meetings in London in May.

26. *Churchman's Monthly Review* (May 1846):378.

27. Dudley Ryder (1798–1882) succeeded to his father's title as Earl of Harrowby in December 1847. He presided at the annual meeting of the BFBS early in May 1846. *Record*, May 9, 1846. See *Dictionary of National Biography*.

28. Robert Grosvenor (1801–1893) was the third son of the first Marquess of Westminster and was created a baron in his own right in 1857. See *Record*, Jan. 28, 1847.

29. Ian S. Rennie, "Evangelicalism and English Public Life, 1823–1850," Ph.D. thesis, University of Toronto, 1962, p. 280.

30. *Record*, Jan. 28, 1847.

31. *Record*, Feb. 25, 1847.

32. *Churchman's Monthly Review* (July 1846):535–536.

33. *Record*, Aug. 17, 1846.

34. "Statement of principles upon which the National Club is founded," *Addresses to the Protestants of the Empire, issued by the Committee of the National Club*, first series, no. 1, London, 1848.

35. Machin, *Politics and the Churches*, p. 176.

36. Among the politicians were the following Evangelicals: George Montagu, 6th Duke of Manchester, chairman of the club; Frederick John William Lambart, 8th Earl of Cavan; Stephen Moore, 3d Earl of Mountcashel; Robert Jocelyn, 3d Earl of Roden; George William Finch-Hatton, 5th Earl of Winchelsea; Robert Edward King, 1st Viscount Lorton; J. W. Blandford, M.P. (later 7th Duke of Marlborough); and J. C. Colquhoun. The Reverend Hugh McNeile was probably the best-known clergyman associated with the club. See *National Club Addresses*, and *Record*, May 6, 1846.

37. *Addresses of the National Club*, no. 1, p. 5.

38. *Record*, July 12, 1847.

39. For a detailed discussion, see Rennie, "Evangelicals and English Public Life," pp. 277–282.

40. Prest, *Lord John Russell*, p. 256.

41. G.I.T. Machin, "The Maynooth Grant, the Dissenters and Disestablishment, 1845–1847," *English Historical Review*, 82 (1967):83.

42. Noel came to reject paedobaptism and underwent baptism by immersion. He became a respected Baptist minister in London.

43. *Record*, Nov. 23, 1848.

44. Under legislation enacted in 1832 a Judicial Committee of the Privy Council was entitled to hear all appeals to the King in Council; in 1840 the Church Discipline Act provided that bishops who were privy councillors would join the committee when ecclesiastical cases were being tried. Machin, *Politics and the Churches*, p. 30.

45. Machin, *Politics and the Churches*, p. 203.

46. Peter Toon, "Evangelical Response to Tractarian Teaching," D.Phil. thesis, Oxford University, 1977, p. 79.

47. *Record*, Aug. 28, 1848.

48. *Record*, Dec. 28, 1848.

49. *The Witness*, Dec. 5, 1848, cited in *Record*, Dec. 28, 1848.

50. B. W. Noel, *The Union of Church and State*, London, 1848.

51. See *Record* from Dec. 28, 1848, to Feb. 5, 1849.

52. *Record*, June 14, 1849.

53. *Record*, Aug. 2, 1849.

54. *Record*, Aug. 13, 1849.

55. *Record*, Aug. 23, 1849.

56. *Record*, Aug. 26, 1849.

57. *Record*, Sept. 10 and Sept. 24, 1849.

58. *Record*, Oct. 8, 1849.

59. See two letters in *Record*, Oct. 8, 1849, and letter in Oct. 18, 1849 edition.

60. *Record*, Dec. 10, 1849.

61. Letter from Bishop Blomfield to R. W. Dibdin, May 30, 1846, *Fulham Palace MSS.*, fiche 107, f. 82 in Lambeth Palace, London.

62. Letter from R. W. Dibdin to the editor of the *Record*, in *Record*, Jan. 14, 1850.

63. *Christian Observer* (Sept. 1849):648.

64. *Christian Observer* (Oct. 1849):720.

65. *Christian Witness* 6 (1849):417.

66. *Christian Witness* 6 (1849):418.

67. *Christian Observer* (Jan. 1850):72.

68. *Christian Observer* (April 1850):289.

69. *Record*, Aug. 6, 1849. Perhaps the person best known for this line of reasoning was William Goode.

70. *Record*, March 7, 1850.

71. *Christian Witness* 7 (1850):220–221.

72. *Christian Witness* 7 (1850):222.

73. Peel, *These Hundred Years*, p. 218.

74. Even the *Record* acknowledged such a possibility. See chapter 10.

75. See Desmond Bowen, *The Protestant Crusade in Ireland, 1800–1870*, Montreal, 1978, pp. 1–3. Bowen's book has some rather curious omissions. He fails to even mention Baptist Noel and Captain James Gordon. Gordon was the leading Evangelical in nineteenth-century English No Popery and had a great deal of influence in Ireland. Bowen also fails to note the operations of the English Reformation Society, a key No Popery organization.

76. See chapter 4.

77. *Record*, Aug. 17, 1846.

78. Alan R. Acheson, "The Evangelicals in the Church of Ireland, 1784–1859," Ph.D. thesis, Queen's University of Belfast, 1967, p. 77. D. H. Akenson maintains that the Irish Church was predominately Evangelical by 1850 and that only after disestablishment was it overwhelmingly so. D. H. Akenson, *The Church of Ireland, Ecclesiastical Reform and Revolution, 1800–1885*, New Haven, 1971, p. 132.

79. Letter from Charlotte Elizabeth to the editor of the *Christian Observer*, December 16, 1835, published posthumously in *Christian Observer* (April 1847):210.

80. Edwin Hodder, *The Life and Work of the Seventh Earl of Shaftesbury*, 2 vols., London, 1887, 1:392.

81. *Record*, Sept. 4, 1848.

82. *Churchman's Monthly Review* (Oct. 1841):544.

83. Ibid., p. 544.

84. *Christian Observer* (1828):239. For a discussion of the Evangelicals' educational efforts in Ireland, see: D. Hempton, *Methodism and Politics*, pp. 152–158 and D. H. Akenson, *Church of Ireland*, pp. 134–142.

85. Letter from James Edward Gordon to Robert Peel, July 9, 1824, British Museum *Peel MSS.*, 40366, f. 255.

86. Letter from the same to the same, May 22, 1823, British Museum *Peel MSS.*, 40356, f. 166.

87. See especially the letters from James E. Gordon to Robert Peel, January 13, 1824, British Museum *Peel MSS.*, 40360, f. 87; and March 23, 1824, 40363, ff. 89–96.

88. *Hansard Parliamentary Debates*, n.s. 12 (1825) col. 216. House of Commons debate on February 10, 1825.

89. *Hansard Parliamentary Debates*, n.s. 12 (1825), cols. 280–281. House of Commons debate on February 11, 1825.

90. *Hansard Parliamentary Debates*, n.s. 12 (1825), col. 259. House of Commons debate on Feb. 10, 1825. Gordon denied having created such a disturbance or even having been in Ireland in connection with any society. See Letter from J. E. Gordon to Robert Peel, British Museum *Peel MSS.*, 40373, f. 240.

91. *Record*, April 29, 1843.

92. The London Hibernian Society's receipts were £8,439 in 1828, £7,330 in 1831; by 1844 they had fallen to £3,876 and the society was deeply in debt. See *Christian Guardian* (June 1828):236; (July 1831):278; and (July 1844):277.

93. *Record*, Jan. 17, 1833.

94. See chapter 2.

95. Rennie, "Evangelicals and English Public Life," chapter on "No Popery."

96. Baptist Noel and Captain Vernon Harcourt were prominent members of the Reformation Society whose views on Ireland were sharply divergent. *Record*, May 17, 1845.

97. *Record*, March 4, 1830, and March 13, 1834.

98. *Sixteenth Annual Report of the LCM* in *LCM Magazine* (1851):114. For details on the Catholic efforts to consolidate the allegiance of the Irish poor to the Church, see Conrad Charles, "The Origins of the Parish Mission in England and the Early Passionist Apostolate," *Journal of Ecclesiastical History* 15 (1964):72–74; and Sheridan Gilley, "Catholic Faith of the Irish Slums, London, 1840–70, in *The Victorian City: Images and Realities*, eds. H. J. Dyos and Michael Wolff, 2 vols., London, 1973.

99. Ibid., p. 113.

100. Wiseman's statement that "Catholic England has been restored to its orbit in the ecclesiastical firmament," especially rankled. See Cardinal Wiseman's letter, "Out of the Flaminian Gate," in *English Historical Documents, 1833–1874*, eds., G. M. Young and W. D. Handcock, vol. 12(1), pp. 364–67.

101. *Record*, Oct. 31, 1850.

102. *LCM Minutes*, Nov. 18, 1850.

103. *Sixteenth Annual Report of LCM* in *LCM Magazine* (1850):113.

104. Rev. William Cunningham, "Popery in Britain, and our Duty to its professors, an address to the Evangelical Alliance in London," quoted in *LCM Magazine* (Nov. 1851):251.

105. *LCM Magazine* (Jan. 1851):2.

106. *LCM Magazine* (Dec. 1850):272. See also *LCM Magazine* (June 1851):117.

107. *LCM Magazine* (Jan. 1851):5.

108. Ibid.

109. Ibid.

110. Ibid., p. 23.

111. Ibid., p. 24.

112. For a contrary view, see E. R. Norman, who maintains that the main body of Nonconformists kept out of the main protests: *Anti-Catholicism in Victorian England*, London, 1968, p. 65.

113. *Record*, Nov. 21, 1850.

114. Ibid.

115. *Record*, Dec. 12, 1850.

116. *Record*, Nov. 21 and Dec. 12, 1850.

117. *Christian Witness* 7 (1850):iii.

118. *Christian Witness* 7 (1850):iii and iv.

119. This is against the views of Gilley and Toon, who both are mistaken in citing the Islington Protestant Institute as example of an interdenominational organization, when it was in fact a strictly Anglican organization. See Sheridan Gilley, "Evangelical and Roman Catholic Missions to the Irish in London, 1830–1870," Ph.D. thesis, Cambridge University, 1970, pp. 89–90; Toon, "Evangelical Response to Tractarian Teaching," p. 86; *First Annual Report of the Islington Protestant Institute*, London, 1847, p. 1. The only copy of the *Annual Report* in the Islington Public Library, London.

120. E. R. Norman, *Anti-Catholicism in Victorian England*, London, 1968, p. 65.

121. *Record*, Oct. 13, 1851, and *Second Annual Report of the Protestant Alliance*, London, 1853.

122. "The Protestant Alliance: Rule, and Address of," *Protestant Magazine* 8 (April 1846):169–173.

123. *Record*, Aug. 11, 1851.

124. Notably the Reverend Richard Burgess, rector of Upper Chelsea, and Francis Close of Cheltenham. *Record*, Dec. 1, 1851.

125. *Record*, Feb. 6, 1856.

126. Bowen, *The Protestant Crusade in Ireland*, p. 183.

127. Ibid., pp. 185–186.

128. Ibid., p. 217. For details on Dallas, see D. H. Akenson, *The Church of Ireland*, pp. 207–8.

129. The principal English societies with long-established missions in Ireland were the Irish Society of London, the London Hibernian Society, and the Reformation Society.

130. *The Nation*, Nov. 20, 1852 quoted in *Record*, Dec. 16, 1852.

131. *Record*, Dec. 13, 1852.

132. Robert Bickersteth's speech to the Society for Irish Church Missions to Roman Catholics in *Record*, Dec. 16, 1852.

133. D. H. Akenson, *The Church of Ireland*, p. 209.

134. *Record*, June 16, 1853.

135. Revenues jumped from £3,876 to £40,718. See *Christian Guardian* (July 1844):277 and *Record*, May 20, 1852.

136. *Record*, June 16, 1853.

137. *Record*, June 23, 1853.

138. *Record*, July 18, 1853.

139. Among these were Lord Shaftesbury and Robert Hanbury, along with the following London clergy: W. Cadman, James Cohen, Samuel Garratt, and J. E. Keane.

140. *LCM Minutes*, Nov. 7, 1851. Hanlow was then sent to a panel of ministers for a more thorough theological examination and then on their recommendation was employed. *LCM Minutes*, March 17 and March 24, 1851.

141. Gilley, "Evangelical and Roman Catholic Missions," p. 8.

142. Charles S. Stanford, *A Handbook to the Romish Controversy; being a refutation in Detail of the Creed of Pope Pius the Fourth, On the Grounds of Scripture and Reason*, Dublin, 1852.

143. See Gilley, "Evangelical and Roman Catholic Missions," pp. 31–32; B. I. Coleman, "Anglican Church Extension, c. 1800–1860, with Special Reference to London," Ph.D. thesis, Cambridge University, 1967, p. 362; G. Kitson Clark, *The Making of Victorian Britain*, London, 1962, p. 21; and G.F.A. Best, "Popular Protestantism in Victorian Britain," in *Ideas and Institutions of Victorian Britain*, ed. R. Robson, London, 1967, p. 142.

144. Gilley, "Evangelical and Roman Catholic Missions," pp. 31–32.

145. Ibid., p. 32.

146. Ibid., pp. 32–33.

147. See J. A. Wylie, "Rome's Grand Missionary Institute, or her use of the Irish in Swamping England," in *Rome and Civil Liberty*, London, 1864, pp. 164–170.

148. Gilley, "Evangelical and Roman Catholic Missions," p. 32, n.2.

149. *LCM Magazine* (June 1853):136.

150. *Churchman's Monthly Review* (1846):936.

151. John Henry Newman, "Logical Inconsistency of the Protestant View," in *Lectures on Catholicism in England . . .*, cheap edition, Birmingham, 1851, p. 187.

152. *LCM Magazine* (June 1853):121 f. and (June 1854):117 f.

153. Gilley, "Evangelical and Roman Catholic Missions," p. 85.

154. For details on the background to this see: G.I.T. Machin, "Lord John Russell and the Prelude to the Ecclesiastical Titles Bill, 1846–1851," *Journal of Ecclesiastical History* 25 (July 1974):277–295.

155. *Record*, March 10, 1851.

156. For a discussion of its impact, see E. R. Norman, *Anti-Catholicism*, p. 79.

157. *Christian Observer* (Aug. 1852):577–578.

158. *Record*, Aug. 9, 1852.

159. *Record*, April 14, 1853.

160. *Record*, Aug. 1, 1850.

161. *Christian Observer* (Aug. 1852):578.

162. *Record*, Oct. 18, 1852.

163. Elliott-Binns, *Religion in the Victorian Era*, London, 1936, p. 126.

164. *Record*, Jan. 1, 1855.

165. *Hansard*, 137, 2074. Cited by Machin, *Politics and the Churches*, p. 273.

166. English giving to evangelistic work in Ireland also fell off during the 1850s. In 1853 the Irish Church Missions amalgamated with the Irish Society of London (*Record*,

Sept. 22, 1853). Its funds apparently peaked in 1855 at £39,489 but dropped to £27,735 in 1860. (*Record*, May 2, 1855, and May 9, 1860). By 1857 the LCM was being forced to withdraw some of its workers who had been trained in anti-Catholic polemics. *LCM Magazine* (Jan. 1857):28f.

167. See chapter 9.
168. *Record*, Feb. 6, 1856.
169. Machin, *Politics and the Churches*, pp. 276–280.
170. Gilley, "Evangelical and Roman Catholic Missions," pp. 96 ff.
171. Ibid., p. 117.
172. Ibid.

CHAPTER 9: Specialization in Evangelism

1. G.I.T. Machin, *Politics and the Churches in Great Britain, 1832–1868*, Oxford, 1977, p. 257. For further details on the census, see Machin, pp. 6–9; the Report on the Census, Parliamentary Papers, 1852–3 (1969), 89; K. S. Inglis, "Patterns of Religious Worship in 1851," *Journal of Ecclesiastical History* 11 (1960):74–86; J. D. Gay, *The Geography of Religion in England*, London, 1971, 55 ff.
2. Inglis, "Patterns of Religious Worship," p. 78.
3. *Record*, Sept. 21, 1854.
4. See chapter 4.
5. *LCM Magazine* (Feb. 1854):44.
6. B. I. Coleman, "Anglican Church Extension, c. 1800–1860, with Special Reference to London," Ph.D. thesis, Cambridge University, 1967, p. 184.
7. Ibid., p. 187.
8. *LCM Magazine* (June 1855):143.
9. Ibid., p. 144.
10. Molesworth had long been the scourge of Evangelicals. See his attack on the CP-AS: J.E.N. Molesworth, *Symptoms of the Dangerous Hand by Which the Insidious Veto of the Pastoral Aid Society may be wielded. . . .*, London, 1841.
11. *Guardian*, Jan. 19, 1855, quoted in *Record*, Feb. 8, 1855.
12. *Record*, Feb. 8, 1855.
13. "Access to the Masses in our Populous Parishes," *Christian Observer* (March 1853):158. This speech was likely delivered to the Islington Clerical Conference.
14. Ibid., p. 159.
15. *LCM Magazine* (June 1858):152 ff.
16. Ibid.
17. An example of this is seen in the Foreigners' Evangelical Society, which in 1848 was appealing to the LCM to take over its work. *LCM Minutes*, Feb. 14 and Feb. 21, 1848.
18. See *LCM Magazine* (Nov. 1844).
19. *LCM Magazine* (Oct. 1851):230–233 and (March 1859):49–88.
20. In 1859 the LCM estimated that only 24.3 percent of the Welsh in London attended church services, whereas the 1851 religious census had reported that 52.4 percent of the population of Wales were attenders. *LCM Magazine* (March 1859):64–65.
21. *LCM Magazine* (Nov. 1858):277–308.
22. See chapter 2.
23. See chapter 4.

24. E. R. Sandeen, *The Roots of Fundamentalism: British and American Millenarianism, 1800–1930*, London, 1969, p. 11.

25. Charles Simeon, Appendix to *Horae Homileticae*, No. 342, London, 1828; and *Christian Observer* (Appendix 1843):801–810.

26. W. H. Oliver, *Prophets and Millenialists*, Oxford, 1978, p. 62.

27. Lord Ashley's Diary, August 24, 1841, quoted in Edwin Hodder, *Life and Work of the Seventh Earl of Shaftesbury*, 2 vols., London, 1887, 1:311. For a detailed discussion of the bishopric, see R. W. Greaves, "The Jerusalem Bishopric, 1841," *English Historical Review* 64 (1949), 328–352; and P. J. Welch, "Anglican Churchmen and the establishment of the Jerusalem Bishopric," *Journal of Ecclesiastical History* 8 (1957):193–204.

28. Shaftesbury Diary, August 1, 1841, quoted in Hodder, *Life of Shaftesbury*, 1:310–311.

29. Diary of Chevalier Bunsen, July 19, 1841, quoted in Hodder, *Life of Shaftesbury*, 1:371.

30. P. J. Welch, "Anglican Churchmen and the Establishment of the Jerusalem Bishopric," *Journal of Ecclesiastical History* 8 (1957):195.

31. In 1845–1846 LSPCJ receipts were £21,253; the CP-AS's, £12,257; and the LCM's, £11,715. *LCM Magazine* (June 1846):127 and (Aug. 1846):187.

32. *LCM Magazine* (June 1845):127.

33. *LCM Magazine* (July 1850):163.

34. *LCM Magazine* (Aug. 1850):179–182.

35. *LCM Magazine* (June 1858):152.

36. *LCM Magazine* (Aug. 1850):178.

37. Ibid.

38. *Record*, May 5, 1849.

39. W. R. Ward, *Religion and Society in England 1790–1850*, London, 1972, pp. 52–53.

40. See "One of the Protestant Party," *Random Recollections of Exeter Hall 1834–1837*, London, 1838, p. 28, and *Record*, April 2, 1849.

41. Letter from the Duke of Wellington to Lord Eldon, November 13, 1820, quoted in Horace Twiss, *The Public and Private Life of Lord Chancellor Eldon with Selections from his Correspondence*, 2 vols., London, 1844, 1:408. This is referred to in the *Record*, April 2, 1849, but is incorrectly cited as being written on Nov. 13, 1819.

42. The Reverend Samuel Briscall was appointed rector of South Kelsey in 1822, a living worth £687. He later also served as Wellington's personal chaplain.

43. Olive Anderson, "The Growth of Christian Militarism in Mid-Victorian Britain," *English Historical Review* 86 (Jan. 1971):46.

44. Ibid., p. 47.

45. *Record*, Oct. 8, 1832, and Nov. 20, 1834.

46. *LCM Magazine* (Oct. 1853):218.

47. *Record*, May 24, 1830. See *New Sailors' Magazine and Naval Chronicle*. This publication, begun in 1827, underwent eight name changes between 1827 and 1862.

48. Leading figures in this society included Thomson Hankey, sometime Liberal M.P. and governor of the Bank of England from 1851–1853, and Henry G.F. Moreton, 2d Earl of Ducie. *Record*, May 20, 1852.

49. These included Sir Jahleel Brenton (1790–1844), Francis Vernon Harcourt (1801–

1880), Sir Henry Hart (1796–1856), Sir W. Edward Parry (1790–1855), and Earl Waldegrave (1788–1859).

50. These included Sir Henry Hope (1787–1863) and Edward Hawker (1782–1860).

51. Lord Gambier (1756–1833) was active in both the CMS and in the pan-evangelical Port of London and Bethel Union. See *Christian Guardian* (June 1830):229 and *Record*, May 13, 1830.

52. Lord Ashley's Diary, December 27, 1843, quoted in Hodder, *Life of Shaftesbury*, 1:284.

53. Lord Ashley's Diary, October 4, 1844, quoted in Hodder, *Life of Shaftesbury*, 1:279–280.

54. See Hodder, *Life of Shaftesbury*, 2:286–287.

55. See [Rear Admiral Sir] Jahleel Brenton, *The Hope of the Navy; . . .* , London, 1839; and [Anonymous], *The Sailor's Hope for Himself AND the Nation: or, a Plea for Religion. . . .* , London, 1846; and a review of the latter work in *Churchman's Monthly Review* (Nov. 1846):853–860.

56. *Record*, May 15, 1855.

57. Anderson, "Christian Militarism," pp. 51–52.

58. Fox Maule (1801–1874). A long-time Scottish M.P. until his succession as Lord Panmure in 1852, the peer was a strong supporter of the Scottish Free Church. See *Record*, April 30, 1849, and *Dictionary of National Biography*. See *Record*, Nov. 21, 1856, for a speech by him entitled "Religion in the Army."

59. For an example of this, see: (Rev.) B. St. John, ed., *All is Well: Letters and Journal of Lieut. H.B.T. St. John. . . .* , London, 1846; and a review of the work in *Churchman's Monthly Review* (March 1847):226–228. See also Anderson, "Christian Militarism," p. 46, n.3.

60. *Record*, May 15, 1855.

61. *Record*, Jan. 11, 1855. See also John Cumming, *The Church in the Army*, London, 1856.

62. Anderson, "Christian Militarism," p. 47, n.3.

63. Ibid., p. 48.

64. Elizabeth Jay, *Religion of the Heart*, Oxford, 1979, p. 9, n.25.

65. Anderson, "Christian Militarism," p. 48.

66. Ibid., p. 48.

67. Ibid.

68. Ibid., p. 49.

69. *Record*, November 21, 1856.

70. Anderson, "Christian Militarism," p. 46.

71. Ibid., p. 49.

72. *Record*, Aug. 7, 1857.

73. Ibid.

74. *Record*, Sept. 11, 1857.

75. Anderson, "Christian Militarism," p. 49.

76. Ibid., p. 51.

77. Ibid., p. 51, n.1.

78. The receipts of the reorganized and renamed Soldiers' Friend and Scripture-readers' Society were £9,359 in the year 1854–1855. (*Record*, May 15, 1855).

79. Anderson, "Christian Militarism," p. 55, n.1.

80. Ibid., p. 55.

81. Ibid., p. 56. Previously recruits had been required to declare themselves as Anglicans, Catholics, or Presbyterians.

82. Ibid., pp. 58–60.

83. Ibid., pp. 60–61.

84. Ibid., pp. 59–60.

85. Ibid., p. 63.

86. For details of the LCM's work among cabmen: *LCM Magazine* (Oct. 1859). For information on the labors among the fire brigade see: *LCM Magazine* (Dec. 1859) and (Jan. 1860):1.

87. *LCM Minutes*, Feb. 10, 1836.

88. F. K. Prochaska, *Women and Philanthropy in Nineteenth Century England*, Oxford, 1978, pp. 182ff.

89. For an overview of such societies and their work see: "Female Penitentiaries," in *LCM Magazine* (Jan. 1849):6–15; and "Female Penitentiaries," *Quarterly Review* 48 (Sept. 1848):359–376.

90. Ralph Wardlaw, *Lectures on Female Prostitution: Its Nature, Extent, Effects, Guilt, Causes and Remedy*, Glasgow, 1842. See *Evangelical Magazine* (Nov. 1842):689–693.

91. *LCM Magazine* (April 1840):58–59.

92. *Parliamentary Papers*, "Reports from Commissioners, Report of the Royal Commission upon the Administration and Operation of the Contagious Diseases Acts," 1871, 19, p. 447. Quoted in Prochaska, *Women and Philanthropy*, p. 185.

93. *LCM Magazine* (Nov. 1842):161–167.

94. Ibid., p. 211.

95. *LCM Magazine* (Aug. 1856):173.

96. Ibid., p. 175.

97. For a study of Victorian efforts to rescue prostitutes, see Prochaska, *Women and Philanthropy*, chapter 6, pp. 183–221.

98. R. W. Vanderkiste, *Notes and Narratives of a Six Years' Mission*, London, 1852, pp. 281–282.

99. Prochaska, *Women and Philanthropy*, p. 186.

100. *LCM Magazine* (Oct. 1860):281–296. Prochaska thinks that the idea for the Midnight Meetings originated with Theophilus Smith of the Female Aid Society. He apparently was unsuccessful with them in 1850, but by 1860 the time for his idea seemed to have come. Prochaska, *Women and Philanthropy*, p. 194.

101. Prochaska, *Women and Philanthropy*, p. 196.

102. In 1853 the LCM received £1,567 from its country associations whereas in 1858–1859 its receipts from this source were estimated at between £5,000 and £6,000, plus almost £700 from Scotland and £100 from Ireland. See *LCM Magazine* (Feb. 1857):42 and (June 1859):156.

103. *LCM Magazine* (Sept. 1854):181–196.

104. Mrs. Emma Sheppard, *An Out-Stretched Hand to the Fallen*, London, 1860, p. 6. Quoted by Prochaska, *Women and Philanthropy*, p. 186.

105. *LCM Minutes*, Feb. 10, 1836.

106. *LCM Magazine* (June 1837):90.

107. Prochaska, *Women and Philanthropy*, p. 38.

108. Ibid., p. 232.

109. See chapter 6, n.8.

110. E. H. Ranyard, *True Institution of Sisterhood*, London, 1862, p. 8.

111. Ibid., p. 24.

112. See Edward Cook, *The Life of Florence Nightingale*, London, 1913, 1:109–111 and 2:249; I. B. O'Malley, *Florence Nightingale, 1820–1856: A Study of her Life Down to the End of the Crimean War*, London, 1932, pp. 129–131 and 168–171; Cecil Woodham-Smith, *Florence Nightingale, 1820–1910*, London, 1952, pp. 69–70.

113. *Christian Observer* (Dec. 1858):904–908.

114. *RBM MSS.*, Council Minutes, July 23, 1860 in Greater London Public Records Office, London.

115. See C. H. Simpkinson, *The Life and Work of Bishop Thorold*, London, 1896, p. 31.

116. *RBM MSS.*, Council Minutes, March 25, 1860.

117. Prochaska, *Women and Philanthropy*, p. 127.

118. Ellen H. Ranyard, *The Missing Link*, London, 1859.

119. *LCM Magazine* (Nov. 1860):322.

120. *RBM MSS.*, Council Minutes, March 26, 1860.

121. Ranyard, *Sisterhood*, p. 15. Of the 154 superintendents in 1862, 40 fit this description.

122. *Parochial Mission Women* (pamphlet), London, 1861, p. 1. A copy of this can be found in the Lambeth Palace *Tait Papers*, Vol. 389, f. 52.

123. Ranyard, *Sisterhood*, p. 20.

124. Ibid., p. 7.

125. Ibid.

126. Ibid., p. 9.

127. Ibid., p. 10.

128. Prochaska, *Women and Philanthropy*, p. 127, and Kathleen Heasman, *Evangelicals in Action*, London, 1962, p. 37.

129. Prochaska, *Women and Philanthropy*, p. 129.

130. Mary Stocks, *A Hundred Years of District Nursing*, London, 1960, p. 25. Quoted by Prochaska, *Women and Philanthropy*, p. 129.

131. *Christian Observer* (Dec. 1856):835.

132. *Christian Observer* (April 1835):252.

133. "A London Churchman," *The Gospel Unfettered; or the Necessity of Open-Air Ministration for the Million*, London, 1849.

134. See *Christian Guardian* (Jan. 1850):27–29; (Feb. 1850):71–73; (March 1850):126–128; (May 1850):213–214; and (June 1850):261–263.

135. *LCM Minutes*, Aug. 6, 1849.

136. See Letter from W. Hewett to editor of *Record* (Nov. 24, 1851); Letter from C.C.F. to editor of *Record* in Supplement to the *Record*, Jan. 12, 1854.

137. *Record*, Aug. 12, 1844, and Jan. 15, 1846.

138. *Record*, Aug. 5, 1850. See also *Record*, April 14, 1851.

139. *LCM Magazine* (Aug. 1852):190.

140. *LCM Magazine* (Feb. 1853):40.

141. *LCM Magazine* (June 1853):112.

142. *LCM Magazine* (June 1854):108. The work was T.W.P. Taylder, *Mormon's Own Book: or Mormonism Tried by its own Standards*, London, 1855.

143. J.F.C. Harrison, *The Second Coming: Popular Millenarianism, 1780–1850*, London, 1979, p. 203.

144. *Christian Observer* (Dec. 1856):845 quoting *First Annual Report of the Open-Air Mission*, London, 1853, pp. 15–16.

145. *LCM Magazine* (June 1854):107.

146. *LCM Minutes*, March 10, 1856.

147. *Christian Observer* (Dec. 1856):851.

148. Ibid., p. 840.

149. Letter from Bishop Blomfield to the Reverend C. F. Childe, May 19, 1855, printed in *Christian Observer* (Dec. 1856):841.

150. *Christian Observer* (May 1853):335.

151. Ibid.

152. Brian Harrison, "The Sunday Trading Riots of 1855," *The Historical Journal*, 8, no. 2 (1965):226.

153. Ibid.

154. *Record*, July 8, 1852.

155. *Christian Observer* (May 1853):334.

156. For an example of these lectures, see Benjamin Scott, *The Catacombs of Rome*, London, 1853. See also the later editions of 1860, 1873, and 1889.

157. B. Scott, *Catacombs at Rome*, 2d ed., London, 1860, p. 146. Eventually the WMEU was taken over by the Religious Tract Society. B. Scott, *Catacombs at Rome*, 4th ed., London, 1889, p. 187.

158. *Record*, Feb. 9, 1854. See *Lloyd's Weekly London Newspaper*, Feb. 5, 1854, p. 7.

159. *Christian Observer* (May 1857):286ff.

160. Clyde Binfield, *George Williams of the YMCA*, London, 1973, pp. 161–162; H. Solly, *Working Men's Social Clubs and Educational Institutes*, London, 1867, p. 5.

161. Binfield, *George Williams*, p. 62.

162. Shaftesbury was personally involved in the planning and organizing of the RBM in 1859. He chaired public meetings of the Open-Air Mission and the WMEU, but the lack of primary material makes it difficult to determine his level of personal involvement in these societies.

163. Arthur Kinnaird (1814–1897), who was later to become Lord Kinnaird, had worked with Shaftesbury in the LCM and in the CMS before acting as treasurer of the RBM. William Dugmore (1800–1871), the treasurer of the Open-Air Mission, was a close associate of Alexander Haldane, Shaftesbury's closest personal friend and advisor in the 1850s. See Frederic Boase, *Modern English Biography*, London, 1896 and Ian S. Rennie, "Evangelicalism and English Public Life, 1823–1850," Ph.D. thesis, University of Toronto, 1962, p. 82. Robert Cooper Lee Bevan (1809–1890), the treasurer of the WMEU, filled the same function in Shaftesbury's favorite concern, the Ragged School Union.

164. See Appendix C. The CP-AS took over the work of the SRA in 1935. "Agreement between the Church of England Scripture Readers' Association and the Church Pastoral-Aid Society, 16 May, 1935," in Papers of the Church of England Scripture Readers' Association, Church Pastoral-Aid Society, Falcon Court, 32 Fleet Street, London.

CHAPTER 10: New Incentives to Unity

1. *Christian Observer* (Jan. 1855):64–65.

2. "On the Progress of True Religion Amongst Our Home Population," *Christian Observer* (March 1856):145–147.

3. Between 1846 and January 1856 seven vacancies in Crown livings occurred, and five of the seven appointees are easily recognizable as Evangelicals. The three canonries of St. Paul's Cathedral that the Crown controlled were given to leading Evangelical clergy in the period, giving them an important say in the appointment of other London clergy. The only appointment that the lord chancellor made during this period was also given to an Evangelical.

4. *Christian Observer* (March 1856):147.

5. "Rope of Sand," *Christian Observer* (Jan. 1858):9.

6. Ian S. Rennie, "Evangelicalism and English Public Life, 1823–1850," Ph.D. thesis, University of Toronto, 1962, p. 212.

7. Ibid.

8. Ibid., p. 209.

9. Letter of Henry Blunt, quoted in *Record*, Dec. 29, 1853.

10. Notably, Sir Andrew Agnew, M.P., Andrew Johnston, M.P., Alexander Gordon, and Alexander Haldane. Rennie, "Evangelicals and English Public Life," p. 216.

11. Ibid., pp. 204–205.

12. Ibid., p. 206.

13. *LCM Minutes*, April 27, 1840.

14. *LCM Magazine* (March 1840):33–36.

15. *LCM Magazine* (Nov. 1847):229–239.

16. *LCM Magazine* (June 1852):135–136.

17. Rennie, "Evangelicals and Public Life," p. 230.

18. *LCM Minutes*, Jan. 10, 1853.

19. For a survey of press opinion, see *Record*, Aug. 26, 1854.

20. *Record*, March 12, 1855.

21. See G. M. Ellis, "The Evangelicals and the Sunday Question, 1830–1860," Ph.D. thesis, Harvard University, 1951, p. 346. Cited by Brian Harrison, "The Sunday Trading Riots of 1855," *The Historical Journal*, 8, no. 2 (1965):242.

22. Harrison, "The Sunday Trading Riots," p. 220.

23. Ibid.

24. Letter from Lord R. Grosvenor, dated June 28, 1855, published in the *Times*, June 29, 1855, cited by Harrison, "The Trading Riots," p. 222, n.17.

25. Ibid., p. 222.

26. *Hansard Parliamentary Debates*, n.s. 137 (1855), col. 527, House of Commons debate on April 18, 1855, Lord Robert Grosvenor's speech.

27. Ibid., n.s. 138 (1855), cols. 57–58. House of Commons debate on May 3, 1855, Sir George Grey's speech.

28. Brian Harrison, "Religion and Recreation in Nineteenth-Century England," *Past and Present*, no. 38 (December 1967), p. 109.

29. *Hansard Parliamentary Debates*, n.s. 149 (1855), cols. 1911–1937. House of Commons debate on June 14, 1855.

30. *Times*, June 15, 1855, p. 7.

31. *Marx and Engels on Britain*, p. 417, cited by Harrison, "The Sunday Trading Riots," p. 223.

32. *Hansard Parliamentary Debates*, n.s. 139 (1855), col. 159, House of Commons debate on June 24, 1855, Sir George Grey's speech.

33. Harrison, "Sunday Trading Riots," p. 235.

34. *Times*, July 2, 1855, p. 12, cited by Harrison, "Sunday Trading Riots," p. 223.

35. Harrison, "Sunday Trading Riots," p. 223.

36. Ibid., p. 225.

37. *Record*, July 30, 1855.

38. *Hansard Parliamentary Debates*, n.s. 139 (1855), col. 159, House of Commons debate on June 24, 1855, Sir George Grey's speech.

39. *Times*, July 3, 1855, p. 8.

40. Harrison, "Sunday Trading Riots," p. 233.

41. Ibid., p. 224.

42. Ibid., p. 227.

43. Ibid.

44. Ibid., pp. 228–229.

45. Ibid., p. 231.

46. Lord Ashley's diary, June 15, 1841, quoted in Edwin Hodder, *The Life and Work of the Seventh Earl of Shaftesbury*, 2 vols., London, 1887, 1:181.

47. Harrison, "Religion and Recreation," p. 104.

48. Ibid., p. 105.

49. Harrison, "The Trading Riots," p. 231.

50. Ibid., p. 230.

51. *Times*, July 2, 1855, p. 9.

52. Harrison, "Religion and Recreation," p. 122.

53. Harrison, "Sunday Trading Riots," pp. 239–240.

54. Lord Shaftesbury's diary, February 11, 1867, cited by Harrison, "Sunday Trading Riots," p. 234.

55. Ibid., p. 235.

56. *Hansard Parliamentary Debates*, n.s. 139 (1855), col. 1850, House of Commons debate on August 5, 1855, Speech of the Marquess of Clanricarde.

57. Harrison, "Sunday Trading Riots," pp. 237–238.

58. Ibid., p. 237.

59. John Wigley, *The Rise and Fall of the Victorian Sunday*, Manchester, 1980, p. 70.

60. *Record*, Oct. 9, 1855.

61. *Record*, Dec. 12, 1855.

62. See chapters 4 and 8, and, in particular, chapter 8, n.22.

63. Clyde Binfield, *So Down to Prayers: Studies in English Nonconformity: 1780–1920*, London, 1977, p. 57.

64. Edward Baines, Sr. (1774–1848) was Liberal M.P. for Leeds, 1834–1841. The elder Baines was converted late in life. See Edward Baines, *The Life of Edward Baines*, London, 1851, pp. 292ff.

65. Matthew T. Baines (1799–1860) was Liberal M.P. for Hull, 1847–1852, and for Leeds, 1852–1859.

66. Binfield, *So Down to Prayers*, p. 58.

67. Edward Baines, *On the Performance of Military Bands in the Parks of London on Sunday*, London, 1856, p. 8.

68. Edward Baines, *The Social, Educational, and Religious State of the Manufacturing Districts . . . In Two letters to Sir Robert Peel*, London, 1843.

69. *Hansard Parliamentary Debates*, n.s. 244 (1856), col. 326, Lord Palmerston's speech in the House of Lords, May 19, 1856.

70. Harrison, "Sunday Trading Riots," p. 241.

71. *Record*, May 16, 1856.

72. *Times*, May 14, 1856, p. 8.

73. *Record*, June 14, 1855.

74. *LCM Magazine* (April 1850):95.

75. *Times*, June 18, 1855, p. 8.

76. *Hansard Parliamentary Debates*, n.s. 139 (1855), col. 494, Lord Derby's speech in House of Lords debate on 6 July 1855.

77. Ibid.

78. *Hansard Parliamentary Debates*, n.s. 139 (1855), col. 502, Lord Shaftesbury's speech in House of Lords debate on July 6, 1855.

79. Ibid., cols. 506–508, Bishop Blomfield's speech on the same day.

80. Ibid., col. 504, Archbishop Sumner's speech on the same day.

81. Ibid., cols. 513–515, Bishop Wilberforce's speech on the same day.

82. *Record*, July 11, 1855.

83. *Record*, July 13, 1855.

84. *Hansard Parliamentary Debates*, n.s. 139 (1855), col. 884, Lord Shaftesbury's speech in House of Lords debate on July 16, 1855.

85. Ibid., col. 509, Lord Broughan's speech to the Lords on July 6, 1855.

86. *LCM Magazine* (Jan. 1846):11.

87. Jeffrey Cox, *Churches in a Secular Society*, Oxford, 1982, p. 123.

88. *LCM Magazine* (Jan. 1846):11.

89. Ibid.

90. *LCM Magazine* (June 1860):184.

91. Ibid., p. 185.

92. *Christian Observer* (Aug. 1853):567.

93. L. E. Elliott-Binns, *Religion in the Victorian Era*, London, 1936, p. 333.

94. *Record*, Feb. 23, 1854, and Robert S. Candlish, *Examination of Mr. Maurice's Theological Essays*, London, 1854.

95. *Christian Observer* (Oct. 1855):649–657.

96. *Record*, July 11 and Oct. 3, 1855.

97. *Record*, Jan. 2, 1856.

98. Elliott-Binns, *Religion in the Victorian Era*, pp. 141–142.

99. Albert Peel, *These Hundred Years*, London, 1931, pp. 221 ff.

100. *Record*, Nov. 12, 1856.

101. G.I.T. Machin, *Politics and the Churches in Great Britain 1832–1868*, Oxford, 1977, p. 255.

102. *Record*, Nov. 12, 1856.

103. *Record*, Feb. 27, 1857.

104. *Edinburgh Review*, 98 (1853):341–342 quoted by Machin, *Politics and the Churches*, p. 256.

105. See chapter 8.

106. *Record*, Sept. 30 and Oct. 4, 1852.

107. *Record*, Oct. 18, 1852.

108. *Christian Observer* (Sept. 1852):649–650.

109. *Record*, Feb. 26, 1852. Since 1846 the Whigs had appointed at least two Evangelical bishops and raised J. B. Sumner to Canterbury. One was W. A. Shirley, bishop of Sodor and Man; the other was Sumner's replacement in Chester, John Graham. See *Record*, March 16, 1848.

110. Machin, *Politics and the Churches*, p. 261.

111. Quoted in ibid.

112. John Jackson, who was successively bishop of Lincoln and then of London, was apparently regarded as a moderate Evangelical at the time of his appointment. He had been a strong supporter of the SRA and had superintended for the LCM. See *LCM Magazine* (Oct. 1856):255, and *Christian Observer* (April 1853):255.

113. *Record*, Sept. 21, 1854.

114. William F. Cowper (1811–1888) was M.P. for Hertford, 1835–1868, and for Hampshire South, 1868–1880.

115. Quoted in Georgina Battiscombe, *A Biography of the Seventh Earl of Shaftesbury, 1801–1885*, London, 1974, p. 249.

116. Edwin Hodder, *The Life and Work of the Seventh Earl of Shaftesbury*, 2 vols., London, 1887, 2:505.

117. Machin, *Politics and the Churches*, pp. 271 and 300.

118. See the *Record*'s editorial of Dec. 19, 1856, for a discussion of the reaction of the popular press.

119. *Record*, Dec. 19, 1856.

120. *Record*, March 16, 1857.

121. Michael Hennell, *Sons of the Prophets*, London, 1979, p. 57.

122. *Record*, March 18, 1857.

123. Ibid.

124. *Record*, Feb. 11, 1857.

125. *Record*, April 3, 1857.

126. *Record*, March 9, 1857. Cited by Machin, *Politics and the Churches*, p. 283.

127. *Record*, April 13, 1857.

128. *Record*, April 20, 1857.

129. *Christian Observer* (April 1857):283.

130. Machin, *Politics and the Churches*, p. 284.

131. Ibid., p. 258.

132. Quoted in Ibid., p. 271.

133. Ibid.

134. Ibid., p. 285.

CHAPTER 11: Bishop Tait's Episcopacy

1. *LCM Magazine* (March 1857):59.

2. *LCM Minutes*, Dec. 4, 1838.

3. *LCM Magazine* (April 1859):93.

4. C. J. Blomfield, *A Charge Delivered to the Clergy of the Diocese of London, at the Visitation in November MDCCCL*, 2d ed., London, 1850.

5. It is questionable whether the "Broad Church" label is appropriate for Tait. He was raised as a Scottish Presbyterian and always remained that kind of Protestant. I am indebted to Dr. P. B. Hinchliff of Balliol College, Oxford, for this observation.

6. Edwin Hodder, *The Life and Work of the Seventh Earl of Shaftesbury*, 2 vols., London, 1886, 3:197, cited by Michael Hennell, *Sons of the Prophets*, London, 1979, p. 58.

7. *Record*, Nov. 14, 1856, and Jan. 2, 1857.

8. *LCM Magazine* (Feb. 1858):40–49.

9. Sir Culling Eardley (Smith), *The Testimony to Christian Union . . . With a Letter to the Rev. Dr. M'Neile of Liverpool*, London, 1859.

10. For the about-face of Close, see chapter 8, n.124; for Stowell, see chapter 9.

11. J. H. Gurney, *The Lost Chief . . .* , London, 1852, pp. 5–6.

12. See Lord Shaftesbury's speech to the Blandford-mews ragged school in *Record*, Nov. 7, 1853.

13. *Clerical Journal*, cited in *Record*, Aug. 15, 1853.

14. *Record*, Aug. 15, 1853.

15. *Record*, Aug. 24, 1859.

16. Brian E. Hardman, "The Evangelical Party in the Church of England, 1855–1865," Ph.D. thesis, Cambridge University, 1963, p. 248, and *Record*, Aug. 30, 1858.

17. *Record*, Jan. 26, 1857.

18. *Record*, May 18, 1857.

19. Ibid.

20. *Record*, July 17, 1857.

21. *Record*, Aug. 28, 1857.

22. *Hansard Parliamentary Debates*, n.s. 148 (1857), col. 325, Lord Shaftesbury's speech in House of Lords on Dec. 8, 1857, and Letter of John Campbell to Charles G. Finney, London, January 5, 1859, cited by Clyde Binfield, *George Williams of the YMCA*, London, 1973, p. 212.

23. *Record*, Dec. 7, 1857.

24. Ibid.

25. *Record*, Dec. 30, 1857.

26. Letter from W. Hale Hale to Bishop Tait, July 15, 1857, *Tait Papers*, vol. 106, f. 238, in Lambeth Palace Library, London.

27. *Record*, April 28, 1858. The *Record* was mistaken as to the mission's responsibility for Villiers and Maurice being involved in the same series, but its criticism of the breadth of the mission was based in fact. See *Record*, April 20, 1858.

28. *Record*, May 10, 1858.

29. Letter from W. Hale Hale to Bishop Tait, July 15, 1857, *Tait Papers*, vol. 106, f. 238.

30. *Record*, July 18, 1859.

31. *First Annual Report of the London Diocesan Home Mission*, London, 1858, p. 6.

32. *Hansard Parliamentary Debates*, n.s. 148 (1858), col. 853–854, Lord Shaftesbury's speech to the House of Lords on Feb. 8, 1858.

33. *Record*, Feb. 8 and 16, 1858.

34. *Record*, June 4, 1858.

35. *Record*, July 9, 1858.

36. See the letters of Edouart and Tait in *Record*, July 16, 1858.

37. *Record*, Aug. 6, 1858.

38. *Record*, Nov. 23, 1859.

39. See the comments of the Reverend Hugh Stovel, a Nonconformist evangelical opposed to the theater services in *Record*, Nov. 23, 1859.

40. *Record*, Feb. 27, 1860.

41. *Hansard Parliamentary Debates*, n.s. 156 (1860), cols. 1662–1668, Lord Dungannon's speech to the House of Lords on February 24, 1860.

42. *Hansard Parliamentary Debates*, n.s. 156 (1860), col. 1668, Archbishop Sumner's speech to the House of Lords on February 24, 1860.

43. Ibid., col. 1692, Bishop Tait's speech to the House of Lords.

44. Ibid., col. 1694.

45. Ibid., cols. 1669–1688, Lord Shaftesbury's speech to the House of Lords. For a graphic description of an evangelical theatre service see the article by Charles Dickens, "The Uncommercial Traveller," *All the Year Around*, Feb. 25, 1860.

46. Hardman, "Evangelical Party 1855–1865," pp. 305–306.

47. John W. White, "The Influence of North American Revivalism in Great Britain between 1830 and 1914 on the Origin and Development of the Ecumenical Movement," D.Phil. thesis, Oxford University, 1963, chapter 1, p. 6.

48. Ibid., chapter 1, p. 42. See C. G. Finney, *Autobiography*, London, 1882, pp. 340–341.

49. See *Times* survey of London clergy in 1844 *Bodley Mss.*: Add. Msc. 290, Bodleian Library, Oxford.

50. *Record*, April 16, 1846.

51. *Record*, April 7, 1858. By "ordinary means" the *Record* specified house-to-house visitation by laymen, preaching, Bible classes, and prayer meetings.

52. *Record*, May 28, 1858.

53. *Record*, Dec. 29, 1858.

54. *Record*, March 11, 1859.

55. *Record*, April 6 and 13, 1859.

56. This is against the view of J. E. Orr, *Second Evangelical Awakening*, London, 1949, chapters 5–7. Orr's view has been challenged by Hardman "Evangelical Party 1855–1865," pp. 296 ff. and by P. Toon, "Evangelical Response to Tractarian Teaching," D.Phil. thesis, Oxford University, 1977, p. 86, n.3.

57. *Times*, Sept. 17, 1859, p. 6.

58. *Record*, Sept. 19, 1859.

59. See *Times*, Sept. 16, 1859, p. 7; Sept. 20, p. 7; and Sept. 23, p. 8. See also J. Edwin Orr, *The Second Evangelical Awakening in Great Britain*, London, 1953, pp. 175–176.

60. For an instance of this, see Letter from "J.C." to the editor of the *Times*, Sept. 21, 1859, p. 12.

61. *Record*, Nov. 7, 1859.

62. Ibid.

63. *Record*, Jan. 16, 1860.

64. *Record*, Nov. 18, 1859.

65. For a contrary view, see Hennell, *Sons of the Prophets*, pp. 87–88. Hennell cites the above passage but misunderstands the context.

66. *Christian Observer* (Sept. 1859):652.

67. Ibid.

68. *Christian Observer* (Nov. 1859):725.

69. Ibid., p. 729.

70. Ibid.

71. *Christian Observer* (Nov. 1859):730.

72. Ibid., pp. 730–731.

73. *Christian Observer* (Dec. 1859):786.

74. John William Cunningham (1780–1861) was Vicar of Harrow from 1811 to 1861 and a leading figure in Anglican Evangelicalism.

75. See Cunningham's obituary in *Christian Observer* (Dec. 1861):878–885.

76. W. J. Clyde Ervine, "Doctrine and Diplomacy: Some Aspects of the Life and Thought of the Anglican Evangelical Clergy, 1797–1838," Ph.D. thesis, Cambridge University, 1979, p. 289.

77. See Marsden's obituary in *Christian Observer* (Aug. 1870):633–634.

78. *Record*, Dec. 28, 1859.

79. *Record*, Jan. 16, 1860.

80. Ibid.

81. *Record*, Jan. 16, 1860.

82. Gilbert, *Religion and Society in Industrial England*, London, 1976, p. 169.

EPILOGUE

1. Geoffrey Best, "Evangelicalism and the Victorians," in *The Victorian Crisis of Faith*, ed. Anthony Symondson, London, 1970, pp. 37–38.

2. Jeffrey Cox, *The Churches in a Secular Society: Lambeth, 1870–1930*, New York, 1982, p. 58, n.13.

3. W. R. Ward, *Religion and Society in England 1790–1850*, New York, 1973, p. 6.

4. Raymond Brown, "Evangelicals Ideas of Perfection: A Comparative Study of the Spirituality of Men and Movements in Nineteenth Century England," Ph.D. thesis, Cambridge University, 1964, p. 178.

5. John Kent, *Holding the Fort: Studies in Victorian Revivalism*, London, 1978, pp. 352–353.

6. See Raymond Brown, "Evangelical Ideas of Perfection."

7. Kent, *Holding the Fort*, p. 299.

8. Ibid.

9. G.I.T. Machin, *Politics and the Churches in Great Britain 1832–1868*, Oxford, 1977, p. 252.

10. J. C. Ryle, *Strike: But Hear!*, London, 1868, p. 4.

11. Between 1864 and 1869 the Liberal party gained about 20 Irish seats, thereby erasing "the political effects of 1850–1." Machin, *Politics and the Churches*, p. 327.

12. Lord Ashley's diary, February 27, 1844, Edwin Hodder, *The Life and Work of the Seventh Earl of Shaftesbury*, vol. 1, London, 1887, p. 307.

13. Lord Ashley's diary, February 24, 1844, in ibid., p. 306.

14. Ryle, *Strike: But Hear!*, p. 10. This "domino theory" regarding the church establishments was not unusual; in the same year the Earl of Clarendon wrote to Lord John Russell, expressing the view that the English Church would perhaps only "last till the end of the century." Machin, *Politics and the Churches*, p. 382. What was peculiar to Ryle's view was the immense importance placed upon the Church of England as a bulwark against Rome.

15. Thomas R. Birks, *Church and State: or, National Religion and Church Establishments, Considered with Reference to Present Controversies . . . with a preface by the Lord Bishop of Lincoln*, London, 1869. I am indebted to Dr. Ian Rennie of Ontario Theological Seminary for this reference.

16. T. J. Roswell, a protégé of E. B. Pusey, and the perpetual curate of St. Peter's, Stepney, insisted to the House of Lords Committee on Spiritual Instruction in 1858 that he saw no need for such paid lay workers, although he admitted that he "should not

close Exeter Hall." *Parliamentary Papers, 1857–8*, 9, Deficiency of the Means of Spiritual Instruction, Select Committee, House of Lords: Report, p. 82.

17. I am indebted to Dr. P. B. Hinchliff of Balliol College, Oxford, for this reference. Letter from Benjamin Jowett to Bishop Tait, October 21, 1862, *Tait Papers*, vol. 79, f. 307.

18. Keith Thomas, *Religion and the Decline of Magic*, New York, 1971, p. 160.

19. Ibid., p. 159.

20. Ibid., p. 166.

21. Cox, *Churches in a Secular Society*, p. 94.

22. Thomas, *Religion and the Decline of Magic*, p. 666.

23. Quoted by Cox, *Churches in a Secular Society*, p. 92.

24. Ibid.

25. See B. R. Wilson, *Religion in a Secular Society*, 1966, pp. 10–12. Cited by K. Thomas, *Religion and the Decline of Magic*, p. 56, n.2.

26. Ibid., p. 98.

27. Charles Booth, *Life and Labour of the People in London*, London, 1902. 3d series, vol. 7, p. 270.

28. Ibid.

29. Ibid., p. 273.

30. I am indebted to Dr. Ian Rennie of Ontario Theological Seminary for his helpful insights on this point.

31. Booth, p. 289.

32. F. K. Prochaska, *Women and Philanthropy in Nineteenth Century England*, Oxford, 1980, p. 227.

33. Ibid., pp. 265–266.

34. Cox, p. 7.

35. "The English Evangelical Clergy," *MacMillan's Magazine*, 3 (December 1860):119–120.

Bibliography

Arranged as follows:

    I. Manuscripts
   II. Unpublished Theses
  III. Printed Primary Sources
       A. Autobiographies, Letters, and Biographies
       B. Books, Pamphlets and Sermons
       C. Parliamentary Reports
       D. Newspapers and Periodicals
       E. Dictionaries of Biography, Handbooks, Clergy Lists,
          and Other Religious Works
  IV. Twentieth-Century Secondary Sources
       A. Books
       B. Articles
       C. Dictionaries of Biography, Handbooks, Clergy Lists,
          and Other Religious Works

AUTHOR'S NOTE

The paucity of manuscript sources is the greatest obstacle facing any historian doing research into nineteenth-century British evangelicalism. Dr. Clyde Ervine spent well over a year in an attempt to track down manuscripts for a study of Edward Bickersteth, but was eventually forced to broaden the scope of his research. I too have made many unsuccessful attempts to locate new manuscript material (often by contacting descendants of important figures). Among my many failures were: John Charles Ryle, first bishop of Liverpool (apparently most material relating to Bishop Ryle was destroyed in a fire during

World War I); Robert Hanbury; John Labouchere; Francis Close; William Weldon Champneys (there are a few letters to and from him in the library of Brasenose College, Oxford);
and Abel Smith, M.P. (a visit to the West Sussex County Record Office in Chichester
revealed that the Smith family records on deposit there relate almost entirely to the High
Church side of the family).

Other manuscript sources have been consulted, and it is hoped that listing them here
may be of some help to others researching into other aspects of Evangelicalism: the
Wilberforce Mss. and the Lord John Russell papers in the Bodley, Oxford; the Thomas
Fowell Buxton papers in Rhodes House, Oxford; and letters of Sir R. H. Inglis, Lady
Olivia Sparrow, G. D. Ryder, M.P., and the Hon. Thomas Erskine in the British Museum.
During my research I compiled the names of several hundred evangelical laymen, including Members of Parliament and peers, but virtually no manuscript material is available
on them. Even Lord Shaftesbury's papers proved to be remarkably unhelpful on the
question of urban evangelism.

There are a few letters from Alexander Haldane to Canon Conway in the Cambridge
University Library, and some in the Charles Clayton papers in the library of Gonville
and Caius College. Edwin Hodder in his biography of Shaftesbury said that he had access
to hundreds of letters of Haldane–Shaftesbury correspondence dating from about 1850,
which had been lent to him by Haldane's daughters (Hodder, 1887, 2, 401n.). Some of
these are now apparently in the hands of one of their descendants in Scotland, but the
gentleman who has them is very reluctant to allow anyone access to them.

The parish records of several London churches held in the Westminster Public Library
in the City of Westminster were also consulted. For information on the records of some
of the leading evangelical societies, one should consult pp. iv and v of R. H. Martin's
D.Phil. thesis on deposit at the Bodley, Oxford ("The Pan-Evangelical Impulse").

Apart from the lack of manuscript material, research into English evangelicalism is
made more difficult by the fact that bombing during World War II destroyed some of
the British Library's printed material relating to religious societies. For instance, the early
annual reports of the Scripture Readers' Association have not survived although they are
listed in the British Museum Catalogue. Similarly other evangelistic societies have left
little printed material (only one annual report of the District Visiting Society has survived).
Of the other evangelistic societies, only the London City Mission and the Church Pastoral-
Aid Society have manuscript material relating to the first half of the century. Thus for
information on the functioning of the Metropolitan City Mission, the District Visiting
Society, and the Young Men's Society for Aiding Missions, one has to glean it from the
pages of the *Record*, the only publication that gives detailed accounts of their meetings
and operations.

I. MANUSCRIPTS

Bodleian Library, University of Oxford
    Additional Manuscript c.290
        "The Principal Clergy of London classified according to their opinions on
           the great Church questions of the day, prepared for Mr. Delane, Edtr.
           of *The Times*," 1844.
    Bickersteth Manuscripts, Box 25, Item 1
    Two Letter Books of Edward Bickersteth

Manuscript Additional English e.9
 The Diary of Daniel Wilson, Bishop of Calcutta
St. Edmund Hall Manuscripts 67/9
 The Diary of John Hill, Vice Principal of St. Edmund Hall, Oxford.
S. L. Gifford Collection
 Letters of R. B. Seeley to S. L. Gifford, Editor of *The Standard*
British Library, Great Russell Square, London
 Gladstone Manuscripts
  Letters from R. B. Seeley to R. F. Bonham
 Peel Manuscripts
  Letters from J. E. Gordon to Sir Robert Peel
  Letters from R. B. Seeley to Lord Ashley
  Letters from R. B. Seeley to Sir Robert Peel
  Letters from R. B. Seeley to Lord Sandon(?)
Church Pastoral-Aid Society, Falcon Court, 32 Fleet Street, London
 Papers of the Church of England Scripture Readers' Association, 1935
Gonville and Caius College Library, Cambridge
 Charles Clayton Diary and Papers
Greater London Public Record Office
 Ranyard Bible Mission Manuscripts, Council Minutes
Home Office, London
 Ecclesiastical Census Returns (H.O. 129/22)
Islington Public Library, Holloway Road, Islington
 Reports of the Islington Protestant Association (1846–1848)
Lambeth Palace Library
 Bishop Blomfield Papers, Bishop Blomfield's Letter Books
 Bishop Tait Papers, Bishop Tait's Letter Books
Leicestershire Record Office, 57 New Walk, Leicester
 Noel Family Collection
London City Mission, 175 Tower Bridge Road, London
 Handlist of London City Missionaries
 Minute Book of the London City Mission Committee, 1835–1860
St. Giles-in-the-Fields Church, London
 Manuscript Journal of Joseph Oppenheimer, City Missionary

II. UNPUBLISHED THESES

Acheson, A. R. "The Evangelicals in the Church of Ireland, 1784–1859." Ph.D. thesis, Queen's University, Belfast, 1968.

Baker, W. J. "The Attitudes of English Churchmen, 1800–1850, towards the Reformation." Ph.D. thesis, Cambridge University, 1966.

Bentley, Anne. "The Transformation of the Evangelical Party in the Church of England in the later 19th century." Ph.D. thesis, Cambridge University, 1966.

Brackwell, Clifford. "The Church of England and Society, 1830–1850." M.A. thesis, University of Birmingham, 1949.

Bradley, Ian C. "The Politics of Godliness: Evangelicals in Parliament, 1784–1832." D.Phil. thesis, Oxford University, 1976.

Brewer, J. "Millenarianism: its development and significance within the Christian Era."
    Ph.D. thesis, Leeds University, 1956.
Brown, Raymond. "Evangelical Ideas of Perfection: a comparative study of the spirituality
    of men and movements in Nineteenth Century England." Ph.D. thesis, Cambridge
    University, 1967.
Coleman, B. I. "Anglican Church Extension, c. 1800–1860, with special reference to
    London." Ph.D. thesis, Cambridge University, 1967.
Coombs, Peter B. "A History of the Church Pastoral-Aid Society, 1836–1861." Uni-
    versity of Bristol, 1961.
Cooper, Peter H. M. "The Church in St. Pancras, 1811–1868: a study of the politics of
    church extension." Ph.D. thesis, University of London (Bedford College), 1976.
Embley, P. L. "The Origins and Early Development of the Plymouth Brethren." Ph.D.
    thesis, Cambridge University, 1966.
Ervine, W.J.C. "Doctrine and Diplomacy: some aspects of the life and thought of the
    Anglican Evangelical Clergy, 1797–1837." Ph.D. thesis, Cambridge University,
    1979.
Gilley, Sheridan W. "Evangelical and Roman Catholic Missions to the Irish in London,
    1830–1870." Ph.D. thesis, Cambridge University, 1970.
Greenfield, R. H. "The Attitude of the Tractarians to the Roman Catholic Church, 1833–
    1850." D.Phil. thesis, Oxford University, 1956.
Hardman, Brian E. "The Evangelical Party in the Church of England 1855–1865." Ph.D.
    thesis, Cambridge University, 1963.
James, M. G. "The Clapham Sect—Its History and Influence." D.Phil. thesis, Oxford
    University, 1950.
McIlhiney, David Brown. "A Gentleman in Every Slum: Church of England Missions
    in East London, 1837–1914." Ph.D. thesis, Princeton University, 1977.
MacIntosh, W. H. "The Agitation for the Disestablishment of the Church of England in
    the Nineteenth Century." D.Phil. thesis, Oxford University, 1955.
Martin, Roger H. "The Pan-Evangelical Impulse in Britain, 1795–1830; with special
    reference to four London Societies." D.Phil. thesis, Oxford University, 1973.
Murray, Nancy U. "The Influence of the French Revolution on the Church of England
    and Its Rivals." D.Phil. thesis, Oxford University, 1975.
Orchard, S. C. "English Evangelical Eschatology, 1790–1850." Ph.D. thesis, Cam-
    bridge University, 1968.
Pope, Norris F. "Charitable Activity and Attitudes in Early Victorian England, with
    special reference to Dickens and the Evangelicals." D.Phil. thesis, Oxford Uni-
    versity, 1975.
Potter, Sarah C. "The Social Origins and Recruitment of English Protestant Missionaries
    in the Nineteenth Century." Ph.D. thesis, University of London, 1974.
Rennie, Ian S. "Evangelicalism and English Public Life, 1823–1850." Ph.D. thesis,
    University of Toronto, 1962.
Sangster, P. E. "The Life of Rowland Hill (1744–1833) and his position in the Evangelical
    Revival." D.Phil. thesis, Oxford University, 1964.
Sceats, D. D. "Perfectionism and the Keswick Convention, 1875–1900." M.A. thesis,
    University of Bristol, 1970.
Toon, Peter. "Evangelical Response to Tractarianism," D.Phil. thesis, Oxford Univer-
    sity, 1977.

Walsh, J. D. "The Yorkshire Evangelicals in the eighteenth century: with special reference to Methodism." Ph.D. thesis, Cambridge University, 1956.

Walsh, J. D. "The Moderate Calvinism of the Early Evangelicals." Unpublished typescript by Dr. John Walsh, Jesus College, Oxford University.

White, John Wesley. "The Influence of North American Evangelism in Great Britain between 1830 and 1914 on the Origin and Development of the Ecumenical Movement." D.Phil. thesis, Oxford University, 1963.

Willmer, Haddon. "Evangelicalism, 1785–1830." Hulsean Prize Essay, Cambridge University, 1962.

Wolffe, John R. "Protestant societies and anti-Catholic agitation in Great Britain, 1829–1860." D.Phil. thesis, Oxford University, 1984.

III. PRINTED PRIMARY SOURCES

A. Autobiographies, Letters, and Biographies

Baines, Edward. *The Life of Edward Baines, Late M.P. for the borough of Leeds* (London, 1851).

Bateman, Josiah. *The Life of the Rev. Henry Venn Elliott* (London, 1868).

Birks, Thomas R. *Memoir of the Rev. Edward Bickersteth*, 2 vols. (London, 1852).

Birrell, C. M. *Life of William Brock* (London, 1878).

Blomfield, Alfred. *Memoir of Bishop Blomfield* (London, 1864).

Braithwaite, Robert. *The Life and Letters of Rev. William Pennefather* (London, 1879).

Brenton, L.C.L. *Memoir of Vice Admiral Sir Jahleel Brenton* (London, 1855).

Bridges, James. *Memoir of Sir Andrew Agnew* (Edinburgh, 1849).

Brief Memoirs of T. F. Buxton and Elizabeth Fry (London, 1845).

Brock, William. *A Biographical Sketch of Sir Henry Havelock* (Leipzig, 1858).

Brown, A. Morton, and Ferguson, Robert. *Life and Labours of John Campbell* (London, 1868).

Budd, Henry. *A Memoir of the Rev. Henry Budd* (London, 1855).

Buxton, Charles, ed. *Memoirs of Sir T. F. Buxton* (London, 1855).

Campbell, John. *Memoirs of David Nasmith: His Labours and Travels in Great Britain, France, the United States and Canada* (London, 1844).

Cecil, Richard. *Memoirs of the late Hon. and Rev. W. B. Cadogan, M.A., John Bacon, Esq., R. A. and the Rev. John Newton* (London, 1812).

Corsbie, A. H. *A Biographical Sketch of Alexander Haldane* (London, 1882).

Dale, R. W. *The Life and Letters of J. A. James: including an Unfinished Biography*, 2d ed. (London, 1861).

Davidson, R. T. *The Life of A. C. Tait* (London, 1891).

Dukinfield, Jane. *A Memoir of the Revd. Sir Henry Robert Dukinfield* (London, 1850).

Eardley, C. E. *A Brief Memoir of the Late Revd. Edward Bickersteth* (London, 1850).

Elliott, E. B. *Memoir of Lord Haddo, in his later years fifth Earl of Aberdeen* (London, 1867).

Ferguson, Robert, and Brown, A. Morton. *Life and Labour of John Campbell* (London, 1868).

Finney, Charles G. *Charles G. Finney: An Autobiography* (London, 1862).

Fowler, J. *Richard Waldo Sibthorp* (London, 1880).

Fraser, William. *Memoir of the Life of David Stow* (London, 1868).

Fremantle, W. R. *Memoir of the Revd. Spencer Thornton* (London, 1850).

Garratt, Evelyn R. *Life and Personal Reflections of Samuel Garrett* (London, 1908).

Haldane, Alexander. *Memoirs of the Lives of Robert and James Haldane*, 2d ed. (Edinburgh, 1855).

Hammond, E. D. *Memoir of Captain M. M. Hammond* (London, 1858).

Hanna, William. *Memoir of Thomas Chalmers* (Edinburgh, 1850).

————. *A Selection of Correspondence of the Late Thomas Chalmers* (London, 1853).

Hill, Thomas. *Letters and Memoirs of the Late Walter Augustus Shirley, Lord Bishop of Sodor and Man* (London, 1849).

Hodder, Edwin. *The Life and Work of the Seventh Earl of Shaftesbury*, 2 vols. (London, 1887).

Hole, Charles. *Life of W. W. Phelps* (London, 1871).

Hopper, Ebenezer, ed. *The Celebrated Coalheaver: or Reminiscences of the Rev. William Huntingdon, S.S.* (London, 1871).

Jerram, J., ed. *Memoirs and a Selection from the Letters of the late Rev. Charles Jerram* (London, 1855).

Kelly, Sophia. *The Life of Mrs. Sherwood* (London, 1854).

Knox, G. *Daniel Wilson, Bishop of Calcutta* (London, 1888).

Liddon, H. P. *Walter Kerr Hamilton, Bishop of Salisbury, a Sketch* (London, 1869).

McCaul, Joseph B. *A Memoiral Sketch of Alexander McCaul* (London, 1863).

McCrie, Thomas. *Memoirs of Sir Andrew Agnew of Lochnow* (London, 1850).

Marsden, J. B. *Memoir of Hugh Stowell* (London, 1868).

Marsh, Catherine. *Life of William Marsh* (London, 1867).

Marshman, John Clark. *Memoirs of Major-General Sir Henry Havelock* (London, 1860).

Maurice, Frederick, ed. *The Life of Frederick Denison Maurice, Chiefly told by his own Letters* (London, 1884).

Memoir of Charlotte Elizabeth (London, 1852).

Mozley, Thomas. *Reminiscences: Chiefly of Oriel College and the Oxford Movement*, 2d ed. (London, 1882).

Naismith, Robert. *Memoir of Rev. James Hamilton* (London, 1895).

Napier, W. *The Life and Opinions of General Sir Charles James Napier* (London, 1857).

Pike, G. Holden, ed. *Valiant for the Truth, being an Autobiography of John Matthias Weylland* (London, 1899).

Pratt, Joseph, Jr., and Pratt, John Henry. *Memoir of the Rev. Josiah Pratt* (London, 1849).

Roberts, Arthur. *The Life, Letters and Opinions of William Roberts, Esq.* (London, 1850).

St. John, B., ed. *All is Well: Letters and Journals of Lieutenant H.B.T. St. John* (London, 1846).

Scholefield, Mrs. James. *Memoirs of the late Rev. James Scholefield* (London, 1855).

Simpkinson, C. H. *The Life and Work of Bishop Thorold* (London, 1896).

The Sinner Saved; or Memoirs of the Life of the Rev. W. W. Huntingdon, the Coal Heaver (London, 1813).

Stanley, Arthur Penrhyn. *Memoirs of Edward and Catherine Stanley* (London, 1879).

Stewart, David Dale. *Memoir of the Life of the Rev. James Haldane Stewart* (London, 1856).

Sumner, G. H. *Life of C. R. Sumner* (London, 1863).

Twiss, Horace. *The Public and Private Life of Lord Chancellor Eldon, with Selections from His Correspondence* (London, 1844).

Wallace, D. E. *The Life and Work of James Alexander Haldane* (London, 1844).

Wilson, William. *Memorials of Robert S. Candlish* (Edinburgh, 1850).

B. Books, Pamphlets, and Sermons

An Argument for Dissenters (London, n.d., ca. 1833).

Arnold, T. K. *Remarks on Elliott's Horae Apocalypticae* (London, 1845).

Ashley, Francis Bumstead. *Mormonism: an exposure of the Impositions adopted by the sect called 'the Latter Day Saints'* (London, 1851).

Auriol, Edward, ed. *Popish Doctrines and Millenial Light, being lectures delivered during Lent, 1851, at St. George's, Bloomsbury, by twelve clergymen of the Church of England* (London, 1851).

Baines, Edward, Jr. *The Social, educational and religious state of the manufacturing districts; in two letters to Sir Robert Peel* (London, 1843).

———. *A Correspondence between Edward Baines and B. Oliveira, M.P. on the Sunday opening of the Crystal Palace* (London, 1854).

———. *On the Performance of Military Bands in the Parks of London on Sundays* (London, 1856).

Bardsley, James. *The Necessity of a Real Revival of Spiritual Religion in the Evangelical Body* (London, 1871).

Barker, W. G. *Friendly Strictures upon Certain Portions of the Rev. E. B. Elliott's Horae Apocalypticae* (London, 1847).

Barnes, Albert. *The Theory and Desirableness of Revivals; being six sermons by the Rev. Albert Barnes, with a preface by the Hon. and Rev. Baptist Noel* (London, 1842).

Bayley, Emilius. *The Signs of the Times* (London, 1858).

Bayly, Mary. *Ragged Homes and How to Mend Them* (London, 1859).

———. *Workmen and their Difficulties* (London, 1861).

Bettering Society. *The First Report of the Society for Bettering the Conditions and Increasing The Comforts of the Poor* (London, 1797).

Bickersteth, Edward. *The Christian Student*, 3d ed. (London, 1832).

———. *The Divine Warning to the Church at This Time, of our Present Enemies, Dangers, and Duties, And to our Future Prospects* (London, 1843).

———. *The Signs of the Times in the East; A Warning to the West: being a Practical view of our Duties in light of the Prophecies which Illustrate the Present State of the Church and of the World* (London, 1844).

———, ed. *The Second Coming, the Judgment, and the Kingdom of Christ: being Lectures Delivered During Lent, 1843 at St. George's, Bloomsbury, by twelve clergymen of the Church of England* (London, 1843).

Bickersteth, Robert. *The London Poor* (London, 1855).

———. *A Charge Delivered to the Clergy of the Diocese of Ripon at his Triennial Visitation* (London, 1861).

Binney, Thomas. *Dissent Not Schism, A Discourse, delivered in the Poultry Chapel, Dec. 12, 1834, at the Monthly Meeting of the Associated Ministers and Churches of the London Congregational Union* (London, 1834).

———. *The Ultimate Object of the Evangelical Dissenters avowed and advocated; a Sermon Preached at the King's Weigh-house Chapel* (London, 1834).

Birks, Thomas R. *The First Elements of Sacred Prophecy* (London, 1843).
————. "Religious State of England, 1851–1855," in *Religious Condition of Christendom*, ed. E. Steane (London, 1857).
————. *Church and State: or, National Religion and Church Establishments, Considered with Reference to Present Controversies . . . with a preface by the Lord Bishop of Lincoln* (London, 1869).
————, ed. *The Hope of the Apostolic Church: Or, the Duties and Privileges of Christians in Connexion with the Second Advent, as unfolded in the First Epistle of St. Paul to the Thessalonians, being lectures delivered during Lent, 1845, at St. George's, Bloomsbury, by twelve clergymen of the Church of England* (London, 1845).
Blackburn, John. *The Three Conferences held by the opponents of the Maynooth-College Endowment Bill, in London and Dublin, in May and June, 1845; containing a Vindication of the author from the aspersions of the Dissenting Press* (London, 1845).
Blomfield, Charles James. *A Charge Delivered to the Clergy of the Diocese of London, at the Visitation in July MDCCCXXXIV* (London, 1834).
————. *A Charge Delivered to the Clergy of the Diocese of London at the Visitation in MDCCCXLII* (London, 1842).
————. *A Charge Delivered to the Clergy of the Diocese of London at the Visitation in November MDCCCL* (London, 1850).
Blunt, John Henry. *Directorium Pastorale: Principles and Practice of Pastoral Work in the Church of England* (London, 1854).
Booth, Charles. *Life and Labour of the People in London 3rd series, Religious Influences*, Vol. 2 (London, 1902).
————. *Life and Labour of the People in London, 3rd series, Religious Influences*, vol. 7 (London, 1902).
————, ed. *Labour and Life of the People*, vol. 1, East London, 3d ed. (London, 1891).
Brenton, Sir Jahleel. *The Hope of the Navy: or the True Source of Discipline and efficiency* (London, 1839).
Bridges, Charles. *The Christian Ministry, With an inquiry into the Causes of its Inefficiency, with an Especial Reference to the Ministry of the Establishment* (London, 1830).
Brindley, John. *A Reply to the Infidelity and Atheism of Socialism* (Birmingham, 1841).
Brooks, Joshua W. *A Dictionary of Writers on Prophecy* (London, 1835).
————. *Elements of Prophetical Interpretation* (London, 1836).
Brown, A. W. *Recollections of the Conversation Parties of the Rev. Charles Simeon* (London, 1863).
Brown, Joseph. *The Cottage of Arreton; Simple Recollections of the Dairyman's Daughter* (London, n.d.).
Budd, Henry. *Infant Baptism the Means of National Reformation* (London, 1827).
Burder, George. *Lawful Amusements* (London, 1805).
Burgess, Richard. *A Letter to the Parishioners of Upper Chelsea* (Not published but printed for private circulation.)(Chelsea, 1827).
————. *A Letter to the Rev. John Morrison* (Chelsea, 1836).
————. *The Fourth Pastoral Letter to the Parishioners of Upper Chelsea* (Chelsea, 1843).
————. *The Sixth Biennial Letter to the Parishioners of Upper Chelsea* (London, 1848).
Burgon, John W. *A Treatise on the Pastoral Office* (London, 1864).

Cadogan, William Bromley. *An Address from a Clergyman to his Parishioners* (London, 1785).

Cairns, Adam. *The Second Woe; A Popular Exposition of the Tenth and Eleventh Chapters of Revelation* (Edinburgh, 1852).

Candlish, Robert S. *Four Letters to the Rev. E. B. Elliott on some Passages in his Horae Apocalypticae relative to the Question of Church Establishments, and the Recent disruption of the Church of Scotland* (London, 1846).

———. *An Examination of Mr. Maurice's Theological Essays* (London, 1854).

Caswell, Henry. *The Prophet of the Nineteenth Century; or, the Rise, Progress, and Present State of the Mormons, or Latter-Day Saints: to which is appended, an Analysis of the Book of Mormon* (London, 1843).

Chalmers, Thomas. *Statement in Regard to the Pauperism of Glasgow from the Experience of the Last Eight Years* (Glasgow, 1823).

———. *Tracts on Pauperism* (Glasgow, 1833).

———. "The Political Economy of the Bible." *North British Review* 2, 3 (Nov. 1844):1–52.

———. *The Works of Thomas Chalmers*, 25 vols. (Edinburgh, 1849).

Chester, Grenville John. *Statute Fairs: Their Evils and their Remedy* (York, 1856).

Christian Instruction Society. *A Statement on the Awful Profanation of the Lord's Day* (London, 1829).

———. *A Course of Lectures to Young Men and Others, by Ministers in Connexion with the Christian Instruction Society* (London, 1838).

Church of England Young Men's Society for Aiding Missions At Home and Abroad. *First to Fifth Annual Reports of* (London, 1845–1849).

———. *Claims of Missions* (London, 1845).

———. *Quarterly Journal of* (London, 1848–1850).

———. *Second Annual Report of the East London Branch of* (London, 1846).

———. *Tenth Annual Report of the City of London Branch of* (London, 1854).

———. *Sixteenth Annual Report of* (London, 1860).

Clarke, J. Erskine. "Plain Papers on the Social Economy of the People." *Recreations of the People Real and Imaginary* (London, 1858).

Clarkson, Thomas. *An Essay on the Doctrines and Practice of the Early Christians as they relate to War* (London, n.d.). (Published by the Society for the Promotion of Permanent and Universal Peace.)

Close, Francis. *The Evil Consequences of Attending the Race Course Exposed* (London, 1827).

———. *The Chartists' Visit to the Parish Church. A Sermon, Addressed to the Chartists of Cheltenham* (London, 1839).

———. *The Female Chartists' Visit to the Parish Church. A Sermon, Addressed to the Female Chartists of Cheltenham* (London, 1839).

Conybeare, W. J. "Church Parties." *Essays Ecclesiastical and Social* (London, 1855).

Cooper, Anthony Ashley. *Moral and Religious Education of the Working Classes; the Speech of Lord Ashley, M.P., in the House of Commons on Tuesday, Feb. 28, 1843* (London, 1843).

A Corrected Report of the Speeches Delivered at a Public Meeting in Behalf of Church Extension (London, 1839).

Correspondence from "The Record" relative to the Establishment of a Scripture Readers' Society (London, 1845).

Cumming, John. *Apocalyptic Sketches; or Lecture on the Book of Revelation* (London, 1848).

——. *The Church in the Army* (London, 1856).

Dale, R. W. *The Evangelical Revival* (London, 1880).

——. *The Old Evangelicalism and the New* (London, 1889).

Dale, Thomas. *National Religion Conducive to the Prosperity of the State* (London, 1837).

——. *The Duty of Considering the Poor* (London, 1839).

——. *The Metropolitan Charities: beng an account of the Charitable, Benevolent, and Religious Societies, Hospitals, Dispensaries, Penitentiaries, Annuity Funds, Asylums, Almshouses, Colleges, and Schools; in London and Its Immediate Vicinity* (London, 1844).

——. *Address to the Parishioners of St. Pancras on the Results of the Parochial System* (London, 1847).

——. *Pastoral Superintendance* (London, 1849).

——. *Five Years of Church Extension in St. Pancras* (London, 1852).

Dallas, Alexander R. C., ed. *Lift Up Your Heads* (London, 1848).

Dalton, W., ed. *God's Dealings with Israel: Being Twelve Lectures delivered during Lent at St. George's, Bloomsbury, by twelve clergymen of the Church of England* (London, 1850).

Davies, C. Maurice. *Unorthodox London: or Phases of Religious Life in the Metropolis* (London, 1873).

——. *Heterodox London* (London, 1874).

——. *Orthodox London: or, Phases of the Religious Life in the Church of England* (London, 1874).

Denton, William. *Displacement of London Poor* (London, 1861).

Dibdin, R. W. *Lectures on Subjects Connected with the Second Coming of Our Lord and Saviour* (London, 1848).

——. *The History of West Street Episcopal Chapel* (London, 1862).

Dillon, R. C. *A Sermon on the Evils of Fairs in General, and of Bartholomew Fair in Particular* (London, 1830).

Dodderidge, Philip. *The Rise and Progress of Religion in the Soul* (London, 1830).

Dukinfield, Henry R. *A Letter to the Inhabitants of the Parish of St. Martin-in-the-Fields* (London, 1847).

Dunston, James. *The History of the Parish of Bromley St. Leonard, Middlesex with Historical Illustrations* (London, 1862).

Eardley, Sir Culling. *Reply to a Letter of the Rev. Peter Hall . . . Assigning His Reasons for not attending the Liverpool Conference* (London, 1845).

——. *The Romanism of Italy* (London, 1845).

——, ed. *The Testimony of Christian Union of Australia, France, and Germany in January, 1859 with a Letter from Sir Culling Eardley to the Rev. Dr. M'Neile of Liverpool* (London, 1859).

An Earnest Persuasive to Unity: Mostly Extracted from the Writings of Pious and Learned Members of the Church (Oxford, 1840).

East, John. *The Theatres; a discourse on Theatrical Amusements and Dramatic Literature* (London, 1844).

Elliott, Edward Bishop. *Horae Apocalypticae* (London, 1844).

————. *Reply to the Rev. T. K. Arnold's Remarks on the 'Horae Apocalypticae'* (London, 1845).

————. *Church History the Key to Prophecy* (London, 1853).

————. *Delusion of the Tractarian Clergy as to the Validity of their Ministerial Orders, Shown, on their own Principles* (London, 1856).

————. *Reply to Dr. Candlish's Four Letters, on certain passages in the 'Horae Apocalypticae'* (London, 1857).

————. *Vindiciae Horariae; or Twelve Letters to the Rev. Dr. Keith, in Reply to his strictures on the "Horae Apocalypticae"* (London, 1858).

Engels, Friedrich. *The Condition of the Working-Class in England in 1844* (London, 1892).

England's New Ally, Who? (London, 1845).

Evangelical Alliance. *Report on the Proceedings of the Conference, held at Freemasons' Hall, London, from August 19th to September 2nd inclusive, 1846* (London, 1847).

Faber, George Stanley. *The Difficulties of Romanism* (London, 1826).

Finney, Charles G. *The Sacred Calendar of Prophecy* (London, 1828).

————. *Two Sermons Preached by the Rev. C. G. Finney at Borough Road Chapel, London, on Nov. 22 and 23, 1849* (Manchester, 1849).

————. *Revivals of Religion*, rev. ed. (London, 1910).

Foster, John. *On the Aversion of Men of Taste to Evangelical Religion* (London, 1872).

Fremantle, W. R., ed. *Present Times and Future Prospects, being Lectures delivered during Lent, 1854 at St. George's, Bloomsbury by twelve Clergymen of the Church of England* (London, 1854).

Frere, James Hatley. *The Harvest of the Earth Prior to the Vintage of Wrath, Considered as Symbolical of the Evangelical Alliance* (London, 1846).

————. *The Great Continental Revolution Marking the Expiration of the Times of the Gentiles, A.D. 1847–1848* (London, 1848).

Garbett, Edward. *Union Among Evangelical Churchmen* (London, 1871).

Garratt, Samuel. *The Irish of London* (London, 1852).

————. *Signs of the Times: Showing that the Coming of the Lord Draweth Near* (London, 1868).

————. *The Lightning Appearance* (London, 1877).

Garwood, John. *Second Pastoral Letter to the Congregation Assemblying at Sir George Wheler's Chapel, Spital Square* (London, 1834).

————. *The Claims of the London City Mission on Members of the Church of England* (London, 1837).

————. *The Million-Peopled City* (London, 1853).

Gathercole, Michael Augustus. *Letters to a Dissenting Minister of the Congregational Independent Denomination, Containing remarks on the Principles of that Sect, and the Author's Reason for leaving it, and conforming to the Church of England* (London, ca. 1834).

————. *A Letter to C. Lushington, Esq. M.P., in reply to a Remonstrance Addressed by Him to the Lord Bishop of London* (London, 1835).

Gavin, Hector. *Sanitary Ramblings* (London, 1848).

General Society for Promoting District Visiting. *The Fourth Annual Report of the Society, to which is prefixed a Sermon by the Rt. Revd. the Lord Bishop of Chester* (London, 1832).

————. *District Visitor's Manual: A Compendium of Practical Information and of Facts for the Use of District Visitors: With a Preface by Thomas Dale, M.A., Vicar of St. Bride's* (London, 1840).

Gilbert, Philip Parker. *A Pastoral Address to the Congregation Assembling at the Church of St. Mary Haggerston and to the inhabitants of the District Parish* (London, 1843).

Girdlestone, Charles. *Letters on the Unhealthy Condition of the Lower Class of Dwellings, Especially in Large Towns* (London, 1845).

———. *The Questions of the Day* (London, 1845).

Gladstone, William E. "The Evangelical Movement, Its Parentage, Progress and Issue." vol. no. 7 of *Past Gleanings* (London, 1879).

Goode, William. *The Modern Claims to the Possession of the Extraordinary Gifts of the Spirit Stated and Examined* (London, 1833).

———. *A Brief History of Church Rates* (London, 1838).

Govett, R. *The Locusts, The Euphratean Horsemen, and the Two Witnesses; or the apocalyptic Systems of the Revds. E. B. Elliott, Dr. Cumming, and Dr. Keith, Proved Unsound* (London, 1852).

Grant, James. *Metropolitan Pulpit* (London, 1839).

———. *Travels in Town* (London, 1839).

———. *The End of All Things* (London, 1866).

Gurney, John Hampden. *The Lost Chief and the Mourning People* (London, 1852).

Haldane, Alexander. *Recollections of the late Andrew Hamilton reprinted from the "Record" newspaper* (London, 1854).

Hall, Peter. *Reasons for declining an Invitation from the Central Anti-Maynooth Committee to Attend . . . a Conference of Protestants . . . to be held in Liverpool . . . in a letter to Sir C. E. Smith* (London, 1845).

Harness, William. *Visiting Societies and Lay Readers: a Letter to the Lord Bishop of London* (London, 1864).

Hill, Rowland. *The First and Last Sermons Delivered in Surrey Chapel by the Rev. Rowland Hill, M.A., To Which is added, the History of Surrey Chapel from the period of its erection to the present time* (London, 1837).

Hoare, Edward. *The Time of the End; or, the Visible Church, and the People of God, at the Advent of the Lord* (London, 1846).

Hole, Charles. *Life of Phelps* (London, 1873).

———. *Manual of English Church History* (London, 1910).

House of Lords. *Report of the Select Committee of the House of Lords on the Coalwhippers' Act; together with the Proceedings of the Committee, Minutes of Evidence, etc.*, Vol. 12, 1857, Session 2.

Hudson, T. H. *Christian Socialism Explained and Enforced, and compared with Infidel Fellowship, especially as pronounced by Robert Owen, Esq., and his Disciples* (London, n.d., ca. 1839).

Huntingdon, George. *Amusements, and the Need for Supplying Healthy Recreations for the People* (London, 1860).

Husenbeth, F. C. *Faberism Exposed and Refuted: and Apostilicity of Catholic Doctrine Vindicated* (Norwich, 1836).

Irving, Edward. *The Last Days: A Discourse on the Evil Character of these our Times: Proving them to be the "Perilous Times" of the "Last Days"* (London, 1828).

———. *The Church and State Responsible to Christ, and to one another. A Series of Discourses on Daniel's Vision of the Four Beasts* (London, 1829).

Jackson, John. *Repentance: Its Necessity, Nature and Aids* (London, 1851).

James, John Angell. *Christian Fellowship, or the Church Member's Guide*, 11th ed. (London, 1859). First published in 1822.

———. *A Pastoral Letter on the Subject of Revivals of Religion*, 3d ed. (Birmingham, 1829).

———. *Dissent and the Church of England; or, a Defence of the Principles of Nonconformity, Contained in "The Church Member's Guide," in reply to a pamphlet, entitled "Church of England and Dissent,"* 3d ed. (London, 1831).

James, Walter. *The Poor of London, A Letter to the Lord Bishop of the Diocese* (London, 1844).

Jowett, William. *The Christian Visitor, or, Scripture Readings, with Expositions and Prayers designed to assist the Friends of the Poor and Afflicted* (London, 1836).

Kingscote, Henry R. *A Letter to His Grace the Archbishop of Canterbury on the Present Wants of the Church* (London, 1846).

———. *Sir John Parkington's Plan. A Reply to the "Remarks" of J. C. Colquhoun, Esq.* (London, 1855).

Labourers' Friend Society. *A Second Series of Useful Hints for Labourers; Selected from the Publications of the Labourers' Friend Society* (London, 1840).

"Laicus." *A Letter, Addressed to the Protestant Electors of England, in Prospect of a Coming Election* (London, 1845).

"Layman." *A Letter to His Grace the Archbishop of Canterbury suggested by the Remarks of Henry Kingscote, Esq., on the Present Wants of the Church* (London, 1846).

"A London Churchman." *The Gospel Unfettered; or the Necessity of Open-Air Ministration for the Million. A Letter respectfully addressed to the Right Hon. and Rt. Rev. the Lord Bishop of London* (London, 1850).

London City Mission. *Annual Reports of* (London, 1835–1860).

———. *Lectures Against Socialism. Delivered Under the Direction of the Committee of the London City Mission* (London, 1840).

London Diocesan Home Mission. *First and Second Annual Reports of* (London, 1858 and 1859).

Low, Sampson. *The Charities of London* (London, 1850).

Lushington, Charles. *A Remonstrance Addressed to the Bishop of London on the sanction given in his late charge to the clergy of that Diocese, to the Calumnies against the Dissenters* (London, 1834).

MacGregor, John. *Ragged Schools; their Rise, Progress and Results* (London, 1852).

McNeile, Hugh. *Lectures on the Church of England* (London, 1840).

———. *The State in Danger: A Letter to the Right Hon. Lord John Russell, M.P.*, 2d ed. (London, 1846).

Mann, Horace. *Sketches of the Religious Denominations of the Day . . . and the Census* (London, 1854).

Marsden, J. B. *Sermons on the Church* (London, 1855).

Marsh, Catherine. *Memorials of Captain Hedley Vicars* (London, 1856).

Marsh, William. *A Few Plain Thoughts on Prophecy* (Colchester, 1843).

———. *The Right Choice; or, the Difference between Worldly Diversions and Rational Recreations* (London, 1857).

Massie, James William. *The Evangelical Alliance; its Origin and Development* (London, 1847).

Maurice, Peter. *Popery in Oxford* (Oxford, 1833).

Mayhew, Henry. *London Labour and the London Poor*, 2 vols. (London, 1851).

Melville, Henry. "Sighing because of Sorrowful Tidings." *The Pulpit* 41 (1841):589–596.

Miller, John Cale. *Home Heathen: An Assize Sermon* (London, 1844).

———. *Special Services in the Church of England; A Letter to the right honourable the Earl of Shaftesbury, etc. etc. on his Lordship's Bill* (London, 1858).

Modern Puritanism, A Review of Present and Prospective Results of the Lord Bishop of London's Late Charge, With Especial Reference to the Recent Pamphlets of Rev. Dr. Holloway, Rev. C. J. Yorke, Dean Cockburn, etc. etc. (London, 1843).

Molesworth, I.E.N. *Symptoms of the Dangerous Hand by which the Insidious Veto of the Pastoral Aid Society may be wielded, set forth in a Letter to the Rev. Caleb Whitefoord, on the Fallacies and Unworthy Acts used by Him and Others in Defence of that Society* (London, 1841).

Molyneux, John W. H. *Preaching the Gospel to the Working Classes impossible under the Pew System* (London, 1858).

Moore, Daniel. *The Obligations Upon all Christians to Propagate the Gospel* (Bath, 1853).

Napier, Charles J. *Remarks on Military Law* (London, 1837).

National Club. *Addresses to the Protestants of the Empire by the Committee of the National Club* (London, 1848–1850).

Newman, John Henry. "The Logical Inconsistency of the Protestant View." *Lectures on the Present Position of the Catholics in England* (London, 1851).

Nicholson, William, and Roberts, William. *The Call Upon the Church Considered in Two Essays* (London, 1838).

Nixon, Edward John. *A Manual of District Visiting with Hints and Directions to Visitors, Being an Address to the Members of the Edge-Hill District Visiting Society* (London, 1848).

Noel, Baptist W. *Remarks on the Revival of Miraculous Powers in the Church* (London, 1831).

———. *The State of the Metropolis Considered in a letter to the Rt. Hon. and Rt. Revd. the Lord Bishop of London* (London, 1835).

———. *The Unity of the Church, another Tract for the Times, addressed especially to members of the Establishment* (London, 1836).

———. *Notes of a Short Tour through the Midland Counties of Ireland in the Summer of 1836* (London, 1837).

———. *A Letter to the Right Honourable Lord Viscount Melbourne on Church Extension* (London, 1839).

———. *A Plea for the Poor, Showing how the Proposed Repeal of the Existing Corn Laws will Affect the Interests of the Working Classes* (London, 1841).

———. *The Catholic Claims: A Letter to the Lord Bishop of Cashel* (London, 1845).

O'Brien, Patrick. *Patrick O'Brien; or the power of the Truth* (London, 1856).

Open-Air Mission. *Third Annual Report* (London, 1856).

Osborne, S. G. *Hints to the Charitable, being Practical Observations on the Proper Regulation of Private Charity* (London, 1838).

Overton, J. H. *The English Church in the Nineteenth Century* (London, 1894).

Owen, William. *The Good Soldier, A Memorial of Major-General Henry Havelock, of Lucknow* (London, 1858).

Oxenden, Ashton. *The Pastoral Office: Its Duties, Difficulties, Privileges, and Prospects* (London, 1857).

Page, Thomas. *Letter to the Right Hon. Lord Ashley, M.P., on the Present Defective State of National Education* (London, 1843).

"A Peasant." *The First Part of Falsehood Exposed* (Cheltenham, 1827).

————. *The Second Part of Falsehood Exposed*, 2d ed. (Cheltenham, 1827).

Pennefather, William. *The Church of the First Born* (London, 1865).

Perry, Charles. *Clerical Education, considered with an especial reference to the Universities; in a letter to the Right Rev. the Lord Bishop of Lichfield* (London, 1841).

"Phillippus." *The Spiritual Quixote, Geoffrey Wildgoose, in Cheltenham: or, a Discourse on a Race-Course* (Cheltenham, 1827).

Phillpotts, Henry. *Letter to the Venerable the Archdeacons of the Diocese of Exeter on the Proposed Office of Scripture Readers*, 3d ed. (London, 1847).

Plumptree, E. H. "Church Parties, Past, Present and Future." *Contemporary Review* 7 (Jan.-April 1868):321–346.

Pratt, John H. *Paraphrase of the Revelation of St. John* (London, 1862).

————. *Eclectic Notes; or Notes of Discussions of Religious Topics at the Meeting of the Eclectic Society, London, During the years 1798 to 1814* (London, 1865).

Proby, W.H.B. *Annals of the Low Church Party in the Church of England* (London, 1888).

Proclamation Society. *Statements and Propositions from the Society for Giving Effect to His Majesty's Proclamation against Vice and Immorality* (London, 1790).

Ranyard, Ellen H. *The Bible Collectors: or Principles in Practice* (London, 1854).

————. *The Missing Link: or, Bible-Women in the Homes of the London Poor* (London, 1859).

————. *The True Institution of Sisterhood: or, A Message and Its Messenger* (London, 1862).

————. *London and Ten Years Work in It* (London, 1868).

————. *Nurses for the Needy* (London, 1875).

Redford, George. *The Church of England Indefensible from the Holy Scriptures; in Reply to Several Recent Defences, and Especially to Two Discourses by the Rev. J. Garbett . . .* (London, 1833).

————. *Christianity Against Coercion* (London, 1840).

Ritchie, James Ewing. *The London Pulpit* (London, 1854).

Roberts, Henry. *Home Reform: Or, What the Working Classes May do to Improve their Dwellings* (London, 1852).

————. *The Dwellings of the Labouring Classes, their Arrangement and Construction* (London, 1854).

————. *The Improvement of the Dwellings of the Labouring Classes through the Operation of Government Measures by those of Public bodies and Benevolent Associations, as well as by Individual Efforts* (London, 1859).

Robinson, William. *History of the Parish of Hackney, 1842–1843* (London, 1843).

Ryle, John Charles. *Strike: But Hear!* (London, 1868).

Sadler, Michael Thomas. *The Law of Population* (London, 1830).

Savage, R. C. *Lay Agency. A Letter to the Rt. Hon. the Earl of Denbigh, on the Importance of the Employment of Scripture Readers'* (London, 1857).

Scott, Benjamin. *The Catacombs at Rome: Three Popular Lectures on Paganism, Chris-

tianity, and Popery; delivered before Working Men; for the Working Men's Educational Union, 1st ed. (London, 1853).

———. *Practical Hints to Unpracticed Lecturers to the Working Classes. With a Catalogue of Diagrams, etc., published to aid the Lecturers; and Lists of Subjects Lectured Upon by Correspondents of the Working Men's Educational Union*, 4th ed. (London, 1858).

———. *The Content and Teachings of the Catacombs at Rome; being a vindication of pure and primitive Christianity, and an exposure of the Corruptions of Popery, derived from the Sepulchral Remains of the early Christians at Rome*, 2d ed. (London, 1860).

———. *The Content and Teachings of the Catacombs at Rome*, 3d ed. (London, 1873).

———. *The Content and Teachings of the Catacombs at Rome; a vindication of pure and primitive Christianity, and an exposure of the Corruptions of Romanism: derived from the Sepulchral Remains of the early Christians*, 4th ed. (London, 1889).

Scott, Thomas. *Treatise on Growth in Grace* (London, 1795).

"Search, John." [Pseudonym] *"What? and Who Says It?" An Exposition of the Statement that the Established Church "destroys more souls than it saves" by the Revd. Thomas Chalmers, D.D.; the Right Revd. the Bishop of Calcutta; the Revd. Samuel Charles Wilks &c.* (London, n.d., but ca. 1834).

———. *Strike, but Hear: a Correspondence between the Compiler of "What and who says it?" and the Editor of the Christian Observer: with a Dedication to the Conductors of that Work* (London, 1838).

———. *John Search's Last Words; with a Letter addressed to the Right Revd. Charles James, Lord Bishop of London. By the Editor of "What and Who says it?" and "Strike: but Hear."* (London, 1839).

Seeley, Robert Benton. *Essays on the Church* (London, 1834).

———. *Memoirs of the Life and Writings of Michael Thomas Sadler* (London, 1842).

———. *Remedies for some of the Evils which constitute the Perils of the Nation* (London, 1843).

Sherwood, M. M. *The History of Henry Milner, a Little Boy who was not brought up according to the Fashions of this world*, 2d ed. (London, 1824).

———. *The Millenium: or, Twelve Stories Designed to explain to young Bible Readers the Scripture and Prophecies concerning the glory of the Latter Days* (London, 1829).

Smith, John Pye. *The Protestant Dissent further Vindicated, on the Grounds of Holy Scripture, the Moral Obligations of Men, and the Liberties of Britons, in a Rejoinder to the Revd. Samuel Lee, D.D., Regious Professor of Hebrew at the University of Cambridge* (London, 1835).

Soldiers' Friend and Army Scripture Readers' Association. *A Letter to Revd. Wm. Marsh, D.D., from the Committee of the "Soldiers' Friend and Army Scripture Readers' Society" in reply to a letter by the Revd. G. A. Rogers, M.A., Later Joint-Secretary of the Above Society* (London, 1856).

Soldiership and Christianity: being a review of the Memoirs of the late Captain Hedley Vicars (London, 1856).

Solly, H. *Working Men's Social Clubs and Educational Institutes* (London, 1867).

Speck, E. J. *The Church Pastoral-Aid Society, A Sketch of its origin and progress* (London, 1881).

Sprague, William Buell. *Letters from Europe* (London, 1828).
———. *Lectures on the Revival of Religion* (London, 1832).
Stanford, Charles. *A Handbook to the Romish Controversy; being a refutation in detail of the Creed of Pope Pius the Fourth, On the Grounds of Scripture and Reason; with an Appendix and Notes* (Dublin, 1852).
Stewart, David Dale. *Evangelical Opinion in the Nineteenth Century* (London, 1879).
Stewart, James Haldane. *Thoughts on the Importance of Special Prayer for the General Outpouring of the Holy Spirit*, 2d ed. (London, 1822).
———, ed. *The Priest Upon His Throne: being lectures delivered during Lent, 1849, at St. George's, Bloomsbury, by twelve clergymen of the Church of England* (London, 1849).
Stock, Eugene. *A History of the Church Missionary Society* (London, 1899).
Stuart, E. A. *Funeral Sermon for the late Revd. Daniel Wilson, Vicar of Islington and Rural Dean* (London, 1886).
Sumner, John Bird. *A Treatise on the Records of Creation*, 2 vols. (London, 1816).
———. *A Charge Delivered to the Clergy of the diocese of Chester, at the Primary Visitation in August and September, MDCCCXXIX by the Right Revd. John Bird, Lord Bishop of Chester* (London, 1829).
Talbot, C. S. *A Servant of the Poor; or, some Account of the Life and Death of a Parochial Mission Woman* (London, 1874).
Taylder, T.W.P. *Mormon's Own Book; or Mormonism Tried by its Own Standards— Reason and Scripture* (London, 1855).
Taylor, Isaac. *Natural History of Enthusiasm* (London, 1829).
———. *Four Lectures on Spiritual Christianity* (London, 1841).
Tonna, Charlotte Elizabeth. *Dangers and Duties* (London, 1841).
———. *Helen Fleetwood* (London, 1841).
———. *Personal Recollections* (London, 1841).
———. *Perils of the Nation* (London, 1842).
Vanderkiste, R. W. *Notes and Narratives of a Six Years' Mission, principally among the Dens of London* (London, 1852).
Vaughan, Robert. *Thoughts on . . . Religious Parties*, 2d ed. (London, 1839).
Vice Society. *Occasional Report of the Society for the Suppression of Vice* (London, 1810).
Villiers, H. M. *The Titles of Christ Viewed Prophetically: being Lectures delivered during Lent, 1857 at St. George's, Bloomsbury, by twelve clergymen of the Church of England* (London, 1857).
———, (ed.) *Balls and Theatres: or, the Duty of Reproving the Works of Darkness* (London, 1846).
A Vindication of Scripture Readers (London, 1848).
Warburton, William. *The Alliance between Church and State, or the necessity and equity of an Established Religion and a Test Law* (London, 1736).
Wardlaw, Ralph. *National Church Establishments Examined: a course of lectures, delivered in London, during April and May, 1839* (London, 1839).
———. *Lectures on Female Prostitution: its Nature, Extent, Effects, Guilt, Causes and Remedy* (Glasgow, 1842).
Weylland, John Matthias. *Round the Tower; or, the story of the London City Mission* (London, 1875).

––––––. *A Thought for the World; or, the Narrative of Christian Effort at the Great Exhibition* (London, 1878).

––––––. *Our Veterans; Or, Life-Stories of the London City Mission* (London, 1881).

––––––. *These Fifty Years, being the Jubilee Volume of the London City Mission* (London, 1884).

Whiteoord, Caleb. *The Animus of Dr. I.E.N. Molesworth, in his late Attacks upon the Church Pastoral-Aid Society and its Defenders, Held up to Public Reprobation: in the preface to the Second Edition of a 'Letter to the Friends and Subscribers of the CP-AS'* (London, 1841).

Why We Are Dissenters (London, n.d., ca. 1833).

Wilberforce, Henry W. *The Parochial System: an appeal to English Churchmen* (London, 1838).

Wilson, Daniel, Jr. *A Revival of Spiritual Religion the only Effectual Remedy for the Dangers which now Threaten the Church of England* (London, 1851).

Wilson, Daniel, Sr. "An Introductory Essay" to *The Reformed Pastor* by Richard Baxter, edited by Rev. William Brown (Glasgow, 1829).

––––––. *A Sermon Occasioned by the Death of Rev. Basil Wood, to which are subjoined Notes on the Controversy between the Professor of Divinity at Oxford and the Rev. Mr. Bulteel* (London, 1831).

Working Men's Educational Union. *First Annual Report* (London, 1853).

Wylie, J. A. *Rome and Civil Liberty* (London, 1861).

Yates, Richard. *Church in Danger* (London, 1815).

C. Parliamentary Reports

Parliamentary Papers, 1852–3, 89, "Religious Worship, England and Wales; Reports; Particular Notice of Different Churches; Spiritual Provision and Destitution; and Appendix, containing Summary Tables and Tabular Results."

Parliamentary Papers, 1857–8, 9, "Deficiency of the Means of Spiritual Instruction," Select Committee, House of Lords, Report.

Parliamentary Papers, 1857, 12, "Select Committee of the House of Lords on the Coalwhipper Act; together with the Proceedings of the Committee, Minutes of Evidence, Appendix and Index.

D. Newspapers and Periodicals

All the Year Around
Antisocialist Gazette and Christian Advocate
The Book and Its Mission
British Banner
British Critic and Quarterly Theological Review
British Foreign Evangelical Review
British Protestant
British Quarterly Review
British Review and London Critical Journal
Christian Guardian and Church of England Magazine
Christian Lady's Magazine

Christian Observer
Christian Witness and Church Member's Guide
Churchman
Churchman's Magazine; a monthly review of Church Progress and General Literature
Churchman's Monthly Penny Magazine
Churchman's Monthly Review and Chronicle
Circular of the Free Church of England
Congregational Magazine
Country Town Mission Record
District Visitor's Record
Eclectic Review
Evangelical Christendom
Evangelical Magazine and Missionary Chronicle
Fraser's Magazine
Free Church Magazine
Gentlemen's Magazine
Gospel Magazine, and Theological Review
Home Missionary Magazine
Labourer's Friend Magazine
London City Mission Magazine
MacMillan's Magazine
Missing Link Magazine; or, Bible Work at Home and Abroad
New Sailor's Magazine and Naval Chronicle
North British Review
Pilot
Protestant Preacher
Publisher's Circular
Pulpit
Quarterly Educational Magazine and Record of the Home and Colonial Missionary Society
Quarterly Journal of Prophecy
Quarterly Review
The Record
Scripture Readers' Journal
The Times
Town and Village Mission Record
Young Men's Magazine and Monthly Record of Christian Young Men's Societies
Young Men's Monthly Magazine

E. Dictionaries of Biography, Handbooks, Clergy Lists, and Other Religious Works

Boase, Frederic, ed. *Modern English Biography* (London, 1892).
The Clergy Lists, 1844–1857. London.
Crockford's Clerical Index (London, 1860).
Gilbert, Richard. *Clerical Guide* (London, 1829).
———. *Clerical Guide* (London, 1836).

IV. TWENTIETH-CENTURY SECONDARY SOURCES

A. Books

Akenson, D. H. *The Church of Ireland: Ecclesiastical Reform and Revolution, 1800–1885* (New Haven, Conn., 1971).

Annan, Noel Gilroy. *Leslie Stephen* (London, 1951).

Baker, Leonard Graham Derek, ed. *Material Sources and Methods of Ecclesiatical History* (Oxford, 1975).

Balleine, George R. *History of the Evangelical Party in the Church of England*, 2d ed. (London, 1933).

Battiscombe, Georgina. *Shaftesbury, A Biography of the Seventh Earl, 1801–1885* (London, 1974).

Bebbington, David W. *The Nonconformist Conscience: Chapel and Politics, 1870–1914*, (London, 1982).

Binfield, John Clyde G. *George Williams of the YMCA, a Study of Victorian Social Attitudes* (London, 1973).

———. *So Down to Prayers, Studies in English Nonconformity, 1780–1920* (London, 1977).

Booth, Charles. *Life and Labour of the People in London*, Vol. 7 (London, 1902).

Bowen, Desmond. *Protestant Crusade in Ireland, 1800–1870* (Montreal, 1978).

———. *Souperism, Myth or Reality?* (Dublin, 1980).

Bradley, Ian. *Call to Seriousness* (London, 1976).

Brilioth, Y. *The Anglican Revival: Studies in the Oxford Movement* (London, 1933).

———. *Evangelicalism and the Oxford Movement* (Oxford, 1934).

Brose, Olive J. *Church and Parliament: The Reshaping of the Church of England, 1828–1860* (London, 1959).

Brown, Ford K. *Fathers of the Victorians* (Cambridge, 1961).

Bryand, G. E., and Baker, G. P., eds. *A Quaker Journal: Being the Diary and Reminiscences of William Lucas of Hitchin (1804–1861), a Member of the Society of Friends* (London, 1974).

Burleigh, J.H.S. *A History of the Church of Scotland* (London, 1960).

Carpenter, S. C. *Church and People, 1789–1889* (London, 1959).

Carwardine, Richard. *Trans-Atlantic Revivalism* (London, 1978).

Chadwick, Owen. *The Victorian Church*, 2 vols. (London, 1970).

Clark, G.S.R. Kitson. *The Making of Victorian Britain* (London, 1962).

———. *Churchmen and the Condition of England, 1832–1885* (London, 1973).

Coleman, B. I., ed. *Idea of the City in Nineteenth Century Britain* (London, 1973).

Cook, Edward. *The Life of Florence Nightingale*, 2 vols (London, 1913).

Cowherd, Raymond G. *The Politics of English Dissent; Religious Aspects of Liberal and Humanitarian Reform Movements from 1815 to 1848* (London, 1959).

Cox, Jeffrey. *The Churches in a Secular Society: Lambeth, 1870–1930* (Oxford, 1982).

Cunningham, Valentine. *Everywhere Spoken Against: Dissent in the Victorian Novel* (Oxford, 1975).

Currie, R., Gilbert, A. D., and Horsley, Lee. *Churches and Churchgoers: Patterns of Church Growth in the British Isles Since 1700* (Oxford, 1977).

Davies, G.C.B. *The Early Cornish Evangelicals* (London, 1951).

————, and Balleine, G. R. *A Popular History of the Church of England* (London, 1976).

Donajgrodzki, A. P., ed. *Social Control in the Nineteenth Century* (London, 1977).

Dyos, H. J. *Victorian Studies* (Leicester, 1961).

————. *The Study of Urban History* (London, 1968).

Elliott-Binns, L. E. *The Evangelical Movement in the English Church* (London, 1928).

————. *Religion in the Victorian Era* (London, 1936).

————. *The Early Evangelicals* (London, 1953).

Foster, Charles. *An Errand of Mercy, the Evangelical United Front, 1790–1837* (Chapel Hill, N.C., 1960).

Free Church of England. *A History of the Free Church of England*, 2d ed. (London, 1960).

Froom, LeRoy Edwin. *The Prophetic Faith of Our Fathers*, 4 vols. (Washington, D.C., 1946–1954).

Furneaux, Robin. *William Wilberforce* (London, 1974).

Gash, Norman. *Sir Robert Peel: The Life of Sir Robert Peel after 1830* (London, 1972).

Gay, John D. *Geography of Religion in England* (London, 1971).

Gidney, W. T. *History of the London Society for Promoting Christianity Amongst the Jews* (London, 1908).

Gilbert, A. D. *Religion and Society in Industrial England: Church, Chapel and Social Change* (London, 1976).

Halévy, Elie. *A History of the English People in 1815* (London, 1924).

Haller, William. *Foxe's Book of Martyrs and the Elect Nation* (London, 1963).

Harrison, Brian Howard. *Drink and the Victorians: the Temperance Question in England, 1815–1872* (London, 1971).

Harrison, J.F.C. *The Second Coming: Popular Millenarianism, 1780–1850* (London, 1979).

Heasman, Kathleen J. *Evangelicals in Action* (London, 1962).

Heeney, Brian. *Mission to the Middle Classes* (London, 1969).

————. *A Different Kind of Gentleman* (Hamden, Conn., 1976).

Hempton, David. *Methodism and Politics in British Society 1750–1850* (London, 1984).

Hennell, Michael. *John Venn and the Clapham Sect* (London, 1958).

————. *Sons of the Prophets* (London, 1979).

Hobsbawm, E. J. *The Labour Aristocracy* (London, 1954).

Hopkins, Hugh Evan. *Charles Simeon of Cambridge* (London, 1977).

Inglis, K. S. *Churches and the Working Classes in Victorian England* (London, 1963).

Insh, George Pratt. *The Life and Work of David Stow* (Edinburgh, 1938).

Isichei, Elizabeth M. A. *Victorian Quakers* (Oxford, 1970).

Jay, Elizabeth, *The Religion of the Heart* (Oxford, 1979).

Kent, John. *Holding the Fort: Studies in Victorian Revivalism* (London, 1978).

Laqueur, Thomas Walter. *Religion and Respectability: Sunday Schools and Working Class Culture, 1780–1850* (London, 1976).

Loane, Marcus. *Oxford and the Evangelical Succession* (London, 1951).

————. *Makers of Our Heritage: a Study of Four Evangelical Leaders* (London, 1967).

Locke, A. Audrey. *The Hanbury Family*, 2 vols. (London, 1910).

Machin, G.I.T. *Politics and the Churches in Great Britain 1832–1868* (Oxford, 1977).

McLeod, D. Hugh. *Class and Religion in the Late Victorian City* (London, 1974).

Malcolmson, Robert W. *Popular Recreations in English Society, 1700–1850* (Cambridge, 1973).

Manning, Bernard Lord. *The Protestant Dissenting Deputies* (Cambridge, 1952).

Marsh, P. T. *The Victorian Church in Decline: Archbishop Tait and the Church of England, 1868–1882* (London, 1969).

Martin, Roger H. *Evangelicals United: Ecumenical Stirrings in Pre-Victorian Britain, 1795–1830* (Metuchen, N.J., 1983).

Masterman, N. *Chalmers on Charity* (London, 1900).

Mathieson, W. L. *English Church Reform, 1815–1840* (London, 1923).

Millicent, Rose. *The East End of London* (London, 1973).

Newsome, David. *The Parting of Friends, A Study of the Wilberforces and Henry Manning* (London, 1966).

Norman, Edward R. *Anti-Catholicism in Victorian England* (London, 1968).

———. *Church and Society in England, 1770–1970: A Historical Study* (Oxford, 1978).

Oliver, W. H. *Prophets and Millennialists: The Uses of Biblical Prophecy in England from the 1790s to the 1840s* (Oxford, 1978).

O'Malley, I. B. *Florence Nightingale, 1820–1856: A Study of her Life Down to the End of the Crimean War* (London, 1932).

Open-Air Mission. *Picture and Stories of Our Work* (London, 1905).

Orr, J. Edwin, *The Second Evangelical Awakening in Great Britain* (London, 1953).

Parker, Charles Stuart. *Sir Robert Peel From His Private Letters*, 3 vols. (London, 1899).

Peel, Albert. *These Hundred Years: A History of the Congregational Union of England and Wales, 1831–1931* (London, 1931).

Pelling, Henry. *Popular Politics and Society in Late Victorian Britain* (London, 1968).

Philpot, J. H. *The Seceders: The Story of J. C. Philpot and William Tiptaft* (London, 1964).

Pollard, Arthur, ed. *Let Wisdom Judge* (London, 1959).

Pollard, Arthur, and Hennell, Michael. *Charles Simeon, 1759–1836* (London, 1959).

Pollock, J. C. *A Cambridge Movement* (London, 1953).

Prest, John. *Lord John Russell* (London, 1972).

———. *Politics in the Age of Cobden* (Basingstoke, 1977).

Pringle, J. C. *Social Work of the London Churchmen* (Oxford, 1937).

Prochaska, F. K. *Women and Philanthropy in Nineteenth Century England* (Oxford, 1980).

Read, Gordon, and Jebson, David. *A Voice in the City: 150 Years History of the Liverpool City Mission* (Liverpool, 1979).

Reynolds, John. *Evangelicals at Oxford, 1735–1871* (Oxford, 1953).

Robson, R., ed. *Ideas and Institutions of Victorian Britain* (London, 1967).

Rosenberg, Carroll S. *Religion and the Rise of the American City* (New York, 1971).

Ross, E. A. *Social Control: A Survey of the Foundations of Order* (New York, 1929).

Rowdon, Harold H. *The Origins of the Brethren* (London, 1967).

Rowell, Geoffrey. *Hell and the Victorians: A Study of the Nineteenth Century Theological Controversies Concerning Eternal Punishment and the Future Life* (Oxford, 1974).

Royle, Edward. *Radical Politics, 1790–1900; Religion and Unbelief* (London, 1971).

———. *The Infidel Tradition from Paine to Bradlaugh* (London, 1976).

Russell, Anthony. *The Clerical Profession* (London, 1980).

Russell, G.W.E. *A Short History of the Evangelical Movement* (London, 1915).

Sandeen, Ernest R. *The Roots of Fundamentalism: British and American Millenarianism,*
    1800–1930 (London, 1970).
Smyth, Charles. *Simeon and Church Order* (Cambridge, 1940).
Soloway, R. A. *Prelates and People* (London, 1969).
Stock, Eugene. *The English Church in the Nineteenth Century* (London, 1910).
Symondson, Anthony, ed. *The Victorian Crisis of Faith* (London, 1970).
Tait, Arthur J. *Simeon and his Trust* (London, 1936).
Thomas, Keith. *Religion and the Decline of Magic* (New York, 1971).
Thompson, David. *Nonconformity in the Nineteenth Century* (London, 1972).
Thompson, E. P. *The Making of the English Working Class* (London, 1963).
Thompson, Kenneth A. *Bureaucracy and Church Reform* (Oxford, 1970).
Thorold, Algar Labouchere. *The Life of Henry Labouchere* (London, 1913).
Ward, W. R. *Religion and Society in England, 1790–1850* (London, 1972).
Wickham, E. R. *Church and People in an Industrial City* (London, 1957).
Wigley, John. *The Rise and Fall of the Victorian Sunday* (Manchester, 1980).
Woodham-Smith, Cecil. *Florence Nightingale, 1820–1910* (London, 1952).
Young, G. M., and Handcock, W. D., eds. *English Historical Documents, 1833–1874,*
    vol. 12 (London, 1956).

B. Articles

Anderson, Olive. "The Reactions of Church and Dissent towards the Crimean War."
    Journal of Ecclesiastical History 16 (1965):209–220.
———. "The Growth of Christian Militarism in Mid-Victorian Britain." *English His-*
    torical Review 86 (Jan. 1971):46–72.
Annan, N. G. "The Intellectual Aristocracy." In *Series in Social History, a Tribute to*
    G. M. Trevelyan, edited by J. H. Plumb (London, 1955).
Balda, Wesley. "Simeon's 'Protestant Papists': A Sampling of Moderate Evangelicalism
    Within the Church of England 1839–1865." *Fides et Historia* 16 (Fall-Winter
    1983):55–67.
Bebbington, David. "The Life of Baptist Noel: Its Setting and Significance." *Baptist*
    Quarterly 24 (1972):389–418.
Berwick, Geoffrey. "Close of Cheltenham." *Theology* 39 (July-Dec., 1939):276–285.
Best, Geoffrey F. A. "The Protestant Constitution and Its Supporters, 1800–1829."
    Transactions of the Royal Historical Society, 5th series, 8 (1958):105–127.
———. "The Evangelicals and the Established Church in the Early Nineteenth Century."
    Journal of Theological Studies, n.s. 10 (1959):63–78.
———. "The Whigs and the Church Establishment in the Age of Grey and Holland."
    History 45 (1960):103–118.
———. "Evangelicalism and the Victorians." In *Victorian Crisis of Faith,* edited by
    Anthony Symondson (London, 1970).
Cahill, Gilbert. "Irish Catholicism and English Toryism." *Review of Politics* 19
    (1957):62–76.
———. "The Protestant Association and the Anti-Maynooth Agitation of 1845." *Cath-*
    olic Historical Review 43 (October 1957):270–308.
Chadwick, Owen. "Established Church Under Attack." In *Victorian Crisis of Faith,*
    edited by Anthony Symondson (London, 1970).

Charles, Conrad. "The Origins of the Parish Mission in England and the Early Passionist Apostolate." *Journal of Ecclesiastical History* 15 (1964):60–75.

Clark, G.S.R. Kitson "The Repeal of the Corn Laws and the Politics of the Forties." *Economic History Review*, 2d series, 4, no. 1 (1951):1–13.

Dell, Robert S. "Social and Economic Theories and Pastoral Concerns of a Victorian Archbishop." *Journal of Ecclesiastical History* 16 (1965):196–208.

Gilley, Sheridan "Papists, Protestants and the Irish in London, 1835–1870." In *Studies in Church History: Popular Practice and Belief*, edited by G. J. Cuming and David Baker (Cambridge, 1972):259–266.

———. "Catholic Faith of the Irish Slums, London, 1840–70." In *The Victorian City: Images and Realities*, edited by H. J. Dyos and Michael Wolff, 2 vols., (London, 1973).

Greaves, R. W. "The Jerusalem Bishopric, 1841." *English Historical Review* 44 (1949):328–352.

Harrison, Brian. "Drunkards and Reformers: Early Victorian Temperance Tracts." *History Today* (March 1963):178–185.

———. "The Sunday Trading Riots of 1855." *The Historical Journal* 8, no. 2 (1965):219–245.

———. "Religion and Recreation in Nineteenth Century England." *Past and Present*, no. 38 (December 1967):98–125.

Hempton, D. N. "Evangelicalism and Eschatology." *Journal of Ecclesiastical History* 31 (April 1980):179–194.

Henriques, Ursula. "How Cruel Was the Victorian Poor Law?" *Historical Journal* 11, no. 2 (1968):365–371.

Homan, Roger. "Sunday Observance and Social Class." *A Sociological Yearbook of Religion in Britain* 3 (1970):78–92.

Inglis, K. S. "Patterns of Religious Worship in 1851." *Journal of Ecclesiastical History* 11, no. 1 (1960):74–86.

Kent, John. "The Victorian Resistance: Comments on Religious Life and Culture, 1840–1880." *Victorian Studies* (Dec. 1968):145–154.

McLeod, Hugh. "Religion in the City." *Urban History Yearbook* (1978):7–22.

———. "The Dechristianization of the Working Class in Western Europe (1850–1900)." *Social Compass* 27 (1980):191–214.

Machin, G.I.T. "The Maynooth Grant, the Dissenters and Disestablishment, 1845–1847." *English Historical Review* 82 (1967):61–85.

———. "Lord John Russell and the Prelude to the Ecclesiastical Titles Bill, 1846–1851." *Journal of Ecclesiastical History* 25 (July 1974):277–295.

Martin, R. H. "The Place of the London Missionary Society in the Ecumenical Movement." *Journal of Ecclesiastical History* 31(July 1980):283–300.

Meacham, Standish. "The Church in the Victorian City." *Victorian Studies* 11 (1968):359–378.

Mole, David E. H. "John Cale Miller: A Victorian Rector of Birmingham." *Journal of Ecclesiastical History* 18 (1966):95–103.

———. "The Victorian Town Parish: Rural Vision and Urban Mission." In *Studies in Church History: The Church in Town and Countryside*, edited by David Baker, vol. 16 (Oxford, 1979):361–371.

Pickering, W.S.F. "The Religious Census of 1851—A Useless Experiment?" *British Journal of Sociology* 18 (1967):382–407.

Piggin, Stuart. "Assessing Nineteenth-century Missionary Motivation: Some Considerations of Theory and Method." In *Religious Motivation: Biographical and Sociological Problems for the Church Historian*, edited by Derek Baker (Oxford, 1978).

Pollard, Arthur. "Evangelical Parish Clergy, 1820–1840." *Church Quarterly Review* 159 (1958):389–395.

Price, Richard N. "The Working Men's Club Movement and Victorian Social Reform Ideology." *Victorian Studies* (Dec. 1971):117–147.

Rack, H. D. "Domestic Visitation: A Chapter in Early Nineteenth Century Evangelism." *Journal of Ecclesiastical History* 24 (October 1973):357–376.

Rennie, Ian S. "Nineteenth Century Roots of Contemporary Prophetic Interpretation." In *Dreams, Visions and Oracles*, edited by Carl E. Armerding and W. Ward Gasque (Grand Rapids, Mich., 1977):41–59.

Roberts, David. "How Cruel was the Victorian Poor Law?" *Historical Journal* 6 (1963):97–107.

Rowdon, H. H. "Secession from the Established Church in the Early Nineteenth Century." *Vox Evangelica* 3 (1964):76–88.

Scott, Patrick. "Victorian Religious Periodicals: Fragments that Remain." In *The Materials, Sources and Methods of Ecclesiastical History*, edited by Derek Baker (Oxford, 1975).

Smyth, Charles. "The Evangelical Movement in Perspective." *Cambridge Historical Journal* 7 (1943):160–174.

Spring, David. "Aristocracy, Social Structure and Religion in the Early Victorian Period." *Victorian Studies* 6 (March 1963):263–280.

Thompson, David M. "The 1851 Religious Census: Problems and Possibilities." *Victorian Studies* 11 (1967):87–97.

———. "The Churches and Society in Nineteenth-Century England: A Rural Perspective." In *Studies in Church History: Popular Practice and Belief*, edited by G. J. Cuming and David Baker (Cambridge, 1972):267–276.

Walsh, John. "Methodism and the Mob in the Eighteenth Century." In *Studies in Church History: Popular Belief and Practice*, edited by David Baker (Cambridge, 1972):213–227.

Ward, W. R. "The Tithe Question in England in the Early Nineteenth Century." *Journal of Ecclesiastical History* 16, no. 1 (April 1965):67–81.

Welch, P. J. "Anglican Churchmen and the Establishment of the Jerusalem Bishopric." *Journal of Ecclesiastical History* 8 (1957):193–204.

———. "Blomfield and Peel: A Study in Co-operation between Church and State, 1841–1846." *Journal of Ecclesiastical History* 12 (1961):71–84.

———. "Difficulties of Church Extension in Victorian London." *Church Quarterly Review* 166 (1965):302–315.

C. Dictionaries of Biography, Handbooks, Clergy Lists, and Other Religious Works

Douglas, J. D., ed. *The New International Dictionary of the Christian Church* (London, 1975).

Stephen, Leslie, and Lee, Sidney, eds. *Dictionary of National Biography* (London, 1908).

Townend, Peter, ed. *Burke's Genealogical and Heraldic History of the Peerage, Baronetage and Knightage*, 150th ed. (London, 1970).

Index

About the Author

DONALD M. LEWIS, who specializes in Victorian evangelism, is Assistant Professor of Church History at Regent College, Vancouver, British Columbia.

Recent Titles in Contributions to the Study of Religion
Series Editor: Henry W. Bowden

Southern Enterprize: The Work of National Evangelical Societies in the Antebellum South
John W. Kuykendall

Facing the Enlightenment and Pietism: Archibald Alexander and the Founding of Princeton Theological Seminary
Lefferts A. Loetscher

Presbyterian Women in America: Two Centuries of a Quest for Status
Lois A. Boyd and R. Douglas Brackenridge

Marchin' the Pilgrims Home: Leadership and Decision-Making in an Afro-Caribbean Faith
Stephen D. Glazier

Exorcising the Trouble Makers: Magic, Science, and Culture
Francis L. K. Hsu

The Cross, The Flag, and The Bomb: American Catholics Debate War and Peace, 1960–1983
William A. Au

Religious Conflict in Social Context: The Resurgence of Orthodox Judaism in Frankfurt Am Main, 1838–1877
Robert Liberles

Triumph over Silence: Women in Protestant History
Richard L. Greaves, editor

Neighbors, Friends, or Madmen: The Puritan Adjustment to Quakerism in Seventeenth-Century Massachusetts Bay
Jonathan M. Chu

Cities of Gods: Faith, Politics and Pluralism in Judaism, Christianity and Islam
Nigel Biggar, Jamie S. Scott, William Schweiker, editors

Theodicies in Conflict: A Dilemma in Puritan Ethics and Nineteenth-Century American Literature
Richard Forrer

Gilbert Tennent, Son of Thunder: A Case Study of Continental Pietism's Impact on the First Great Awakening in the Middle Colonies
Milton J Coalter, Jr.